The Future of the Self

The publisher and the University of California Press Foundation gratefully acknowledge the generous support of the Simpson Imprint in Humanities.

The Future of the Self

*An Interdisciplinary Approach to Personhood
and Identity in the Digital Age*

JAY FRIEDENBERG

UNIVERSITY OF CALIFORNIA PRESS

University of California Press
Oakland, California

© 2020 by Jay Friedenberg

Library of Congress Cataloging-in-Publication Data

Names: Friedenberg, Jay, author.
Title: The future of the self : an interdisciplinary approach to personhood and identity in the
    digital age / Jay Friedenberg.
Description: Oakland, California : University of California Press, [2020] | Includes bibliographical
    references and index.
Identifiers: LCCN 2019048352 (print) | LCCN 2019048353 (ebook) | ISBN 9780520302426 (cloth) |
    ISBN 9780520298484 (paperback) | ISBN 9780520970595 (ebook)
Subjects: LCSH: Self-presentation. | Identity (Psychology) | Brain. | Information technology—
    Social aspects. | Online identities. | Avatars (Virtual reality)
Classification: LCC BF697.5.S44 F75 2020 (print) | LCC BF697.5.S44 (ebook) | DDC 155.2—dc23
LC record available at https://lccn.loc.gov/2019048352
LC ebook record available at https://lccn.loc.gov/2019048353

Manufactured in the United States of America

29 28 27 26 25 24 23 22 21 20
10 9 8 7 6 5 4 3 2 1

CONTENTS

List of Figures   viii

List of Tables   x

Acknowledgments   xi

1   Introduction   1

Primary Terms: *Personhood, Self,* and *Identity*   2

The Psychology of Personhood   3

Perspectives on Personhood   3

Non-Western Views of Self   9

A Few More Ideas on the Self   10

The Artificial Self   11

Book Overview   19

2   The Philosophy of Self   21

Historical Conceptions of Personhood and Self   22

Three Additional Philosophical Conceptions of the Self   30

Personal Identity   33

Knowledge of the Self   38

Free Will and Determinism   42

The Extended-Mind Thesis   45

3   The Psychology of Self   48

Varieties of Self: The Modern Approach   49

Psychological Theories of Self   54

Disorders of Self   71

4   Brain 79

       The Neuroscience of Self 80

       Is There a Specialized Brain System for Self? 80

       One or Many Neural Selves? 86

       Neural Models of the Self 90

       Problems with the Neuroscientific Study of Self 99

       Responses to Problems with the Neuroscientific Study of Self 100

5   Brain + Hardware 102

       Cyborgs 103

       Prosthetics 108

       Neural Prosthetics (Brain-Machine Interfaces or Brain-Computer Interfaces) 119

       Artificial Memories 124

       Robotics 125

6   Brain + Software 138

       Technology 139

       Cyberpsychology 143

       Varieties of Online Behavior 148

       Video Games 169

7   Avatars 176

       What Is an Avatar? 176

       Avatar Typologies 178

       Avatar Behavior in the Palace 179

       Avatar Embodiment 184

       Points of View 184

       The Proteus Effect 186

       Representing and Creating the Online Self 186

       Avatars at Play 189

       Avatars and Video Role-Playing Games 190

       Avatars and Identity 191

       Avatar Case Studies 193

       The Future of Avatars 197

8   Virtual Worlds 198

       Augmented Reality 199

       Virtual Worlds 200

       Virtual Spaces 201

A Brief History of Virtual Worlds   205

Presence and the Ultimate Display   206

A Chronology of VR Systems   207

Second Life   210

Avatars, Virtual Worlds, and the Digital Self   222

Benefits of VR and Virtual Worlds   223

Problems with VR and Virtual Worlds   226

The Future of the Virtual World   227

9   Software Selves   228

What Is Life?   229

Artificial Life   229

Life and Consciousness   233

Consciousness   234

Artificial Consciousness   235

Is Artificial Consciousness Possible? Some Ideas   243

Artificial Intelligence   244

Artificial Selves as Mindclones and Bemans   256

Digital Identity, Personhood, and Rights   258

Human Attitudes and Behaviors toward Artificial Selves   259

Digital Immortality   262

10   Conclusion   267

Changing the Self   267

The Future of the Self   272

The Far Future   282

Summary and Main Issues   289

References   291

Index   321

FIGURES

1.   Varieties of artificial beings   12

2.   A depiction of the golem, a mythical being from Jewish folklore   14

3.   A cyborg is a hybrid of biological and technological parts   31

4.   Modern computer architectures contain drives and processing chips   32

5.   The persistence question addresses how or if we remain the same despite drastic changes   34

6.   Human left and right cerebral hemispheres are dominant for different cognitive functions   36

7.   Metacognition is defined as "thinking about thinking"   40

8.   Organisms that are increasingly complex demonstrate more internalized control over their behavior and are less governed by external environmental forces   44

9.   According to the extended-mind thesis, our mind is not just in our brain or body   46

10.   The interplay between the id, ego, and superego aspects of our self, according to Freud   55

11.   Psychological health according to Carl Rogers   59

12.   Abraham Maslow's hierarchy of needs   60

13.   Reciprocal determinism.   68

14.   A chimp touches its forehead during the mirror test   82

15.   The Cartesian theater model of consciousness   87

16.   The multiple-drafts model of consciousness   88

17.   Location of some protoself structures in the brain   92

18.   The formation of core consciousness   94

19. The locations of second-order map brain structures.   94

20. Brain structures in the medial prefrontal cortex corresponding to the EAM, SAM, and CS   98

21. Robo Rat   105

22. A retinal prosthetic system   109

23. A cochlear implant   110

24. Robonaut   114

25. A powered exoskeleton to assist those with walking disabilities   118

26. A brain-computer interface allowing a monkey to operate a robotic arm   121

27. A plot showing the effect of the uncanny valley   128

28. How many of these devices do you own?   140

29. Texting is a predominant form of communication, especially among younger Americans   149

30. A selfie   151

31. Facebook is one of the most popular social networking sites on the internet   154

32. This is your brain on social media   155

33. The brain's dopamine reward network gets activated   167

34. Mobile smartphone games like Candy Crush Saga are currently popular   171

35. A computer avatar used in a video game   177

36. First- and third-person point of view (POV) in video games   185

37. The Proteus effect   187

38. Avatar customization in the video game *The Elder Scrolls III: Morrowmind*   188

39. The five analytical planes of video game spaces   204

40. A woman using a virtual reality headset   210

41. A Second Life avatar   214

42. A romantic moment by the sea in Second Life   218

43. A Sansar avatar in an environment   222

44. A screen shot from a Game of Life simulation   231

45. Agents can take in information about their environment, perform computations on that information, and then use it as the basis of acting   236

46. John Searle's Chinese room scenario   239

47. A simplified version of a cognitive architecture of an artificial general intelligence program   246

48. The Turing Test scenario   247

TABLES

1. Arguments and counterarguments for the ability to replicate complex systems   19

2. Different definitions of personhood   29

3. Self-related constructs, processes, and phenomena   52

4. The different psychodynamic personality types and how they may be expressed online   57

5. The six major facets of identity   62

6. Cattell's sixteen personality factors   64

7. The "Big Five" personality factors in the five-factor model (FFM)   65

8. The factors involved in internet addictive disorder (IAD)   76

9. Different techniques for measuring brain electrical activity, their measuring areas, and neural regions   120

10. Reasons for the online disinhibition effect   153

11. Three proposed brain networks that may be involved in the use of social media   156

12. The twelve different types of video games   170

13. Criteria for internet gaming disorder   172

14. Types of abnormal avatars in the Palace virtual world   183

15. The eleven different types of video game spaces   202

16. The seven properties of life   230

17. Various aspects of consciousness and whether those may exist in the internet/machines   240

18. The computational capacity needed to simulate the human brain   265

19. Kurzweil's past and projected stages of informational complexity   284

ACKNOWLEDGMENTS

I wish to thank the reviewers of this book, Christopher Ferguson, Jacqui Taylor, Jens Binder, Leon James, Narendra Neel Khichi, Jr, Kent Norman, Thomas D. Parsons, Titus Asbury, and Nicholas Bowman, for their efforts in reading and providing comments on the early drafts. Kudos also to Tim Sullivan, Enrique Ochoa-Kaup, and Lyn Uhl at UC Press for their patience and assistance in the many editorial stages, and to Elisabeth Magnus for her razor-sharp copy editor's eye.

CHAPTER ONE

Introduction

CONTENTS

Primary Terms: *Personhood*, *Self*, and *Identity*

The Psychology of Personhood

Perspectives on Personhood

   Historical Perspectives

   Evolutionary Perspectives

   Social-Developmental Perspectives

Non-Western Views of Self

A Few More Ideas on the Self

The Artificial Self

   Varieties of Artificial Selves

The Artificial Self in Mythology, Literature, and Art

Theology and Artificial Selves

Early Attempts at Constructing an Artificial Self

The Artificial and the Natural—Not So Different after All

Replication

Book Overview

This book is about many things. It is about who we are and who we might be, given our current and future interactions with technology. It delves into what a person is as well as what a person might become. It is also about the descriptions we provide for ourselves, what we call our self or identity. These are complex topics and have been addressed from many different disciplinary perspectives. As a result we discuss them from the point of view of philosophy, psychology, neuroscience, artificial intelligence, and robotics.

This introductory chapter is designed as an orientation and springing-off point. We begin by defining essential terms. In particular we look at what it means to be human from philosophical, historical, evolutionary, and social-developmental approaches. We then introduce the concept of the artificial self and differentiate it from other similar concepts.

An artificial self is an agent that acts and experiences the world the same way biological selves do and that from a behavioral point of view cannot be distinguished from a "real" person.

Artificial selves in various incarnations have been a popular topic in mythology, literature, and film. We therefore provide a brief history of their appearance in these media. Following this we describe early attempts to build artificial selves. We finish with the hypothesis that it should be possible for an artificial self either to be constructed or to emerge spontaneously in complex systems. Friedenberg (2008) contains a more extended argument for the existence of artificial selves.

PRIMARY TERMS: PERSONHOOD, SELF, AND IDENTITY

Throughout this book we will use several primary terms. These are *person, human, self,* and *identity.* These four terms are interrelated, and at times it can become difficult to tell them apart. Even researchers sometimes use the terms interchangeably. We will make an attempt to differentiate between them here. To be human is to be a member of the species *Homo sapiens.* This is a biological and genetic standard. It is equivalent to saying that being human is what makes you different from other animals. *Human* and *person* are mostly equivalent terms. Almost all people are human. It might be argued, however, that a fetus, although human, is not a person and therefore does not have a right to life. This is a legalistic standard. Note also that a human under this notion becomes a person once he or she undergoes sufficient developmental change. When exactly one crosses this border from human to person is of course the topic of strenuous debate.

Some writers equate *human* and *person* with *self* and *identity.* However, it is generally acknowledged now that a single person can have multiple selves or identities. Thus *human* and *person* are the more general terms while *self* and *identity* are more specific. Despite some distinctions in the literature, we will equate the concepts of human and person in this book, treating them as the same thing. We will also equate the concepts of self and identity, treating them as the same thing. A good heuristic is to think of human/person as what makes us collectively different from animals and to think of identity/self as what makes an individual person different from other individual people.

Identity and self provide an answer to the question "Who am I?" They are descriptions of individual nature. Identity and self can be described using a list of attributes, values, and motives. Constancy versus change is a common theme in identity research. Does one stay the same or change as time goes by? If one changes, then the term *dynamic identity* is sometimes used. Identity can also be thought of as the image one projects to family, friends, and society. Note the similarity here with roles and role playing from sociology. We may often struggle internally when forming our identity, but what others think of us is certainly important. Thus we have a personal identity and a social identity, the former being who we think we are, the latter being who other people think we are.

THE PSYCHOLOGY OF PERSONHOOD

Before understanding self and identity we need to gain a fuller comprehension of personhood. The primary question here is, "What does it mean to be a person?" or "How do we define a person?" The question is not an easy one and requires the adoption of multiple perspectives. In the following sections we will sketch out some answers from historical, evolutionary, and social-developmental approaches.

It is remarkable that over its extended history psychology has had relatively little to say about people, even though this is what the discipline professes to study. This is because psychology traditionally has been reductionist in its approach. It has focused on the thoughts, emotions, and actions that make up a person but not on the person as an integrated whole. This has changed in recent years, and many researchers across the discipline are now studying the person from a holistic and more integrated perspective.

Human beings are now understood as social beings who are members of a community. It is understood that while they have bodies with biological features, these features are expressed within a sociocultural world. Some of the properties considered vital to humans are self-awareness and self-understanding, a reasoning intelligence, the use of language, the ability to take and integrate different perspectives, a moral concern, agency including intentionality and the ability to act or refrain from acting, and finally the creation of culture (Martin & Bickhard, 2013).

People can also be described in terms of five main concepts. The first is personality, which is a unique combination of temperament and dispositions. We examine the personality approach extensively in chapter 3. The second is identity, which is anchored by physical characteristics, social positioning, and circumstances. The third is autobiographical memories, which are recollections and reflections from our past. There is also character, which is judged by conduct and circumstances (Martin & Bickhard, 2013). Finally, people are considered to be morally responsible, meaning that they need to answer for their deeds.

PERSPECTIVES ON PERSONHOOD

Historical Perspectives

The study of personhood has been going on for a long time, at least as far back as ancient Greece and Rome. The Romans thought of a person as a legal entity. In 160 CE the scholar Gaius said that the law pertains to persons, things, or actions. In the case of theft, the thief and the victim would be the persons, the things would be the objects stolen, and the action would be the theft itself. In Roman society, young children and women were considered minors and under the guardianship of their husband or father. Slaves were not considered people at all. Personhood was only something males could attain by reaching a certain age of maturity. At this age, the man could be held responsible for his actions.

The legal concept of a person may be revisited in the near future. If we consider robots to be people, then they are responsible for their actions. That means if they steal they can be "punished" or treated equivalently in some way by a system of law. If they are deemed nonpersons, then they are nothing more than objects and can be considered property, being owned and controlled by people—that is, slaves. Critical in determining personhood here is the notion of moral responsibility. If a robot knows that stealing is bad but does it anyway, then culpability can be more readily assigned. Also, if robot or software selves must undergo a learning period before they can acquire full cognitive capability, then legally they might be treated as "minors," and their primary caregivers would thus be held responsible for their actions.

Cicero (106–43 BCE) was among the first to note that a person, like an actor, puts on different masks to play different roles in society. These different roles come with different obligations or social duties. For example, a father has the obligation to care for his family. Cicero mentions four kinds of responsibility. The first is that a man ought to be a rational human being, not like an animal governed only by impulses. Second, he needs to be true to his own unique makeup. Third, his social position, such as coming from a rich or poor family, or being a figure in public office, imposes social responsibilities. Fourth, we need to recognize the consequences of our own life choices, such as deciding on a particular career. Cicero believed that each person ought to act as well as possible, always trying to improve or perfect himself. What is interesting about this conception is that there is no real notion of the individual as apart from a person's roles and obligations to society.

This notion of a person as a social construct will come up again in the philosophy chapter. An artificial or digital self, such as a robot or software program, will most likely need to interact with people. Thus it will need to be able to "put on different faces" to play different roles in society, and to interact effectively it will need to be able to read social cues such as facial expression and vocal intonation. Programs such as this already exist and can even recognize fake smiles, as not every human can do. Artificial people that are special purpose and perform only one function may not need to play different roles. Domain-specific AIs that can only play games or pick stocks do not possess general intelligence and as a consequence seem less human. It may be that playing different social roles and accommodating to the complex and changing needs of those around us is what drove the evolution of intelligence and personhood in our species.

Later, with the rise of the Catholic Church, persons were considered only those with rationality. An essential feature of a person was his or her immortal soul. Although God was assumed to give everyone a soul, it could also be qualified with regard to baptismal status, in the sense that the process of being baptized could confer complete personhood and acceptance within the religion for those who came from outside the faith. Perfection was also emphasized in medieval theology. A person was regarded as imperfect but could potentially become perfectible. This is evident in confessional texts where individuals compare themselves to beings more perfect than they are, such as saints. Imperfect beings could attain various degrees of worthiness depending on their social standing and moral conduct.

By the seventeenth century there was for the first time an emphasis upon the individual. René Descartes (1596–1650) focused upon thinking as the standard of personhood in his famous quote "I think, therefore I am." Thomas Hobbes (1588–1679) claimed that people are naturally solitary but are forced to interact with others. He said that people need what others have and that to get what they need they enter into "bonds" or contracts, restricting power and obliging some to render services to others. It is these contracts that enable people to live with one another, since otherwise humans have inherently antisocial tendencies. Despite this social approach, Hobbes believed that a person as an individual was responsible for his actions.

John Locke (1632–1704) and Jean-Jacques Rousseau (1712–78) wrote about the complex inner life of individuals. It was this "inner life," filled with perceptions, thoughts, and feelings, that would dominate the view of a person well into the twentieth century. Locke believed "consciousness" was the inherent characteristic of an individual. What made a person in his view was a constant awareness of oneself as being the same entity now as in the past, emphasizing continuity over time. Locke distinguished between consciousness and a religious soul, saying consciousness was a feature of reality and thus amenable to introspection and scientific study. Locke influenced Thomas Jefferson (1743–1826) and the founding fathers in the US to conceive of people as having individual rights such as freedom of speech and the right to bear arms. They believed the primary function of government was to defend these rights. A society in their view was supposed to be free, allowing people to pursue their own ends, among these being the pursuit of happiness.

Evolutionary Perspectives on Personhood

We commonly understand ourselves to be the same as others, yet different from others. This is reflected in our use of the words *self* and *other*. We can say, I am a "self" to me and an "other" to you, while you are a "self" to you and an "other" to me. There is an implicit understanding in these statements that people all belong to the same class or category but that we can still differ from each other. This ability to differentiate self from other, and in particular to know that others are like us mentally, is a key development in the process of personhood. One of the goals of psychology is to explain how we come to acquire this belief (Barresi, Moore, & Martin, 2013).

The philosopher Peter Strawson (1919–2006) conceived of people as objects with material properties that apply to all objects (M-predicates) and psychological properties that apply specifically to persons (P-predicates). He thus acknowledged that humans are physical creatures that differ from other creatures in such abilities as reason and language. In simple actions like walking, according to Strawson, physical movements (M-predicates) and psychological properties (P-predicates) are mixed, and the intentionality of the person (his or her goal-directed behavior) can be seen directly in that person's movement. We can compare such behavior to our own and realize that other people can have the same goals (walking to get somewhere) as we do. But in other, more complex group actions, other people's behaviors and goals can differ. So in those cases, how can we understand other people's goals?

Of importance here is reciprocal altruism. Simply stated, this is the notion that if you treat someone well, that person will generally return the favor and treat you well. It was the need to engage in joint cooperative activities and mutual aid over time with the same partners, where self and other were treated equally, that made the concept of person necessary (Barresi, Moore, & Martin, 2013). In this view the practice of reciprocal altruism among hominids in early human history laid the basis for the concepts of self and personhood. It enabled us to differentiate between self and other and to determine that other people can have goals or mental states like our own. The notion that other people have minds and intentions like our own is called a theory of mind. The ability to have a theory of mind is a necessary ingredient for being a person, according to this view.

Comparing the abilities of chimps, our nearest genetic animal relatives, can help to clarify the development of personhood. Chimps live mainly in the present, and although they live in social groups with unrelated individuals, their cooperative actions tend be with fellow family members only. They tend to ignore or compete with fellow chimps who are not members of their family. Chimps do not act with regard to a distant past or future. In contrast, people cooperate with others who are not family members. We can also think about the far past and future. We can engage in "mental time travel" to imagine past and future events from different points of view, our own and that of others (Moore & Lemmon, 2001).

In addition, chimpanzees can act now for goals that will be achieved in the future, but they can't do so by delaying gratification of any current desire. In comparison, a four-year-old human child can suppress an immediate desire for a greater future desire. In the classic "marshmallow" test, children are told they can have a small amount of candy now or, if they wait, a greater amount of candy later (Mischel, 1968). Despite individual differences, nearly all children above the age of four are able to wait for a greater future reward. This is something no known animal can do and like rationality is an important feature of being human.

Let us illustrate this with an example. Two genetically unrelated cavemen, "Og" and "Ug," are out hunting. Og sees a group of gazelles nearby, and if he immediately throws his spear he will be able to kill one and get the meat. However, he and Ug have agreed beforehand on a plan. He has agreed to drive the group of gazelle toward Ug, who has several spears and will be able to kill three gazelles as they run past in a panic. In this way the two of them will be able to bring back more meat than if either one acted alone. So Og delays gratification of his immediate desire and follows the plan.

This example illustrates all of the skills we noted above. Og and Ug are engaging in cooperative behavior even though they are not genetically related. They can suppress their immediate desires. They are able to imagine what the future is like, and this imagination takes both their own individual perspective and the other's perspective into account. Ug must imagine Og scaring the group of gazelles to stampede before he has actually done it. Og must imagine Ug spearing them as they run past. They also must both understand that this behavior will result in more game animals killed and will produce more meat not only for the two of them but for the greater tribe to which they belong. To engage in such behavior requires an understanding that other people have minds and intentions similar to our own, theory of mind. Og must know that Ug thinks as he does, gets hungry as he does, and so on. In other words, Og knows Ug is human, like himself. Each has acquired that status of personhood, of having selves.

What is unique about human reciprocal altruism is its basis upon a concept of person that can be applied equally to ourselves and others, that involves a common ability to calculate costs and benefits across different perspectives, and that extends across time. With these abilities in place, even long-term relationships of reciprocal altruism are possible. This produces a sense of justice, whereby large groups of individuals that mutually recognize each other as persons can act cooperatively. Justice may also allow us to treat strangers in a kindly manner. Also of note here is that future planning becomes much easier with the use of language. Language of course presupposes the idea of personhood and a theory of mind because it is a way of communicating thoughts between different minds. It is not clear which of these skills came first: planning and a sense of the future, a theory of mind, or language. They may have all coevolved, reinforcing each other over time.

Imagine an agent that exists with others of its kind in a world. This agent values its own survival but needs to acquire resources from its environment in order to do so. This resource acquisition requires work. The agent has several options. The first is that it can go it alone without dealing with others. This has some advantages, namely that the agent can do what it likes and not take others into account. However, it will probably die because the benefits of working in a group in most situations are so much greater. So the second option is group interaction. In this case there are two primary forms of interaction: competition and cooperation.

Competition means taking what one wants from someone else and not caring about the consequences. The primary drives here are aggression and domination. This approach also has mixed benefits. Bullies and dictators often get what they want this way. But they rarely do it alone. They must recruit others to their cause to support them and partake in the spoils while at the same time having others, such as slaves, do their work. The downside of this approach is that one makes enemies, and this can often get the bully deposed and killed. The second group option of cooperation means working together with others to obtain survival needs. Here the primary drives may be considered love, empathy, and other qualities that result in group bonding. In cooperative societies there are also downsides, like conformity and the suppression of individual deviance. Reciprocal altruism probably operates in both forms of societies. As mentioned above, the formation of identity and self is most likely to occur in groups where agents must interact in order to survive.

In natural ecosystems we see competition and cooperation at the individual and group levels, so all of these possibilities seem to exist in nature. There may be some optimal mixture of these strategies that promotes survival, but it is always dependent on current environmental demands in the form of selection forces. One factor not mentioned yet is reproduction. If an agent needs to mix its genes or coding instructions with others, then it is forced to interact and must live in a group setting (sexual reproduction). This is not a strict requirement, and loners that can reproduce on their own with some variation, like whiptail lizards and stick insects, are possible (asexual reproduction).

Although we think of groups and evolution mostly in terms of biological evolution, this need not be the case. Robotic and software agents can have artificial origins. They can exist in real or virtual environments and be subject to evolutionary pressures in the same way live organisms are. All three possibilities are also open to such agents. They can live autonomously or in groups with a competitive or cooperative basis. In fact, evolutionary simulations of artificial agents have been studied for quite some time, and the ways they organize and behave are quite similar to those seen in nature. See the discussion on evolution and robotics in chapter 5 and the section on artificial life in chapter 9 for more on this topic.

A question we can ask in this context is whether an artificial agent could, on its own and without prior programming, develop a sense of self and identity. Imagine a computer simulation of such agents. Would they be more likely to acquire a self if they evolved in a group as opposed to an individualist setting? One could vary different parameters to see their effect. For example, one might predict that as the amount of communication and mutual dependency between members increases, the likelihood of identity development should also increase.

Many of these issues also come up in our usage of social media. Most of us get onto platforms like Twitter, Facebook, and LinkedIn to meet others, solidify our group bonds, and promote our success and social standing. Meeting others can be for reproductive or nonreproductive reasons. Stronger social bonds means that someone may be more likely to come to your aid in the future. Promotion of social status can help others to think more favorably of you, which can increase your chances of getting interviewed or hired for a job, for example. This can also lead to greater prospects of future survival and flourishing. Digital meeting places serve many needs, but it is interesting (perhaps disheartening) to see that most of us devolve back to these most basic forms of group interaction when we go online.

Social-Developmental Perspectives on Personhood

Social psychology looks at how our interaction with others affects what we think, feel, and do. The theory of reciprocal altruism described above is thus both a social and an evolutionary theory. Developmental psychology looks at changes over the life span of individuals. This is in contrast to evolutionary psychology, which examines changes over the time span of species. In this section we will examine a social theory, called position exchange theory (PET), and show how it can account for the development of personhood, that is, within a life span (Gillespie & Martin, 2014). PET is not only a social or developmental theory. It can be applied equally to the evolutionary cases we have just considered.

Many social activities consist of different yet complementary positions. For example, talking involves being both a speaker and a listener; negotiating involves proposing and considering; and nurturing involves caring and being cared for. Each action involves a specific social role and set of expectations about what each person will do in each position. Buying food involves two social positions, a buyer and a seller. Each position involves the other position, because one cannot be a buyer without there being a seller. Both people, to successfully carry out their role, must appreciate the perspective of the other. Being a buyer makes us a better seller, for instance, because we can appreciate the motivation to save money. PET says that the exchange of social positions forces the adoption of alternate perspective taking, which drives the development of personhood.

We begin to exchange positions very early in development. This may involve leading and following in exchanges of facial expression, imitating during peek-a-boo, hiding and seeking, or catching and throwing a ball. This may explain the importance of games for children. Later in development the use of language also requires position exchange. When speaking, one must imagine what it is like to adopt the perspective of our conversational partner. After acquiring language a child can participate in various media like books, films, and the internet that call on even greater position exchange. When reading a novel, we adopt the position of the hero and the various characters. When playing a video game we adopt the position of the avatar. PET forces us to know what it is like to be someone (or in the case of avatars also something), thus helping us to create a theory of mind and to know that we, like the others around us, are human.

NON-WESTERN VIEWS OF SELF

Many of the views on self in this book come from the Western and scientific traditions. However it is worth delving at least briefly into the ways other cultures understand this concept. Western notions of self center on an internal "man," or homunculus (Mosig, 2006). It is this figure that does the thinking, doing, and feeling of the self. This figure appears in many guises. It can be Freud's id/ego/superego combination, Adler's (1927) creative self, or Rogers's (1961) ideal and real self. Each of these posits an internalized central figure that is the source of experience and action. In theistic conceptions, this homunculus is roughly equivalent to the soul.

In the Buddhist tradition there is no such thing. The personal self is believed to be an imaginary false belief for which there is no corresponding reality (Rahula, 1974). This incorrect view of self is believed to produce harmful thoughts of "me" and "mine" and to produce selfish desires, attachments, and other negative ideas like pride, hatred, and conceit that are considered the source of the world's problems. Much of Buddhist practice is aimed at eliminating the personal self, resulting in happiness at the individual and social levels.

The self, like everything else in the universe, is conceived of less as an object than as a composite relation or configuration. Humans, like all "things," are made up of parts. It is the relationships between these parts that determine something. These relations are like gestalts in psychology. By the Gestalt law of proximity we can perceive three dots as forming a whole only because they are close together. The whole in this case is "more than the sum of the parts": it consists also of the spatial properties that link the parts together. This view is similar to patternism and functionalism, which define self not as material parts but as the patterns and functions they perform.

In Buddhist psychology, a "person" is a composite of five groups of elements called skandhas that make up form, feelings, perceptions, impulses, and consciousness. When these are working together we have a person. If they are removed, the person and corresponding sense of self disappears. The skandhas themselves also exist relationally: any single one exists because of the other four (Mosig, 2006). All of what we think are things are there only because of other things. When these arrangements cease, so does the "thing." This notion of impermanence is central in Buddhist belief. The temporary gestalt formed by the skandhas that produces the illusory self is called the anatta. Realization of this does not diminish the self but instead is supposed to empower a person, as one now understands that one is part of a larger interconnected world. One's self effectively disappears and becomes the universe. The realization of this is called enlightenment. It is supposed to bring about increased compassion for others, since there is no difference between one's self and others.

A FEW MORE IDEAS ON THE SELF

One very important issue concerning the self has to do with materiality and the physical world. It might be quite easy to think that our self is our brain or our brain plus our bodies. However, the chemicals and molecules that make up our bodies are constantly being changed and renewed. Even in the brain, where neurons have a fairly long life, the components that make up the neurons are being replenished. One way around this is to adopt a position known as patternism. In this view our selves are the patterns of neural activation that occur in our brains. It is this pattern, presumably unique in each individual, that captures the nature of self, not the materials that make it up. Some transhumanists go even further by saying that this pattern can be copied and placed in another substrate like a computer so that the self can live on after death.

A number of other definitions of self have been proposed. One is that we are defined through our memories, that our history is who we are. There is some merit to this notion. There is no doubt our past has influenced who we are, but many forces shape our identity, including the present. An argument against this is that the past is who we *were*, not necessarily who we *are*. It is perhaps more accurate to say the self is our characteristic way of responding at any given moment in time. This is the view of personality theorists who measure the self in terms of traits. Traits are simple one-word descriptions, like "outgoing" or "perseverant," that describe the way a person would act in a given situation.

Another, more social concept of the self can be measured as the effect we have on the world. Each of us in a lifetime affects the environment in some way. We get married, have children, and forge a career. All of this adds up to a constellation of changes in the world. We affect the way other people think and the way our children act. We write poetry and books, paint paintings, compose music, or help build a skyscraper. Many of these achievements are a legacy that has drawn on our unique creativity as individuals acting alone or in conjunction with others. According to this definition the self is the legacy we leave behind. Some individuals may opt to preserve the things they have created in a time capsule. Alternatively, an electronic version of our accomplishments could be created and shared with others.

We have a lot more to say about the self later. Chapter 2 provides a philosophical introduction to this topic, surveying historical theories on personhood, self, and identity. Chapter

3 provide a similar treatment from a psychological point of view. We next intro͏ more modern take on the self, which is whether a technological or artificial v͏ could exist.

THE ARTIFICIAL SELF

Varieties of Artificial Selves

Before continuing, it is worth defining several important terms, as we refer to them repeatedly throughout the book. In the definitions listed below we start with the most general and farthest removed from what might be considered human and work our way slowly toward the concept of an artificial person or self. Figure 1 shows examples of artificial beings.

A machine is any mechanical or organic device that transmits or modifies energy to perform or assist in the execution of tasks. Machines typically require some energy as input and accomplish some sort of work. People have designed and used mechanisms and machines throughout much of recent human history to facilitate the performance of jobs. Note that work in this sense can be physical, as is the case with an elevator that can lift loads, or purely computational, as is the case with a calculator that is used to add a list of numbers. Note also that according to this definition a machine can be mechanical, made of fabricated or synthetic parts like gears or circuits, or biological, consisting of organic molecules.

A computer in the most general sense is a device designed to represent and compute information. The hallmark of a computer is that it is incapable of interacting with the physical world. A computer can pass information back and forth through space with other computers via a network, but unless connected to some sort of actuator, like an artificial limb, it is incapable of acting on objects in the world. A computer can therefore manipulate information but not material objects.

An avatar is a representation of an entity, human or otherwise, that exists inside a software program like a computer game. Avatars are controlled using a joystick, game controller, or virtual reality glove. Avatars can also be controlled by artificial intelligences. It may be possible to upload or transfer an individual's mind into an avatar, in which case the person might be considered as having become the avatar (Damer, 1998).

A robot, on the other hand, is a construct that is capable of moving around and/or interacting with the physical world with some degree of autonomy. Some robots are in a fixed position (such as those in an assembly line) but can move objects using arms or other effectors. Others are capable of moving about under their own power and are called mobile robots. Likewise, human operators control some robots while others have autonomous control over their own actions. Robots can but need not look like people (Ichbiah, 2005).

A cyborg or cybernetic organism is a creature that is a mix of organic and mechanical parts (Benford & Malartre, 2007). By the stricter definition of the term, a human cyborg is someone who has had some basic physiological function replaced by an embedded machine part. A person with a pacemaker thus qualifies, but someone wearing contact lenses or using a mobile phone does not. Cyborgs bring up many interesting questions. Imagine a

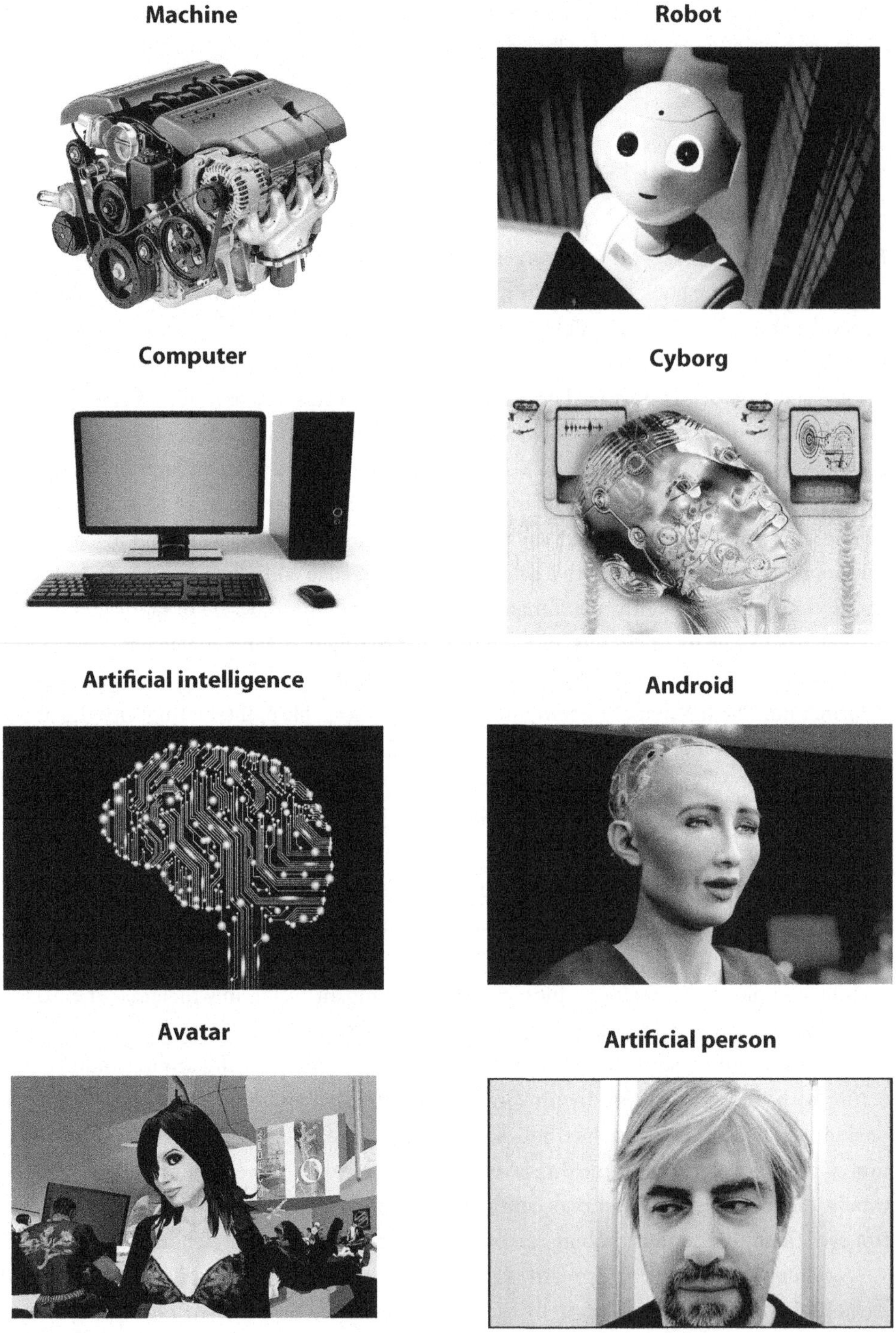

FIGURE 1 Varieties of artificial beings include machines, computers, artificial intelligence, avatars, robots, cyborgs, androids, and artificial selves. Public domain images courtesy of pixneo.com.

cybernetic person named John who is continually augmented with technology. At some point, does John stop becoming a person? If more than half of John were mechanical, would you say he was no longer human? What if all of John's body but not his brain were mechanical? If we gradually replaced more and more of John's brain with functionally equivalent computer parts, would he at some point cease to be human?

An android is an artificially created being that resembles a human being. In literature and other media an android is loosely defined in the sense that it can be entirely mechanical, entirely organic, or some combination thereof. Thus a robot or a cyborg that looks human can be considered an android. Androids as they are customarily treated in the literature, although resembling people, need not act or be exactly like people (Ishiguro, 2007).

An artificial self is an artificially created or emergent being that is by its nature and actions indistinguishable from a human but need not look exactly like one (Friedenberg, 2008). An artificial self is functionally no different from a real person. Its behavior in any given situation or test cannot be reliably differentiated from that of an actual person. Although an artificial self may look different on the inside or the outside, from a behavioral standpoint it is identical in every respect to a person. Like an android, an artificial self may be mechanical, organic, or some combination of the two. An artificial self is capable of having subjective conscious experience.

A key concept when discussing these various incarnations of self is that of an agent. Russell and Norvig (2003) define an agent as anything that perceives its environment through sensors and acts on the environment through actuators or effectors in order to achieve purposive, goal-directed action. People, AI programs, and autonomous robots are all examples of agents. A person takes in information through senses like eyes and ears, then acts on the basis of this information using legs, arms, and hands. An AI program receives input in the form of file contents and network data and acts by transmitting information or operating a remote device. A robot perceives through electronic senses like video cameras and microphones and acts using robotic arms and manipulators.

The Artificial Self in Mythology, Literature, and Art

The history of storytelling is replete with human attempts to construct an artificial self. One of the earliest of these comes from ancient Greece. Hephaestus was a god born as the son of the goddess Hera, wife of Zeus. He became the gods' mechanical assistant, creating the various contraptions they needed with his forge. These included Achilles's shield and Apollo's chariot. His most complex creation was Talos, a bronze robot that guarded the island of Crete. Talos roamed the island and could throw large rocks at passing ships. Talos is the earliest mention in human history of a being that resembles a robot.

During the Middle Ages a work attributed to the alchemist Paracelsus was is the first to use the term *homunculus*, which literally translated from the Latin means "little man." The author reports having made a one-foot-tall homunculus using bones, sperm, pieces of skin, and animal hair. This was then laid in the ground and surrounded by horse manure. After forty days, an embryonic version would form. Another equally ludicrous

FIGURE 2 A depiction of the golem, a
mythical being from Jewish folklore.

recipe involves poking a hole in the shell of an egg laid by a black hen, inserting human
sperm, and sealing the opening with parchment. Thirty days after burial in the ground, a
small person would emerge who would serve his or her creator in exchange for being fed lavender seeds and earthworms! These homunculi were more likely to be imagined creatures.
It is not clear whether any systematic experiments were conducted in the quest to create
them.

Later in Europe we find the golem, an animated being crafted from inanimate material
(figure 2). The story of the golem originates in Jewish folklore. According to these tales,
golems are crafted from mud. They are unintelligent, usually lack the ability to speak, and
are used primarily for menial labor, where they are assigned to perform some simple task
repetitively. Only a holy person such as a rabbi is capable of creating a golem. Because rabbis
were close to God, they gained some of God's power and were able to create these limited
versions of people. One of the better-known golem stories concerns Rabbi Judah Low ben
Bezalel, who in the sixteenth century produced a golem to defend the Prague ghetto against
anti-Semitic assaults (Bloch, 1972).

Frankenstein is a novel written by Mary Wollstonecraft Shelley and first published in
1818. In it, she relates the story of Victor Frankenstein, a protoscientist who creates a manlike creature from corpses. Horrified at its appearance, he runs away, whereupon the creature itself also disappears. Later events find the creature asking Frankenstein to build him
a female partner. After Frankenstein destroys the partially made female in disgust, the creature seeks revenge and kills Frankenstein's wife. Frankenstein himself now hunts the creature down, pursuing him through the Arctic wastes and ultimately perishing in the attempt.

A prominent theme in this classic is the loneliness and isolation of the creature that wants companionship from humanity and from a kindred creature like itself.

The first use of the word *robot* comes from a play by the Czech Karel Čapek called *Rossum's Universal Robots*, first performed in 1921. Čapek tells the story of beings who are manufactured for the sole purpose of work. These creatures are created in a large factory out of organic materials. They both look and act like people but have no feelings. The wife of the factory owner takes pity on them and asks the factory manager to instill feelings in them so that they will be happier and can get along better with their human counterparts. He agrees, but the robots, now realizing their superiority, revolt and massacre almost everyone. The play ends with a truce between the robots and humankind and a hope for a better future.

Modern science fiction of course offers us many instances of artificial persons along with morality tales warning us of the consequences. In Arthur C. Clarke's *2001: A Space Odyssey*, the computer HAL suffers a breakdown and murders the crew of a spaceship because of an inability to resolve conflicting mission instructions. In the *Terminator* movies, intelligent machines designed for national defense fulfill their duty too well by deciding to wipe out the human race. A similar theme is echoed in the *Matrix* films, where computers win a war against people by imprisoning them in an artificial virtual reality.

The apocalyptic visions portrayed in these stories reflect our fear that in constructing an artificial person we will also bring about our own demise. In other words, our mechanical reproductions will not only possess what makes us great but contain our flaws as well. There is also the lurking anxiety that they may become smarter or better than we are, deciding to ignore or do away with us entirely. The quest to create an artificial person thus has a light and a dark side. By creating an artificial person we are able to figure ourselves out and thus transcend ourselves. But in so doing, we run the risk of becoming obsolete and insignificant.

Theology and Artificial Selves

Anne Foerst, in her 2004 book *God in the Machine*, discusses the theological implications of constructing an artificial self. The first question she addresses is why we should even want to engage in such an endeavor. Most people have mixed feelings about humanlike robots. Many are scared of them and perceive them as a threat. They trigger in some of us a sense of insecurity because of the possibility that they might equal or exceed our own abilities. Artificial people thus jeopardize our sense of uniqueness, the idea that humans are special or privileged in some way.

However, we are also attracted to the notion of interacting with beings similar to ourselves. It seems we humans are lonely. We have a strong desire to share experiences and interact not only with one another but with others like us. This is evident in the quest to communicate with other animal species like chimpanzees and dolphins and in the search for extraterrestrial intelligence. Curiosity about our nature seems to be another underlying factor. The process will undoubtedly teach us more about who we are and how we work.

Perhaps another reason for desiring to recreate ourselves is that in so doing we seem to transcend our own limitations and become like gods. Most religions have a god figure that creates humankind. These acts of creation are related in the form of stories depicting how the gods or a god created humans. If we ever become capable of such a feat, it might imply that we too have achieved a godlike status. Some may interpret this notion as heretical because by acquiring some of God's powers we usurp him.

Foerst (2004) provides a contrary theological interpretation in which recreating our own likeness is not a transgression against God but a celebration of him. She argues that the construction of an artificial person such as a golem is an act of prayer. By engaging in golem building, we learn more about God's creation of people and about our special abilities. Because God created us in his image, participating in this particular version of God's creativity allows us to celebrate God and to better appreciate the wonder of his creation. In this view, creativity becomes an act of prayer. The more complex the creative act, the stronger the prayer becomes and the more we praise God. Because humans are the most complex things we know about, constructing them is the ultimate creative act and therefore the highest form of worship.

In this view, rather than make us arrogant, golem building makes us humble. By understanding the incredible complexity and intricacy that make us up, we gain a newfound appreciation of ourselves and of God's ability. The result is not a sense of superiority but feelings of modesty and humility. This same sentiment has been expressed by a number of scientists. The astronomer Carl Sagan describes the awe he and others have felt when appreciating the amazing workings of the universe. The physicist Albert Einstein, when crossing the Atlantic on a ship, realized how small he and the ship were in comparison to the vast surrounding ocean. He relates the feeling as humbling and awe-inspiring.

Early Attempts at Constructing an Artificial Self

Although there were a number of attempts at constructing artificial beings prior to the eighteenth century, they were somewhat crude. The level of sophistication increased dramatically with the automatons of the French engineer and inventor Jacques de Vaucanson (1709–82). An automaton is a self-operating mechanical moving machine designed to resemble human or animal actions. In a more general sense, an automaton is a device or system that acts in a completely well understood manner. Vaucanson created a flute player who by accounts could play twelve different tunes by moving his fingers, lips, and tongue. Vaucanson's most memorable creation was an artificial duck. Made of copper and rubber tubing, it could drink, quack, and flap its wings. Flying was apparently not part of its behavioral repertoire.

The most sophisticated automaton of this period is attributed to the Swiss clockmaker Henri Maillardet, born in 1745. Spring-driven cams power this "Draughtsman-Writer." The automaton is in the form of a girl that sits in front of a desk with her right hand grasping a pen. When wound up, it looks down and writes poems in French and English and draws several elaborate pictures, including a sailing ship and a pagoda. In 1928, the automaton was first presented to the Franklin Institute in Philadelphia, where it exists to this day.

The 1939 World's Fair in New York was the showcase for one of eight robots built by Westinghouse Corporation. It was seven feet tall and weighed three hundred pounds but appeared humanlike. Elektro could walk forwards and backwards, dance, and even smoke a cigarette. With the aid of a record player, it could count to ten and say seventy-seven words. Elektro even had a companion, Sparko the robot dog, who could bark, sit, and beg.

Several themes run through these early creations. We can see that as new technology develops it gets incorporated into artificial people. Eighteenth-century automatons operated using springs, gears, and cams. Their internal workings resembled those of a complex clock. Later, when electricity became available, it served as a power source. Robots like Elektro were controlled by electric relays and vacuum tubes. Notice also that all of these artificial people were created for the purpose of entertainment. It wasn't until later in the twentieth century that robots would be designed for labor or as investigative research tools. More modern robots are discussed in chapter 5.

The Artificial and the Natural—Not So Different after All

Most of us tend to think of the natural and the artificial as being two very different sorts of things. However, from a scientific perspective, they are best characterized as being the same. The scientific worldview is that the universe is entirely physical or material in nature, being made up of matter and energy (although at a fundamental level matter and energy are identical). Everything in the universe can be understood through physical laws. These laws describe the way any physical system, no matter how complex, should operate.

If this assumption is correct, we can use the laws of the different sciences to explain what a computer is doing at any given moment. Our knowledge of the architecture and operating characteristics of the electronic circuits and other parts allow us to give a very good account of the computer's behavior. The human brain, like a computer, is a physical system governed by known laws. Given a sufficient understanding of the laws that govern it, among them neuroscience and molecular biology, we could also explain what a person is doing at any given moment.

There are two philosophical views that reflect these ideas. According to universal mechanism, everything in the universe can be understood as a completely mechanical system: that is, a system made up entirely of matter in motion, governed by natural laws. All phenomena can be explained by the collision of matter, where one particle or object moves and induces some effect in another. This view has sometimes been described by the phrase "clockwork universe," in which the universe is like a giant clock, filled with springs and gears, each moving in an orderly, understandable way. The French mathematician Pierre-Simon Laplace (1749–1827) was a proponent of this view.

Another version of this perspective is called anthropic mechanism. Anthropic mechanists believe that although everything in the universe may not be explicable as a mechanism, everything about human beings is. In this view everything about the brain and body, including consciousness and free will, can be reduced to the operation of mechanistic forces. The French philosopher Julien Offray de La Mettrie (1709–51) was an anthropic mechanist. He advocates the position in his book *Man and Machine*, written in 1748. Both forms of mechanism imply determinism: if everything about either the universe or people can be explained, then everything about that particular system must also be determined. Determinism poses a problem for freedom and free will. It is discussed at greater length in chapter 2.

The basic premise of this book on the digital self is that there is no reason in principle why people should be treated any differently in terms of the way they are understood than a computer or robot. Technological devices, which are mechanistic, have been shown to be very good models for how the body and the brain operate. Recent years have seen the development of more sophisticated prosthetic limbs and artificial organs. These devices demonstrate that the functioning of body parts can be effectively carried out in a mechanistic fashion. The same also appears true for the brain. The field of cognitive psychology views the mind as a mechanistic information processor and was influenced by the rise of the computer. It has been very successful in explaining mental functions like perception, memory, and reasoning using models where information is represented and processed in a formal mechanistic way.

Replication

Replication is the idea that if we understand something well enough, then we can recreate it and expect it to act the same as its original version. This principle is known as replication. The concept of replication can in principle be extended to the reproduction of any system, no matter how complex. If we understand the system well enough—that is, if we can describe, explain, and predict it—then we should also be able to reproduce the system and expect our reproduction to act in the same way as the original. We can apply these principles to the creation of an artificial person. Assume first that we can sufficiently understand Eve. Next assume we are capable of creating an artificially engineered version of Eve based on this understanding. The reproduction of Eve can then be expected to act in a way that is nearly indistinguishable from the original.

There are two ways to create an artificial Eve that acts like the original. First, we can create an identical copy or duplication. That is, we can reproduce, exactly as possible, all aspects of the original Eve. Identical twins are nature's way of accomplishing this. An artificial means of producing it is through cloning. We could also reproduce Eve by creating a nonidentical copy. In this case, the artificial Eve could be constructed differently from the original. We could do this using nanoelectronics or any other advanced engineering techniques. This version of Eve would act in the same way as the biological Eve but would not resemble Eve in terms of its parts and the way those parts interact. Two systems with differing architectures but similar processes possess functional equivalence. They differ in their hardware or internal organization but produce the same behavior when exposed to the same environments.

The central argument put forth here can be stated in three parts. (1) There is no difference between what we call natural and artificial systems because all systems are made up of matter and energy and are governed by universal physical laws. (2) Sufficient understanding

TABLE 1   Arguments and counterarguments for the ability to replicate complex systems: that is, for the ability to create an artificial person

Objection	Argument	Counterargument
1. Incompleteness	Science has yet to provide a complete description of even relatively simple systems.	Increased understanding will enable better reproductions of systems.
2. Complexity	Complex systems with emergent properties cannot easily be explained by an understanding of their component parts (reductionism).	Future methods of measurement or mathematical modeling may be able to demystify complex systems.
3. Quantum indeterminancy	We may never be able to sufficiently measure the activity of small-scale physics, which could affect larger phenomena.	Certain large-scale events may not be affected by what is happening at the quantum level.
4. Engineering limitation	We may lack the sophistication to engineer things that are either very complex or very small.	It may be possible to replicate complex systems without having to reproduce these aspects.

Source: Friedenberg (2008).

of a system in the form of description, explanation, and prediction allows us to replicate or reproduce it. (3) Exact or functionally equivalent reproductions of an original system will exhibit similar behavior. If these three propositions are true, then the existence of an artificial self is possible. These are very controversial statements, and there are quite a few objections to them. Table 1 lists these arguments as well as the arguments against them.

BOOK OVERVIEW

This book is divided into four main sections. The first section includes this introduction along with a chapter on the philosophy of self and a chapter on the psychology of self. These three chapters together provide a summary of historical and contemporary thought on personhood, self, and identity. They serve as a foundation upon which the remaining parts of the book rest. Readers who are familiar with these topics or are interested more in issues of science and technology can skip them and progress to later sections of the book.

The second section consists of three chapters. These are titled in order: "The Brain," "The Brain + Hardware," and "The Brain + Software." These topics can be thought of as concentric rings of self that radiate outward from the brain and body to include prosthetics and robotics (hardware) and then computer programs and artificial intelligence (software). In the third section are four chapters. The first is on avatars, which are software manifestations of self. The second is on virtual worlds, which are the environments that avatars inhabit. The third is on software selves, beings that might exist as entirely electronic.

The fourth chapter of this section, which concludes the book, is more speculative and describes what future selves might be like. Most of what we present up until this point is factual or plausible, based on scientific research or near-term future predictions. But in the last chapter all bets are off. There we speculate on what might occur either within the next century or beyond. We live in exciting times where technology is accelerating exponentially. Many of us will live to see some of these ideas realized.

CHAPTER TWO

The Philosophy of Self

CONTENTS

Historical Conceptions of Personhood and Self

  Socrates

  Plato

  Aristotle

  René Descartes

  John Locke

  David Hume

  William James

  Daniel Dennett

  Postmodernism and Human Nature

Three Additional Philosophical Conceptions of the Self

  The Bodily Conception of the Self

  The Psychological Conception of the Self

  The Executive Conception of the Self

Personal Identity

Problems of Identity

  The Persistence Question

  Views of How Identity Changes through Time

  Fission

  The Too-Many-Thinkers Problem

  Time and Indeterminacy

Knowledge of the Self

  Self-Identification

  Agency

  Self-Consciousness

  Pre-reflective Self-Consciousness

Free Will and Determinism

  Self and the Free Will/Determinism Debate

  Evolution and Freedom

  The Illusion of Free Will

The Extended-Mind Thesis

In this chapter we sketch out various theories of personhood and self that have been proposed by major Western philosophers throughout history. Following this we more closely examine specific topics including personal identity, knowledge of the self, free will, and the extended-mind thesis. We discuss technology where it is relevant to these issues. The understanding of these ideas will be foundational for interpreting the psychological theories of mind presented in the next chapter.

HISTORICAL CONCEPTIONS OF PERSONHOOD AND SELF

Torchia (2008) provides a description of what various Western philosophers have thought about personhood, self, and identity over the past several thousand years. He starts with the Socratic ancient Greek thinkers and works his way historically up to the present day. In what follows we provide a summary of this history, drawing from his work and other sources.

Socrates

The ancient Greek philosopher Socrates (470–399 BCE) was known for his questioning method of getting at the truth (Brickhouse, 2000). He was concerned with "the good" and how humans should achieve it. He believed that correct knowledge of what to do in a situation should be translated into correct action. A person was morally good only so far as he or she understood what was good intellectually and could then act on it. Socrates looked forward to death because he thought good people were rewarded after death. Death to him was the point at which the soul departs the body, ending physical life but beginning a new life in a different world. For Socrates the soul operates best by avoiding excessive contact with the body. The body in some sense "contaminates" the soul and makes reasoning more difficult. Some of these ideas translated forward into Christian religious beliefs about the afterworld.

One cannot help but notice the similarity of these views to the modern-day transhumanist belief in mind uploading that we discuss in detail later. In mind uploading or whole-brain emulation, a copy of the mind is made and "uploaded" to a computer, where it can reside indefinitely and experience greater intellectual powers. The mind here becomes the soul, and the computer systems in which it can live after death become an ideal world of forms, a place of pure reason and perfection. In Christian theology that world is heaven for those who pursued the good and hell for those who did not. Many modern-day thinkers argue that uploaded minds will have vastly increased intelligence and be able to interact with other similarly uploaded minds (Moravec, 1990). One detects in these modern ideas a disdain for the physical and the elevation of the soul in the form of abstract information and computation. The so-called "rapture of the nerds" is the ascendency to this greater state of being.

Plato

In dualism, one believes that both mental and physical substances are possible (Armstrong, 1968/1993). Plato, the well-known ancient Greek philosopher (427–347 BCE), was a dualist

(Cooper & Hutchinson, 1997). He believed that the mind and the body exist in two separate worlds. Knowledge of the mind, he thought, exists in an ideal world of forms, which is immaterial (nonphysical), nonextended (not occupying space), and eternal (lasting forever). The body instead resides in a world that is material, extended, and perishable. There are crucial differences between the objects of one world and those of the other. Mental ideas that reside in the ideal world of forms are perfect, whereas concrete examples of those ideas that we find in the real world are always imperfect. For instance, in the world of forms the "circle" is perfectly round, but if we examine an actual circle, at some level of magnification the circle's edge will lose its circular curvature.

To Plato, as to his instructor Socrates, the self is divided in two. On the one side we have the body, which is corrupt and imperfect. On the other side we have the soul, which is perfect and rules over the body. Plato believed that we are fundamentally our souls and that the body must always be subordinate and inferior to the soul. The soul is the seat of reason and through reason is able to access the ideal world of forms. One question here is what the soul will be like after death. Will it still have the personality that belonged to its physical body? Or will it be an abstract form devoid of any human traits?

Plato later differentiated the soul into three parts. The spirited soul is the most elevated or noble. The rational soul is the part that thinks and governs the body. At the lowest level is the appetitive soul, the seat of physical desires such as hunger and sex. If the soul were not regulated by reason it would give in to all the impulses and whims of the appetites, the part closest to the physical body. There is a noticeable similarity here to the id, ego, and superego aspects of the self in Freud's theory of personality. The superego that strives to do "good" corresponds to the spirited soul, the rational ego is equivalent to the reasoning soul, and the impulsive animalistic id is like the appetitive soul. We discuss Freud's theory at greater length in the psychology chapter that follows.

Aristotle

According to monism, there is only one kind of state or substance in the universe. The ancient Greek philosopher Aristotle (384–322 BCE) was a monist (Ackrill, 1981). Plato was Aristotle's teacher, but the two held quite different views. Aristotle did not believe in an ideal world of forms and thought that abstract phenomena were grounded in reality. To him the soul was intricately bound up with and inseparable from the body. Aristotle characterized the difference between mind and body as the difference between form and matter. One way to think of his notion is to consider a lump of clay. It is made up of physical matter, and we can think of it as corresponding to the brain. We can shape the clay with our hands into different forms—for example, we can roll it into a ball or flatten it into a pancake. The shapes the clay can assume, Aristotle implied, are like the different thoughts the mind can take on when it undergoes different patterns of activity. These shapes are just different physical states and do not constitute any nonphysical or spiritual substance.

This view is not too far from our physical understanding of the brain. Whenever we think, different sets of neurons activate and send messages to one another. These require actual changes in the physical state of the brain where ions flow through membranes and neurotransmitters flow across synapses. With repeated stimulation we see an increase in dendritic spines and in some cases the growth of new neurons in areas like the hippocampus. So thought does correspond to physical changes in the brain. These changes are more subtle and microscopic than a lump of clay changing shape, but they do occur. Our sense of self may reside in the unique ways our brains change and respond to experiences. In the future it may be possible to have a neural signature of self consisting of a precise 3-D spatial and temporal map depicting the unfolding of these processes.

Aristotle believed in a hierarchy of souls, with plants at the lowest level, followed by animals at the second level and then by humans at the highest level. Each level inherits the psychic qualities of the levels beneath it, so animals inherit the capabilities of plants, and humans inherit the capabilities of plants and animals. Plants can grow, decay, and reproduce. Animals have sense perception and movement, but only humans have all of these abilities and in addition to them reason and will.

For Aristotle, the senses provide raw information that is used for concept formation. Concepts then serve as the basis for more advanced forms of learning. Active intellect makes knowledge possible, and knowledge is the highest aim. According to him all humans desire knowledge. This is acquired directly through sensation but also through the exercise of memory. Aristotle also thought that people were motivated to create knowledge through productive means like art. The ideal for him was the wise man who is capable of learning difficult topics, of being precise, and of understanding the underlying causes of things.

René Descartes

The French philosopher René Descartes (1596–1650) starts his view of the self from an understanding of existence (Cottingham, 2013). He argues that he may doubt everything, and may be deceived about the existence of all other things, but he can't doubt that he exists. In fact, merely being able to think shows that he exists, hence his quote "I think therefore I am." Descartes next asks himself what he is and concludes that he is a thinking thing. But what is a thinking thing? He believes the mind is a type of substance. Substances are things that are capable of existing independently of other things. Clearly the mind can be seen as a substance, Descartes thought, because we can see that it exists independently. Each substance has an essence, and for Descartes the essence of the mind is thought. Thought as a substance has modes, the different states or actions it can produce. These modes are processes like judging, doubting, and affirming.

So Descartes concludes now that he is a thing that thinks. But what is the nature of a thinking thing? In order to discover this he examines a piece of wax. His senses tell him it is hard and solid, smells slightly of flowers, and tastes slightly like honey. Then he applies a flame to the wax and it changes. It is now soft and has a different smell. He concludes that things in the world can change. What did not change in this situation, however, was his mind. It was capable of perceiving changes that happened to objects, but it remained the same during these changes. He concludes that he can never know anything better than his own mind. This is because whenever he understands some aspect of a material thing like shape or size, he also becomes aware of the ability of his mind to perceive and understand that aspect. Whenever he learns things about the physical world, he also learns things about his mind. But he can learn aspects of his mind without learning anything new about the world. Thus he knows his mind better than anything else.

Descartes's view may be put to the test given advances in technology. We now access vast amounts of information and computation through various devices like smartphones and computers. But in these cases, the devices often "think" for us. When we want to determine the tip for a bill, we use a calculator app. When we want to check grammar or spelling, we let writing software do it for us. In these situations "we" are not the ones doing the thinking. Does that then mean that our self has disappeared during those moments? According to Descartes these are changes or different circumstances during which we may not have full conscious awareness that we are thinking, so by his definition our selves may diminish or vanish. We explore this "outsourcing" of the mind in greater detail later in this chapter in the discussion of the extended-mind thesis.

John Locke

The English philosopher John Locke (1632–1704) considered a person to be a thinking, intelligent being that has reason and reflection (Chappell, 1999). He proposed several other criteria as well. In sum, he believed that to be human one must have the capacity for (1) reason or rationality; (2) mental states like beliefs, intentions, desires, and emotions; (3) language; (4) entering into social relationships with other persons; and (5) being considered a responsible moral agent.

Locke argued that a stable and unified sense of self arises from considering ourselves as the same beings in different times and places. It is the consciousness we experience whenever we experience anything that tells us we are the same being on different occasions. Thus an ever-present sense of personal consciousness is what unifies all of our different experiences and tells us that we are the same "I" existing now that existed a minute ago.

So Locke's argument for self is based on some constancy of being in the presence of changing places and times. We know we are the same person because we feel the same in some sense wherever we go or no matter what time it is. However, in video games and virtual reality we can stay in the same place but occupy different virtual spaces and times. For example, I can walk around a Greek island even though I am sitting at home in New York. I can also exist in a time that does not correspond to the present by playing the role of a thief or assassin during the period of the Persian Empire. In these situations we often aren't even ourselves. We take on characters or avatars with personalities and abilities that can be quite different from our own. So our constancy of being as well as our perceived spatial and temporal experiences change in these digital worlds. According to Locke this might mean our real self is temporarily suspended while we take on other selves.

David Hume

The Scottish philosopher David Hume (1711–76) had a detailed theory of the self, firmly based on the traditions of Newtonian physics and science (Wiley, 2012). He believed that only the scientific method could yield a true understanding of self. Hume was an empiricist, believing that ideas enter the mind through the senses. He thought we should doubt the existence of very abstract concepts like the soul or the self because these ideas are very far removed from the senses. Hume believed that we make associations between ideas on the basis of resemblance (two things being similar to each other), spatial and temporal proximity (two things being close together in space or time), and causality (one causing the other). These associations are mediated by experience. For example, if we smell smoke, we assume that there is a fire nearby because in the past we have associated the two together and know that one causes the other.

Hume doubted that a single unified self could exist. He claimed that the only things we can believe with certainty are sense perceptions because those are directly experienced. Self is no more than a "bundle" of perceptions. On each occasion we have different experiences, and there is little to link them together. Life is just a rapid succession of sights and sounds. What we think is identity is actually relation. In other words, two things may be related to one another on the basis of perceptual association, but that does not mean they are necessarily the same thing. So I may see a horse one day and another similar-looking horse in the same place the following day, but that does not mean they are the same horse.

Hume also noted the relations between parts and how those make up wholes. How many parts does one have to change in a whole before it loses its identity and becomes something else? A ship like the USS *Constitution* has over the centuries had nearly all of its parts replaced. Does this mean we should still refer to it as the same ship, simply because it still floats (Torchia, 2008)? Likewise, the human body has many of its cells replaced over time, yet we still claim to have the same bodies in spite of this change. Is a middle-aged woman still the same person she was as a child? Is an elderly man still the same person he was when middle-aged? Functionality and the relations between parts seem to be the answer here. If our bodies still function in largely the same way and our behaviors and personalities are also largely similar, then we may still be judged as being the same person. Likewise if the relationship between parts is preserved even though the parts themselves change, identity is preserved.

To Hume memory was an important way to preserve past impressions and so produce a sense of identity. If we can remember going to bed last night in this particular bedroom and compare it to waking up this morning in the same bedroom, then this suggests we must be the same person. Memory gives us historical continuity even in the face of gaps. Hume believed that without memory there would be little to indicate identity and self.

William James

One of the most prominent early American psychologists was William James (1842–1910). He had a well-developed theory of Self (he uses a capital "S"). James thought the understanding of Self could be broken into three categories (James, 1892). First are the constituents or parts of Self. Second are the feelings and emotions they arouse, what he calls Self-feelings. Third come the actions that they prompt, what he calls Self-seeking and Self-preservation. The first category of constituents can themselves be broken into another four categories: the material Self, the social Self, the spiritual Self, and the pure Ego. Echoing modern sentiments, James acknowledges that Self consists of these multiple Selves that interact and that Self is not a single, monolithic construct.

The material Self is made up of our bodies, clothes, immediate family, and home. These things affect us deeply because we are the most invested in them. The more we invest in them the more attached to them we become. The social Self comes from our interactions with other people. What other people think about us and the reactions they have to us are analyzed and shape this sense of ourselves. Multiple aspects of social Self get actuated depending on our social context. James seems to be repeating here the notion of social roles or masks that one can put on to play different roles in society, like that of "father" at home and "professor" at work. Because it may be possible to assume more than one possible social role in a given situation, and because the options may conflict, James says we use a sense of "fame" or "honor" to determine, on the basis of morality and reason, what roles are appropriate in any given situation. Next comes the spiritual Self, our awareness of religious beliefs and our evaluation of them.

The last aspect of Self to James is the Pure Ego. This is the subjective part of Self, the part that is self-aware. The Pure Ego has awareness of its own thoughts: these have a particular warmth to them because they are our own. The Pure Ego operates using a process called subjective synthesis, which brings thoughts together so they can be contrasted or processed further. This cognitive operation seems to temporarily unify what might normally be different aspects of consciousness.

In neuroscience this binding role of the Pure Ego seems to be the function of the frontal lobes. During some states of conscious experience there are patterns of neural synchrony in which prefrontal areas seem to coordinate activity in other brain regions. The Pure Ego may also correspond to working memory. In cognitive psychology this is the place where information we are currently aware of gets processed, as when we are solving a problem or trying to remember a fact. A focused state of self may require a "coordinator" or "integrator" that brings information together in one place. Our self may vanish or be more diffuse when we are daydreaming or in some other nonfocused state.

James also noted that self-esteem (feeling good or bad about the Self) is dependent on what he called pretensions (our aspirations) and successes (our perceived accomplishments). For example, if Michelle aspires to attend medical school, then failing her organic chemistry course will affect her self-esteem negatively. In contrast, Bill has no such aspirations. If he were to fail the course it would be less upsetting to him. Self-esteem is thus the difference between our pretensions and present behavior. Note the similarity of this view to the real self and ideal self proposed by the psychologist Carl Rogers. We describe the Rogerian view of self in the next chapter.

Daniel Dennett

The contemporary philosopher of mind Daniel Dennett presents six necessary conditions of personhood (Dennett, 1978). Some of these overlap with those proposed by Locke. These are as follows:

1. Persons are rational beings. We are capable of thinking rationally and logically.

2. Persons are beings to which states of consciousness are attributed, or to which psychological or mental states are ascribed.

3. A person is a being to which an attitude or stance of personhood is taken, i.e., a person is someone who is treated as a person by others.

4. The object to which the stance ascribed in number three above must be capable of reciprocating in some way. In other words, to be a person is to treat others as persons, perhaps in a moral way.

5. Persons must be capable of verbal communication or language. This excludes all nonhuman animals.

6. Persons are conscious in some special way that other species are not.

Notice that conditions 2 through 5 are not intrinsic properties of an individual. They require a social level of description. For number 2, mental states, because of their subjective and psychological character, cannot be proven objectively. Partly for this reason, Dennett proposes that others ascribe them. This theme is echoed in condition 3, where we see that personhood is again extrinsic, a property attributed to one by others. Condition 4 simply makes this a two-way street: a person is someone who not only is considered by others as human but in turn treats them as if they too were people. Condition 5 is also social, as the purpose of language is to exchange information between individuals. For additional conceptions of personhood, see table 2.

An important issue concerning what it means to be a person centers on the body. Is a body necessary in order to be human? Nowhere in any of the definitions given above do we see that having arms, legs, internal organs, or for that matter even a brain is necessary. There is no mention of what exact physical form a person needs to take. Instead, Dunnett emphasizes the capacity of a being to have mental states. If this is the case, then a being with the right sorts of mental states is human regardless of its physical structure. People can be made of nonbiological parts as long as the system as a whole is capable of supporting the appropriate mental states.

If Dennett's conditions 3 and 4 are true, then it is possible for artificial beings like robots and androids to attain personhood. It is not difficult to imagine a constructed being that is treated by others as a person because it may look and act very much like a real person. This being may also be fully capable of treating others as people and acting in a moral way. We as

TABLE 2   Different definitions of personhood according to Foerst (2004)

Homo Type	Definition	Description
Homo sapiens	The thinker	Having the ability to think and be intelligent.
Homo faber	The builder	Capable of constructing things and shaping the world with the help of tools and technology.
Homo ludens	The player	Being playful but also taking on a role in a society such as father.
Homo economicus	The economist	Engaging in economic activity. Trading goods and services. But also being self-centered and pleasure seeking.
Homo religiosus	The spiritualist	Practicing religion. Praying, worshipping, and exhibiting spiritual beliefs.
Homo narrans	The storyteller	Constructing narratives or stories.
Homo objectivus et rationalis	The objective rationalist	Being objective and rational. Capable of using reason and logic.

humans are very prone to anthropomorphizing and will quite easily attribute human qualities to inanimate objects and animals, so it is likely that we will consider such beings as people, even if they lack intrinsic human qualities like consciousness.

Postmodernism and Human Nature

The postmodernist movement in philosophy raises several interesting issues regarding personhood. The first is whether an extraterrestrial alien or a robot could be considered human. If one of these entities was capable of expressing any of the fundamental attributes of personhood we have examined so far, like reason, empathy, and morality, would it be human? Some scholars have argued that what may matter is not the intrinsic features of such a being but its treatment by others. Dolby (1989) believes that if people are willing to accept robots or aliens as persons then they should be treated as such (this corresponds to Dennett's third criterion above). In this view, it is not inner processes that count but whether the entity in question meets certain behavioral criteria that are agreed upon by a significant majority.

This view, that personhood is a matter of subjective opinion, is characteristic of the postmodern approach. Postmodernism challenges that there is any such thing as objective truth, knowledge, or meaning. Postmodernists like Rorty (1980) believe that reducing ourselves to a list of features treats human beings as objects rather than subjects. The problem with this subjective postmodern approach, though, is that personhood and self can be anything we want them to be. It stretches the understanding of these ideas so far that they begin to lose any sort of meaning.

A second and related issue is whether some individuals, although having human bodies, can lose the status of being human. If an individual loses reason, autonomy, conscious experience, and moral agency, is that person human anymore? This question can apply to individuals who have gone into a coma, and to a lesser extent to the mentally disabled, the very young, and the senile. In contrast to aliens and robots, who may have nonhuman bodies but human traits, individuals in this category have human bodies but nonhuman traits. Engelhardt (1988) believes that moral agency is necessary for personhood. Those who are unable to understand their choices, or to appreciate whether their actions are good or bad, in his view are not human.

THREE ADDITIONAL PHILOSOPHICAL CONCEPTIONS OF THE SELF

Knobe and Nichols (2011) outline three major philosophical conceptions of the self. These are called the bodily, psychological, and executive. Each can be thought of as delving deeper inward into the source of what controls our actions, starting with the larger body, moving from there to general psychological mechanisms of mind and brain, and from there to the specific parts of our brain that make decisions.

The Bodily Conception of the Self

In this view, the self is everything "from the skin in." It would include not just the brain but internal organs, arms and legs, and so on. This view is commonsensical. If Mary sprains her ankle, we know that *Mary* has suffered the injury, not somebody else like her sister. Nietzsche supports this position, but so do several contemporary philosophers (Carter, 1990; Nietzsche 1883/1999; Olson, 1997). This later work endorses the view that humans are animals, or, more generally, organisms with bodies, and that this is fundamental to determining the self. No prominent accounts of self would deny that decisions and commands to move are generated by mechanisms inside our bodies.

However, there are still problems with this view dating as far back as Socrates. Socrates said that after he died his body would still be present but Socrates himself would no longer be present. Thus his body and his self would be two separate things. This at least means that a functioning body is necessary for self, because after death a body no longer functions. Modern-day cyborgs also pose a challenge to this argument because they are a mixed system of machine and biological parts that act together. Does a person with a majority of his body parts replaced with mechanical or electronic equivalents have a self (figure 3)? What if significant parts of a person's brain are replaced with artificial parts, including those areas like the frontal lobes that make decisions? Cyborgs thus pose a problem for all three conceptions of self outlined here. Another related issue here is whether we even need bodies to have selves. Some have suggested that software entities that are noncorporeal can be alive. See chapter 9's section on cellular automata and artificial life for more on this.

The Psychological Conception of the Self

This second view is more restrictive and states that many parts of the body are irrelevant to the self. People can have their limbs removed, for example, and their self seems to remain mostly

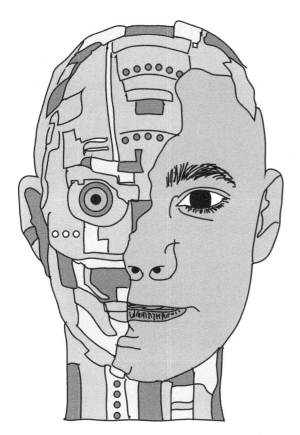

FIGURE 3 A cyborg is a hybrid of biological and technological parts. Are cyborgs human?

the same. What is important here are psychological characteristics, things like our thoughts, memories, beliefs, and desires. These seem to be more localized to the brain and perhaps the enteric nervous system (that governs our digestive system) and endocrine system (glands that regulate body and brain function) than they are to body organs like the pancreas or intestine. John Locke and more recent thinkers support this view (Locke, 1847/1979; Parfit, 1986).

The Executive Conception of the Self

We can continue to get more specific and localized with regard to the location of the self and say only the part of the brain that actually makes decisions is the real self. In this view, other psychological attributes and their corresponding brain areas might not be needed. The executive part of our brain is closely allied with the frontal lobes. This area can take psychological factors like fear and desire into consideration before making a decision. For example, Mary may want to be a teacher but may be very introverted and may fear what students may think of her. In the end she may decide that she will go ahead and teach anyway because that is more important than her personal feelings. The executive therefore considers psychological states, but it is the executive itself and not the states that make the decision. This would make the executive and not the states the source of self.

FIGURE 4 Modern computer architectures contain drives and processing chips. There are analogous operations in the human brain. Can a self be located somewhere in here? Public domain image courtesy of pixneo.com.

The ancient Stoic philosophers would agree with this conception. They saw the soul as the source of human action. This "soul" was viewed as a commanding faculty, the part of the person that thinks, plans, and decides (Baltzly, 2008). This faculty was thought to be separable from the body (Sextus Empiricus, 1949/2000). Other scholars like Reid have echoed this view, emphasizing that the self is the thing that *does* the thinking, deciding, and acting, not the thought, decision, or action itself (T. Reid, 1785/1969). According to this perspective, psychological states are not *the* self, they merely *belong* to the self.

This difference is similar to the data/processing distinction in computer science (Hill, Jouppi, & Sohi, 2000). *Data* refers to information that is internally stored on hard drives or cached in memory or externally input from sources through devices like cameras. These data are ultimately fed to processors. Processors are chips like the central processing unit (CPU) in a computer (figure 4). The way in which the data are processed is determined by the code that makes up the software. Code consists of lines of instruction written in a computer language like C++. One could imagine psychological states as being like the data in a computer and the executive as being like the processing chips or instructions in the software. This would localize the self as being in the chips or code since they are doing the processing rather than the data, as the data are merely "consulted" to determine some processing goal.

Under scrutiny, however, this view is unlikely, for both brains and computers. In brains, psychological states and other inputs to a decision-making mechanism are necessary for making that decision. The decision could not be made without them. It is therefore better to think of the accessed states and the executive device *together* as the seat of self. This conforms more with what we know from brain-imaging studies, where the frontal lobes and other brain areas are all active simultaneously during decision-making. It is the totality of all these systems that is best thought of as the self. For example, if memories were part of making a decision, we would see activity in the frontal lobes and brain areas that underlie memory.

Similarly, in computer science, it would be the activity of the CPU and other systems inside the computer working concurrently that could be best conceptualized as the computer's "self." For example, if the CPU needed to consult some data to make a decision, it might activate the hard drive to access these data. The CPU, the hard drive, and the other systems needed to support this function considered as a whole might then be the self. If data are necessary for making a decision, then data cannot be considered separate from it. If ancillary hardware systems are necessary for performing a computation, those too cannot be considered separate from it. In this view it is the totality of processing systems, hardware and software, that holistically and integrally constitutes the self.

PERSONAL IDENTITY

Philosophical inquiry into personal identity attempts to answer such questions as: Who am I? When did I begin? What is it like to be me? With regard to the first question, we describe ourselves using phrases such as "likes opera" or "is tall." These are called properties of the self and correspond roughly to personality traits in psychology. Of course, people are always changing, so the properties by which we define our identity will change as well. In this section we provide a summary of the account of personal identity provided by Olson (2015).

Problems of Identity

One recurring problem in the philosophy of self is persistence. This looks at how identity persists over time. Why are you the same person today as you were yesterday? Are we completely different people now than we were as children (figure 5)? Persistence after death also comes up here. When would your self or identity end completely? Is it possible to persist after death? Immortality and mind uploading are important theoretical issues that neuroscientists and transhumanists are also now studying. Later in the book we will examine technological forms of immortality and how these may be attained.

Persistence requires evidence of a past (Shoemaker, 1970). One form of evidence is first-person memory. If you remember doing something in the past and someone really did do it, then that is evidence in support of your having done it, and hence your having existed in the past. Memory can be problematic, though. We now live in an age where it may be possible to delete, change, or substitute memories in an individual. If you erased Laura's memories and replaced them with Lucy's, would Laura still be Laura? Or would she now be Lucy? Another form of evidence is physical continuity. If the person that did something looked like you or was physically continuous with you, then that could also be evidence that it was you that did the deed.

Next is the problem of properties or parts (Olson, 2007). What are we made of? What particular configuration of parts defines who you are? Where do our boundaries end? Can your self or identity exist spatially beyond your body? If so, what are its boundaries? Are we made of substances or states or processes or events? There are lots of questions here, with different answers to each of them from different philosophers. Regarding the digital world, does the substrate matter? In other words, in order for something to have a self, does it need to be constructed of a particular type of matter? Is a robot not a person simply because it is made of metal and plastic? If you subscribe to the school of patternism, then you believe it is the patterns of energy and matter flow in a system that will produce things like sentience, while the "stuff" itself can be irrelevant.

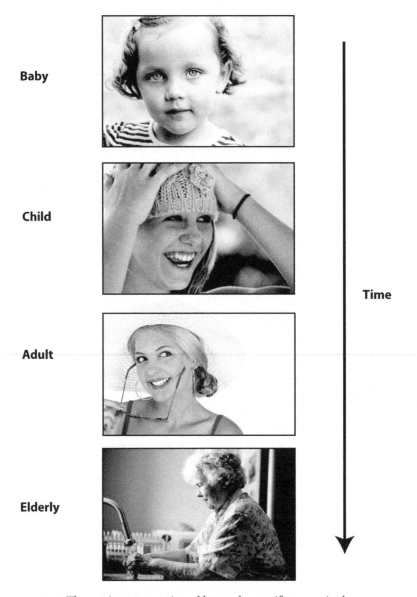

Baby

Child

Time

Adult

Elderly

FIGURE 5 The persistence question addresses how or if we remain the same despite drastic changes to our physical makeup and behavior with development. Public domain images courtesy of pixneo.com.

A final major issue here is what matters in identity. Why should we care if our identity changes over time? Should you care if you have a clone or mental version of a clone made of you? The crux of the matter here is whether the new person in question really is you. If it is someone different, then we will care about this entity in an entirely different way. We will see later in the book that it may be possible to create an electronic or biological duplicate of you. Should such entities exist, they will change the way we think about ourselves in a very radical way.

The Persistence Question

The persistence question is sometimes phrased as: If a person X exists at one time and a person Y exists at another time, under what possible circumstances is it the case that X is Y? It is the equivalent of asking what it takes for a past or future person to be you, or whether two people existing at different times are the same. As mentioned above, memory is one answer to this question. If X can remember something that happened to Y in the past from a first-person perspective, then X and Y may have the same identity.

One way to answer this question coming from psychology is whether the two people in question have the same traits. If they do or if they share a large number of traits according to the results of an objective test, then we might consider them to be the same. Another answer from neuroscience is whether the two people show the same pattern of brain activation. If there are persistent ways individual brains operate over time and these can be measured using techniques like fMRI, then we can use the neuroimaging technology to assess whether Bob in the present is the same as Bob from the past.

Views of How Identity Changes through Time

There are three philosophical responses to the persistence question. The most popular is the psychological continuity view (Hudson, 2001). If you inherit mental features from the past or pass them on into the future, then a past "you" or a future "you" may be said to be the same as the current "you." Mental features are things like preferences, beliefs, memories, or the ability to reason in a particular way. A number of philosophers hold this position.

A second response is the brute physical view (Mackie, 1999). This says you are the same you over time if you have the same body or relation of body parts. Physical and mental continuity can be considered separately. If we transplanted Michael's brain into Mark's body, who would now be the new "you"? Would it be Mark with Michael's brain or Michael with Mark's body? If psychological properties matter and these are mostly in the brain, then Michael would become the new self. If it the physical properties matter and these are mostly in the body, then it would be Mark. The anticritical view says that mental and physical features can constitute evidence for identity but are not necessary (Merricks, 1998). What the third plausible alternative to these might be is not well stated. It may involve nonmaterial properties.

The replacement of body parts is now currently a reality. Three-dimensional printed lungs and other organs are being manufactured that can be used to swap out damaged or diseased organs. Is a person the same if he or she has a new biologically grown or mechanical heart and liver? If all of a person's organs are replaced with updated versions that operate differently from their prior counterparts and have different relations to one another? What if a complete reproduction of a person's brain could be replaced as well? In a well-known philosophical thought experiment, a person's neurons are replaced one by one with artificial silicon versions. At what point is the person transformed from biological to technological human?

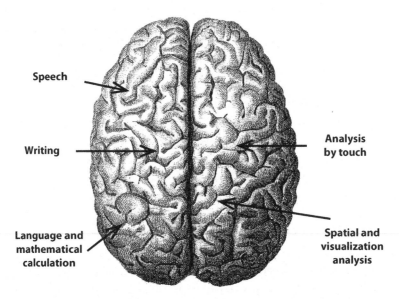

Left Hemisphere

- Processes input sequentially and analytically
- Time sensitive
- Recognizes words and numbers

Right Hemisphere

- Processes input more holistically and abstractly
- Space sensitive
- Recognizes faces, places, objects, and music

Speech

Writing

Language and mathematical calculation

Analysis by touch

Spatial and visualization analysis

FIGURE 6 Human left and right cerebral hemispheres are dominant for different cognitive functions. Under certain conditions these can be dissociated showing we may have two biologically distinct selves "under one roof."

Fission

One critique of the psychological continuity argument involves another thought experiment. Imagine that we take your left hemisphere and transplant it into somebody else called Lefty. We then take your right hemisphere and transplant it into another person called Righty. By this proposal you would have split into two different people. You would be psychologically continuous with them both because each would share one half of your brain, thus inheriting some of your mental features. This situation is referred to as "fission," meaning a splitting. Something analogous to this occurs within a single individual in dissociative identity disorder when distinct selves are formed, each with its own personality traits.

One solution to this problem is called the "multiple occupancy view." It states that with two hemispheres, each one of us already has two selves or identities. The hemispheres do indeed have different cognitive skills, and with split-brain patients these become dissociable (figure 6). For example, some split-brain patients can lift one arm to perform an action.

Their other arm then grabs this arm and redirects it toward another action. Under particular conditions these people can be seen as being "at war" with themselves. This view says that you already have two selves (H. Noonan, 2003). An alternate argument says this situation is like two roads that coincide at first but then diverge, so that they at first share spatial and temporal elements in common but then dislocate (Hudson, 2001).

Multiagent systems are software programs that consist of separate software components called agents. Each agent is capable of perceiving, computing, and acting in the software world. Their interactions lead to unpredicted emergent phenomena. What is the "self" in this situation? Is it the individual agents? Groups of them that interact to form subminds? The entire program considered as a whole? The human brain already contains this kind of modularity (Fodor, 1983). Neuroscience reveals that some brain areas act more independently than others. They are less responsive to inputs from other areas that can modulate their function. The brain as a whole, however, seems to be more "quasi-modular," consisting of networks of areas that interact. For example, to regulate attention seems to require at least six distinct brain structures (Posner & Peterson, 1990). It may be more accurate to portray the self as a collection of subselves that work together in a ballet of fission and fusion.

The Too-Many-Thinkers Problem

Another objection to the continuity proposal is that you should stay you as long as you remain a biological organism. A brain or hemisphere transplant removes only an organ; the rest of you remains, and it is this organism that determines identity. The organism would for all intents and purposes be nonfunctional but it would still be alive or in a vegetative state. The organism has a brute-physical persistence, and it would in some sense still maintain identity in the absence of being able to think. This and other arguments like it are called the "too-many-thinkers" problem (Snowdon, 1990).

The argument against this is that being in a vegetative state is not really being a self. Being able to think, as Descartes says, is the foundation of identity. Without thought we are not a self. A more realistic alternative would be the creation of a clone or a duplicate digital mind that was a thinking being sharing your mental properties. Under these circumstances we could say that two selves were created. Another example would be identical twins: they start off as the same because they have identical genes but then diverge to differing degrees depending on how different their environments are.

Time and Indeterminacy

A metaphysical view on the issue of persistence states that identity is in constant flux. One way to state this is that "you are you now, only now." An instant later you are a different you because you will have existed at a different moment in time and will have changed. Identity in this view is like a water fountain. If you take a picture of a water fountain at time t and then wait and take a second picture of it at time t + 1, it will be different. In addition many different aspects of your identity might get expressed at any moment. Which one gets expressed depends on a variety of factors, including the environment, your mood, and your cognitive capacities. This view is similar to quantum theories in which there are multiple universes of possibility and in which free will or choice determines the one that gets actualized.

KNOWLEDGE OF THE SELF

Here we will examine knowledge of the self, meaning knowledge of one's own mental states. Mental states are things like attitudes, beliefs, and thoughts. They can also include sensations like the feeling of something rough against your skin or the taste of coffee. Emotions also qualify as mental states. Knowledge of self also refers to how we distinguish ourselves from others, self-awareness, and issues related to the use of reason and agency. In this section we will summarize some of the content described by Gertler (2015).

Self-Identification

To self-identify is to have a mental state such as a thought and to know that the state belongs to you. This is also to know that the state does not belong to anybody else. On one view, you first grasp that you have psychological properties and then by analogy conclude that other people do too. You might, for example, notice the similarity between yourself and others (you and someone else both having facial reactions like smiling in certain circumstances) and then realize that if you feel happy when you smile then other people do too. There is a relation here to the psychological idea called theory of mind. You have a theory of mind if you know that you yourself and others both have minds, the capacity to have subjective experiences.

Access to self-knowledge may be direct and immediate (Evans, 1982). Alternatively it can occur as the result of a longer descriptive process (R. Howell, 2006). Proprioceptive awareness that your arm is raised is given as an example of immediate self-knowledge because it happens quickly. Proprioception is based on receptors inside our own body. If our arm is raised, we know that "from the inside" without even having to even look at our arm. These processes are immune to the error of mistaking they might come from someone else (Brewer, 1995). They are also direct and immediate. However, they may still be inaccurate, as in the case of phantom limb syndrome, where individuals still feel sensations from a missing arm or leg.

Self-identification can also come from visual perception. Visual experience is always from a certain perspective. It tells us the location of objects, but these are always in relation to a particular point of view. You can, for instance, see the door as in front of *you*, the bed to *your* right, and so on. The body is thus experienced as an object too, the object that is the point of origin of egocentric perception. Objects are also coded relative to self-directed motion. When you turn your head to the left, the world moves to the right. When you move forward there is a point of radial expansion where objects move away from the point of fixation. This motion of the world relative to oneself is called optic flow, and it also helps you to maintain your balance. (Try standing on one foot with and without your eyes shut for a dramatic demonstration.) Optic flow is an example of ecological perception, a form of perception that tells you properties of the world immediately and without inference (Gibson, 2014). It also by default provides you with information about yourself.

In the modern world, self-identity is put to the test. It is possible now for two or more people to share identical experiences. For example, if a video is live streaming, the video and audio can be experienced by millions. In this case one is distal from both the source event and the others experiencing it. Would we say that this now becomes a "shared self"? We know that the mental state belongs to us but also that it belongs to others.

The psychological process of introspection used by the early psychologists like Wilhem Wundt illustrates the difference between direct and indirect self-awareness. Wundt's method was introspection, or internal perception. *Introspection* literally means "inward looking." Just as one can look out at the external world to see various objects, such as a chair or table, Wundt believed that one could also look inward to experience and describe mental objects. He presented the students in his lab with various stimuli, such as colored shapes, and asked them to introspect. The students then recorded their subjective experiences of the stimuli. Although philosophers have used various forms of introspection for centuries, Wundt attempted to systematize and objectify the technique. He had his students put themselves in a ready state of attention prior to their introspecting and repeat their observations several times as he varied specific physical aspects of the stimulus, such as size and exposure duration. This kind of methodological exactness exemplifies the influence of the scientific method.

Wundt believed that psychology should study consciousness. However, he distinguished between two types of conscious experience. Immediate experience is our direct awareness of something. For example, if we see a rose, our perception of the rose as red is immediate. It is the redness that we experience directly while we are looking at it. If someone then asked us what we were looking at and we responded, "A red rose," then that thought would be a mediate experience (it was a thought about the rose). Mediate experiences are those that come from mental reflection about an object. Wundt emphasized the study of immediate experiences. He believed that they were the best way to describe the basic elements of the mind since they were "untainted" by elaborate thought processes.

Agency

Agency refers to the capacity to make decisions and then act upon them. It also refers to our capacity to know that we ourselves are the source of that action (this can be equated under some circumstances with free will). Some philosophers argue that agency and a sense of being human requires knowledge of our traits and dispositions (C. Taylor, 1977). Others state that we need to rationally evaluate our desires in order to have freedom of the will. Frankfurt (1971) believes this rational evaluation produces second-order desires. These are desires concerning which desires to have or to act upon. As an example we may have the desire to sleep because we are tired but then not act upon this desire because we need to stay up to study for an exam. The desire to not sleep in order to study is a second-order desire.

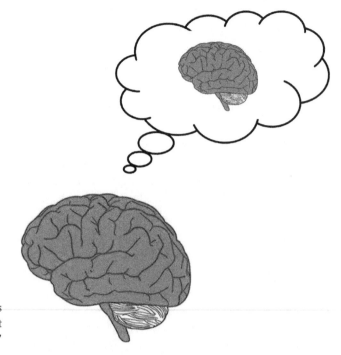

"I have a brain, therefore I am"

FIGURE 7 Metacognition is defined as "thinking about thinking."

Second-order desires of this type are similar to the process of metacognition in cognitive psychology. *Metacognition* refers to any process that monitors, regulates, or controls any aspect of cognition (figure 7). Metacognitive regulation includes planning, resource allocation, checking, error detection, and error correction (Brown, Bransford, Ferrara, & Campione, 1983). The prefrontal cortex is believed to be the site of the metacognitive system. In a problem-solving situation, metacognitive processing evaluates whether a particular strategy is working and, if it is decided that it is not working, initiates another strategy. Individuals lacking metacognitive control persist in their applications of inappropriate strategies, meaning that they get stuck on one approach to a problem and fail to consider other options.

Most computers as we now know them have a single source of "agency," which is their central processing unit (CPU). Many commands and regulation of information flow issue from this centralized chip. This limits the processing capacity of the computer because all commands must be executed in order, in what is called serial processing. However, new personal computers are now being made that are dual- or multichip. This increases their processing power and is known as parallel processing. The brain is considered to be a massively parallel processor, as it performs many calculations at the same time. Neural network software is modeled on this premise and can perform certain tasks, like pattern recognition, faster than traditional serial models. The question remains, though, as to what type of agency is necessary for a self. Can a person with a self exist with only one source of agency, or does selfhood require multiple forms of agency?

Self-Consciousness

Consciousness is defined as subjective awareness. We can be conscious of the world around us but also be aware of our body states and mental content. Self-conscious subjects are aware of themselves as themselves. In other words, we are aware of ourselves, and we are aware that *we* are the ones doing the "awareing." We use first-person pronouns like *I, me*, and *my* to refer to ourselves in this way (Sainsbury, 2011). The difference between having thoughts and knowing that we are the one having the thoughts can be summed up in the following anecdote: "I once followed a trail of sugar on a supermarket floor, pushing my cart down the aisle on one side of a tall counter and back the aisle on the other, seeking the shopper with the torn sack to tell him he was making a mess. With each trip around the counter, the trail became thicker. But I seemed unable to catch up. Finally it dawned on me. I was the shopper I was trying to catch" (J. Perry 1979/1993, p. 33).

Perry's awareness that someone was trailing sugar is equivalent to basic level awareness of a thought. Knowing that he was the one trailing the sugar is equivalent to the self-conscious perception of that fact. The topic of self-consciousness has been studied by philosophers for centuries. Here we provide a summary on various issues by Smith (2017).

An issue debated by philosophers is whether self-consciousness is a default type of consciousness that runs in the background. If this were the case, effort would not be needed for it to occur. So if it were "prereflective" it would not require one to explicitly reflect on one's own mental states or to take them as objects of attention. It would be manifest even in situations where we direct our attention outward to objects and events in the world. It would be implicit in all conscious awareness, providing us with continuous awareness of ourselves as the subject of our experiences. Prereflective self-consciousness in this sense would be somewhat like the operating system of a computer: always running in the background and serving as the basis for the operation of individual software applications.

Another analogy with visual perception is necessary here. In vision research, one makes the distinction between preattentive and attentive processing. When searching for an object, we can see certain things without any effort all. Examples include a red object in a field of green objects or a vertical line among horizontal lines. These are examples where the target differs from the distractors in a single way. Preattentive search is fast, parallel (occurring over the entire visual display at once), and effortless. In comparison, when we are searching for a red vertical line among red horizontal lines and vertical green lines, the search becomes more difficult. We must focally gaze at every item in the array to locate the target. Attentive search is characterized as slow, serial (one object at a time), and effortful. These two forms of attention are for outwardly directed consciousness, not internal, but the presence of a prereflective form for extrospective vision suggests there may be an equivalent for introspective self-consciousness.

FREE WILL AND DETERMINISM

According to the doctrine of free will, a person is the sole cause of his or her actions (Kane, 2005). Any single action stems from a decision or act of will on the part of the individual and was not caused by other preceding factors. Free will puts control and responsibility in the mind and hands of the individual. It suggests that things could have been otherwise, that a murderer could have killed someone but then decided not to. Determinism instead claims that the brain is a physical system. In physical systems any event is always caused by other prior events. Since decision-making is a brain process, any decision is always caused by preceding events. Eventually we will be able to understand what these prior events are, and when we do we can predict behavior. What we are calling free will is just a chain of causal, understandable events. Human actions are therefore determined. Many people find determinism disturbing because it suggests that we have no control over our choices and therefore have no moral responsibility. In other words, a murderer didn't have a choice as to whether he could kill or not: it was already preordained on the basis of preceding factors in his genes or in the environment.

Self and the Free Will/Determinism Debate

But what role does the self play in this debate? Nahmias (2006) provides experimental evidence that people's worry about moral responsibility comes from a fear that there may be no self that thinks and acts, that determinism does away with the self as a moral agent. We want to believe that Bill had a choice in doing what he did. If he didn't, Bill and the rest of us become zombies. Systems of law are also predicated on moral responsibility. Whom would we punish when crimes were committed? If everybody believes that nobody is at fault there is a danger that people may run amok and feel free to do whatever they please. The result could be anarchy and a breakdown in social order.

Knobe and Nichols (2011) show that people think differently about self in different situations. When they think about an individual microscopically in terms of cognitive states and processes, they believe that the self isn't part of that individual. They don't want to reduce the self to being atomistic or merely the operation of parts. They think that the self must be something more than this. Such a view doesn't hold individuals responsible for their actions, fits with determinism, and makes people feel threatened. When people are asked to think about an individual from a broad point of view, one that includes other individuals and the surrounding environment but not the brain, they are more likely to attribute self to the individual and think of individuals as being morally responsible. This perspective preserves free will and is the perspective most people feel more comfortable with.

Evolution and Freedom

Daniel Dennett in his 2003 book *Freedom Evolves* sketches out a view of how free will evolved. Five billion years ago, he says, there was no freedom because there was no life.

Without life you can't have an agent that perceives, thinks, or acts. Therefore inanimate objects possess no freedom whatsoever. He then progresses through the evolution of more complex life forms, showing that increased freedom comes with increased complexity and a flexible ability to deal with a dynamic environment.

Single-celled organisms like bacteria may be said to have a small amount of freedom because they can detect food or danger and swim either toward or away from it in either case. Animals that move can thus be said to have greater freedom than those that are sessile, like plants. Locomotion means that animals must anticipate where they need to go next and then figure out how to get there. This calls on planning, or at least the generation of an expectation about what is going to happen next.

So we can conceive of free will and determinism as lying along a continuum (figure 8). Determinism is at the starting point of this continuum. Here we have lifeless objects like rocks not capable of any internal computation to guide their behavior. Their actions are entirely determined by causal factors impinging upon them from the outside environment. Next we have simple organisms like amebas that have reflex-type reactions to stimuli in their environment. They have a bit more control over what they do, but this is no more than a mapping of a specific stimulus onto a specific response (a reflex). After this we have more complex animals like mammals. They possess cognition and can decide between alternatives. So they have more centralized control over their actions. At the end of the continuum are humans. Our problem-solving and decision-making capacity exceeds that of all other animals and so concentrates behavioral control even further inside the agent.

According to this view determinism in humans is the result of suspending centralized control over our actions. It amounts to "letting go" and being influenced by factors that we could have suppressed or activated. Free will involves a conscious consideration of possible courses of action and an evaluation of their possible outcomes. We determine what each of these courses of action means for us, followed by a choice to actualize one outcome and an action to bring it about. This ability to anticipate what the world would be like "if" something were the case is unique to humans. We can hypothesize or construct what are called counterfactuals and pick one to guide our action. People who focus and perform this process are exercising free will. Those who don't are not and hence become subject to other more deterministic influences. If we believe this view, then it is the self that can perform this thinking, with some people choosing to think before they act and others not doing so or doing so less often. An interesting question we can ask here is whether the suspension of free will corresponds to the suspension of self.

The Illusion of Free Will

A number of investigators argue that our concept of free will is illusory. Wegner (2002) says that the experience of willing an act comes from interpreting one's thought as the cause of the act when in fact it is caused by other factors. He says there are three steps in producing an action. First, our brain plans the action and issues the command to start doing it. Second, we become aware of thinking about the action. This is an intention. Third, the action

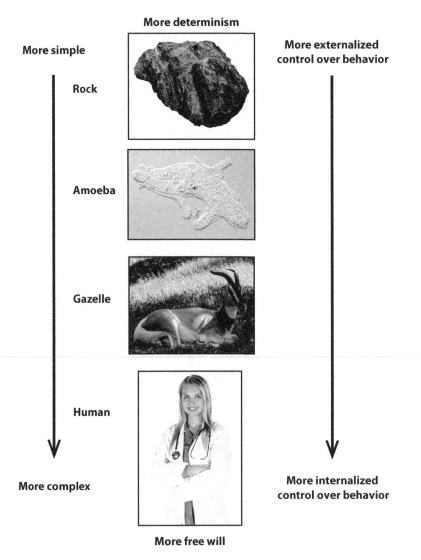

More determinism

More simple

More externalized control over behavior

Rock

Amoeba

Gazelle

Human

More complex

More internalized control over behavior

More free will

FIGURE 8 Organisms that are increasingly complex demonstrate more internalized control over their behavior and are less governed by external environmental forces. This can be interpreted to mean that they have more free will and that their behavior is less determined. After Dennett (2003). Images sourced from publicdomainpictures.net.

happens. Our introspective experience informs us only of the intent and the action itself. Because we are not aware of the subconscious planning and initiation, we mistakenly attribute the cause to conscious intention.

Experimental evidence supports this idea (Libet, 2004). Brain activity to initiate an action actually occurs before we are aware of having initiated it, during the first of the above stages. This suggests that causal factors other than intention are at work: that is, the choice was determined by subconscious events and not the act of will we experience. In this view either there is no self to do the deciding or the unconscious aspect of our self decides for us, an aspect we have less control over. This is just the sort of outcome that people fear, given the research cited earlier.

Currently, we cannot completely understand human choice. There are two primary reasons for this. The first is that we lack knowledge about all the inputs that go into a decision, including environmental conditions and a person's life history. The second is that we also lack knowledge about the brain mechanisms that produce decisions, which themselves may be quite complicated. This does not, however, mean that we can't someday explain most or even all of these phenomena.

THE EXTENDED-MIND THESIS

Where is the mind? Most of us would probably say in the brain or at most the body, what might be referred to as internalism. Externalism, on the other hand, is the view that the mind can exist outside the body. In this perspective, when we are reading a book our mind extends outward to include the book because we are thinking about it. A. Clark and Chalmers (1998) propose a view called active externalism, based on the active role the environment plays in driving cognitive processes. This view of active externalism is the extended-mind thesis.

In the extended-mind thesis, the mind can be seen as partially "outsourced" to technological or other environmental processes that perform a cognitive task for us (figure 9). For example, when we look up something on Google using our smartphone, the internet has de facto become our semantic long-term memory. When calculating a tip we use a calculator app on our iPhone, replacing the mathematical part of our brain. When editing a draft of a paper we use a spellcheck function in word-processing software, replacing the linguistic part of our brain. In all of these cases a task that could have been performed entirely inside our heads was performed to at least a partial extent externally.

Active externalism sees the human organism as linked with an external entity in a two-way interaction, resulting in a coupled information-processing system. All of the parts in this system interact causally, and if one part is removed from the system its efficacy will suffer. If you did not consult Google search, you might not have been able to understand something. Without the calculator you could have estimated too small of a tip, and without the spellcheck function you might have overlooked a typo.

Not everybody agrees with this position. If we equate consciousness with cognition then it would seem unlikely that consciousness could extend outside our heads. However many cognitive processes or components of cognitive processing take place subconsciously. Some examples include memory retrieval, aspects of reading or writing, and motor skill acquisition.

Another objection is that cognitive processes should be portable. In this view we can always use our heads to try and solve a problem, regardless of what external environment we

Computer server

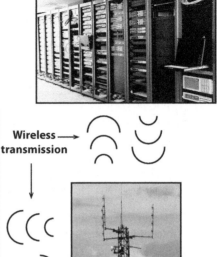

Wireless → transmission

Human and smartphone

Cell phone tower

FIGURE 9 According to the extended-mind thesis, our mind is not just in our brain or body. It consists of the technological systems we use when routinely processing information. Images sourced from publicdomainpictures.net.

find ourselves in. This means that the mind is always inside the head because environments change and cannot be consistently relied upon. A bad wireless connection decouples the external system, but we can still use our brains to try and get things done. The core system of mind in this view is what stays the same: anything else can be considered an add-on or extra.

However, technology is also portable. We could in the future plug modules directly into our brain to assist cognition. Or more simply, we could walk around with a slide rule or pocket calculator. Clark and Chalmers (1998) argue that reliable coupling is what matters. If most of the time we are able to perform a cognitive task with the assistance of an outside device, then that device can still count as mind. Even our own brains are not reliable all the time—for instance, when we are tired or hung over or when we have a stroke.

Evolution may have already selected for our brain to rely on aspects of the environment. The visual system uses certain regularities in the environment (Ullman & Richards, 1984). Body motion and locomotion also produce changes that are used as heuristics to solve perceptual problems (Blake & Yuille, 1992). In fact a whole school of perception has arisen that claims the environment is part of visual processing (Gibson, 2014). For example, we can estimate the height of objects by noting where our eye height intersects the object. If vision can accommodate the external world, then additional cognitive processes may be able to as well.

An objection to this is that selection would need to have acted on the mind much earlier in our evolutionary history, prior to modern-day electronic aids, prior to even writing. Selection could have acted on vision or linguistic capabilities, since these have been part of the human mental package for millennia or longer. The use of language is primarily to exchange ideas, so language ability, although localized in the brain, could not function in its more broad sense without the presence of others. This means that the mind could be extended to social groups or at least to a conversational partner. Learning within the lifetime of the organism also needs to be considered. The current "iGeneration" of "digital natives" who have experienced digital devices from birth onwards could be learning to "unload" parts of their thinking to the environment more than older generations have.

Does an extended mind mean an extended self? Clark and Chalmers (1998) believe so. If we consider what we think and the way we think to be part of our self, and if these are crucially dependent upon technology, then the technology becomes part of our self too. Evidence in support of this comes from the anxiety people have when they lose their smartphone. The anxiety is more than what might be experienced than if they lost a pencil. For a more extended critique on the extended-mind thesis, see Fahim and Mehrgan (2013).

CHAPTER THREE

The Psychology of Self

CONTENTS

Varieties of Self: The Modern Approach

Five Aspects of Self . . .

. . . Reduced to Three

Self-Motivation and Emotion

More Multitudes

Four Perspectives

Contrasts in the Study of Self

Psychological Theories of Self

Sigmund Freud and Psychodynamic Psychology

Erik Erikson and the Developmental Approach

Humanist and Motivational Approaches to Self

Narrative Perspectives on Identity and Self

Trait Theories of Self

Douglas Hofstadter's Cognitive Theory of Self

Modernist versus Postmodernist Theories of Self

Social-Cognitive Theories of Self

John Suler and Digital Selves

Evaluating Psychological Theories of Self

Disorders of Self

Dissociative Disorders

Dissociative Amnesia

Dissociative Fugue

Depersonalization Disorder

Dissociative Identity Disorder

Narcissistic Personality Disorder

Disorders of the Digital Self

Compromised Identities

Internet Addiction Disorder

The Brain and Internet Addiction Disorder

But Is It Real?

Evaluating Disorders of Self

VARIETIES OF SELF: THE MODERN APPROACH

In this chapter we turn to modern perspectives of self. These are theories and ideas of what self is from a psychological perspective. Most of these theories posit the existence of more than one self. We will briefly sketch out the views on this subject from psychologists of many orientations including the psychodynamic, developmental, humanist, narrative, trait, cognitive, and digital approaches. We will show that many of the psychological qualities of self also apply to artificial and digital selves. The chapter concludes with a section on the disorders of the self.

Five Aspects of Self . . .

Since the 1970s the topic of the self has received increased research attention. A large number of psychologists of all types have turned investigatory efforts toward this topic. Thinking about oneself is a fundamental characteristic of being human and affects the way we think and act, both consciously and nonconsciously. Thus the self is important to understand, and the past few decades have seen an accumulation of published papers.

One of the major issues in the study of self is coming to terms with the plethora of self-related concepts studied by psychologists. Multiple subtopics of self-based research exist, including the study of self-esteem, self-awareness, self-control, and identity. There is unfortunately no single, agreed-upon definition of self. Leary and Tangney (2012, pp. 3–5) have identified five distinct ways in which researchers in the behavioral and social science communities use the term *self*.

The first of use of the term *self* refers to the entire person, that is, it equates self and person. This idea is generally not supported because most people seem to think, not that a person *is* a self, but rather that each person *has* a self or can have multiple selves. The second meaning refers to all or part of an individual's personality. *Personality* in this case refers to the collection of traits or terms that one can use to describe oneself (Tesser, 2002). This also does not seem to be a useful meaning. If a person's self is his or her personality, it would mean that all personality researchers are studying the self, which is clearly not the case. Personality instead is best understood as the sum of a person's aspects that make him or her distinct from others.

The third notion is self as the experiencing subject. This is the part of our self that is subjectively aware of itself. We have here the self as subject, which is the "I" of first-person perspective. This is in contrast to the self as object, as studied by someone else, in which case we can use *him*, *her*, or another third-person pronoun. The fourth meaning of *self* is that of the beliefs we have about ourselves. This refers to one's perceptions, thoughts, and feelings about oneself. This is equivalent to asking the questions "Who am I?" or "What am I like?" Finally, we arrive at the self as executive agent. This is the self that is the decision maker or doer. It is the part of us that plans and makes decisions. Notice that philosophers have already addressed many of these themes.

. . . Reduced to Three

Leary and Tangney (2012, p. 6) argue that writers should stop using the term *self* to apply to the first two aspects of self as outlined above. There are more clear and precise words than *self* for these constructs. Also, most of the work in the social sciences that studies self deals with something other than the total person or the personality. The third, fourth, and fifth aspects above do have some merit, however. Unfortunately, none of these three ideas captures the nature of self in a way that encompasses all of the others. Thus we must admit that *self* has these three distinctive meanings or otherwise come up with some definition that can include all three.

One idea that does take all into account is the capacity for reflexive thinking. This is the ability to take oneself as the object of one's attention and thought. Reflexive consciousness involves subjective awareness of mental content and the capability of thinking about it in the service of action. Perhaps the best modern definition of *self* then is "the set of psychological mechanisms or processes that allows organisms to think consciously about themselves (Leary & Tangney, 2012, p. 6).

It is entirely possible to build a machine that has the capability for reflexive thinking. Most thoughts are about something. We can think about something in the world, a fact or concept, or even something imaginary. When we think about ourselves, the object of our thoughts simply gets directed to some representation of our self. This can be the state of our body, our mood or emotional outlook, or a memory. The same goes for machines. A computer can have a representation of its internal state such as the charge on its battery, the amount remaining in its memory buffers, or awareness of its external surroundings. It can then use this information in the same way that we do, to make decisions about plans and how to act. There is nothing special about reflexive thinking other than that the subject of computation is self-related.

Most psychological topics that have been studied by modern researchers involve one of three interrelated psychological processes: attention, cognition, and regulation. It is rare for one of these processes to occur without the other. For example, if we are aware of something we tend to think about it, and if we think about it we are likely to act upon it. So becoming aware that we are hungry makes us realize that it is now one hour later than the time we normally have lunch. Therefore, we decide to walk down to the corner deli to buy a sandwich.

Let's describe each of these processes briefly. Attention is that aspect of a person that allows one to direct conscious attention to oneself. Only a few other animals on the planet seem to have this capacity, and they have it only in a more rudimentary form. These are orangutans, chimpanzees, elephants, and dolphins (Gallup 1979). Cognitive processes are those that allow us to think consciously about ourselves. We can think about our current state or situation, about our attributes or roles, or about our memories and imagination— that is, what we did in the past or what we might do in the future. *Cognition* is what allows for the construction of a self-concept and identity. *Executive processes* refers to our capacity to regulate ourselves. Unlike humans, other animals lack the ability to control their impulses, feelings, and actions. *Self-control* means that we are not entirely under the control of environmental forces or internal biological urges and that we are capable of acting in an autonomous, self-directed way (Vohs & Baumeister, 2011).

Artificial selves would need to have attention, cognition, and regulation. In fact these abilities are already part of most robotic and AI systems. Attention is the equivalent of where processing resources are devoted. Cognition is the capacity to compute in general, and regulation is the ability to control internal states. To illustrate, a self-driving car would need to pay attention to the location of other cars and pedestrians on the road, it would need to be able to compute their projected locations, and it would need to regulate the location of the vehicle so that it proceeds forward without hitting any of these objects.

Self-Motivation and Emotion

Motivation and emotion have also been considered to be aspects of the self, with writers mentioning self-enhancement and self-verification as motives and mentioning emotions like shame, pride, and guilt as self-relevant. Various self-related motives have been studied, among them self-appraisal, self-actualization, self-affirmation, and self-esteem maintenance (ego defense in psychodynamic terms). Self-based emotions like embarrassment occur when people either judge themselves relative to their own personal standards or imagine how others judge them (Tracy, Robins, & Tangney, 2007). Although such motivations and emotions seem intimately tied to the self, the conclusion is that they are not an inherent part of it (Leary & Tangney, 2012, p. 8).

More Multitudes

As mentioned earlier, modern researchers have studied many self-related concepts. Table 3 lists just a few of these. A search using *self* as a keyword topic in 2011 revealed over 260,000 abstracts that contained a hyphenated *self-* term. The most frequent terms to come up were *self-awareness, self-monitoring, self-control, self-actualization, self-confidence, self-disclosure, self-concept*, and *self-esteem*. Sadly, little has been done to explore how these different aspects of self relate to one another. We are currently left with individual trees and not a forest. Going back to our trio of attention, cognition, and execution, and to self-motivations and emotions, many of these constructs involve at least two and sometimes three or four of these characteristics.

Four Perspectives

Summarizing modern research on self, Leary and Tangney (2012, pp. 10–15) note four emergent themes. These can be considered perspectives or disciplinary approaches to the study of self. They are evolution, development, culture, and neuroscience. The evolutionary aspect of self refers to questions like "What is the adaptive purpose of self?" or "Why is it helpful to have a self?" Theorists have proposed several possible answers to such questions (Leary & Buttermore, 2003; Sedikides & Skowronski, 2003). In evolutionary theory the shift from a hunter-gatherer style of living to agriculture meant staying in one place for an extended period of time. This allowed communities to specialize into different roles like toolmaker,

TABLE 3 Self-related constructs, processes, and phenomena

Desired/undesired self	Self-blame	Self-handicapping
Ego	Self-care	Self-help
Ego defense	Self-categorization	Self-identification
Ego extension	Self-completion	Self-identity
Ego ideal	Self-complexity	Self-image
Ego identity	Self-concept	Self-management
Ego integrity	Self-confidence	Self-monitoring
Ego strength	Self-conscious emotions	Self-organization
Ego threat	Self-consciousness	Self-perception
Feared self	Self-control	Self-preservation
Future/past self	Self-criticism	Self-presentation
Ideal self	Self-deception	Self-protection
Identity	Self-defeating behavior	Self-reference
Identity orientation	Self-definition	Self-regard
Ought/should self	Self-development	Self-regulation
Possible selves	Self-disclosure	Self-reliance
Self-acceptance	Self-discrepancy	Self-schema
Self-actualization	Self-doubt	Self-silencing
Self-affirmation	Self-efficacy	Self-talk
Self-appraisal	Self-enhancement	Self-trust
Self-assessment	Self-esteem	Self-verification
Self-awareness	Self-evaluation	Self-worth

Source: After Leary and Tangney (2012, p. 10).

farmer, weaver, or merchant. This would then allow for an individual to think of himself as "the person who bakes," or "the person who farms." It would also allow for someone to think of someone else's identity in this way: she is "the person who sells." A sedentary existence also allows for the accrual of personal possessions and ownership of a particular space and of objects that then also help to define identity. We examined evolutionary theories on personhood and self in chapter 1.

The second perspective is developmental, looking at how self-related qualities change over time. For example, one could look at how self-esteem changes before, during, and after adolescence and the factors that influence it at each stage. Developmental psychologists look at individual differences as well: why some people have higher self-esteem than others, for instance. The third approach looks at the influence of culture on self. One here can look at how shame is experienced across cultures and see how being raised in one culture like Japan would make people experience shame differently than in other cultures.

The neuroscience perspective looks at the brain structures underlying various self-constructs. Given the large number of self-constructs, this has been a difficult task. For instance, researchers have looked at the neural substrates of self-referential processing (Beer & Hughes, 2010), autobiographical memory (Cabeza et al., 2004), executive processes and self-regulation (Brass & Haggard, 2007), self-esteem (Eisenberger, Inagaki, Muscatell, Bryrn Haltom, & Leary, 2011), and mind wandering (Mason et al., 2007). Our current understanding is that there are many self-systems, each subserved by overlapping neural systems. In chapter 4 we provide a summary of theories of self that attempt to incorporate these disparate selves.

Contrasts in the Study of Self

Morf and Mischel (2012) provide an overview of modern psychological studies of self and identify a number of contrasting ideas. To begin, modern studies of self are now distributed across multiple disciplines. The study of self was a unidisciplinary affair for much of history, being studied almost entirely by philosophers for millennia. Modern-day studies of the self are multidisciplinary. Just within the field of psychology alone they span work in the fields of social cognition, social psychology, personality, clinical psychology, psychiatry, developmental psychology, neuroscience, cognitive science, and cultural psychology. Second, there is a debate over whether the self is a unitary integrated structure or a plurality of distributed multiselves. It is generally acknowledged that the self is not a single system but a set of interrelated but functionally independent systems that interact with each other in complex ways (Klein & Gangi, 2010).

Another contrast is between "hot" and "cool" systems. It is now acknowledged that the self is made of both. These are independent of one another but are continuously interacting (Strack & Deutsch, 2004). The "hot" system is based on emotions. It is more automatic, impulsive, and quick to respond. The "cool" system is based on reason and logic. It operates more slowly, is more reflective, and requires greater attentional resources. The "hot" system uses affect-laden representations. Stress increases activation of this system. The "cool" system contains knowledge representations of the self and of situations, goals and values that are relevant to the self, expectations of how events should transpire, plans, and strategies to control attention. The two systems have different biological substrates but can interact (Posner & Rothbart, 2000). If Rachel expects to get an "A" on her next exam, the expectation and the studying would be part of the "cool" system. If her expectation was violated and she received a "C," she might get angry. The anger she experienced would be part of the "hot" system. The anger and disappointment she felt might, however, motivate her to study more next time, so the "hot" would be influencing the "cold" in this instance.

When it comes to artificial selves, we seem to have less difficulty imagining them with "cool" systems than with "hot" systems. Computation in a computer seems akin to the sort of thinking and cognition that we do ourselves. However, "hot" systems are also computationally based. In biological organisms they involve patterns of activation among neurons in the brain, just in areas different from (and in some cases even overlapping) those involved in cognition. In artificial beings they involve electrical impulses traveling through circuits. The only real difference between the two is in how they are experienced. A "hot" computation involves a subjective emotional response while a "cool" one does not. There are robots now that can detect, think, and act emotionally, just as we do. Kismet, discussed later, is one of these. The key difference between these selves and humans is in the experience. We do not yet know whether machines may someday themselves feel emotionally as we do. It cannot yet be ruled out.

There are also implicit and explicit systems of self. Implicit aspects of self involve processes that are less controlled and more automatic, some of which may be subconscious (Devos, Huynh, & Banaji, 2012). Explicit systems are more conscious and subject to top-down control. For example, Bill may hold implicit stereotypes about blacks that are expressed verbally to his friends only when he is drunk and less inhibited. Bill would never normally make these remarks in other social situations for fear of other people's reactions.

Another contrast in the study of the self is that of an individual or a social self. Humans are social creatures. We live in societies characterized by relations with coworkers, friends, and family. The extent to which these interpersonal interactions influence the self varies from person to person and with the situation. The consensus view in psychology now is that the self does not just passively react to the social world. Instead, it is proactive and motivated in the way it interacts with others. What we think of ourselves is built and evaluated against other people's opinions (Morf, Torchetti, & Schürch, 2011).

Meta-analysis and literature reviews of the self tend to show a broad agreement regarding the features of the self. They acknowledge that self is a complex phenomenon and that it consists of many contrasting elements. For some reviews, see Leary and Tangney (2012) and Swann and Bosson (2010). These studies show that self is both a knowledge structure (personality traits) that is "known" and a process-driven system that is a "doer." The self both "knows" and "feels," being driven by understanding and emotion. The self is also stable and variable (the state-trait debate in personality theory); it is consistent and inconsistent; it plans and reacts; it is rational and irrational; it actively make decisions as an agent and automatically follows routines. The self is also self-aware and other-aware.

PSYCHOLOGICAL THEORIES OF SELF

In this section we will outline several of the major theories of self that have been developed by psychologists and researchers in other fields. Each has a slightly different take on what constitutes identity and self. Some, like Sigmund Freud, see the self as being in constant conflict with itself. Others, like the humanists Carl Rogers and Abraham Maslow, see the self as striving toward fulfilling its potential and improving itself. Erik Erikson describes how identity may be formed, while trait theorists are concerned mainly with accurate word-like descriptions of self. Some of these theories are an attempt to explain human personality. *Personality* is defined as a unique and relatively stable pattern of thoughts, feelings, and actions (Huffman & Dowdell, 2015). Personality describes how we are different from others

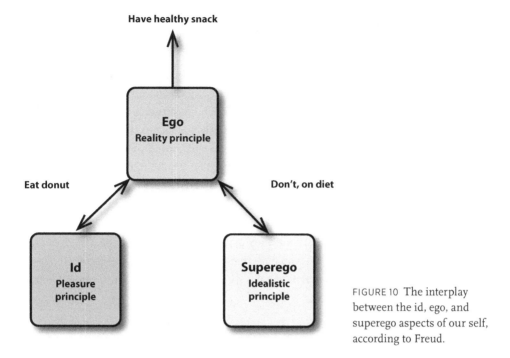

Have healthy snack

Ego
Reality principle

Eat donut

Don't, on diet

Id
Pleasure principle

Superego
Idealistic principle

FIGURE 10 The interplay between the id, ego, and superego aspects of our self, according to Freud.

and what makes each individual unique. For our purposes we are equating the psychological concept of personality with self and identity.

Sigmund Freud and Psychodynamic Psychology

Psychodynamic psychology as promulgated by Sigmund Freud (1856–1939) saw the mind as being made up of distinct components (Barenbaum & Winter, 2013). Each of these components competes with the others and attempts to control behavior. Psychodynamic psychology posited not just one state of consciousness but three and emphasized the role of the unconscious mind, of which the individual has little awareness and over which he or she has little control, in influencing thought and action. Freud also thought that sex, pleasure, aggression, and other primitive motivations and emotions were powerful influences on personality, as were early childhood experiences.

Freud described three other mental structures, each having a different operating principle. The id contains unconscious impulses and desires such as sex and hunger. It operates on the pleasure principle and attempts to attain gratification for its desires immediately. The superego is responsible for our ethical sense. It operates on the idealistic principle and motivates the individual to do what it considers morally sound or proper. The ego balances the competing demands of the id and superego. It operates on the reality principle, spurring one to act in a rational and pragmatic fashion.

A crucial part of this perspective is the dynamic interplay between the id, ego, and superego (figure 10). The id demands immediate satisfaction of its appetite for pleasure, while the superego in most cases advocates controlling or suppressing such urges in the name of decency. It then falls to the ego to attempt a rational and viable solution to the conflict. The ego is thus being barraged with the id's impulses and the superego's restraints. If it fails to satisfy either one, the result is anxiety. To alleviate its anxiety it constructs defense mechanisms that channel or dissipate the anxiety.

The id, ego, and superego in Freud's theory can each be considered a different self that dominates to a greater or lesser degree depending on various factors. If one is very hungry, then the "id self" gains greater dominance. If one feels very strongly about being ethical in a given situation, then the "superego self" dominates. The "ego self" may be in some ways considered the master self, as it always needs to satisfy and balance the demands of the other two selves.

Psychodynamic theory can be used to explore how people act online. McWilliams (2011), in her book *Psychoanalytic Diagnosis*, outlines psychodynamic theory's basic personality types and what motivates the people who have them; and Suler (2016) provide examples of how these may be expressed in cyberspace (table 4). Keep in mind that any given individual can be more just one of these types.

Erik Erikson and the Developmental Approach

Erik Erikson (1902–94) was a social developmental psychologist. As such he was interested in how identity develops. He formulated an eight-stage theory of development where each stage was marked by a crisis or conflict (Erikson, 1989). How people deal with the crisis determines their personality. If they deal with it successfully they will develop a positive outcome and be psychologically healthy. If they fail to deal with it successfully, they will develop a negative personality outcome.

We will not detail all eight of Erikson's stages, only the one that concerns identity. His stage 5 is characterized as "identity versus role confusion" and occurs at twelve to twenty years of age. Erikson believed that adolescents at this age develop a coherent and stable self-concept by exploring different roles and then deciding which ones fit them best. For example, they may try being an artist by taking painting classes. If they like painting, then they will have discovered that, for example, creativity and visual thinking are part of who they are. If they don't like these classes, then they will have discovered that those traits are not to their liking, and they will not include them in their self-concept. According to Erikson, individuals who do not determine a fitting set of roles for themselves by the end of this stage will develop an identity crisis. This could lead to apathy, social withdrawal, and role confusion. Should they find a fitting set of roles then they will have begun to form a stable identity or sense of self.

The stage labels Erikson uses may not apply to all cultures. For example, in societies where group harmony and cooperation are stressed the preferred outcome at certain stages might be dependence rather than autonomy (Berry, Poortinga, Breugelmans, Chasiotis, & Sam, 2011). This means that individuals in some Asian societies may develop a sense of self that is more open and connected to others. They may be more willing, for instance, to seek

TABLE 4   The different psychodynamic personality types and how they may be expressed online

Type	Description	Online Behavior
Psychopathic	Motivated by the need to control and manipulate others, to "get over on" them; impulsive, self-centered, unreliable, and irresponsible; has difficulty experiencing social conscience and deep emotions.	Do online anonymity and the power to manipulate environments encourage psychopathic personalities? Are they the malicious hackers of cyberspace? Out of a need to dominate people, do they become the "trolls" who deliberately stir up distress in others? Some people believe the internet has become the playground of psychopaths.
Narcissistic	Motivated by the need to maintain a valued sense of self; has tendencies toward feeling privileged, special, grandiose, and self-centered; craves admiration and expects favors; inattentive to the needs and feelings of others.	Do narcissistic personalities use cyberspace as a means to build an admiring audience? Do they create habitats where they display themselves while caring less about listening to others? Are they what traditionally was called the "newsgroup personality"—the person who always argued, who always had to be right in an online discussion?
Schizoid	Motivated by a need to preserve a sense of safety by avoiding intimacy with others; prefers being alone; has difficulty forming close relationships and showing warmth or tender feelings; has a tendency to withdraw into internal fantasies.	Are schizoid people attracted to the reduced intimacy resulting from partial or complete online anonymity? Do they tend to be lurkers?
Paranoid	Motivated by a need to avoid feeling vulnerable and helpless; has tendencies toward being suspicious, guarded, irritable, cold, humorless, and argumentative; has a tendency to blame, criticize, or project onto others.	Feeling vulnerable and helpless, do paranoid people take extreme measures to protect their machines, security, and privacy in cyberspace? Are they the people who distrust the internet, perhaps avoiding it completely?
Depressive	Motivated by the need to grapple with feelings of somehow being bad; has tendencies toward gloominess, guilt, a lack of energy, difficulty in enjoying the pleasures of life, self-criticism, feeling rejected, and low self-esteem.	Would depressive types seek help in online groups? Would they seek out support from others by text, email, or other forms of electronic communication? Or would they abandon all usage of these media?
Manic	Motivated by a need to defend against underlying feelings of depression; has tendencies toward being elated, energetic, impulsive, mobile, distractible, self-promoting, highly social, witty, and entertaining.	Do manic people take advantage of asynchronous communication as a means to send more measured responses to others, or do they naturally prefer the terse, immediate, and spontaneous conversations of chat and texting?

(continued)

TABLE 4   *(continued)*

Type	Description	Online Behavior
Masochistic	Motivated by the need to endure pain and suffering for the purpose of attaining some greater moral good; has a tendency toward feeling depressed, but also experiencing resentment, indignation, and moralization on his or her own behalf.	Might masochistic types complain excessively online to others about their woes? Would opinions or viewpoints that disagree with their own outrage them?
Obsessive/ Compulsive	Motivated by a need to maintain emotional security and self-esteem; perfectionist, preoccupied with details and rules, more concerned with work than with pleasure; has a tendency to be serious and formal; has a need to be in control.	Are compulsives drawn to computers and cyberspace for the control it gives them over their relationships and environment? Are they meticulous in how they manage their computers, online habitats, and relationships?
Histrionic	Motivated by a need for attention, love, and dependency; has tendencies toward being highly sociable, expressive of emotions, dramatic, attention-seeking, hypersensitive, and seductive; has a tendency to repress negative emotions and deny problems.	Do histrionic people enjoy the opportunities for theatrical displays that are possible in social media, especially in environments that provide tools for creative and dramatic self-expression?
Dissociative	Motivated by a need to compartmentalize anxiety-provoking experiences by splitting identity into separate parts; has tendencies toward being resourceful, interpersonally sensitive, creative, sociable, and susceptible to hypnotic states; has a complex fantasy life.	Do people with dissociative personalities tend to isolate their cyberspace lifestyles from their in-person lives? Are they especially attracted to the creation of multiple, compartmentalized online identities, as in online role-playing games?

Sources: After McWilliams (2011) and Suler (2016).

advice from coworkers when confronting a problem. In Western societies like the US where independence is valued, people may be more likely to see their self as closed off from others. Such individuals may try to solve a problem entirely on their own without asking for help.

Humanist and Motivational Approaches to Self

Carl Rogers (1902–87) was a humanist psychologist. The humanists emphasize a person's internal feelings and thoughts and how they view themselves, what is called a self-concept. In this perspective people are naturally good and have a tendency toward self-actualization:

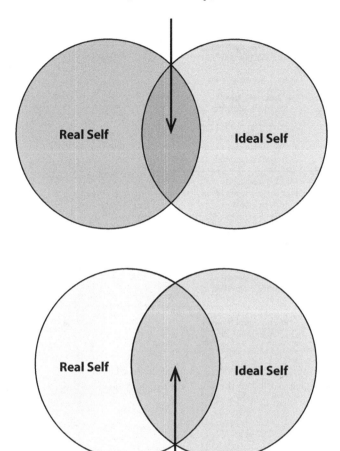

**Poorly adjusted individual
(Small overlap)**

Real Self

Ideal Self

Real Self

Ideal Self

**Better adjusted individual
(Greater overlap)**

FIGURE 11 Psychological health according to Carl Rogers was determined by the amount of overlap between the real and ideal selves.

a drive to develop all of their talents and abilities. Psychological health and adjustment according to Rogers are determined by the degree of overlap or congruence between two selves (Rogers, 1961). The real self is how you perceive yourself to actually be. The ideal self is the type of person that you want to be. If there is a lot of overlap between these selves, the result is a well-adjusted individual. If there is just a little overlap between them, the result is a poorly adjusted individual (figure 11).

To illustrate this, take Jed. Jed perceives himself to be a good student but wants to be an outstanding one. His ideal is getting a perfect 4.00 grade point average (GPA). In this example Jed's real and ideal selves are in strong congruence because he has a 3.7 GPA, close to his

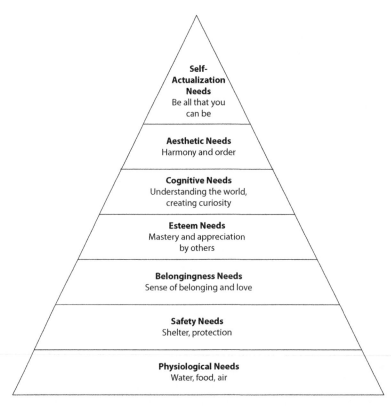

FIGURE 12 Abraham Maslow's hierarchy of needs can be visualized as a pyramid. When lower needs are satisfied, the self seeks to satisfy needs at the next level up.

ideal. Now let's take Bill. Bill perceives himself as an average student, but his ideal is also to be an outstanding one. In his case there is less overlap between his real and ideal selves because his actual GPA is 3.00 but his ideal is a 4.00 GPA. Jed, according to Rogers, would be psychologically healthy, while Bill would not.

Abraham Maslow (1908–70) was another humanist psychologist who believed that people seek to actualize their potential, what he called self-actualization. He formulated a hierarchy-of-needs theory (Maslow, 1970). In his view, whenever we satisfy a set of lower needs we are next motivated to attain a higher set of needs. Lower, more primitive needs occupy the base of the hierarchy, which is shaped like a pyramid (see figure 12). Higher needs occupy levels farther up. A healthy individual strives to make it all the way to the top, assuming each level is satisfied.

In order from low to high are physiological needs like food and water, followed by safety needs for shelter and protection. Then come belongingness needs such as love. Those are followed by esteem needs, the desire to achieve mastery and to be appreciated by others. After this are cognitive needs such as understanding the world along with curiosity. Then there are aesthetic needs, which are a desire to achieve harmony and order. At the very top on the last level is self-actualization, which means achieving those goals that are uniquely yours, based on your own individual skills and interests.

Hierarchical lists of needs such as those proposed by Maslow can also be implemented in machines. The question is what needs we want to put in or what needs might evolve on their own in such systems. Self-preservation would seem the most basic, but this must not conflict with causing harm to others. In Asimov's laws of robotics, self-preservation is secondary to fulfilling the wishes of humans and preventing them harm. The issue when implementing pursuit of needs is what to do when two or more conflict. This is not an easy problem. Ethicists who have been studying these issues for millennia cannot agree on how to prioritize values. Perhaps a superintelligent AI may be able to solve these problems for us.

Deci and Ryan (2008) advocate a tripartite theory of self similar in many ways to the views of Rogers and Maslow. It is called self-determination theory (SDT). From this perspective there are three basic psychological needs that all people strive to achieve. Our well-being and self-esteem are dependent on the extent to which they are satisfied. *Competence* refers to our need to feel capable of performing various tasks. If we excel at work and hobbies, this need will be satisfied. *Autonomy* refers to our need to feel in control of our actions and goals. If we feel that our lives are beyond our control or are influenced by outside factors, this need will go unsatisfied. The third need, called *relatedness*, refers to the desire for social contact and emotional connections with others. Spending quality time with friends, family, and lovers could satisfy this. These three needs together have been found to predict how enjoyable people find games (Ryan, Rigby, & Przybylski, 2006).

Narrative Perspectives on Identity and Self

Narration refers to the act of producing a story, either oral or written. Narration is about the self and involves personal accounts, life stories, or autobiographies. It involves any verbal utterance, talk, or text. However, the use of technology allows us to tell narratives in other media like movies and games. Narratives involve events that are selected, organized, connected, and evaluated in a story that has a beginning and end. Typically there is some meaning or lesson for a particular audience. As such, narratives have both "sequence" and "consequence" (Reissman, 2004). Narratives tell us something about the narrator. They are believed to reveal something about his or her identity. They also usually reflect the culture or context in which they are produced. It is generally acknowledged that narratives can't be generated until adolescence because preadolescents lack the necessary motivation and abilities (Habermas & Bluck, 2000).

Narratives are subjective, which makes them difficult to study scientifically. This is because scientists are used to dealing with objective phenomena that can be more easily measured. Despite this, narrative research is on the rise in psychology. Investigators have found that first-person narratives are an effective way to understand identity and how the self evolves over time. In fact, many researchers even say that telling narratives actually

TABLE 5   The six major facets of identity

	Name	Definition	Example
1.	The body	How the body changes or develops over the life span	Illness or aging
2.	Individual traits	Features or characteristics of identity	Achievement or redemption
3.	Human relations	How characters are depicted in one's life story and how they reflect on identity	Relationships with parents or siblings in a family, with friends, with a romantic partner or spouse
4.	Social reality	The narrator's roles or scripts in his or her particular social-cultural setting	Social class and gender
5.	Cultural environment or historical time	Selection of time and culture	Choice of a culture or time period to present as a narrative
6.	Religion or spiritual concerns	Values the individual adopts as a guide for his or her life	Converting to Buddhism; following a spiritual leader

Source: After Lieblich and Josselson (2013).

creates identity. There are at least six distinct facets to identity. These and some examples are listed in table 5 (Lieblich & Josselson, 2013).

Bruner (1986) distinguishes between two types of cognitive functioning. Paradigmatic functioning is based on logic, numbers, and formulas. It is objective and relies on establishing the truth or falsity of propositions, which are sentence-like statements. Narrative functioning, in comparison, is demonstrated in stories. It is subjective and oriented toward what might be or might have been, not what is true or not. Stories are not strict reproductions of someone's experiences. They are colored by our personality, emotions, and other psychological variables. Especially important is what is chosen or left out of our stories. The events we choose to include in our narratives are of great importance to understanding identity.

Bruner claimed that life stories contain a lesson the story teaches the listener in much the same way that a folktale or fable has a moral. This lesson may be considered the leitmotif of the individual's identity. The dramatic effect in a story occurs through a crisis or problem, an event that poses some challenge to the hero or protagonist. Life stories, like their fiction counterparts, can have a theme, form, and style. Likewise they can be a tragedy, a comedy, or another literary form. Bruner is a postmodernist when it comes to narratives. He believes there is no such thing as a static self. The dynamic self is constantly being constructed by the telling of our stories.

Narratives are not just a series of events that we string together. What events we choose, what theme or lesson there is to learn, all say a lot about the person's identity. Someone who feels insecure and must prove himself, for example, may choose to tell a story of how he stood up to a bully or was admitted to Stanford Medical School while waiting tables. Narratives must therefore be interpreted appropriately to make sense. In this regard they share something with psychoanalysis or psychotherapy, where the therapist must interpret what the patient says. However, there are now more scientific ways, like keyword coding, to interpret narratives objectively.

A person's life stories that mirror his or her identity are to some extent a product of the culture and society in which they are embedded. They can reflect social divisions of power like class and gender that prevail in society at a certain time in history (Franz & Stewart, 1994). However, genetic predispositions probably also play a role (or in this case create a role). Somebody that is predisposed toward extroversion would have stories filled with more characters than someone who is more introverted, where introversion and extroversion are genetically influenced.

In the digital world narratives have taken on greater importance. We are no longer limited to listening to stories around the campfire or reading books. We can experience narratives online in blogs, stream movies on Netflix, or watch videos on YouTube. We can play characters in video and VR games. There has never been a moment in history during which we can experience as many stories as we do now. These stories are no doubt shaping our selves in complex ways. Digitally experiencing the story of an immigrant, for example, may help us to become more empathetic and perhaps change our political views. "Stepping into someone's shoes" digitally and experiencing the world the way that person does will hopefully help us to understand the other's personality and motives. This is a good first step toward getting along with him or her.

Trait Theories of Self

Traits are typically single words or phrases that are used to describe an individual. The number of traits that can be used to describe people is quite large, so the task of the trait theorist is to find a smaller set of traits that can be used to accurately characterize someone's personality (Allport & Odbert, 1936). One way to do this is to employ a statistical technique called factor analysis that takes a large number of variables in a data set and condenses them into a smaller set of factors.

Raymond Cattell (1990) reduced a large list of personality traits obtained from numerous experiments into a basic set of sixteen. Table 6 shows Cattell's sixteen basic traits. Each is listed as a continuum from low to high. So, for example, somebody who doesn't like to go out and keeps to herself might be listed as reserved, being low on that continuum. Someone who enjoys parties and talking to others could be listed as outgoing and high on that continuum. If the points along each continuum are connected, the result is a personality profile. People with similar personalities have similar profiles. People from certain occupations such as airline pilots also tend to have similar personality profiles. As a result profiles can be used practically, for example to help narrow down the field of crime suspects.

McCrae and Costa (2013) reduced personality traits even further, into five basic factors, what are sometimes called the "Big Five." These are shown in table 7 and are also represented

TABLE 6   Cattell's sixteen personality factors

	Low	High
1.	Reserved	Outgoing
2.	Less intelligent	More intelligent
3.	Affected by feelings	Emotionally stable
4.	Submissive	Dominant
5.	Serious	Happy-go-lucky
6.	Expedient	Conscientious
7.	Timid	Venturesome
8.	Tough-minded	Sensitive
9.	Trusting	Suspicious
10.	Practical	Imaginative
11.	Forthright	Shrewd
12.	Self-assured	Apprehensive
13.	Conservative	Experimenting
14.	Group-dependent	Self-sufficient
15.	Uncontrolled	Controlled
16.	Relaxed	Tense

Source: Cattell (1990).

as continua. This has since been known as the five-factor model or FFM. These five traits appear continually even when different tests are used. They are generally value neutral, meaning it isn't necessarily "better" to be higher along a continuum. For example, there are advantages that come from being introverted, because it could lead one to be studious. Similarly, it might be good to be critical, as it would lead to better critical thinking skills. The exception to this is the last trait, neuroticism, which it would be generally better to score low on.

One debate among trait theorists is known as the state-trait debate. This centers on the issue of whether traits are inherently stable across the life span or whether they vary with situations. If a trait is stable, a person with it will exhibit that trait all the time regardless of the context or environment. If, on the other hand, a person varies in a trait depending upon the situation, then the trait is more malleable and less "set in stone." For example, if Laura is calm in all situations, then her neuroticism can be considered stable. Should Laura be calm all the time except when facing job interviews, then that trait can be considered more variable.

Factor models like the FFM have been shown to predict mate preference (Buss, 2003). Such results have been demonstrated to be true cross-culturally in a number of studies (Brumbaugh & Wood, 2013). The FFM has also been found to predict preferences and behaviors. For instance, people who score high in extroversion like music that is more energetic

TABLE 7 The "Big Five" personality factors in the five-factor model (FFM)

	Factor	Low Score	High Score
1.	Openness	Down to earth Uncreative Conventional Not curious	Imaginative Creative Original Curious
2.	Conscientiousness	Negligent Lazy Disorganized Late	Conscientious Hardworking Well organized Punctual
3.	Extroversion	Loner Quiet Passive Reserved	Joiner Talkative Active Affectionate
4.	Agreeableness	Suspicious Critical Ruthless Irritable	Trusting Lenient Soft-hearted Good-natured
5.	Neuroticism	Calm Even-tempered Comfortable Unemotional	Worried Temperamental Self-conscious Emotional

and upbeat like hip-hop and rap. People who are open to experience prefer complex and intense music like rock and classical. However, traits by their very nature lose specificity and fail to capture the more subtle details of someone's personality. They also fail to describe how traits are formed or how they may interact with one another. Still, they are a compact way of describing what is meant by "self." Each of the "Big Five" or Cattell's sixteen traits can be considered as a separate self or as facets of a single self.

Should we give artificial people traits? Since traits enable us to do well in certain situations, it makes sense to enable such agents to have characteristics that will optimize their performance in a given domain. For example, a receptionist android should be "extroverted" and "friendly," while a search algorithm designed to look up information ought to be "curious." As was the case with emotions, there is a difference between actions that reflect traits and subjective experience of those traits. We can program in any trait we desire into a machine, but whether it actually feels what it is like to be neurotic or conscientious is another issue.

Traits can also be left open-ended in such agents. If we want them to have a variety of traits, then agents can learn them through experience the way we do. For instance, agents could be programmed to simply "like" what they have experienced. Those experiences could then foster the development of related traits. An android that takes art classes in this scenario would end up becoming more creative. Humans tend to like things that are more familiar to them. Once we start acting in ways consonant with those things, we are more likely to pick up the associated traits and skills.

Douglas Hofstadter's Cognitive Theory of Self

Douglas Hofstadter, in his 2007 book titled *I Am a Strange Loop*, proposes several interesting ideas regarding the self. He believes that our subjective self can exist in substrates other than the brain. This view in the philosophy of mind is known as functionalism. Functionalists argue that a mind could conceivably be implemented in any physical system, artificial or natural, as long as certain critical processes or functions are preserved. According to functionalists a mind or self could exist in a computer or an alien brain. It is not the specific hardware that matters here but the pattern of action or process that the mind performs. This view is sometimes known as patternism. If this is correct, one could transfer one's self or identity into a computer or other biological equivalent and in so doing perhaps attain immortality. One process by which this might take place is called whole-brain emulation. This involves taking a detailed scan of a brain and replicating it in another substrate. We discuss this approach in greater detail later.

According to Hofstadter, our creative outputs contain a trace of who we are. Poems, paintings, or novels created by different individuals reflect an aspect of their selves. When we experience these works, we also experience what it is like to be the artist. Hofstadter believes that the pattern of neural activity in a person corresponding to a subjective experience can be represented symbolically. Similarly the objective notation to a musical score or the text in a poem is also represented symbolically. Although one is subjective and the other is objective, the notes in the score or the words in the poem can be converted to a subjective experience when another person interprets them correctly. In this way when we read Keats or listen to Bach we in some sense become the artist and share in the state of mind that created the work.

Hofstadter subscribes to the notion of the narrative self. His take on this is that the self is actually a hypothetical construct. It is a story our brains create that generates the illusion of a single stable self. We have no single self because it is a constantly changing narrative that we implicitly create and believe in. We are also not born with a self, writes Hofstadter. Our ego, or sense of having an "I," gradually emerges as we form internal concepts through learning. Eventually these concepts become so complex and interrelated that they begin to loop back on themselves. This looping back is a form of self-reference and is also seen in mathematics and logic, where such loops are called "strange loops." In these systems there are propositions (sentence-like statements) that refer to truths and also to the symbols systems that express those truths. In other words, they refer to things and to themselves.

Self-reference can be implemented in a computer system fairly easily. All one has to do is make a function or expression that takes some other aspect of the system (a symbol or proposition or function itself) as its object. Let "A" stand for "Apple" and function "I" be a perceptual operation that allows one to "Imagine" or see an object visually in one's imagination (with eyes closed). We can then let I(A) be the imagination of an apple. We could then imagine imagining an apple, represented as I(I(A)). This process could be repeated, each time getting a representation of the former representation. It is possible because the function "I" can take the former imagination as its own subject or variable. Another way to think of self-reference is to think of a camera that is pointed at itself. It can view the world, but it can also view itself viewing the world. In cognitive science, self-referentiality is usually discussed in the context of metacognition.

Like other theorists, Hofstadter argues that we contain within us many selves. There is a core self that we identify as "I." There are also internal representations of other people, meaning we may have selves that mirror our mother, our spouse, our best friend, and so on. Extensive familiarity with others allows us to adopt other people's subjective perspective and to see the world in much the same way they do. It is this process that allows us to empathize with others and to get along with them. These simulated subjectivities of others, however, will probably not be as strong as the core self.

Modernist versus Postmodernist Theories of Self

Modernist views of self and identity place a heavy emphasis on the individual, who is a subject of action and is capable of purposive and meaningful behavior (Melucci, 1997). Individuals have a unitary consciousness that is capable of knowing the self and the world, in other words is aware of internal and external events (Faigley, 1992). The modernist view is best expressed by Giddens (1991), who believes that an individual has a single core self-identity rather than multiple identities. This identity is determined by a person's life narrative. All of us construct a narrative about ourselves based on what we have done or accomplished. New actions must be able to be integrated with the identity we have already created: matches can support the existing identity, while mismatches can trigger changes to it. In Giddens's perspective what other people think is not important to identity. It is what the individual thinks that matters.

Postmodernists instead view identity as fragmented and multiple. They question whether there is any such thing as a single or core identity. Fuss (1989, 1995) believes that both internal (psychical) and external (social) stimuli contribute to the multiplicity of identities within an individual. Some postmodern theorists would go so far as to say there is no such thing as identity. Identity is in such constant change based on situational and environmental factors that it can't be defined for any individual. This debate between the primacy of internal dispositional factors and external situational factors is echoed in the state-trait debate.

It can probably be safely said that elements of both modern and postmodern theories are correct. Identity is the product of both internal and external forces. There are elements of identity that are stable and persistent through the life span. At the same time there are elements that are changeable. This view is echoed by Haraway (1991), who describes identity as consisting of many distinct and unique parts (division) that share enough in common to be able to join together (merger).

Modernists emphasize a single central self (ego) that either exists by itself or directs and coordinates other selves. Postmodernists argue that there is no central self, only multiple

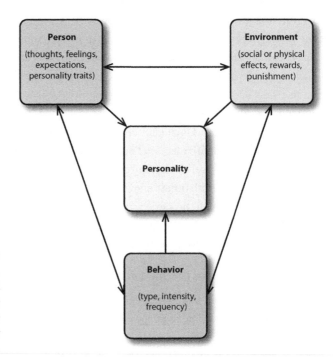

FIGURE 13 According to the idea of reciprocal determinism, our self-efficacy is affected by how the person, the person's behavior, and the environment all interact. After Bandura (2012).

selves that change over time. Modernists emphasize the cognitive or information-processing perspective in which a single individual thinks on his or her own, regardless of others. Post-modernists emphasize the social perspective in which our interactions with others and what others think about us affect our self. In short, modernists are cognitive and postmodernists are social.

Social-Cognitive Theories of Self

Social-cognitive theories of the self take both cognition and social interaction into account and help to resolve the modernist versus postmodernist debate. Albert Bandura is a prominent advocate of this approach. Bandura (2012) introduces the concept of self-efficacy. This is similar to the everyday notion of self-confidence. Individuals with a strong sense of self-efficacy will be more likely to take on challenges. Self-efficacy can affect our personality through the process of reciprocal determinism. This is how the person, the environment, and behavior all interact to affect self. Figure 13 depicts this interaction. To illustrate, a person's belief ("I can succeed") will influence behaviors ("I will work hard and ask for a raise") that will then influence the environment ("My boss gave me the raise"). Instead of seeing the individual or the context as primary, reciprocal determinism shows that both interact with one another in conjunction with behaviors.

Rotter (1990) is also a social-cognitive theorist. He states that cognitive expectancies guide what we do and affect our surroundings. In his view our behavior and sense of self are determined by what we expect to happen after a certain action and the reinforcement that action receives. Rotter introduced the idea of locus of control. People with an internal locus of control think that they can personally control events in their own lives on the basis of their own efforts. Those with an external locus of control think that forces outside themselves control what they do. These two forms of control echo the philosophical debate between free will and determinism.

A person with an internal locus of control attributes outcomes to him- or herself: "If I got into graduate school it is because I prepared hard on my own." That person will then prepare harder in a similar situation in the future. Someone with an external locus individuals attributes outcomes to the environment: "If I didn't get into graduate school it was because I received poor advising." That person may then see a different adviser. In the first case, the individual's actions will get him or her into a graduate program. In the second, someone else's actions will. But in either case, expectations influence thoughts, which stimulate actions, which affect the environment. These then affect future events. Again, we see a three-way causal linkage between the person, the environment, and the behavior, all affecting personality and self.

John Suler and Digital Selves

John R. Suler is one of the founders of the field of cyberpsychology and has spent considerable time studying people's behavior online. In his 2016 book *Psychology of the Digital Age,* he outlines various types of "online" selves. In this section we will review some of his proposed digital or online selves. Online selves refer to the different ways that people think, feel, and act online. Sometimes our offline and online selves are the same, but in many cases they are not. Think about this. Do you react to people the same way in person as you do online? Why or why not?

The first of Suler's online selves is the molecular self. This refers to all of the "things" or elements of our online experience. If we gathered together all of your texts, selfies, Facebook and Twitter posts, et cetera and just considered these as a group, they would constitute the molecular digital "you." There is an analogy here with biology. Just as all the physical molecules that make up your body constitute your physical self, all the digital "molecules" that you create online constitute your online self.

The molecular self can also be thought of as the self-as-structure, a complicated aggregate of memories, thoughts, and emotions defining who you are.

In the late nineteenth century there was a movement in psychology called structuralism that advocated much the same thing. Structuralists believed in cataloging what they thought were mental "atoms" and "molecules." These were basic perceptual experiences like the color red or more complex entities like thoughts, memories, and emotions. A challenge for this view, though, is to specify how all these different parts fit together to create a unified self. A digital structural self is one made up of our online components and how they relate to our internal mental states.

One answer to this comes from Suler's next online self, what he calls the transcendent me. In this view there is a force, ground, or organizing energy that gives rise to and unifies all the different molecules of self. This force binds the disparate parts of our digital experience together. However, this whole is more than just the sum or aggregate of its parts. It says something about how parts relate to one another. Again there is a historical precedent here. The Gestalt psychologists believed that mental wholes were more than just the sum of their parts. For instance, imagine three dots in a line. The first two dots are red and next to one another, while the third is blue. How would you see them? The answer is that your visual system would group the two red dots together on the basis of proximity and similarity. You would see them as a whole and separate from the blue dot. Similarly, there may be a digital Gestalt psychology that groups similar items together. For instance, your online posts about your best friend might group together based on similarity.

The sentient self is the part of the self that is self-aware. This self is equivalent to subjective consciousness and holds as its object the contents of mind, things like thoughts or emotions. In psychodynamic psychology it is called the observing ego. It also corresponds to William James's Pure Ego. This self occurs in cyberspace when we use a tool that makes us aware of the contents of the online environment. This content can be the other people in cyberspace as participants in that space. The content of the online environment could be web pages, photos, and text. We may be more aware of this content and of ourselves when we read an online news item about a terrorist attack in the city where we live.

The willing and doing self is the part of the self that initiates online action. It provides intention, direction, and meaning to what we do in cyberspace. It is thus the motivating part of self. This corresponds roughly to Maslow's motivating self, only in this case we are talking about what motivates online behavior. For example, self-actualizing forces might motivate us to post artwork online so that we could receive feedback and share it with others.

Next there is the "me that is a we" online self, perhaps thought of as our digital social selves. This refers to the different social roles that we play in our lives. Examples include being a child, parent, student, worker, neighbor, friend, or lover. Thus we can say that it is equivalent to Cicero's social actors. However, in this case it is our online actions in each of these guises. For example, we would take on the digital social role of friend when texting back and forth with our best friend Lauren. Alternatively we would take on the digital role of son or daughter when emailing a message to our mother. An important issue here is the integration of all these selves. For some people they may remain dissociated, or split apart. This might not be good for optimum mental health. A goal of therapy would then be to try to integrate them together using a core self or transcendent self (Kohut, 1977).

Anyone who has been online knows that there is both a positive and a negative side to human nature. The positive digital self would make donations to a charity online or respond to help others in a chat room. The negative digital self would attack people online for their political views by saying they are stupid. Good examples of the negative digital self are internet trolls. These are people who sow discord on the internet by starting quarrels or upsetting people. They post inflammatory, extraneous, or off-topic messages in online communities such as blogs or newsgroups. Their goal is to induce an emotional response or to disrupt discussions, often for their own amusement. We should keep in mind that everyone has these two sides to their personality to a greater or lesser degree and will sometimes express them in cyberspace.

Another important distinction is between real and fantasy selves online (Suler, 2016). Our real self online is how we normally interact with others in a social or business setting. So this would correspond, for example, to sending an email to a colleague at work. Our fantasy self is that part that would be expressed by playing an Orc in an online role-playing game like *World of Warcraft* or participating in a blog about the *Star Wars* science fiction films. We wouldn't normally express these desires to others in our everyday lives, but they can be a powerful aspect of our personality and they find expression in cyberspace.

Finally we can turn to our controlled and out-of-control selves. Normally we regulate our behavior. This self-regulating function in Freudian psychodynamic theory is the ego, which is rational and balances the needs of the id and superego. If we completely give in to our base emotional desires, then we are acting in an out-of-control manner. Sometimes adolescents will post an inappropriate photo of themselves naked or partying because they thought it was funny or cool at the time but later will regret it. Even so-called mature adults have done this. A case in point is the politician Anthony Wiener, who for months carried on an online sexual relationship with a fifteen-year-old high school girl, sending her pictures of himself without clothes on and pressing her to engage in "rape fantasies." We should remember that pretty much all of what we do online, including our search histories, is recorded and preserved indefinitely on computer servers in "the cloud."

Evaluating Psychological Theories of Self

We've covered a lot of different theories so far. Although these theories differ, there are also some common threads. Most posit the existence of multiple types of self within a single individual. These selves can take many forms. They can be internal representations of one's self, typically posited as the ego. They can also be representations of other people, of our base "animal" natures, of our conscience or ethical sense, or of different traits we have within us. Some of the theories specify how these selves interact. In some cases they fight one another for dominance; in others they can work together toward improving and self-actualizing.

Another common theme that runs through these theories is the role that the person or the environment has in influencing the self. If the person has more influence, then their thoughts or cognitions are emphasized. If the environment has more influence, then what is salient is the social realm, the thoughts and actions of others. Modernists argue for the former, postmodernists for the latter. Social-cognitive theories combine these two and specify ways in which individual and social factors together affect behaviors, which in turn affect the environment. Many of these selves will reappear in various guises in later chapters.

DISORDERS OF SELF

We can learn something about the self when it goes wrong, as is the case for psychological disorders. In this section we describe disorders of the self, those that affect our sense of who we are and what we do. Each of these disorders can affect our identity as well as our memories.

Dissociative Disorders

Dissociative disorders are characterized by a disruption in one or more of the integrated functions of consciousness, memory, and identity, usually caused by a traumatic or stressful event. These disruptions can be very brief or long lasting and their appearance can be swift or gradual. They can lead to the following symptoms (Steinberg, 1994):

- Identity confusion, a state of uncertainty about one's identity
- Identity alteration, the adoption of a new identity
- Derealization, the sense that familiar objects have changed or seem "unreal"
- Depersonalization, the experience of observing oneself as if from the outside
- Amnesia, loss of memory

There are four primary types of dissociative disorders: dissociative amnesia, dissociative fugue, depersonalization disorder, and dissociative identity disorder.

Dissociative Amnesia

Dissociative amnesia is marked by amnesia for important personal information, usually about a traumatic or very stressful event (Staniloiu & Markowitsch, 2014). People with this may experience "gaps" in their memory, periods that are lost to them. For example, a soldier that has been fighting in battle may not recall certain aspects of the battle. Some people may later recall this missing information. Others never can. Dissociative amnesia is usually localized to a particular event or time. It is rare that a complete loss of identity and life history occurs, although it is possible. This disorder is associated with childhood trauma, particularly emotional abuse and neglect. People may not be aware of the memory loss.

Dissociative Fugue

Dissociative fugue is an inability to remember some or even all of one's past history in combination with a sudden, unexpected disappearance from work or home (Coons, 1999). This period of time can last up to several months in duration. During the altered state individuals act completely normal and there are no signs of abnormality. They also do not create a new identity for themselves. It is extremely rare, at least in the US population.

Depersonalization Disorder

Depersonalization disorder involves an ongoing recurrence of two states (Phillips et al., 2001). The first is depersonalization, an experience of unreality or detachment from one's mind, self, or body. People may feel as if they are outside their bodies and watching events happen to them from a third-person point of view. The second is derealization, the experience of unreality or detachment from one's surroundings. People may feel as if things and the people in the world around them are not real. Individuals are aware of reality and know their experience is unusual. It is quite distressful to them, even though there can be a lack of emotion. Symptoms can start in early childhood, on average around the age of sixteen.

Dissociative Identity Disorder

Dissociative identity disorder (DID) formerly went by the name of multiple personality disorder (MPD). It is associated with overwhelming experiences, traumatic events, and/or abuse that happened during childhood (Ross, Miller, Bjornson, Reagor, & Fraser, 1991). Symptoms include the existence of two or more distinct identities or personality states. Each identity is accompanied by alterations in actions, memory, and thoughts. Ongoing gaps in memory for events and personal information can occur. The symptoms cause distress or problems functioning correctly in everyday aspects of life like work or social situations. Suicide attempts and attempts to injure oneself are common in those with DID and happen in more than 70 percent of these patients.

Attitude and personal preference for such things like clothing, food, and activities can suddenly shift in patients with DID. These shifts occur involuntarily and are unwanted and distressful. There are states of depersonalization. Some people report feeling as if they are a small child, the opposite gender, or huge and muscular. The alternate selves are sometimes referred to as "alters." Each alter can be experienced with a distinct self-image, personal history, and identity, including a separate name, distinctive mannerisms, and a particular way of speaking. Some alters are aware of the existence of other alters and can share their memories (Huntjens et al., 2005). Some are completely isolated from other alters. People with DID have been reported to have as many as one hundred alters, although ten or fewer are commonly reported. Stress can trigger the transition from one alter to another.

DID is believed to be caused by childhood trauma, particularly physical and emotional abuse. Children who experience abuse report that their mind left their bodies so that they could endure the pain. In other words, they dissociate or split into an alter as a defense mechanism. Continued abuse can produce multiple alters with unique histories, caused by each alter remembering and developing during discrete periods of time. Children who have been severely traumatized have been found to have a tendency to dissociate or to become aroused in response to negative stimuli (B. Perry et al., 1995).

Despite this, DID is a controversial diagnosis. Research on the topic has been characterized by poor methodology (E. Howell, 2010). It has been suggested that DID is caused by therapists, especially those using hypnosis (Reinders, 2008). There is also no clear agreement among mental health professionals on how to diagnose or treat it. There is no experimentally supported definition of what dissociation even is (Lynn et al., 2012). Diagnosis is difficult because of a high rate of comorbidity (prevalence of other disorders).

Narcissistic Personality Disorder

Narcissistic personality disorder (NPD) is separate from the dissociative disorders because it does not involve fugue, dissociation, or alternate personalities. NPD is exemplified by an exaggerated sense of self-importance, an excessive need for admiration, and an inability to empathize with others (Caligor, Levy, & Yeomans, 2015). These individuals spend a lot of time thinking about their appearance, power, and success. They usually take advantage of the other people in their lives for their own personal gain. They have a sense of entitlement and expect special treatment and obedience from others. Many are pompous and arrogant. The disorder begins in early adulthood.

Causes of NPD are not well known. The disorder is heritable with increased likelihood if a family member is diagnosed (Paris, 2014). The genes that may contribute are not yet known. Environment also has an influence. It may develop from an impaired attachment to parents or primary caregivers that causes the child to think of him- or herself as unimportant and disconnected from others. Overindulgent and overly permissive parenting as well as insensitive and overcontrolling parents may also contribute (F. Berger, 2014).

Most aggressive people, contrary to popular belief, do not feel bad about themselves and act aggressively toward others as a way of boosting their self-image. The research shows that aggressors actually think very highly of themselves and of what they can do: in other words they have high self-esteem (Morf & Rhodewalt, 2001). It may be that such people view a threat to their positive self-image as leading to a drop in self-esteem. Thus they defend against this decline and the ensuing shame or depression by acting aggressively (Twenge & Campbell, 2003).

Disorders of the Digital Self

Compromised Identities

Modern digital life can compromise our identities in a number of ways. Technology use can affect the self negatively and produce psychological problems. Suler (2016) has explored three ways that cybertechnology can compromise our identities. These might be considered as new disorders of the self, in contrast to the established disorders we have already listed. The first of these as-yet-to-be-recognized problems we can label "the symbiotic me" (Suler, 2016). Symbiosis is a mutual codependence seen in ecosystems, as is the case with flowers and honeybees. Many people now are dependent on constant communication with others or with digital content. This can be demonstrated by people who barely glance up from their smartphones, even to walk up or down stairs. It is also shown by the phantom vibration phenomenon in which a person feels a phone vibrating when it isn't. Many individuals also don't feel complete without their smartphone. When it is removed, sometimes even for short periods, they suffer what might be termed separation anxiety. More specifically, the symbiotic self is defined by a need for approval from others in the form of Facebook "likes" or Twitter retweets. Turkle (2011) argues that many people have now lost the ability to be alone and to reflect in solitude, activities that may be essential for identity formation and growth.

A second potential disorder of the self that is brought on by technology has been labeled by Suler as "the shallow me." This is the trend toward online relationships that lack emotional depth. Turkle (2011) refers to this as the Goldilocks Effect, where people multitask in their online and offline relationships so that they can be not too close but not too far from connectedness with others. This is characterized by a switching back and forth between in-person and online conversations and between multiple relationships as a way of avoiding true intimacy. It may also be motivated by boredom and as a means of avoiding conflict. These people seem to want an admiring audience, but they also seem to fear deeper social attachments.

Then there is "the disillusioned me." Imagine posting a photo from your recent vacation to a social networking site. You check back a day later, only to discover that nobody has "liked" or posted comments. How would you feel? Many feel anxious or depressed under such conditions in what has been deemed a black hole experience. A number of us can suffer a significant loss in self-esteem when we see our friends and family getting more approval than we do. Such individuals may resort to desperate attempts to shape and present their identity online in a way that will receive approval.

As is the case with all psychological disorders, there are individual differences, meaning that some people will be much more likely to suffer from these problems than others. A person with healthy self-esteem who has significant real-world connections with others might not get upset if he or she is unpopular on social media. Some people may be more emotionally needy than others and have a greater desire to receive approval. This is the case for people with narcissistic personality traits, as mentioned above. See chapter 7's section on disorders in the Palace for a glimpse at how some of these traditional personality disorders can make their way into virtual worlds.

Internet Addiction Disorder

Internet addiction disorder (IAD) is also referred to as compulsive internet use (CIU). It is characterized as usage that interferes with daily life or that causes harm or even death. Several deaths have been attributed to internet and video game overuse. IAD is divided into different subtypes based on gaming, social networking, blogging, email, pornography, or shopping. IAD is marked by changes in mood or reliance on the internet to achieve a desired mood, an inability to control time spent on the internet, and continuation despite negative consequences.

Part of what may make the internet addictive is that the rewards operate on a variable-ratio reinforcement schedule. This means that the rewards are both unpredictable and variable. This schedule makes users want to strongly continue their behavior in order to obtain the next reward. The rewards vary depending on the subtype: sexual stimulation for porn, social rewards for gaming, romantic fantasy with dating sites, financial gain with online poker or gambling, and a sense of belonging for chat rooms. Table 8 shows the factors involved in IAD (Greenfield, 2011).

Fortunately, there are multiple documented cases of successful treatment. Cognitive behavioral therapy (CBT) in particular has been found to be useful (Cash, Rae, Steel, &

TABLE 8 The factors involved in internet addictive disorder (IAD)

	Factor	Description
1.	Content factors	The content found on the internet (music, videos, games) is inherently pleasurable in nature.
2.	Process and access/availability factors	The availability of opportunities for the user to experience a fantasy (e.g., enacting a sexual fantasy with relative ease, disinhibition, and anonymity) or to act out a persona is highly attractive.
3.	Reinforcement/reward factors	The internet operates on a variable-ratio reinforcement schedule. Users are rewarded at both unpredictable frequencies (e.g., receiving of Facebook "likes") and unpredictable magnitudes (e.g., Google search matches).
4.	Social factors	The internet is both socially connecting and socially isolating. It affords titrated social connection within a highly circumscribed social networking medium. Hence, users can tailor their degree of social interaction in a way that maximizes comfort and mediates connection.
5.	Gen-D factors	Generation-Digital users are persons who have been raised with this technology.

Source: After Greenfield (2011).

Winkler, 2012). The prevalence for IAD varies considerably across nations and is inversely correlated to quality of life (Cheng & Li, 2014). One 2007 estimate has 17 percent of Chinese citizens aged thirteen to seventeen years of age as sufferers. Estimates for Europe and the US are lower.

The Brain and Internet Addiction Disorder The frontal lobes and other associated regions constitute what is called the executive system. These parts of the brain are responsible for selectively attending to events, inhibiting responses, planning, and problem-solving (Diamond, 2013). The orbitofrontal cortex is part of this system, as is the ventromedial prefrontal cortex. They transmit reward information and allow flexible responding in the face of changing events (M. Noonan, Kolling, Walton, & Rushworth, 2012). Online social interaction requires executive functioning (Ybarra & Winkielman, 2012).

The failure of the frontal lobe system to inhibit or control behavior is a key factor in IAD and internet gaming disorder (IGD). Individuals suffering from these maladies have decreased cortical thickness in frontal areas (Hong et al., 2013). Individuals with lower levels of self-control are more likely to suffer Facebook addiction (Blachnio & Przepiorka, 2015). Furthermore, high levels of self-control are associated with healthy internet use (Muusses, Finkenauer, Kerkhof, & Righetti, 2013).

Another collection of brain structures involved in addiction is the salience network. It consists of the anterior insula and the dorsal anterior cingulate cortex among other areas. It activates in response to salient sensory events, task initiation and switching, and transitions from inward-looking mental activities to task performance (Sridharan, Levitin, & Menon, 2008). It is responsible for identifying the most important or relevant stimuli on a moment-to-moment basis (Seeley et al., 2007).

If there is a dysfunction in the salience system, people will have difficulty determining what is important or in reallocating attention away from something that is irrelevant, both of which are characteristics of internet and gaming addicts, who can't tear their eyes away from the screen. Yuan, Qin, Yu, et al. (2015) studied people diagnosed with IGD and found abnormal connectivity between the executive network and the salience network. In these participants, important stimuli like a reminder to do homework either are not noted or are noted but are not passed to the executive system to affect behavior. In effect, there has been a disconnection between the part of their brain that identifies what is important and the part that would decide to act on it.

People with cyber addictions often lack self-control. They have smaller volumes in the dorsolateral prefrontal cortex (dlPFC), orbitofrontal cortex (OFC), anterior cingulate cortex (ACC), and supplemental motor area (SMA). These are all regions that underlie self-control (Yuan, Qin, Wang, et al., 2011). Other associated structures that mediate this skill and that are implicated in cyber addictions are the dorsomedial prefrontal cortex (dmPFC), ventromedial prefrontal cortex (vmPFC), nucleus accumbens (NC), and ventral tegmental area (VTA) (Brand, Young, & Laier, 2014).

But Is It Real? Currently there is a debate about whether IAD is a legitimate phenomenon. Some investigators doubt its existence. Others think it is a symptom of other disorders. Many internet "addicts" can be classified as falling under other diagnostic labels like depression, anxiety, or impaired impulse control. However, it is not clear whether IAD is the cause of these disorders or the effect. For some of these individuals, internet usage may be a form of self-medicating or of avoidance. Regardless of whether IAD is real or not, the likelihood of a prospective virtual reality addiction disorder (VRAD) may be much greater, given its potential for increased immersion and satisfaction.

The Society of Media Psychology and Technology, which is division 46 of the American Psychological Association, has doubts about whether gaming-related disorders are real. They have written a statement opposing the World Health Organization's intent to include them in the International Classification of Diseases, the ICD-11. The reasons they cite are that there is currently insufficient research on the topic and that this move may be a result of moral panic, an unjustified social concern with the potential dangers of new technology.

The APA proposal has examined the literature on IAD and similar supposed disorders and concludes that there are many open questions, including how best to define it, what the symptoms are, and how widespread it may be. One study found that participants scoring high on a video game addiction (VGA) measure were not significantly more comorbid for other physical and mental problems (Przybylski, Weinstein, & Murayama, 2017). Other research has found that VGA-related issues may dissipate with time (Scharkow, Festl, &

Quandt, 2014). So the issue of whether IAD and VGA are legitimate psychological disorders is still on the table.

Evaluating Disorders of Self

Dissociative disorders suggest that it is possible to split into separate selves and that this may be caused by childhood trauma. The splitting into alters has been explained as a need to escape suffering. However, one should take these conclusions with a grain of salt, especially with DID, which may be falsely diagnosed or therapeutically induced. If these disorders are real, they provide additional support for the multiple-selves hypothesis, which states that all of us, even those who are psychologically healthy, have alternate facets of our selves. It may be that people with DID have weak egos that are unable to coordinate or regulate alternate selves. If this is the case, it would suggest that having multiple selves is normal and even adaptive, as alters could be called up to deal with different life situations. For example, an outgoing self could be conjured up for a job interview, while a more introverted self could be used for studying alone at home. This notion of alternate selves for different social roles fits with ideas in sociology and with historical conceptions of personhood.

NPD seems to be an obsession with one's self caused by either overindulgent or disconnected parents. However, the etiology and diagnosis of this disorder are tentative. If DID is characterized by a weak ego, it seems that NPD is characterized by an overly strong (yet fragile) ego. It could be that NPD patients are unable to form alternate selves during development, especially selves that might represent others close to them. This inability to create social selves may explain their lack of empathy because they cannot see the world through other people's eyes.

CHAPTER FOUR

Brain

CONTENTS

The Neuroscience of Self

Is There a Specialized Brain System for Self?

  The Physical Self

    Face Recognition

    Body Recognition

    Agency

  The Digital Physical Self

  The Psychological Self

    Traits

    Autobiographical Memory

    First-Person Perspective

  Summary of Studies on Self-Specialized Brain Systems

One or Many Neural Selves?

  Daniel Dennett's Multiple-Drafts Model

Solving the Coordination Problem: Neural Synchrony and Reentrant Processing

Neural Models of the Self

  Antonio Damasio's Neural Model of Self

    The Somatosensory System

    The Protoself (Nonconscious)

    The Core Self (Core Consciousness)

    The Extended or Autobiographical Self (Extended Consciousness)

  A Neural Model of Self-Referential Processing

  A Neural Self-Memory System Model

Problems with the Neuroscientific Study of Self

Responses to Problems with the Neuroscientific Study of Self

THE NEUROSCIENCE OF SELF

In this chapter we examine how the self can reside in the human brain. We start by providing a review of the literature centered on the question of whether there is a specialized self-brain system. As we will see, there are multiple aspects of self and multiple ways self-related processing can occur in the brain. The rest of the chapter is devoted to models of self. These models are in most cases based on meta-analyses of multiple studies or on experimental or clinical data. They are thus very general and capture the "bigger picture." Finally, we wrap up by examining some of the problems in this field of research. Some familiarity with brain anatomy and physiology is assumed for this chapter.

Craik et al. (1999) were the first to examine the neural basis of self using brain-imaging technology. Since then, the number of researchers doing this has exploded, so much so that meta-analytic reviews of the data were being written just a few years later (Northoff et al., 2006). To provide an overview, we will list here some of the studies investigating specific topics. A number of researchers have focused on trying to find the "self" in the brain (Gillihan & Farah, 2005; Northoff et al., 2006). At least six functionally independent subsystems have been identified (Klein, 2010; Klein, 2013; Martinelli, Sperduti, & Piolino, 2013; Picard et al., 2013). Other researchers have focused on the cortical machinery responsible for self-reflection (Herwig, Kaffenberger, Schell, Jancke, & Bruhl, 2012; Jenkins & Mitchell, 2011; M. Johnson, Nolan-Hoeksema, Mitchell, & Levin, 2009; M. Johnson et al., 2006). Other topical areas are the neural basis of self-knowledge (Moran, Kelley, & Heatherton, 2013; Ochsner et al., 2005), self-referential thought (Abraham, 2013; Gusnard, Akbudak, Shulman, & Raichle, 2001; Leshikar & Duarte, 2013), the self-concept (Heatherton, Macrae, & Kelley, 2004; K. Kim & Johnson, 2010), self/other differences (P. Chen, Wagner, Kelley, Powers, & Heatherton, 2013), trait self-knowledge (Ma et al., 2013), and self-regulation (Beauregard, Lévesque, & Bourgouin, 2001; Heatherton, 2011). We do not attempt to provide an exhaustive review of all of this work in this chapter but provide these references for those who want to pursue further.

IS THERE A SPECIALIZED BRAIN SYSTEM FOR SELF?

Gillihan and Farah (2005) review a wide body of literature in several domains to assess whether there is a specialized brain system that represents the self. A specialized system is distinct from other systems used for more general-purpose cognitive processes. Language and face recognition are both examples of specialized systems. Systems are considered special on the basis of four criteria. The first is anatomical. Does the system engage distinct brain areas? The second is functional uniqueness. Is information processed in the system differently than in other areas? Third is functional independence. Does the system's operation depend upon others? A double dissociation (A does not depend on B and B does not depend on A) is considered evidence for independence. Finally there is species specificity: whether the ability is seen in only one or several other species.

There have been several proposed locations for self-related processing. The left hemisphere is supposedly where recognition of our own face as well as autobiographical knowledge, personal beliefs, active goal states, and conceptions of self is located (Turk et al., 2002). The right frontal cortex has been proposed as the location for autobiographical memory, self-face identification, and theory of mind (Platek, Myers, Critton, & Gallup, 2003). The right lateral parietal cortex is implicated in representation of the physical and mental self (Lou et al., 2004). The medial prefrontal cortex in both hemispheres has been proposed as a site of the "self model," a construct containing features like continuity and unity, experience of agency, and a body-centered perspective (P. Fossati et al., 2003).

Unlike Klein (2013), Gillihan and Farah (2005) argue that the absence of a good definition for self may actually be a good thing. They state that the research literature has clarified these terms and that a better definition may occur over the course of future work. In this review they focus on two aspects of self, each with different subtypes: the physical self, including face recognition, body recognition, and agency; and the psychological self, including traits, autobiographical memory, and first-person perspective. In what follows we will summarize research in each of these areas to see if they support the notion of a specialized neural system for self.

The Physical Self

Face Recognition

Gallup (1979) performed several classic studies to operationalize self-awareness in animals. The subject's face is marked, for example with rouge applied to the forehead, with or without the subject's awareness; the subject then views him- or herself in a mirror (figure 14). Self-awareness is indicated if the subject then touches his or her face. Humans, along with chimpanzees and orangutans, but not monkeys, pass this test. In humans the ability first manifests at the age of eighteen to twenty-four months (Anderson, 1984). This demonstrates the species specificity criterion. However, the test could be failed for a number of reasons other than absence of a self-concept. For instance, the test requires understanding the relation between real and reflected space (Heyes, 1995).

Sperry, Zaidel, and Zaidel (1979) presented face images of self and other people to the hemispheres of split-brain patients and found that skin conductance was greatest when images of the patient's own face were presented to the right hemisphere. This suggests that the right hemisphere and accompanying emotional centers may be responsible for processing images of our own face. Keenan et al. (1999) presented upright and inverted pictures of faces corresponding to the self, a familiar face, and a stranger's face. There was a reaction time advantage for self faces when subjects responded with their left hand, which is controlled by the right hemisphere. At least two other studies have found speeded responses to images of one's own face with the left hand (Keenan, Freund, Hamilton, Ganis, & Pascual-Leone, 2000; Platek & Gallup, 2002). However, other studies using PET and fMRI show activation of both hemispheres in response to self face information. Areas in these studies included the left anterior insula, putamen, and pulvinar as well as the right anterior

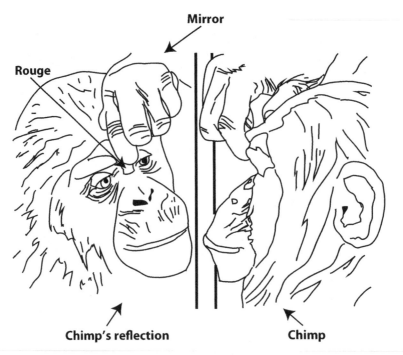

Mirror

Rouge

Chimp's reflection

Chimp

FIGURE 14 A chimp touches its forehead during the mirror test. Does this mean that it has a self?

cingulate and globus pallidus in one case and the right limbic system, middle temporal gyrus and left prefrontal cortex, cerebellum, parietal lobe, and lingual gyrus in the other case (Kircher et al., 2000; Sugiura et al., 2000). As a result of this research we cannot conclude that any one hemisphere or part of the brain responds selectively to images of one's own face. All we can definitively say is that both hemispheres are involved.

Body Recognition

Is the internal representation of our own bodies and body actions distinct from representations used for other people? Brain disorders can help answer this question. In autotopagnosia there is a loss of knowledge of the spatial locations of, and relations among, one's own body parts. But in these patients there is also an impairment of knowing the spatial layout of other people's bodies (Goldenberg, 2003). Patients with this disorder cannot point to named body parts on command, either on themselves, the experimenter, a mannequin, or a picture. So this disorder fails to show the existence of a specialized system for self body representation.

Another disorder though, called asomatognosia, does show a clear distinction between self and other. In these patients brain damage causes arm paralysis, yet they will deny that this same arm belongs to them. They will say their own paralyzed arm belongs to a friend, family member, or the questioning clinician! Asomatognosia thus does show selectivity. The areas of damage in these cases, specifically the right supramarginal gyrus and adjacent white matter, seem to hold awareness of one's own arm.

Reed and Farah (1995) had normal participants view a model in one position, then had them try to remember it over a brief delay. They then viewed the model again and had them determine if any part of the model's body had moved. When the participants moved their arms during the delay they were more accurate in judging whether the model's arms had moved. Likewise, when they were moving their legs during the delay they were more accurate in judging movements of the model's legs. This result shows that the body representation system is not specialized only for one's own body: it codes for other bodies as well. This is the opposite of a specialized system devoted only to the self.

Agency

Agency is the recognition of being the cause of an action (Blakemore & Frith, 2003). It requires both recognition of one's body and awareness that one's body is the cause of an action, what has been called "ownership" and "authorship." For example, if you moved your right arm to grasp a coffee mug, normally you would both recognize the arm as your own and recognize that it was you that decided to perform the action. The disorder of schizophrenia in some cases involves an overextension of agency to the actions of others. Some schizophrenic patients believe aliens are controlling their thoughts and/or their actions, for instance. Spence et al. (1997) found that the delusion of alien control in a schizophrenic sample was associated with right parietal cortex hyperactivation.

Ruby and Decety (2001) instructed subjects undergoing PET scans to imagine either themselves or the experimenter performing actions like peeling a banana or stapling a sheet of paper. The imagined self-action condition showed activation of the bilateral inferior occipital gyrus, postcentral gyrus, posterior insula, and left inferior parietal lobule. The imagined experimenter action showed activation of the frontopolar gyrus, inferior parietal cortex, right precuneus, and left posterior cingulate cortex. These results suggest separate neural mechanisms for self versus imagined actions.

Farrer and Frith (2002) performed brain scans on participants while they used a joystick to control the motion of an onscreen cursor in one condition or used a disconnected joystick while watching the cursor move under the experimenter's control. The first condition involves agency while the second does not. They found bilateral insula activity in the agency condition and left lateral premotor cortex, right inferior parietal cortex, and bilateral parietal activity in the nonagency condition. In a related study using a different behavior, McGuire, Silbersweig, and Frith (1996) contrasted reading aloud while hearing one's own voice to reading aloud while hearing a transformed voice or the voice of the experimenter. There was greater right-side lateral temporal cortex activation in the mismatched voice conditions. The results show that agency is special with regard to anatomical specificity.

So is there a specialized system for the physical self? The results are mixed. Taken together, the research does not support the notion of a single physical self system that incorporates face recognition, body layout, ownership, and agency. Face recognition appears to involve areas in both hemispheres. For movement the system clearly codes for the layout of both one's own body and that of others. However, for part ownership and agency there do appear to be specialized neural systems.

The Digital Physical Self

Artificial agents will certainly need to recognize themselves in multiple modalities, whether visual, somatic, or self-initiated action. It is difficult to move around in the world if you don't know where your legs are. Robots are thus equipped with sensors that tell them the position of their limbs and other body parts in space. This mimics the proprioceptive and vestibular senses found in humans and other animals.

Issues of body recognition also come into play when we inhabit avatars. While playing such characters, we project ourselves into the body of the character, seeing what it sees and controlling its movements. While this happens we may temporarily lose sense of our own bodies and in effect inhabit a new virtual body. This is probably more likely to occur during a first-person view than a third-person view, since the former is closer to the way we experience the world. It is also more likely to occur in virtual reality games where the visual environment reacts to our head movements. We more fully address what it is like to bodily inhabit an avatar in chapter 7.

The Psychological Self

Traits

We now focus on aspects of the psychological self as manifested in traits, autobiographical memory, and first-person perspective. Miller et al. (2001) found a high rate of change in normally stable traits like political and religious attitudes in patients who had right hemisphere disease. They state that maintenance of enduring personality traits is moderated by the right frontotemporal regions. The self-reference effect (SRE) is the beneficial effect of encoding information related to oneself. The SRE supports the idea of a distinct memory system for self-knowledge. The SRE has been replicated by numerous researchers (Symons & Johnson, 1997). For example, Platek, Myers, Critton, and Gallup (2003) asked subjects to indicate with one of two hands whether a trait word described themselves, someone they knew, or neither. They obtained a left-hand advantage, suggesting right-hemisphere control. Craik et al. (1999) used PET to study individuals judging whether a trait adjective described themselves or a famous person, whether the word was positive or negative, or how many syllables it had. The self condition showed greater activation of the right anterior cingulate area. Unfortunately much of this research suffers from lack of adequate control conditions and alternate interpretations of the results, so it is still unclear whether such studies support the existence of a special self memory.

Autobiographical Memory

Autobiographical memory is memory for personal events. It is considered a subset of episodic memory, which is memory for all events. Events in this context refer to episodes from a specific place and time. Episodic and semantic memory (memory for facts) constitute the two types of long-term memory. De Renzi, Liotti, and Nichelli (1987) report on the case study of a woman who had encephalitis that caused severe impairments in semantic memory but whose memory for personal events was still quite good. This case suggests a neuro-anatomical dissociation between semantic and episodic memory. However, it does not imply that personal event memory is distinct from event memory in general. Fink et al. (1996) gathered brain images of participants while they listened to a narrative describing one of their own memories and another person's memory. When the narrative described participants' own memories, participants showed greater activation in the anterior insula, right temporal lobe, and other right-hemisphere regions. This study is also problematic, though, as the greater right-hemisphere activation could have been due to retrieval of episodic memories in general, a function for which it is known, rather than a specific type of memory that operates only on personal episodic information. Given the problems with these and related studies, we cannot yet conclude that there is a separate neural system devoted to an autobiographical self.

Can a digital person have a sense of self without an autobiographical memory? Is a recorded history of an experienced past necessary for an agent to achieve selfhood? On the one hand, having such a memory tells us about who we are. If we recall standing up to a bully, then we consider ourselves brave. If we remember caring for a father with cancer, then we consider ourselves empathetic and kind. So this type of past informs us about who we are and would be useful to have in an agent to enable it to better understand itself. On the other hand, however, we might say that it is our actions and the way we respond to the world that determine self. In this case it is not the memory of what we have done but what we do now that matters. An agent that possesses a particular character will act in accordance with it even if it has no memory of its previous actions. It could form a sense of self moment to moment based on evaluations of its behavior. The autobiographical account conforms to the narrative approach to self, while the action-based one is more in line with trait-based approaches.

First-Person Perspective

First-person perspective is a memory defined by a centeredness in one's own body, operating in an egocentric reference frame (Vogeley & Fink, 2003). It roughly corresponds to the first-person POV in a video game of looking out through one's own eyes. Third-person perspective is objective rather than subjective and involves experiencing an event from outside one's body. There is also a more abstract narrative sense of first-person perspective in which one understands a story as happening to "I" instead of "he" or "she." These latter two impersonal pronouns are the way a story is related using a third-person perspective. Vogeley et al. (2001) had subjects read a story told in either the first- or third-person perspective. In the self condition subjects read stories and were asked questions about their own actions, beliefs, and perceptions within the stories. In the other condition, the story was about someone else and subjects were asked similar questions, but this time about the other person. There were some common areas of brain activation for both conditions, but in the self condition unique activation was found in the bilateral anterior cingulate cortex and the right temporoparietal junction.

Gusnard, Akbudak, Shulman, and Raichle (2001) had viewers judge whether images gave them a pleasant, a neutral, or an unpleasant feeling (first-person, emotional) or whether the image's locale was in or out-of-doors (third-person, neutral). The first-person condition produced greater activation in the medial prefrontal area and in the frontal operculum/left insula. An earlier similar study found greater activation in the anterior cingulate cortex when subjects' responses were based on their own emotional reactions (Lane, Fink, Chau, and Dolan, 1997). Unfortunately there are methodological issues with these studies. The Vogeley experiment had a small number of subjects and stories per condition. In studies using emotion-based images, activation could be based on the images' affective component alone and not on any first-person perspective per se.

Summary of Studies on Self-Specialized Brain Systems

Interpretation of the literature shows there is no single, across-the-board brain system corresponding to all aspects of the self, physical or psychological. In fact, just the opposite was obtained for body representation, which appears to code for the body layout of both others and ourselves. Many of the studies cited in the previous sections suffer from methodological flaws such as inappropriate control stimuli. It is difficult to equate "other" and "self" stimuli in the case of words because of the many ways words can vary, particularly in familiarity and affective content. So the jury is still out on whether there is a specialized neural system for self.

Part of the problem is that there are so many aspects of self. Each aspect, such as face recognition or body representation, has a different underlying neural system. It may be costly for the brain to evolve many separate self-based systems. Instead it may have adopted a more efficient processing strategy of attaching a special code or tag to self-related information or according it greater attention or priority. These measures could be implemented more easily across systems and would not require having to build separate processing mechanisms. However, as we shall see in the sections that follow, researchers have formulated many models that describe how a self system might be implemented in the brain. Not all of these suffer the problems described in the Gillihan and Farah (2005) review. Most have substantial corroborating experimental support. Let's turn to these next.

ONE OR MANY NEURAL SELVES?

Daniel Dennett's Multiple-Drafts Model

In his book *Consciousness Explained,* Dennett (1991) outlines a theory on the nature of consciousness. He begins by refuting the classical view of consciousness. The classical view, promoted by Descartes, posits a single point in the brain where all information funnels in. This area is a supposed center of consciousness or self, where we experience the external contents of the world or the internal contents of our thoughts in a coherent, unified way.

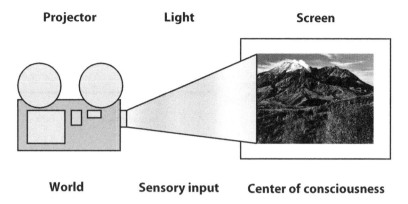

Projector   **Light**   **Screen**

World   **Sensory input**   **Center of consciousness**

FIGURE 15 The Cartesian theater model of consciousness. After Friedenberg and Silverman (2016).

Dennett calls this center the "Cartesian theater." It is as though our consciousness were the result of a projector displaying information on a movie screen. The individual sitting in the theater watching the screen then has a single conscious experience of what is playing. Although this is a theory of consciousness, we can also use the arguments here and apply them to the notion of self. We experience a single unified self subjectively, so it would seem logical for there to be a single place in the brain where information is displayed and where our "self" is able to experience it. Figure 15 shows a representation of the Cartesian theater.

However, there are a number of problems with the Cartesian theater. To start, linked modes of information do not arrive within the brain simultaneously. Light from an event, because it travels faster, precedes the arrival of sound. The sight of a fireworks display, for example, reaches the mind prior to the sound of the explosion, yet we experience the two in unison. This suggests that our consciousness is constructed; the visual experience is kept in check or delayed until arrival of the sound, at which point the two are integrated into a unified percept of the fireworks. This example and others imply that the experience of the conscious self occurs, not in real time, but (in many instances) several fractions of a second or so after an event. Our experience of consciousness as direct and immediate seems to be an illusion.

Another problem with the Cartesian theater is that anatomically it is difficult to find a brain region that links incoming sensory inputs and outgoing motor outputs. There is no central processing unit (CPU) in the brain as there is in a computer. The task of a computer's CPU is to schedule and coordinate ongoing activity. If a computer were to have a self, the CPU might be where it was located. Processing in the brain, however, is "massively parallel." Most tasks are split into multiple subtasks where computation occurs simultaneously. Some of these subtasks get completed or may arrive at a solution before the others. Exactly how information in separate streams gets coordinated is not entirely known. Neural synchronization is one possibility, discussed later.

The Cartesian theater analogy requires an observer in the audience watching the screen. This observer is the subjective self who experiences the screen's contents. But how is this

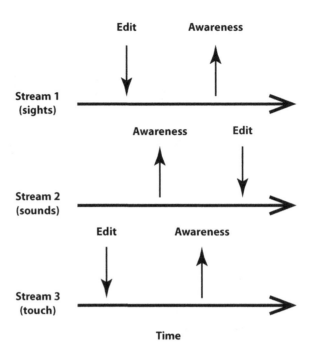

Stream 1
(sights)

Edit   Awareness

Stream 2
(sounds)

Awareness   Edit

Stream 3
(touch)

Edit   Awareness

Time

• Mental activity occurs in parallel

FIGURE 16 The multiple-drafts model of consciousness. After Friedenberg and Silverman (2016). Based on Dennett (1991).

• Streams correspond to different sensory inputs or thoughts

• Editing can consist of subtractions, additions, and changes

• Consciousness can happen anywhere, not just at the end

person inside one's head interpreting the image and having the conscious experience? To explain this, we need to posit another mechanism or theater inside this person's head with another, even smaller person, and so on ad infinitum. This is known as the homunculus problem in psychology and philosophy. *Homunculus* translated means "little man." An effective theory of consciousness must avoid the logical conundrum of homunculi nested inside each other.

Dennett replaces this problematic formulation with a multiple-drafts model of consciousness (see figure 16). In this model, mental activity occurs in parallel. Rather than projecting to a single location for processing in unison, different ongoing streams of information are processed at different times. Each of these streams can correspond to different sensory inputs or thoughts. Processing or editing of the streams can occur, which may change their content. Editing can consist of subtractions, additions, and changes to the information. Awareness of a stream's content can happen before or after editing takes place. To illustrate, take our fireworks example. One mental stream would contain the visual experience of the fireworks, while another would contain its auditory representation. The visual stream would undergo editing in the form of a delay to synchronize it with the auditory stream. Then the information from both streams could be tapped to produce awareness.

Dennett's theory also allows for different levels of awareness. Some information that is part of a stream may be available to conscious awareness and could be verbally described by the individual experiencing it. Other data streams we may be only vaguely aware of, but they can persist and influence additional mental processes. Still other information may simply fade into the background. We may never be aware of this information. These three levels of awareness are comparable to Freud's conscious, preconscious, and subconscious aspects of mind.

Solving the Coordination Problem: Neural Synchrony and Reentrant Processing

The visual system is a good example of parallel processing. It adopts a "divide-and-conquer" strategy. The visual system carves up different aspects of an object during pattern recognition. These aspects are each processed separately in different parts of the brain by anatomically distinct pathways. This information is later combined to yield a unitary percept, but we are not aware that the information has been separated and then united. To illustrate this, imagine that you are looking a red Porsche moving down the street. The shape (curves), color (red), and movement (left to right) of the car would each be processed in different streams. The shape of the car would be represented by neurons in the temporal lobe, the color by V4 neurons in the occipital lobe, and the movement by neurons in the medial temporal region.

If a task is split into so many streams, how does the information in all of them get unified or coordinated? To perceive the car we need to combine the color red, the shape of the curves, and the direction of movement. Only then could we know that the properties applied to the same object and only then would we be able to recognize or act sensibly to it. If there is no homunculus or CPU for the results of the different streams to feed into, how do the object properties get combined? This is known as the binding problem in vision.

One way is to coordinate the activity between a group of neurons. A perceptual object can be represented by the joined and coordinated activity of a group of cells, a concept known as neural synchrony (Singer, 1996). Subgroups can stand for individual features and may be separated by relatively large physical distances in the brain, but the dynamic activities of all of them serve to represent an entire object. The same group of neurons that code for a particular feature in one object can participate in different cell assemblies and thus stand for this same feature in other objects. For example, a network of cells representing the color red can participate in the assembly for a stop sign. These same cells can then participate in the assembly for a tomato.

What happens in neural synchrony is that all the participating neurons fire, or initiate action potentials, at the same time. It is helpful to use an analogy here. Imagine a group of drummers in a band. If all the drummers banged out different rhythms, the result would be a chaotic mess. But if the drummers all beat the drums at the same time they would stand out and thus become salient. Neural synchrony could be the basis for many cognitive phenomena such as memory formation and attentional effects. Synchronized neurons that stand out from background activity enough to enter conscious awareness could be the contents of the subjective self. In other words, they could be what the self is aware of at any given time.

More recent research on this topic shows that the brain can synchronize far-flung activity in a much more flexible way than previously assumed. Guttman, Gilroy, and Blake (2007) differentiate between temporal synchrony and temporal structure. In the first case, neurons must be in phase with one another. The impulses or spikes representing action potentials have to occur at the same moment, either for the entire pattern or for subsets within the pattern. In the second case, there can be similar patterns of impulses over time in either location, and these can be linked. Imagine that neurons in one brain area fire two bursts of high-frequency impulses followed by one burst of low-frequency impulses. In another area, this same pattern occurs but several seconds later. Even though the impulses don't happen at exactly the same time, their similar patterning or temporal structure can still serve as a basis for the synchronization.

For a long time it was believed that signals in the visual system were feed-forward only, meaning they traveled from one layer of neurons to the next, in an upward or bottom-up style from the eye to ever higher levels in the brain. We now know that signals in the visual system can also travel in the opposite direction, downward or top-down (van Kerkoerle et al., 2014). Feedback activity of this sort is also referred to as reentrant. It could be that we become consciously aware of visual content when these two directions of activity merge, when the forward and backward sweeps overlap. Reentrant signaling and synchrony between different parts of the brain, especially between the frontal cortex and other areas, might be the mechanism behind conscious awareness and could explain what the self is aware of (Tononi & Koch, 2008).

NEURAL MODELS OF THE SELF

In this section we examine neural models of the self. These are comprehensive models that specify how the self could be instantiated in the human brain. We look first at Damasio's extensive model and turn after that to a self-referential model and a model for self-memory. These are not an extensive list of all such models but serve as examples.

Antonio Damasio's Neural Model of Self

The neuroscientist Antonio Damasio, in his 1999 book *The Feeling of What Happens*, outlines an extensive neuroscientific account of consciousness. In what follows we will provide a somewhat detailed description of his theory. For Damasio there are two key players, the organism and the object. The organism is the person whose self we are attempting to explain. The object is what that person is either perceiving in the outside world (Aunt Sally sitting on the chair in front of him or her) or remembering from internal recollection (a memory of Aunt Sally at the person's birthday party last year). Also important is the relationship between organism and object. This refers to the change that occurs in the organism when it takes the object into account. Objects in the world or in our memories are subject to ongoing change and transformation. In contrast our bodies tend to be stable. In fact, our bodies spend a lot of time trying to keep things like temperature and blood pressure within a narrow range of tolerances. The organism actively regulates internal states to produce stability. This stability is necessary to maintain life.

To begin, all organisms have a boundary that separates them from the environment and creates an inside relative to an outside. Changes in the outside usually do not cause a correspondingly large amount of variation within. In a single cell this boundary is called a membrane. In an animal it is the skin. The boundary and the area inside of it are the body. Bodies are essential for personhood. According to Damasio there is always a one-to-one correspondence between body and being a person. He says it is not possible to have a single person with two bodies and that neither is it generally true that there can be multiple people inside one body. One possible exception to the latter is multiple personality disorder, or, as it is now called, dissociative identity disorder, which we discussed in detail in chapter 3. Digital technologies may also prove this assumption incorrect, as it may be possible for software, which has no physical boundary to be a self. We discuss this further in the section on artificial life in chapter 9.

To perceive an object the organism requires sensory signals, like the pattern of activation in the visual system in response to light that falls on the retina. Secondarily, it needs the pattern of activity in the body that is normally generated when it monitors itself. Our body then undergoes a reactive change in response to a new object. This change is part of a sequence that ultimately culminates in our feeling of self. But before we get to that, let's describe how the body monitors itself. It does this through the somatosensory system.

The Somatosensory System

The somatosensory system consists of the neural and hormonal systems that monitor the body's state and convey this information to the brain. For Damasio, the somatosensory system has three subsystems. These are the visceral/interoceptive division (monitors internal organs); the vestibular (maintains balance) and musculoskeletal/proprioceptive system (senses changes in the skeleton and bones); and fine touch (processes information from the skin). The visceral division is in charge of sensing changes mostly from our internal organs like the stomach or small intestine. Chemicals in the bloodstream caused by changes in these organs, such as low blood glucose levels, are sensed by nuclei of neurons in areas of the brain stem, hypothalamus, and telencephalon. If the concentration of these chemicals is too high or too low, neurons will respond, attempting to correct the imbalance. Messages in this system can also be sent by neurons to the brain, producing a reaction there. Being hungry and wanting to have sex are two possible consequences of this reaction.

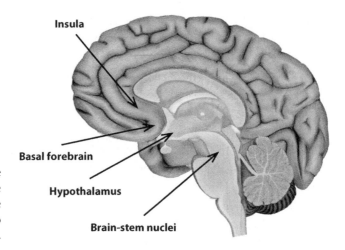

Insula

Basal forebrain

Hypothalamus

Brain-stem nuclei

FIGURE 17 Location of some protoself structures in the brain. Regions are approximate. After Damasio (1999).

The vestibular system helps maintain our balance. It tells us where we are positioned in space. It does this using the semicircular canals, three fluid-filled loops in the inner ear. Movement in one of the three axes in space causes this fluid to flow and to bend tiny hairs. The musculoskeletal category conveys to the brain the state of muscles that are being moved by the body. It senses the tension and length of muscles and the angle of limbs at joints. The third and final category of somatosensation is for fine touch. Signals in this division become activated when we make contact with another object—for example, when our hand reaches out to grab an apple. They carry information about temperature, texture, weight, temperature, and other features.

The Protoself (Nonconscious)

For Damasio, information from the somatosensory system is used to generate the protoself. He defines the protoself as a coherent collection of neural patterns that map ongoing changes in the state of the physical structure of the organism in its many dimensions. It is located in many different parts of the brain and at many different levels of spatial scale. We are not conscious of the protoself, and it does not contain knowledge. It simply serves as a baseline or referent condition against which an object is contrasted. Figure 17 shows the location of some of this system's structures. We next describe the three main structures that make it up.

First comes the brain stem. This region contains a collection of nuclei receiving information concerning the overall current body state as mediated by the spinal cord pathways, the trigeminal nerve, the vagus complex, and the area postrema. Included in this region are reticular nuclei. The second is the hypothalamus. This helps monitor and control pH levels and circulating nutrients like glucose sodium, and several hormones. The third and last structure of the protoself comprises the insular cortex, the secondary somatosensory cortices, and the medial parietal cortices.

The Core Self (Core Consciousness)

The core self results from core consciousness. This consciousness occurs when the brain's representation devices generate an imaged, nonverbal account of how the organism's own state is affected by the organism's processing of an object. The following is a statement of some of the premises in Damasio's words. First, the organism as a unit is mapped in the organism's brain, within structures that regulate the organism's life and signal its internal state continuously. The object is also mapped within the brain, in the sensory and motor structures activated by the interaction of the organism with the object. Both organism and object are mapped as neural patterns, in what Damasio calls first-order maps. The sensori-motor maps pertaining to the object cause changes in the maps pertaining to the organism. These changes are now rerepresented in still other, second-order maps that thus represent the relationship of object and organism. The mental images that describe the relationship are feelings.

Figure 18 shows a step-by-step process of how core consciousness is formed. First there is a neural map of an object. This is either a representation of a perceived object, such as a friend's house that one is currently looking at, or a representation of a recalled object from memory, such as an image of what one's childhood house looked like. The neural map triggers the formation of a map of the inaugural protoself at that instant. This is the set of neural patterns representing what the state of one's body is like at the moment the object is processed. That in turn leads to a map of the protoself modified, which is the state of one's body after the object is processed. All of this information, the object map, and the two protoself maps are examples of first-order maps. They have inputs to other brain regions that then use it to assemble a second-order map. Damasio allows for the possibility of multiple second-order maps corresponding to different aspects of an object, such as the color, shape, and movement of a car. Figure 19 shows the location of candidate brain regions for these second-order maps. They include the cingulate, thalamus, and superior colliculus.

The core self is a direct conscious experience of an object with the knowledge that *you* are having the experience: for instance, awareness of a car and awareness that *you* are perceiving the car. Damasio believes this mental experience of self can be had only by realizing there is an object while realizing there is a you doing the experiencing of that object. The awareness occurs through the contrast of the "me" in the protoself and the way this "me" gets changed by awareness of the object. Core self lives in the moment. It doesn't have access to memories or to higher-order cognitive processing. That type of awareness would require additional conscious processing

The Extended or Autobiographical Self (Extended Consciousness)

Extended consciousness goes beyond the here and now of core consciousness. It is based on the core self but is now connected to the lived past and anticipated future. Rather than just being aware of pain (core self), you can now also survey facts concerning where the pain is (the elbow), what caused it (playing tennis), and how that might affect future plans (canceling a game for tomorrow). This is all possible because you can access memories of

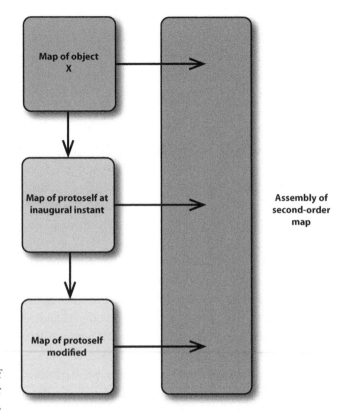

FIGURE 18 The formation of core consciousness. After Damasio (1999).

Map of object X

Map of protoself at inaugural instant

Map of protoself modified

Assembly of second-order map

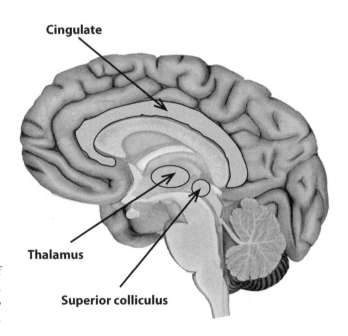

Cingulate

Thalamus

Superior colliculus

FIGURE 19 The location of second-order map brain structures. After Damasio (1999).

the past and thoughts about the object. In extended consciousness the sense of self arises in the repeated display of one's own personal memories, the objects of one's personal past.

Working memory is what holds these objects and makes them more than just fleeting sensations. It must hold active, simultaneously and for a substantial amount of time, the many images of the autobiographical self and the images that define the object. Awareness here is thus taking place over a period of several seconds or minutes. For Damasio extended consciousness occurs when working memory holds in place at the same time both a particular object and the autobiographical self: in other words, when both a particular object and the objects in one's autobiography simultaneously generate core consciousness. Other areas that subsume the neuroanatomical basis of the extended self are early sensory cortices of varied modalities (the primary visual cortex in the occipital lobe; the primary auditory cortex in the temporal lobe), higher-order cortices, and varied subcortical nuclei.

An autobiographical self can occur only in organisms with sufficient memory and reasoning capacity. However, language is not required, as nonverbal images of memories can be used. It is possible that in humans this type of memory forms as early as eighteen months. Damasio believes that apes such as bonobo chimpanzees have this kind of self and that dogs may as well. However, these animals do not possess personhood. For that, language is necessary along with more memory and reasoning capacity. So far as we know, only humans have these gifts.

A Neural Model of Self-Referential Processing

In an attempt to make sense of the vast literature on self, several researchers have performed meta-analyses. In this approach, data across multiple studies are analyzed to look for commonalities and differences. Northoff et al. (2006) propose a model of self-referential processing in the human brain based on a meta-analysis. This model, they believe, can link the various aspects of self that have been proposed in the philosophical, psychological, and neurological literature. Examples of multiple aspects of self include the physical self, the mental self, and the spiritual self, the protoself or minimal self, the core or mental self, the autobiographical self, and the narrative self (Damasio, 1999; Gallagher & Frith, 2003; James, 1892). Other aspects of self include the emotional self (P. Fossati et al., 2003), the spatial self (Vogeley & May, 2004), the facial self (Keenan & Wheeler, 2003), the verbal or interpreting self (Turk & Heatherton, 2003), and the social self (Frith & Frith, 2003). Some of these are discussed in other parts of the book in further detail, and we don't elaborate upon them here.

What unites these different ideas of self is self-referential processing, also known as self-related or self-relevant processing. It concerns stimuli that are experienced as strongly related to ourselves, such as our own picture or the picture of a close friend in contrast to the picture of a stranger. Stimuli experienced this way are considered to be implicit, subjective, and phenomenal and have been deemed self-qualia (David & Kircher, 2003). They are also value-laden and emotionally colored. Self-referential processing concerns multiple kinds of stimuli, including autobiographical, emotional, motor, and facial.

The model is based around a cluster of brain structures in the cortical midline area, called the cortical midline structures (CMS). The CMS consist of the medial orbital prefrontal cortex (MOFC), the ventromedial prefrontal cortex (VMPFC), the sub/pre- and supragenual anterior cingulate cortex (PACC, SACC), the dorsomedial prefrontal cortex (DMPFC), the medial parietal cortex (MPC), the posterior cingulate cortex (PCC), and the retrosplenial cortex (RSC). These structures are believed to function as a cohesive anatomical and functional unit. The CMS are the structures hypothesized to perform self-referential processing. If they perform this task, then activation in these areas should be observed regardless of the type of task (face recognition, memory, emotion) and also across sensory modalities (visual, auditory, tactile).

Twenty-seven PET and fMRI studies on self-related tasks published between 2000 and 2004 were analyzed. Activation peaks for xyz coordinates across studies were plotted onto medial and lateral views of a 3-D brain image. The studies were divided into several categories based on the type of domain. These domains were verbal (judgment of sentences like "I can be trusted"), spatial (egocentric processing of one's own body), memory (retrieval of self- vs. non-self-related adjectives), emotional (judging whether emotional, positive, or negative personality traits apply to oneself), facial (distinguishing one's face from other faces), social (attributing emotions, thoughts, attitudes, and beliefs to other persons), and movement (the feeling of being causally involved in an action).

The results showed that the CMS were activated across a diverse set of sensory modalities, showing that they were modality independent. For example, emotional tasks caused activation in the CMS regardless of whether the task in the study was olfactory, gustatory, auditory, or visual. This makes sense, as the CMS receive afferent inputs from the parts of the brain that process these different modalities. CMS structures were also activated regardless of task, whether it was verbal, memory, emotional, or social. This shows that CMS activation is also task independent.

The CMS are also connected to cortical and subcortical regions like the insula, hypothalamus, periaqueductal gray (PAG), and colliculi, which process interoceptive signals. These signals include the vestibular, proprioceptive, and visceral senses that provide information about the internal state of the body. Studies investigating outputs to body regulation or exteroception such as biofeedback arousal, regulation of heart rate, relaxation, and affective control of pain show activation in CMS structures. The MOFC and VMPFC have been called polymodal convergent zones. As such they seem to be the place where different sensory stimuli are determined to be self-referential. Stimuli that are strongly related to oneself show activation in the CMS, while those that are unrelated show low activation or even deactivation.

Subcortical midline regions are associated with the bodily self or protoself (Damasio, 1999; Panksepp, 2005). These older parts of the brain may instantiate a "virtual body." The linkage of sensory processing in these areas with self-referential processing in the CMS may cause the creation of the core or mental self. Note the similarity here with Damasio's neural model, in which there is a contrast between sensory processing of an object and the protoself. This study additionally showed a high resting level of neural activity in the CMS. This resting-level activity may constitute our constant background awareness of self, akin to James's "stream of consciousness."

Lateral prefrontal cortical regions are activated in self-related tasks where there is a cognitive component (Steele & Lawrie, 2004). Examples include deciphering the meaning of a word (verbal domain), performing judgments, making inferences, thinking and imagining (emotions and theory-of-mind tasks), and encoding, retrieving, and recognizing information (memory). In the model the CMS are assumed to filter, select, and provide higher-order cognitive areas with stimuli that are self-relevant. These stimuli can then be elaborated upon and processed further once they reach these areas. In this sense, the CMS act as a gate, opening to allow self-relevant stimuli through and closing to block off non-self-relevant material.

The CMS may also be the key to understanding the different types of self. Damasio's autobiographical self may be the result of linkage between self-referential stimuli and memory processes—that is, between the CMS and other parts of the brain that process memories. The best elaboration of how this might take place is in the Martinelli, Sperduti, and Piolino (2013) self-memory model described below. The interpreter (Turk et al., 2002) or narrative self (Gallagher & Frith, 2003) or dialogical self (Dimaggio et al., 2003) could be the result of linkage between the CMS and various parts of the brain that process verbal information. The emotional self (H. Fossati et al., 2004) could result from linkage to emotional centers, and the spatial self (Vogeley & May, 2004) to areas for processing spatial awareness.

The CMS model is attractive in that it is general. It can account for stimuli across the sensory domain and across task domain. The CMS sit "midway" between incoming sensory messages and outgoing signals to higher cognitive areas and so logically are in a position to assign self-referentiality to sensory information prior to cognitive processing. As a result, they could be the basis for a three-layer model of self, which going from bottom to top would be sensory self, experiential self, and cognitive self. These three layers in order correspond to the protoself, the core self, and the autobiographical self that have been hypothesized by Damasio and other earlier researchers.

A Neural Self-Memory System Model

Martinelli, Sperduti, and Piolino (2013) also adopted the meta-analysis approach, performing an analysis of thirty-eight studies on the self-memory system. They adopted a model of self-memory processing based on three components of explicit, or declarative, memory. These memory systems are conscious and require high-level cognitive processes. This is in contrast to implicit self-memory processes that are largely unconscious, like body ownership and agency. Such processes are linked to proprioception and action planning and were not the focus of this study.

The three components in Martinelli et al.'s model are the episodic autobiographical memory (EAM), the semantic autobiographical memory (SAM), and the conceptual self (CS). The

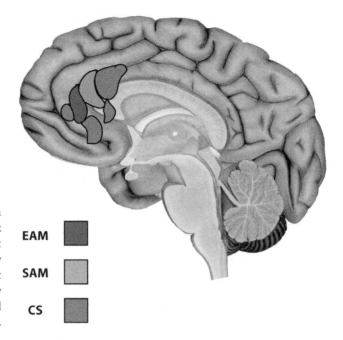

FIGURE 20 Brain structures in the medial prefrontal cortex corresponding to the episodic autobiographical memory (EAM), the semantic autobiographical memory (SAM), and the conceptual self (CS).

EAM ☐

SAM ☐

CS ☐

EAM consists of concrete and specific items of personal information that are closely related to unique autobiographical events situated in a specific time and place. This would include examples like "the first time somebody kissed a girlfriend on a warm evening in August." The SAM contains semantic personal information comprising general knowledge of personal facts. This would include information about friends and common locations but also general events like "first job," "weekends at the country house," and "that holiday in Italy." The CS stores semantic memory in the form of personal beliefs, values, and attitudes. It contains self-knowledge of personality traits and judgments on a number of categories of self-identity. This would include, for instance, knowledge that "I am anxious," or "I work hard."

The statistical method used in the researchers' study was called activation likelihood estimation (ALE). It models all coordinates of maximum activation for a given study as the peaks of a 3-D Gaussian probability distribution. A single map for that study is computed, and the union of all these maps across studies is determined on a voxel-by-voxel basis. A voxel is a 3-D pixel that contains activation values for an xyz coordinate space. The result is a map of the brain that can show which areas were most active across a set of studies. Figure 20 shows the three components of their model based on their results.

The results for the EAM showed the greatest activation in the limbic structures, midline cortical structures, and left middle temporal gyrus. For SAM tasks, the regions were the ACC and PCC, MPFC, left middle and inferior frontal gyrus, left superior and middle temporal gyrus, left thalamus, left fusiform gyrus, and parahippocampus. For the CS the regions of greatest activation were in the vMPFC and dMPFC, lateral frontal cortex in both hemispheres, and ACC. To summarize a different way, the EAM activated predominantly posterior and limbic structures, including the hippocampus; the SAM was associated with anterior, posterior, and limbic activations; and the CS recruited medial prefrontal structures. The mPFC was activated for all three types of self-representation. It was engaged in all three conditions but in slightly different locations for each.

The researchers confirmed their hypothesis that there would be a shift in processing from posterior to anterior (back to front of the brain) with increased abstraction of representation. This means that more specific and concrete items would be likely to be processed in the back part of the brain where primary sensory cortices are located. Processing would then shift toward midline and frontal structures. The front of the brain contains executive systems and so is better equipped to handle abstract representations. Posterior regions are more involved in reviviscence (retrieval) and access to autobiographical information, while frontal areas are more involved with self-referential assessment.

This meta-analysis shows that no single brain region processes declarative self-memory. Instead, processing is spread throughout the brain. The mPFC seems to play a crucial role in self-representation independent of the level of abstraction, as it was activated in all cases. Separate centers exist for different types of self-memory information. The extent of their functional independence has yet to be determined, as well as the way in which they are coordinated or organized.

PROBLEMS WITH THE NEUROSCIENTIFIC STUDY OF SELF

Klein (2013) points out several difficulties with the scientific study of self. The first and most important is that the concept of self is underspecified. In other words, researchers don't do a good job of defining what they mean by self or of linking it to theory. He argues that currently we lack a theoretically compelling answer. A possible explanation coming from Eastern philosophy and other thinkers is that there may be no such thing as self at all, that it is simply an illusion (Hood, 2012; Siderits, Thompson, & Zahavi, 2011). However, if the self is an illusion, an illusion is an experience, and an experience requires an experiencer (Schwerin, 2012).

Despite these issues, psychologists have not stopped studying the self, formulated by many in the form of hyphenated terms. These include *self-comparison, self-concept, self-complexity, self-deception, self-esteem, self-handicapping, self-image, self-perception, self-regulation, self-reference,* and *self-verification.* Leary and Tangney (2012) provide a review. Models of self have been proposed in psychology for over one hundred years (Conway, 2005; Samsonovich & Nadel, 2005). Examples include contextualized selves, cultural selves, social selves, cognitive selves, embodied selves, situational selves, autobiographical selves, relational selves, narrative selves, and collective selves.

This multiplicity of terms suggests there is not a single self to describe (Legrand & Ruby, 2009). In most of these discussions at least two selves come up. The first is the third-person neurally instantiated systems of self. The second is the subjective first-person self (Strawson, 2009). The former consists of things such as personal memory, body image, and emotions. The activity corresponding to these can be localized in the brain and is capable of objective scientific study. The latter is the subjective having of that experience and may not be amenable to study. Some have proposed that this aspect of self cannot be directly known by an act of perception or introspection (Swinburne, 2013). To others, these two aspects of self, object and subject, must interact because there can be no object without a subject and no subject without an object (Neuhouser, 1990). In this view there must be *someone* (the self) to be aware of *something* (some aspect of mental content).

The problem with the multiplicity of self appears in recent neuroimaging studies. Within the study of self-referential memory, at least three different types of self-knowledge have been found that are both within and across different systems of long-term memory. These include semantic factual self-knowledge, semantic trait self-knowledge, and episodic personal memories (Martinelli, Sperduti, & Piolino, 2013). These aspects of self are considered to be conceptually and functionally independent. Research to date shows at least six different functionally independent systems of self-knowledge. Within those there a variety of subsystems that are also functionally independent (Renoult, Davidson, Palombo, Moscovitch, & Levine, 2012). To complicate matters, the same result can be mediated by more than one kind of self-memory. Both semantic memory (for facts) and episodic memory (for personal events) can be used to judge a trait's self-relevance.

RESPONSES TO PROBLEMS WITH THE NEUROSCIENTIFIC STUDY OF SELF

At a micro level one can say that there is a self for every piece of mental content we are aware of: a self that is aware of a butterfly, a self that is aware of a kitchen spoon, and so on. But certainly this is multiplying the number of selves out of proportion. Instead we must work upwards from this level, clustering selves that correspond to types of mental content or types of mental processes. At the same time we can work from the macro level downward, investigating selves that correspond to higher-order categories or phenomena: a self of visual imagery, a self of imageless verbal thought, et cetera. Somewhere these lines of investigation would meet in the middle and corroborate one another. Neuroscience research imposes constraints on this endeavor. If one part of the brain lights up only for a specific subprocess A, then it is implicated only in that subprocess. If another part of the brain lights up for A and for another subprocess B, then it plays an organizational or coordinating role for those two. In this way investigators can slowly ascertain the mechanistic basis for the self phenomenon in question.

Of course, critics can say in response to this that at the end we have all the mechanisms of self but still not the subjective self that is aware of these mental contents or that directs these mental processes. In the end science can provide us only with the objective representations and functions, not the subjective experience. However, much can be gleaned from similar work being done on the neural correlates of consciousness (NCC). There one can isolate those regions that are active when we are aware and those that seem to play a more subconscious role (Koch, 2004). If we assume that awareness is necessary for self, then consciousness neurons should be active during self-awareness, and those not linked to awareness should not. Better linkage between researchers in these two areas is needed.

Klein (2013) points out that better linkage is needed with philosophy as well. Philosophers are giving more thought to what self is and are starting to take neuroscience findings into account (Flanagan, 2002; Klein & Nichols, 2012; Knobe & Nichols, 2008). Philosophers are good at defining terms and at theorizing. They may be able to construct better theoretical constructs of self that can then be tested experimentally. Scientists in particular need to do a better job connecting the variables they operationalize in their studies with the theories they use.

CHAPTER FIVE

Brain + Hardware

CONTENTS

Cyborgs

    Examples of Animal Cyborgs

    Examples of Human Cyborgs

    Implantable Chips: Convenience versus Privacy

    Deep-Brain Stimulation

Prosthetics

    Sensory Prosthetics

        Retinal Implants (Prosthetic Vision)

        Cochlear Implants (Prosthetic Hearing)

        Artificial Skin

    Motor Prosthetics

        Reaching and Arms

        Grasping, Manipulation, and Hands

        Artificial Arms and Hands

        Walking and Artificial Legs

    Illusory Body Perception

    Powered Exoskeletons

Neural Prosthetics (Brain-Machine Interfaces or Brain-Computer Interfaces)

Animal Research

Human Research

Cognitive-Based "Mind-Reading" Techniques

Other BCI/BMI Applications

Artificial Memories

Robotics

    Telerobotics

    Personal Robotics (Social Robotics)

        Keeping Up Appearances

        Social Perception of Machines

        Kismet: The Emotional Robot

        ISAC—A Robot with Social Skills

    Robots and Ethics

    Collective Robotics

    Evolution and Robotics

        The Golem Project

        Evolvable Hardware

Nanorobotics and Nanomedicine

In this chapter we will examine a wide variety of subjects related to technology and its relation to our bodies. We start by discussing cyborgs, which are blends of people and machines. We then provide examples of how intelligent machines are being used to help us perceive and move and how this changes our perception of self. Following this we describe several fields in robotics that involve our control of or interaction with robots and the implications of these for our sense of self and identity.

CYBORGS

The term *cyborg* was coined by Manfred Clynes and Nathan Kline in 1960. Human space travel at that time was just becoming a reality, and these researchers proposed that we could adapt the human body to deal with the environments of outer space and new worlds. They proposed the addition of machine components that would monitor and control biological organisms so they could exist in any theoretical environment. These devices would be integrated into animals or people and allow their bodies to function without their having to think about it, thus freeing them up to explore and perform other functions.

For example, an osmotic pressure pump capsule could be implanted under the skin and used to inject a person with biochemically active substances at the right dose over time. A similar device might be used to supply oxygen into the blood and remove carbon dioxide so that someone could breathe in a vacuum. Other mechanical components could keep astronauts awake, protect them from radiation, monitor their metabolism and fluid intake, regulate enzyme systems, and perform a whole host of other tasks related to vestibular and cardiovascular function, changes in temperature, pressure, gravitation, and magnetic fields. In short, they saw humans as becoming biological/machine hybrids (Clynes & Kline, 1960).

Cyborg is short for *cybernetic organism* and means a being with both organic biological parts and mechanical/technological parts. It refers to an organism that has restored function or enhanced abilities due to the integration of some artificial component. Note the use of the word *organism* in this definition. It means animals as well as people can be cyborgs. *Restored function* means that the added artificial parts can be included in order to make up for some deficit or disorder, as when a war veteran is missing a leg and receives a prosthetic one. The phrase *enhanced abilities* means that the artificial parts can be added in order to improve or make the organism better, as in the hypothetical case when someone is given an artificial eye that allows better vision than he or she had before, perhaps extending into the infrared and ultraviolet portions of the electromagnetic spectrum.

Feedback is an inherent characteristic of cyborg parts. *Feedback* means that the part in question receives sensory input of some sort and uses this to modify its behavior. An artificial cardiac pacemaker uses feedback because it measures the electrical potential of the heart and on the basis of these inputs can stimulate and regulate the rate at which it beats. A person who wears contact lens or glasses would not be considered a cyborg by this definition because the lens does not change the person's behavior. However, cell phones do receive inputs both from other machines (an incoming call) and from people (the user hitting keys) that change the user's behavior. So the use of cell phones fulfills the feedback part of the definition. However, cell phones are not surgically attached or otherwise physically integrated with our bodies. A conservative definition would thus include integral attachment as well as feedback.

A more general definition of *cyborg* includes human-technology mixtures in which the device is not physically integrated into the body. A cell phone falls into this category. Mixtures may be considered cybernetic because they involve feedback and enhance the user. By this definition all tool-like artifacts make humans cyborgs, including low-tech items like pen and paper. Note the similarity between this mixture idea and the extended-mind hypothesis we encountered in chapter 2.

Cyborgs bring up philosophical questions. When does a person stop becoming a person? Where do we draw the line between the real and the artificial? Perhaps a thought experiment will help. Imagine that we take a single neuron belonging to a man and replace it with an electronic chip that performs the same function. We might all agree that this individual was still human, as most of his brain would still be biological. But what if we continued this thought experiment, replacing neurons one by one until all of his one hundred billion brain cells were converted into circuits? Would this person still be a person? At what point in this process would the man transition from being human to being machine? Is there a gray area in between where it would be a true cyborg, part man, part machine, but not either? What rights would we accord such halfway entities?

How does the addition of nonhuman parts to the body affect our sense of self? If we define ourselves by our physical bodies, then a replacement body part will surely change our self-conception. However, individuals fitted with quality prosthetics can adapt to them and in some cases fail to even notice they are there. One reason for this is that the somatosensory and motor cortices reorganize themselves in response to such changes. Newer limb prosthetics have the capability to allow sensory perception and motor control directly from the brain or by nerve connections and so reproduce the way we would normally perceive and move an arm or leg.

Examples of Animal Cyborgs

The US company Backyard Brains has manufactured a commercially available kit that allows one to control the movements of a cockroach (Gage & Marzullo, n.d.). Called "Roboroach," the kit allows the user to briefly make the cockroach walk either to the left or to the right by microstimulation of the antenna nerves. An electronic "backpack" is attached to the roach, and the movement is controlled using a smartphone. The effect is only temporary (two to seven days), and the device can be removed with little harm done to the roach. As of this writing, the kit costs US$150. Roaches are not included and must be purchased separately. Many other insects and animals have been remote controlled, including beetles, flies, sharks, turtles, geckos, pigeons, mice, and dogs.

Roboroach is an example of a bio-robot or robo-animal. Several studies examining the remote control of rats have also been performed (Harder 2002). Two electrodes are implanted in the ventral posterolateral nucleus of the thalamus, which conveys facial sensory

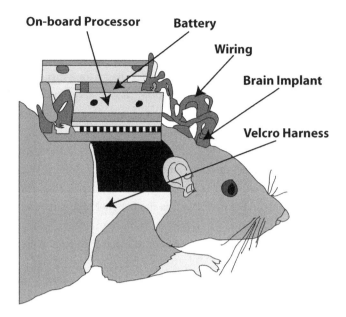

FIGURE 21 Robo Rat.

information from the left and right whiskers. A third electrode is implanted in the medial forebrain bundle, involved in the reward process. During training, one of the whisker electrodes can be stimulated to make the rat feel as if it has encountered an obstacle on one side of its body. When the rat turns to the opposite side, a signal is sent to the reward center. In 2002, researchers at the State University of New York were able to remote-control rats using a laptop from a distance of up to five hundred meters. The rats were made to turn left or right, navigate piles of rubble, climb ladders and trees, and jump from different heights. One benefit of this technology is that rats could be used to carry cameras to discover people trapped in collapsed buildings (figure 21).

There are obvious ethical concerns about remote-controlling animals. Even the developers have said that a debate on the topic is necessary. Implanting the controllers causes the animal discomfort. One of the developers, Sanjiv Talwar, has stated that the rat, given its "native intelligence," can overcome the directives to move but that with enough stimulation this hesitation can be overridden in some conditions. This resistance suggests that the rat is aware its actions are coming from outside its body, does not like the feeling, and attempts to redirect control to itself. This brings up interesting questions about self and identity. Is control over our own actions the most primary sense of self? Does an animal under remote control relinquish its sense of self? Should the human controllers and the animal together be considered as an extended "metaself"?

Examples of Human Cyborgs

Kevin Warwick is deputy vice-chancellor of research at Coventry University and before this was professor of cybernetics at the University of Reading. In 1998 he underwent surgery to implant a silicon chip transponder into his forearm. This allowed his movements to be tracked by a computer as he moved about Reading University. It also allowed him to turn lights on and off and to operate doors, heaters, and computers without having to operate them by hand. In the second phase of this experiment, Warwick had a one-hundred-electrode array implanted into the nerves of his left arm. Reading these nerve impulses, Warwick was able to control an electric wheelchair and an artificial hand. He could receive sensory inputs from the fingertips of this hand in order to adjust the grip. This allowed him to "feel" objects that he wasn't actually touching. He was later able to receive ultrasonic inputs to remotely detect the distance to objects, in effect a new form of perception. War-wick's wife next volunteered to have a similar electrode implanted in her arm (Warwick, 2004). Signals from her finger movements were transmitted via the internet to Kevin's electrodes, causing stimulation of her nervous system. Then signals from her nervous system were similarly sent to stimulate Kevin's nervous system. The result was that each person was able to "feel" the other's movements.

The British artist Neil Harbisson in 2004 had an antenna implanted in his head that allows to him to perceive colors beyond the human visual spectrum on the basis of vibrations in his skull (Ronchi, 2009). He can also use the system to wirelessly receive phone calls, music, and even images. All of the signals are translated into sound information. He is officially recognized as a cyborg by the government. In 2010 he founded the Cyborg Foundation, an international organization that defends cyborg rights, supports individuals who want to become cyborgs, and recognizes the trend as an art movement.

These experiments demonstrate several things. The first is that it is possible to perceive sensory information that is beyond our own innate biological senses. Information about one part of the electromagnetic spectrum, such as the infrared, can be picked up by a sensor and then transmitted to the brain in a different modality like vibrations or sound. This can allow us to perceive aspects of the environment to which we were formerly blind. It can ultimately allow us to "see" objects in the dark and even to hear radio stations. One can imagine a future in which smartphones are embedded in our brains. We could perceive and operate such devices using thought alone. If self is defined by what we can experience and do, then these clearly extend the boundaries of self and identity.

A second implication of such studies is that it is possible to send signals back and forth between two bodies or brains. In the future it may be possible in principle to "see" in detail what someone else is seeing or to "hear" what another person are hearing. One person's perceptions or thoughts could be directed to one or many others, allowing us to in essence see the world through that person's eyes and to be aware of the contents of his or her mind. The implications of this for identity and self are profound. It would allow two people to communicate by thought alone. Such dialogues or the mutual experience of one another's cognition could be seen as the formation of a group self, defined not by the physical boundaries of one's body but by a shared information exchange. Because neural activity corresponds to conscious experience and this process occurs through neural stimulation, the people in the group mind are having a shared conscious experience.

Implantable Chips: Convenience versus Privacy

In 2017, Three Square Market, a company in Wisconsin, partnered with another company, called Biohax, to offer chip implantation to its employees (Noe, 2017). The chip is the size of a grain of rice and is implanted between one's thumb and index finger. The chip allows any task involving radio-frequency identification (RFID) technology, such as passing through security to get into a building or paying for food in the cafeteria, to be done with a wave of the hand. RFID is the use of radio waves to read and capture information stored on a tag attached to an object. The program is voluntary, but as of July 25, 2017, fifty out of eighty employees had the procedure performed. The response among the employees was mostly positive, perhaps because Three Square Market is a technology company.

Such chips are certainly convenient. A general-purpose device of this sort could allow you to be hands-free for most of life's little tasks, like getting into and out of your car or apartment. It could be used to pay for items at the local drug store without your having to remove a wallet or purse. There are, however, several downsides to the use of such chips, the first of which is encryption. The company claims the tags are secure, but they could be hacked and information about the wearer obtained. Also, employers could potentially use these chips to obtain wearers' location and other information without their consent. They could, for example, determine how long people spend on bathroom breaks. There are also health risks. Although the FDA approved the chips, it is still possible for the site of the implantation to become infected. The long-term effects of radio transmission on human tissue are also not fully understood.

Deep-Brain Stimulation

A much more radical type of cyborg implantation is used in a technique called deep-brain stimulation (DBS), which involves implanting a medical device called a neurostimulator. This sends electrical impulses via electrodes to specific areas of the brain. It is used to treat various disorders, including obsessive-compulsive disorder (OCD), major depression, Parkinson's disease, and chronic pain (Appleby, Duggan, Regenberg, & Rabins, 2007). The FDA approved DBS to treat certain disorders in 2009. There are three major components to the system, the implanted pulse generator (IPG), the lead, and an extension. The IPG is battery powered and transmits the electrical impulses. The lead is an insulated wire with four electrodes that can be placed in one or two target locations in the brain. The lead is connected to the IPG by the extension. The IPG is implanted subcutaneously below the shoulder bone or in the abdomen. All components are covered in titanium or platinum to ensure biocompatibility.

The location of the lead electrodes varies depending upon the disorder treated. For OCD it is placed in the nucleus accumbens. For Parkinson's tremor it is placed in the globus pallidus and the subthalamic nucleus, and for pain in the periaqueductal gray. Since these locations are deep inside the brain they require invasive surgery. The mechanism by which DBS works is not well understood. It is believed to interfere with the normal function of the target brain regions and because of its invasiveness is used only when patients are unresponsive to traditional treatments like medication.

PROSTHETICS

The field of prosthetics is the study and construction of prostheses. A prosthesis is an artificial extension that replaces a missing part of the body. Prostheses must be integrated into a living person, so they effectively turn their users into cyborgs. Many of the latest creations are neural prostheses, which send and receive signals from the person's nervous system. Some prostheses also have onboard computers and electronics to process sensorimotor information. We will present in this section examples of sensory prosthetics, those that assist in visual, auditory, and other types of perception. Next we will present prosthetics that facilitate movements such as reaching, grasping, walking, and running.

Sensory Prosthetics

Retinal Implants (Prosthetic Vision)

Vision in a healthy adult is the product of light reflecting from surfaces in the environment. This image is focused by the eye onto the retina, a layer of photoreceptors located on the inside of the back of each eye. Photoreceptors in one layer of the retina are connected to ganglion cells in another layer. The pattern of retinal stimulation indicates the distribution of light intensities in the image, in essence capturing a "snapshot" of the visual scene. This information is then passed along the optic nerve to brain areas like the visual cortex in the occipital lobe that process it, further allowing sight. However, in some patients with disorders like retinitis pigmentosa and age-related macular degeneration, the retina degenerates, resulting in visual impairments and blindness. In these sorts of disorders the photoreceptor cells are damaged but in some cases the ganglion cells are not. If the ganglion cells can be stimulated in the right way, they can send a message back to the brain, restoring sight.

Retinal prosthetic systems consist of a miniature video camera that is housed in the patient's glasses (see figure 22). The camera captures the scene the patient is looking at. The video is sent to a small computer or video-processing unit that is also worn by the patient. The images are processed, then sent back to the glasses and transmitted wirelessly from there to the implant. The implant then stimulates the retinal cells to reproduce the pattern of light the scene would normally cast on the retina. Over time and with training, the user can learn to discriminate visual patterns. Some patients have been able to read again with enlarged text (Fornos, Sommerhalder, & Pelizzone, 2011). Examples of current retinal prosthetics in development include the Second Sight Argus II (which was FDA approved in 2013 and has met with some success in clinical trials), the Retina Implant AG, and Bionic Vision Australia.

Cochlear Implants (Prosthetic Hearing)

Prosthetic ears in the form of cochlear implants have been around for quite some time now (G. Clark, 2003). These devices work on much the same principle as retinal

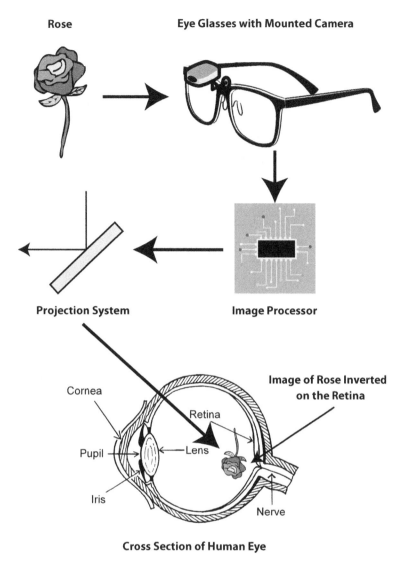

Rose

Eye Glasses with Mounted Camera

Projection System

Image Processor

Cornea

Retina

Image of Rose Inverted
on the Retina

Pupil

Lens

Iris

Nerve

Cross Section of Human Eye

FIGURE 22 A retinal prosthetic system.

implants. They use sound information to stimulate neurons representing different kinds of sounds. The cochlea is a curled, fluid-filled structure located in the inner ear. Different areas of the cochlea contain neurons that code for distinct frequencies. Sound vibrations in the air induce a wave to travel through the cochlear fluid. This wave will maximally stimulate the cochlear region corresponding to its largest frequency component. High-frequency sounds produce a peak wave and greatest neural stimulation close to where the cochlea starts. The waves from low-frequency sounds peak later, closer to where it ends. The cochlea is thus somewhat like a piano keyboard, where sounds "play" the keyboard to produce our perception.

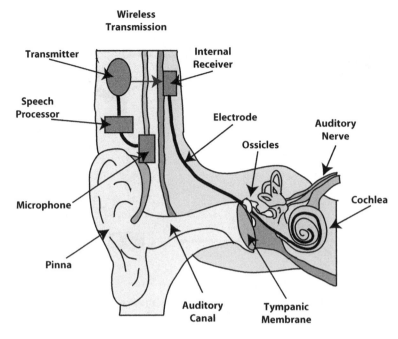

FIGURE 23 A cochlear implant.

Cochlear implants are used in patients who have suffered damage to the hair cells that stimulate cochlear neurons. The device consists of a number of parts (figure 23). A microphone behind the ear picks up sounds and transmits this information to an external processor. The processor amplifies, filters out noise, and converts the sound into an electronic signal. This signal is then broadcast as radio waves to an internal receiver located under the skin. The receiver transmits the signal along wires to a tube inside the cochlea. The tube stimulates the different cochlear regions corresponding to the frequency characteristics of the sound. In this way, the implant mimics the way the ear would normally process sound.

Cochlear implants have restored hearing to those with full or partial deafness. However, the success of the procedure depends on a number of factors such as the duration and age of deafness onset in the patient, how long the implant is used, and the extent of initial damage. The quality of hearing from these devices is also less than optimal. Some patients report speech as sounding disconnected and artificial. Future models may eliminate this by increasing the number of stimulated regions and incorporating more sophisticated processing algorithms.

Artificial Skin

Perhaps the senses most people think the least about are those of somatosensation. These are senses related to the body. Somatosensation includes information about the world conveyed to us by our skin as well as information about the position and movement of our limbs. These last two kinds of information are referred to as proprioception and kinesthesis.

The skin provides us with a wealth of data about the environment. We have pressure receptors there that tell us about an object's weight or roughness and so aid in our ability to manipulate. There are also sensory neurons for temperature and pain. These are crucial for survival, as we need to maintain a proper body temperature and avoid pain if we are to function properly. The proprioceptive and kinesthetic senses originate from receptors inside the body and are necessary for maintaining balance and moving around. Impulses from all these sensory neurons, whether from the skin or inside the body, pass to the spinal cord and brain, where they undergo further processing.

One approach to the creation of an artificial pressure sensor is to embed a polarized crystal between two membranes. When force is applied to the surface, the crystal inside bends and its electrical properties change. This is known as the piezoelectric effect. The greater the force applied, the greater the change in electrical charge. This change is measured and indicative of the amount of applied pressure. Identification of an object can then proceed through a 2-D map of the conductive differences and how they change over time.

Researchers at the University of Tokyo have used a related technique (Someya et al., 2004). They created a flexible film or sensor skin with a half-millimeter-thick layer of rubber embedded with electrically conductive graphite particles. When the layer bends, its conductive properties alter and are processed by an array of organic transistors that are cheap and easy to manufacture. The film can be rolled around a narrow cylinder and can serve as a robotic finger covering. It can also be placed in floors to identify people or to sense when a hospital patient collapses.

Skin serves a number of purposes other than perception. It provides a protective covering that prevents damage to internal parts, regulates temperature, and keeps out bacteria. But to be effective at these tasks a skin has to be able to repair itself. A team at the University of Illinois has produced a material that like human skin can repair itself when scraped or torn. The material is filled with small capsules of polymer building blocks and catalysts. When the material is damaged, the capsules rupture and release their contents, which then bind the fractured areas together.

Motor Prosthetics

Reaching and Arms

Getting an arm to reach out toward an object may seem easy, but the problem is really quite complex and not yet fully understood. To begin, a moving limb does not just traverse a path through space. It must move in a certain direction with a given force and speed. If you were reaching to catch a moving fly ball in a baseball game, you would move differently than you would when picking up a stationary glass of water. This information on how a limb should move constitutes a motor goal or command issued by the brain. This abstract command must then be converted into a pattern of signals that control the muscles during movement execution. The human arm is articulated by a number of different muscle groups such as the bicep and triceps. Each of these must be activated in a particular sequence in order to produce a given motion.

Specifying an arm movement requires several pieces of information (Bizzi, Mussa-Ivaldi, & Giszter, 1991). First, there is the initial location of the arm. Then there is the location of the object. These two constitute starting and end points. Finally, there is the trajectory the arm must pass through. Human arm location is provided by proprioception and other cues. Object location is for the most part visually determined. The brain then computes the trajectory on the basis of these cues. However, as mentioned earlier, the movement is dynamic in the sense that it can be altered during execution. When reaching for something, we can swerve to avoid obstacles or to compensate for sudden object movement. An artificial person's reach would need this capability.

In this section, we will consider arms apart from hands, even though the two are sometimes used in concert. That is because arms are typically employed for reaching while hands are used for manipulating. The primary function of an arm is to place a hand at an object location. The primary function of a hand or other effector is to then manipulate the object.

Arms are articulated, meaning they have different parts divided into sections by joints. Robot arms can contain more joints than a human arm, although they can be made with three major joints, in which case these could be labeled as "shoulder," "elbow," and "wrist." Robot arms with more joints have a corresponding increase in the number of different ways they can move.

The term *degrees of freedom* is used to measure arm mobility. There are three primary ways to move in 3-D space: up and down, or pitch; left and right, or yaw; and rotation, or roll. A joint that can move in all three of these ways possesses three degrees of freedom. The shoulder has three degrees of freedom, while the elbow has only one, since if the shoulder is fixed you can only move your elbow up and down. The total degrees of freedom for an arm is the sum of the degrees of freedom for all its joints.

Grasping, Manipulation, and Hands

Once a hand or gripper has been directed to an object by reaching, it can be grasped. Grasping requires that fingers hold an object securely. A secure grip is one where the object won't slip or move, especially when displaced by an external force. Your grasp on a hammer, for example, would not be secure if bumping against something caused you to drop it. One precondition of a firm grasp is when the forces exerted by the fingers balance each other so as not to disturb the object's position (Mishra & Silver, 1989). The characteristics of an object such as its geometric configuration and mass distribution may demand that some fingers exert greater force than others to maintain stability. The grasp and support forces must also match overall object mass and fragility. An egg requires a more delicate touch than a rock.

Another factor to be considered is finger positioning. Two fingers are in equilibrium when they oppose each other and share the same line of action: that is, when they are oriented 180 degrees apart and push toward one another. Three fingers are in equilibrium when their forces add to zero and their lines of action intersect at a point (Ponce, 1999). An object's center of mass affects stable finger positioning (Bingham & Muchisky, 1993). If mass distribution is low down on an object, as it is in a half-filled glass, then the grip should be lowered to be closer to the center. Texture also influences finger positioning and force. Adjustments may be necessary to accommodate smooth and rough surfaces that are more or less slippery. In robots, this is accomplished with texture sensing. A laser beam is bounced off a surface. Smooth, shiny surfaces scatter less light back to detectors than rougher matte surfaces.

A stable grasp is necessary for manipulation, which can take many forms. An object can be rotated by turning the wrist or by finger repositioning. Three-dimensional translations through space can be accomplished by moving the hand and arm. Objects can also be pushed or pulled across a surface (Lynch & Mason, 1995). Twirling and rolling are further examples of complex manipulation.

For both grasping and manipulating, sensory information needs to be monitored constantly. Feedback from hand sensors plays a critical role in setting and adjusting grip force to prevent slipping (Johannson & Westling, 1987). This is true for people and machines. Robots that perform complex manipulations use closed-loop control systems where sensory input from a limb is sent back to regulate its motion. A good example of this is a back-pressure sensor that sends a signal registering the amount of mechanical resistance encountered. The greater the resistance, the greater the motor force applied to the limb. In this way, a robot arm will work harder to lift a heavier load, or will grip more strongly to maintain a grasp on a heavier object.

Of all the limbs we consider, hands are the most challenging to engineer artificially. Unlike an arm or leg, the hand, considered together with wrist and fingers, has twenty-two degrees of freedom. Each finger can be considered a limb unto itself and has some amount of independent motion. The opposable thumb also characterizes the human hand. We can place our thumb against each of the other fingers, increasing the dexterity with which we can hold or orient objects. The opposable thumb may have even driven the evolution of intelligence in early humans because it enabled us to create and use tools (Napier, 1980). Coupled with this complex manipulator capacity is the hand's high concentration of tactile sensory neurons in the fingertips and palms. A complete reproduction of this amazing structure's motor and sensory function may take some time.

Artificial Arms and Hands

Many war veterans come home missing arms and legs because of explosive devices. Regular prosthetic attachments allow minimal movement and control. Fortunately, developments in microelectronics are allowing for the construction of robotic arms and hands that allow for a much greater range of movement. These arms can be controlled by the mind and can even sense the weight and texture of objects because they are connected directly to the brain for both sensory and motor function.

The Defense Advanced Research Projects Agency (DARPA) announced in 2015 that it has created a robotic arm that can be moved by thought. The user is also able to feel with the device. The arm is connected by wires to the user's sensory cortex (which processes tactile information) and motor cortex (which controls muscles). The first person to use the arm was blindfolded. His fingers were then touched. He was able to tell which fingers were touched,

FIGURE 24 Robonaut. Photo courtesy of NASA (nasa.gov).

even when two fingers were touched at the same time. Ultimately, users would be able to discriminate textures with the arm.

A research team at John Hopkins University is also working on a mind-controlled prosthetic arm, revealed to the public in 2016. The arm attaches directly to the patient's bone at the end of the remaining limb. Nerves from this stump are then connected to the prosthetic. It has enabled patients to move individual fingers and grasp small objects. One of the test subjects is Johnny Matheny, who lost his arm to cancer in 2008. He is now able to reach over his head and even behind his back with the arm. In order to make it work, the patient must first undergo targeted muscle reinnervation, which reassigns nerves that controlled the arm or hand to effectors in the prosthetic. The researchers call this arm a modular prosthetic limb (MPL). Some of its other capabilities are being able to move two fingers simultaneously and to grasp objects. It allocates two degrees of control at the wrist.

One example of a robotic hand unattached to a person is Robonaut (figure 24). A joint development project of the National Aeronautics and Space Administration (NASA) and DARPA, Robonaut consists of a torso with a head and two attached arms with hands. Astronauts operate it remotely by viewing what Robonaut sees through his stereoscopically mounted twin cameras. They move his hand through a "data glove" that mimics the operator's hand motions. His anthropomorphic design enables natural and intuitive control by human tele-operators. Robonaut was designed to perform maintenance and repair in the dangerous work environment of space outside the International Space Station.

Robonaut's hand looks much like its human equivalent. It has four fingers and an opposable thumb that can touch the forefinger and index finger. The fingers roll at the base and pitch at all three joints, allowing fourteen degrees of freedom. A forearm houses the motor and drive electronics. The hand currently provides no tactile feedback to the operator, but research is ongoing to provide this capability. It does have a grasping algorithm that clasps the hand about certain objects automatically once it is prepositioned by the tele-operator. Future hands will utilize finger tendon sensors that allow the grasp to adjust to a wider range of objects.

More recently, Disney has developed a humanoid robot capable of playing catch and juggling. It is enabled with a vision system that can track the three-dimensional location of a ball as it is moving. Since this robot must interact with a human partner, it is programmed to orient its head and "look" at the person it is playing with. It is also programmed to look down when it misses a ball. Neither of these is necessary, but both make it easier for a human to play with the robot. Systems that interact with people must be able not only to perform the required physical actions but also to understand and use the prerequisite social skills.

Walking and Artificial Legs

Systems for walking with legs can be divided into two categories (Boone & Hodgins, 1998). In a passively stable system, the body's center of mass stays within a well-defined region formed by the points where the feet touch the ground. Because the body's center is always centered over the feet, these machines can stop at any time and still maintain their balance. In dynamically stable systems, the body is balanced and remains upright only during a given portion of the gait cycle. This inherent instability makes such systems more difficult to design. Bipedal human locomotion is dynamically stable. Try pausing at different times while walking to discover for yourself where the greatest instability is.

Many terrestrial locomotion demands are satisfied by the use of wheeled or tracked vehicles. Wheels are the best way to move on flat surfaces with good traction. Tracks are better for soft or sandy ground and for dealing with small obstructions like rocks. Legs, though, are the best solution for traversing rough terrain. They can be used to step across or jump over obstacles. In conjunction with arms, legs also enable climbing vertical or near-vertical surfaces. Legs, whether bipedal, quadrupedal, or more, are nature's solution to getting around in difficult environments. Researchers have therefore devoted a considerable amount of effort into designing artificial legs that can mimic these feats.

An example of a simple leg prosthetic is the two curved springy metal blades used by the runner Oscar Pistorius. He has been running with them to some success, winning several races against other unenhanced runners. The use of prosthetics to restore normal function is generally uncontroversial, but not when it gives someone a competitive edge. Do you think Pistorius should be allowed to compete in the Olympics and other races against so-called normal runners? Is this the mechanical equivalent of doping?

Otto Bock HealthCare's C-leg is a big step toward a fully functioning artificial leg. It has microprocessors and sensors that reproduce the stability and stepping motion of a real leg.

One of its features is an electronically controlled hydraulic knee that adapts to different movements. A strain sensor measures the load on the foot. Other measures track characteristics like knee angle and motion more than fifty times a second. Algorithms then process these data to determine the current phase of the gait cycle and make adjustments. The result is that patients don't have to think about how to use the leg, as they do with a normal "dumb" prosthetic. The C-leg enables patients to walk normally down ramps, down stairs, or on uneven terrain. Curtis Grimsley, a computer analyst for the Port Authority of New York and New Jersey, used the leg to walk down seventy flights of stairs at the same speed as other evacuees to escape from the World Trade Center disaster (Karoub, 2002).

Illusory Body Perception

The use of prosthetics seems to extend the boundaries of our bodies and hence our selves. Blind people who use a cane to aid in walking often report sensation not where their hand grasps the cane, but at its tip, where it touches the ground and other objects. It is as if the cane gets incorporated into the body and becomes an extension of a limb and they are now able to feel with it in the same way one would feel with one's own biological hand.

The body transfer illusion is the perception of owning a body part or an entire body that does not belong to us. It is typically elicited by stimulating subjects into thinking they are feeling one thing but seeing something else. A good illustration of this phenomenon is the rubber hand illusion (Ehrsson, Spence, & Passingham, 2004). Here subjects are positioned with their left hand hidden from sight. They then view a realistic rubber left hand in front of them. An experimenter next strokes both the real hand and the rubber hand at the same time. The strokes are made with a paintbrush and are synchronized to occur in the same direction. Under these conditions participants experience the rubber hand as belonging to their own body. When asked which is their left hand, participants will even point to the rubber hand with the right hand. In this study MRI recording showed activation in the premotor cortex during the feeling of body ownership. This area is involved in planning body movements.

Other studies have shown that different brain areas are also involved (Ehrsson, Wiech, Weiskopf, Dolan, & Passingham, 2007; M. Slater, Perez-Marcos, Ehrsson, & Sanchez-Vives, 2009). When researchers made a stabbing movement toward the rubber hand with a needle, MRI scans showed increased activity in the anterior cingulate cortex. This region is normally activated when a person anticipates pain. They also found activation in the supplementary motor area that activates in response to an urge to move the arm. Anticipating the stab of pain from the needle caused the subjects to treat the rubber hand as their own, moving their real hand, even though that was in a different place and not actually threatened.

Additional research in this area has shown we can experience other changes to imaginary limbs, including the perception of limbs we don't even have. Schaefer, Flor, Heinze, and Rotte (2007) connected an artificial arm and hand to subjects' bodies, giving them the impression of having an extended second arm. The participants reported feeling that the arm and hand were their own and were longer than their normal arm. Brain imaging showed changes in the activity of the primary somatosensory cortex (which contains an internal map of the body) corresponding to the illusory elongation. In a related study these researchers again connected an artificial hand and arm to subjects' bodies, but this time to create the illusion of a third supernumerary arm. The participants viewed and felt that they now had a third arm. The researchers again found changes in the somatosensory cortex that corresponded to this experience (Schaefer, Heinze, & Rotte, 2009).

M. Slater, Spanlang, Sanchez-Vives, and Blanke (2010) used a virtual reality simulation to show that our entire bodies can be transferred into someone else's body. They had male participants perceive a room from the perspective of a seated girl. In front of the girl was a woman who was stroking the girl's shoulder and who then unexpectedly struck the girl three times in the face. The participants experienced this situation from either a first- or a third-person perspective, seeing the situation from the girl's own eyes and body or seeing it from a point several feet over her head and looking down. The participants reported that they had in effect "become the girl" and that they were inhabiting her body. The results showed that the first-person perspective condition was more powerful in inducing this effect than the third-person condition. Touch information was included and found to be more significant than head-movement synchrony.

What all of this work shows is that our brains can be easily fooled into believing what the bodily self is. We rely on haptic, visual, and other inputs to tell us where and what our limbs and body are like. Although we are physically bound by our bodies and we understand this at the cognitive level, this information can be easily overridden by perceptual information. Future technologies will be able to bend our brain's concept of what constitutes the body even more. For example, full VR that simulates all of the senses may enable us to slip inside virtual (or simulated real) bodies so that we can completely experience what it is like to be our friends, lovers, or family members. If software can copy the actions of other animals or creatures, then we could experience what it is like to be an eagle, a mountain lion, or an imaginary alien. We could even know what it might be like to be a cloud or to have no body at all.

Powered Exoskeletons

A powered exoskeleton is a wearable mobile machine powered by electric motors, pneumatics, hydraulics, or some combination of technologies that allows the wearer increased limb movement and endurance (figure 25). It may also go by the name of power armor, hardsuit, or exosuit (Bellis, 2017). A wearer with such a suit can lift heavier than normal objects for a longer period of time or perform other such work without getting fatigued. Powered exoskeletons have applications in the military, where, for example, they can be used to load supplies or allow troops to march long distances. The current military LIFESUIT prototype 14 can walk one mile on a full charge and lift 203 pounds.

Powered exoskeletons can provide assisted walking to those suffering damage from stroke or spinal cord injury. Some of these rehabilitation exoskeletons can provide a continuum of assistance to patients from full power to free walking, thus tailoring the suit to the specific needs of the wearer. Suits such as these in Japan have also been used to help nurses

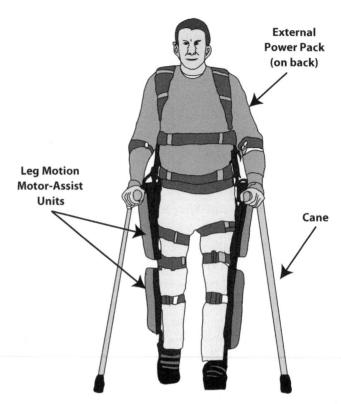

External
Power Pack
(on back)

Leg Motion
Motor-Assist
Units

Cane

FIGURE 25 A powered
exoskeleton to assist those
with walking disabilities.

move heavy patients. Other civilian applications include use by firefighters and other rescue
personnel to help survive dangerous environments.

A number of problems need to be overcome before exosuits are capable of quick and agile
movements. Current models are slow and lack extended endurance in the field. Few independent power supplies are available that can sustain a full-body powered exoskeleton for
more than a few hours. Electrical batteries need recharging, which requires the transport of
charging units out along with the suits. Internal combustion engines have good energy output but consume large quantities of fuel and run hot. Current models are tethered to external power sources. Strong but lightweight materials like titanium must be used in the frame
or skeleton. Steel is strong but too heavy. Aluminum is light but too weak. Compressed air
(pneumatics) and compressed fluids (hydraulics) for use as an actuator (the part of a machine
that is responsible for moving or controlling a mechanism) are unacceptable. The former is
too unpredictable and the latter too heavy.

Another problem is getting the suit to match the motion of ball-and-socket joints like the
hips and shoulders. This limits the suit's flexibility. Further, no suits now can match the
flexibility of the human spine. Any powered suit of this nature must limit its range of motion
to prevent damage to the wearer or the suit itself. To overcome this problem requires an
onboard computer that can track limb positions. Finally there is the issue of size. People

come in a variety of sizes. To fit everyone, suits of multiple sizes or adjustable-length limbs and frames must be constructed.

Unless these limitations are overcome, an adequate model of a powered exoskeleton is still some years into the future. However, there has been no shortage of powered exoskeletons used in movies. One prominent example is when the character Ripley, played by Sigourney Weaver, fights the alien queen in the 1986 film *Aliens*. Another is when the character Max, played by Matt Damon, uses one to overcome his physical disability in the 2013 movie *Elysium*.

NEURAL PROSTHETICS (BRAIN-MACHINE INTERFACES OR BRAIN-COMPUTER INTERFACES)

Motor neural prostheses also go by the term *brain-machine interfaces* (*BMIs*) or sometimes *brain-computer interfaces* (*BCIs*). These are devices that help bring motor function to patients who are paralyzed or for other reasons have difficulty moving their limbs. They convert electrical activity measured from neurons into signals used to control assistive devices like robotic arms. Electrodes typically implanted in the motor cortex read the intent to move. The information picked up by the electrodes is fed to neural "decoder" algorithms, which are then sent to the device. If the intent is interpreted as reaching out with the right arm to grasp a ball, then commands are sent to move a prosthetic arm to perform this action, for example. After training with the devices, patients can perform these acts on their own just by thinking about them.

The Utah array is a 10 by 10 array of silicon microelectrodes (Nordhausen, Maynard, & Normann, 1996). Wires from the back of the array feed recorded signals to a connector pedestal that is attached to the skull. The entire device is coated in a material that prevents the body's immune system from rejecting it. Nevertheless, scar tissue does form on the electrodes, though it usually does not impede data acquisition (Chestek et al., 2011). Alternately, individual microwires can be inserted one at a time or in groups. This requires a much more complex surgical process but has the advantage of being able to record from different brain locations (Nicolelis et al., 2003). Electrodes have been used successfully over a period of seven years (Kruger, Caruana, Dalla Volta, & Rizzolatti, 2010).

Electrical signals can be recorded in BMI techniques without electrode implantation. The advantage is that they are less invasive and do not require surgery. The disadvantage is lost resolution, as these procedures record over a larger area. Table 9 shows this trade-off. Electroencephalography (EEG) recordings can measure neural signals over a 3 cm region and are applied to the scalp. Subdural electrocorticography (ECoG) electrodes are placed just above the cortex, and epidural ECoG are placed above the dura. Recording with these techniques is within a 0.5 cm region. Electrodes within the cortex that measure signals from a population of neurons within a 1 mm area record what is called a local field potential. Finally, single-cell electrodes, inserted in or near an individual neuron, record the neuron's action potentials (the electrical signals sent down its axon).

TABLE 9 Different techniques for measuring brain electrical activity, their measuring areas, and neural regions

Recording Device	Measuring Area	Neural Region
EEG	3 cm	Cortical area
ECoG	0.5 cm	Narrow cortical area
Local field potential	1 mm	Neural group
Single-unit action potential	0.2 mm	Individual neuron

Hardware systems amplify, digitize, and filter the neural signals. These are then passed to the decoding software on a computer that processes the data in real time. Some signal processing must occur before decoding and can consist of extracting the "spikes" of action potentials. Filtering can extract firing within different frequency ranges: for example, approximately thirty to one hundred Hertz for the gamma band. These systems are sometimes integrated with the electrodes. Power consumption for these devices must be low because the tissue surrounding the area is sensitive to temperature and can be damaged if they get too hot. Data from the pedestal or implant can be transmitted wirelessly to the computer with the decoding software and from the computer to hardware like robotic arms.

Animal Research

Researchers at several labs have recorded signals from the cortex of rats and monkeys. Carmena et al. (2003) used a BCI to get a rhesus monkey to reach and grasp using a robotic arm. The animals were trained to perform these motions visually using a joystick and computer screen (see figure 26). In those experiments the movements of the robotic arm were hidden from the monkey. In later studies the monkey viewed the robotic arm directly while performing the task. The BCI was able to determine arm velocity and hand gripping force. O'Doherty, Ifft, Zhuang, Lebedev, and Nicolelis (2010) had a monkey control the location of an avatar arm while getting sensory feedback through direct intracortical stimulation in the part of the sensory cortex representing the arm. Optimal movement and control require this kind of feedback. Whenever a healthy person picks up a cup of coffee, that person feels his or her arm extend as well as feeling the weight and texture of the cup when grasping.

Other investigators have used BCI successfully when recording from a surprisingly small number of cells, fifteen to thirty neurons compared to fifty to two hundred in earlier studies. One group was able to use a BCI to have a monkey track visual targets on a computer screen with and without the use of a joystick (Serruya, Hatsopoulos, Paninski, Fellows, & Donoghue, 2002). BCIs have been used to allow three-dimensional tracking of arm control with a virtual reality system (D. Taylor, Tillery, & Schwartz, 2002). Also impressive was the use of a BCI allowing a monkey to feed itself pieces of fruit and marshmallows (Velliste, Perel, Spalding, Whitford, & Schwartz, 2008). Not all recording is done in the motor cortex.

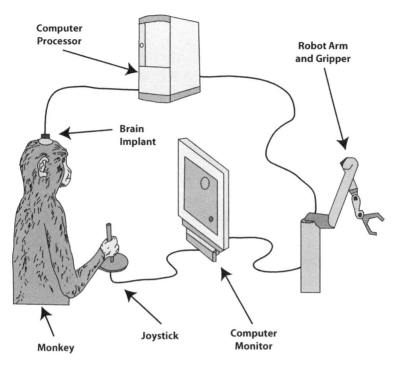

Computer
Processor

Robot Arm
and Gripper

Brain
Implant

Monkey

Joystick

Computer
Monitor

FIGURE 26 A brain-computer interface allowing a monkey to operate a
robotic arm.

Other studies have controlled monkey reaching from premovement activity in the posterior
parietal lobe and when animals anticipated getting a reward.

Human Research

Matt Nagle was stabbed. The knife severed his spinal cord and paralyzed him from the neck
down. He used a BCI called BrainGate to control a robotic arm in 2005. The electrodes were
implanted into the precentral gyrus region of the motor cortex. He was able to use the
ninety-six-electrode implant to control the robotic arm by thinking about moving his hand.
He was also able to control a computer cursor, lights, and a television. This initial success
has been followed up by researchers at the University of Pittsburgh Medical Center who have
been able to get tetraplegic patients to move robotic prosthetic limbs in many directions
using the BrainGate system (Collinger et al., 2013).

As mentioned above, ECoG is less invasive than direct electrode implantation into brain
tissue. It involves placing electrodes in a thin plastic pad above the cortex, beneath the dura
mater membrane. Having the electrodes under the skull provides better signal reception, as
the skull partially blocks the signal. ECoG methods were first tried in 2004 by a team at
Washington University in St. Louis. In a later study they were able to get a teenage boy to
play the game Space Invaders using an ECoG implant. Since this procedure is less physically

damaging to the patient and still provides a fairly good level of control, it is a good trade-off.

EEGs are the noninvasive procedure for BCI. These are easy to apply, as the electrodes go directly on the scalp and do not require surgery. But they have poor spatial resolution, and some higher frequencies in the signal are obscured by the skull. Temporal resolution is good. Most BCI studies have been done using EEGs. Application of the electrodes takes trained personnel. Doud, Lucas, and Pisansky (2011) used an EEG-based BCI that allowed participants to control the motion of a virtual helicopter in three-dimensional space. Participants using a similar method were later able to guide a real remote-controlled helicopter through an obstacle course.

Cognitive-Based "Mind-Reading" Techniques

Dr. Stanislas Dehaene of the Collège de France in Paris had participants in one study look at a number while recording parietal lobe MRI data. On the basis of the pattern of the MRI data, they were able to determine what number the participants were looking at. Each number corresponded to a specific pattern of neural activation. In another study Dr. Brian Pasley and colleagues used ECoG to measure brain responses to words. Their technique involved placing sixty-four electrodes directly on the cortical surface. They also found distinct patterns of electrical activity that corresponded to hearing individual words. Eventually the researchers were able to determine, solely on the basis of the activity data, what word a participant was thinking about. In yet another study, scientists at the University of Utah in 2011 placed electrodes over the portion of the motor cortex that controls facial muscles. They recorded activity as participants spoke specific words like *hello* and *goodbye*. The researchers were able, on the basis of activation patterns, to determine what word a person would speak. Paralytics could use this procedure for dictation.

Dr. Jerry Shih at the Mayo Clinic in Minnesota has used ECoG BCI techniques with epileptic patients. Epilepsy is a brain disorder in which neurons fire uncontrollably, causing spasms, seizures, and in some cases death. His patients focused on individual letters from the alphabet while brain activity was recorded. Later, they were able to type words on a computer screen with 100 percent accuracy simply by thinking about each letter. Less accurate EEG typewriters are currently available. By one estimate they can be used to type at a rate of five to ten words per minute. Paralyzed patients can use the procedure.

Similar techniques have been used to record visual image data. Dr. Gallant at the University of California at Berkeley had participants in one study lie in an fMRI scanner and watch YouTube videos. A three-dimensional video of brain activity made up of voxels was recorded. A voxel is a three-dimensional "pixel" that can light up a given brightness or color to represent brain activity at an xyz coordinate space. Voxel videos thus show how the brain's activity changes over time. Gallant found a correlation between the features in the videos and brain activity. This research team was able to use the brain-imaging data to recreate a video of what the participants were looking at. It could also do this procedure in reverse, taking the video and using it to predict the voxel-based images. For example, when participants were asked to imagine the Mona Lisa, the program pulled up a picture of Salma Hayek, so it is not perfectly accurate yet.

So mind-reading devices are already here. They are not solely in science fiction stories anymore. Using current technology it is possible to create a weak magnetic field MRI scanner the size of a cell phone. One could scan one's brain anywhere using this device. The recorded signal could then be broadcast wirelessly to a computer to decode and generate a three-dimensional image. Patients could do this at home and send the information to their doctors, thus performing near real-time monitoring of their medical conditions. Future possibilities are exciting. One could implant a "neural lace" of nano-sized electrodes in a person's brain. The person could then think out entire sentences to a "robo secretary," who could take dictation for emails, book reservations for dinner, or schedule events on a calendar.

Other BCI/BMI Applications

As alluded to above, BCIs have also been used to play video games and virtual reality simulations. This activity is known as neurogaming. In 2009 the company NeuroSky marketed its system called Mindflex, which used EEG sensors to move a ball through a maze. So it is now possible to use your mind to control an avatar's actions like firing weapons or evading enemies, just as if one were playing a real video game using a traditional controller or joystick. Portable EEG sensors can also detect when workers like bus drivers are dozing off and then wake them to prevent accidents. In Japan a goofy version of this looks like bunny rabbit ears when worn. The ears rise when the person is interested and fall when there is less interest. These could be used to indicate romantic interest at a party!

We mentioned earlier that sensory feedback can be used to enable patients to modify their movements and thus perform them with greater precision and control. Dr. Nicolelis at Duke University has developed a sensory feedback version of BMI used to control a prosthetic arm. A brain sensor sends motor commands to the arm, which then moves and sends sensory feedback back to the brain. The feedback can inform the user if a surface is rough or smooth, for instance. This technique is called a Brain Machine Brain Interface (BMBI) because motor signals are first sent from the brain to control an effector. The effector based on the movement then sends the commands back to the brain so they can be interpreted. This, of course, is what happens when a normal person moves a limb.

Researchers at the University of Washington in 2013 were able to use BMIs to directly control another person's actions. One user played a BMI video game, and when his right arm fired a cannon a signal was sent over the internet that was used to move a second person's arm so that he also fired the cannon. A paralyzed patient could also remotely control a robot, seeing through the robot's cameras and moving its arms and legs to locomote and manipulate objects. Future wars may be fought this way so that soldiers don't get injured or killed. In the future, actors wearing BMIs/BCIs could record their experiences for all five senses. This information could then be transmitted to users in a theater so that they too could have the same experiences, such as climbing a mountain. Ultimately there may be a brain-net in which people could exchange thoughts and experiences by thought alone. Such a network could lead to "group minds," minds made up of the interactions of many different individuals all thinking together.

ARTIFICIAL MEMORIES

The hippocampus creates memories by taking an experience and breaking it down into different sensory modalities. These are then stored in different parts of the cortex and brain. For example, emotions are stored in the amygdala, words in the temporal lobe, visual information in the occipital lobe, and information regarding touch and movement in the parietal lobe. The level of specificity for storing information is fairly fine-grained. There are locations in the cortex where our concepts of fruits and vegetables, plants, animals, and facial expressions are all stored, much the way somebody might store glasses, mugs, plates, et cetera in different shelves in a cupboard.

During recall the brain needs some way of reactivating all of these different parts of a memory. This is called the binding problem. One way it may do this is through the frequency of neural activity. One memory fragment may for instance vibrate at a particular frequency (say 40 Hz) and reactivate another memory fragment also vibrating at that frequency. Electrical stimulation by BMIs at these frequencies could trigger retrieval of the relevant information.

In 2011 researchers at Wake Forest University recorded a memory from a mouse and stored it digitally in a computer. The memory was a particular pattern of activity in the hippocampus representing a task they had taught it. They then injected the mouse with a chemical that made it forget how to perform the task. Next, they reactivated the hippocampus using the digitally stored memory. After this, the mouse was able to perform the task again. This technology has some interesting implications. It suggests that someday we may be able to insert new memories into people, ones they never actually experienced. This technique could be used to train workers or educate people about facts they didn't know. An artificial hippocampus could be implanted into the brains of people with Alzheimer's disease or stroke who had damaged hippocampi. Skill knowledge (like knowing how to fly a helicopter or fight using jujitsu, as happens in the movie *The Matrix*) involves other parts of the brain like the basal ganglia, cerebellum, and motor cortex, but in principle this could be reproduced as well.

Speculating on future possibilities, we may be able to have memories of vacations we never took (as happens to the protagonist in the movie *Total Recall*) or even of lives we never lived (as occurs to the Major in the 1995/2017 movies *Ghost in the Shell*). We may be able to record our entire lives and upload them into a computer network so that they can be shared by others. As we note later in this book, personal information might be loaded into a software avatar or an android robot to create a new you, one that would be similar in what it knew and what it did. Other interesting possibilities include having Jake commit a crime and then erasing the memory of the crime in his brain, replacing it with a false, alibi memory. Jake could also insert a memory of a crime Jake had committed into Jack's brain. Jack would now think that he had committed the crime. Alternatively, the criminal Jake could commit a crime but then insert false memories into the brains of the eyewitnesses so that they wouldn't remember seeing it.

ROBOTICS

Robotics is an interdisciplinary field made up of computer scientists, engineers, and people from other fields. The field addresses the construction, operation, and use of robots. A robot can take on any form, including humanoid. Robots have been made that mimic snakes, four-legged animals, even jellyfish and insects. Robots are machines that can interact with an environment in an autonomous manner, meaning they are capable of sensing, thinking, and acting on their own. Typically they are created to perform some specific task like defusing bombs or cleaning a floor. Regardless of their shape or task, all robots share three features: (1) a mechanical frame or construction, (2) electrical components that power and control the machinery, and (3) some level of computer programming code.

In this section we will first discuss semiautonomous robots that can be controlled by humans. Then we will take an extended look at the field of personal robotics where humans and robots interact. Following this we will examine how robots interact with one another and how their behavior can be governed by evolutionary and genetic principles. We finish with a section on the role of nanorobots and medicine. All of these applications have implications for the self. They serve to project the self outside the human body and show that we consider machines that look or act human to be human.

Telerobotics

Telerobotics is the area of robotics that is concerned with the control of semiautonomous robots from a distance using wireless communications. It is a combination of two fields, telepresence and teleoperation. *Telepresence* refers to technologies that allow one to feel as if one were present or to give the appearance of being present at a place other than one's true location. A common example of telepresence is videoconferencing, which allows a distant person to participate in a business meeting. The application Skype allows for this, but other, more sophisticated software tools are available. Telepresence permits you to create a "copy" of yourself so that you are informationally present at two locations simultaneously. How might telepresence affect your sense of self? When Skyping do you feel as if you are in more than one place? Is the projected self at the distant location more prominent when you are engaging someone there in social discourse?

Teleoperation is the operation of a machine at a distance and can be considered equivalent to the remote control of a machine by a human from another location. Examples of teleoperation include radio-controlled model aircraft or drones and attack or spy aircraft like the Predator drone used by the military. In cases where distances are too great to allow fast communications, such as planetary rovers, the device must be given some degree of autonomy.

Usually an operator sees what the robots "sees" through a camera mounted on the robot. It can control the robot's movements using a joystick or a simple monitor-mouse-keyboard (MMK) interface. Virtual reality goggles and gloves can also be used as an interface and can allow a greater degree of immersion and control. One prominent example of telerobotics is when police or the military use a robot to defuse or forcibly explode a bomb. When a user is remote-controlling a robot, the robot becomes the user's avatar, as it serves as the representation of the user's actions. Autonomous roaming telepresence robots like the iRobot Ava 500 can move down hallways and into rooms, allowing their operators to view and communicate with people via a computer display.

Human surgeons can teleoperate surgical robots. These robots reproduce the operator's movements with greater precision than the human hand, allowing more precise cutting and suturing. Surgical robots have been in use for some time now and have been employed in almost every area of surgery, including cardiology, gastroenterology, neurosurgery, ophthalmology, and orthopedics. The advantages of using these systems are smaller incisions, decreased blood loss, less pain, and faster wound recovery. There are also downsides. The systems are expensive, the cost of the procedure is higher, and more training is needed for the surgeons and support staff.

Telerobotics and other forms of remote control actually create an "out-of-body experience." When operating devices remotely, we "see" through distant cameras and operate robotic arms that respond to our commands. The result is the feeling that we are not "here," where our bodies are located, but instead "elsewhere," the location where the robot is located. By experiencing the world through its sensors and acting on the world through its effectors, we in effect "become" the robot, transforming our self into that of the machine.

Personal Robotics (Social Robotics)

In this section we discuss the interaction between robots and humans, what is known as personal or social robotics. Robotics is taking a new turn. Throughout most of its history robots were designed for use in highly structured environments that did not require direct human oversight or interaction. They functioned well in places like factories and power plants where they performed the same repetitive action over and over again. But the growing number of elderly in industrialized nations has placed an increased demand on robotics to design robots for the home environment where they can assist the aged and/or disabled. This calls for a new kind of robot, one that can perform a variety of different tasks and that can function safely in the presence of humans. The objective of personal robotics is to design and manufacture intelligent machines that can interact with and assist human beings in many different everyday circumstances.

One of the most important challenges in personal robotics is not technological but psychological. The robots must be designed in such a way that they are accepted and used by people. Dario, Guglielmelli, and Laschi (2001) bring up several points in this regard. They argue that personal robots, like a home appliance, must be evaluated according to their usefulness, pleasure of interaction, safety, cost, and other criteria. For instance, it may not be desirable to make a humanlike personal robot because it could be perceived as an invasion of a person's personal environment. It is also important that the robot not be perceived as threatening, so it would be designed to not show movements or expressions indicative of aggression. A further consideration is that people may not like a personal robot with a high degree of autonomy and initiative because this could also be perceived as threatening. To avoid this, the robot would need to be designed to optimize rather than minimize user involvement.

Keeping Up Appearances

What should personal robots look like? This is an important consideration if we are going to be interacting with them on a daily basis. A personal robot ought to be about the same size as a person or smaller. Any larger and they would be perceived as threatening. The Honda Corporation robot Asimo was designed to be smaller so that it could effectively access door handles, countertops, and other work areas that are just a few feet off the ground. Although it is not a strict requirement, personal robots also ought to look at least somewhat human to facilitate social interaction.

Although we humans certainly have a tendency to attribute human qualities to machines, other research shows that when inanimate objects appear to be somewhat but not too lifelike the result can be shocking. Robotics professor Masahiro Mori first found in 1970 that if a robot is made increasingly humanlike in the way it appears and moves, the human emotional response to it increases, becoming more positive and empathetic. However, when the robot is at about 75 percent of the likeness of a person, there is a dramatic negative emotional response. It is now perceived as inhuman and repulsive. At about 85 percent of human likeness, the emotional response becomes positive once more (Mori, 2012). Figure 27 shows the function depicting this drop, which has been coined the "uncanny valley."

Clearly, people will not want to interact with robots with the uncanny appearance of being "almost human." But how can we explain this phenomenon? In one account, humanlike characteristics stand out and are noticed more with entities that look distinctly nonhuman, generating empathy. But in entities that look almost human, the nonhuman features become salient, generating revulsion. Another explanation is that things that look almost human resemble corpses, while quasi-human motion is indicative of illness or neurological or psychological dysfunction. This latter account may have an evolutionary basis, since it would be a survival advantage to avoid disease-bearing bodies.

Given these results, personal robots of the future should be designed to avoid the uncanny valley and should appear either extremely humanlike or just somewhat human. In the first case, we would have robots that might be indistinguishable from humans. This could cause another set of problems, as people would certainly want to be able to know whether they were dealing with a natural person or a robot. The second case thus seems the most likely outcome.

Social Perception of Machines

Researchers have also investigated people's reactions to computers, which bear little physical resemblance to humans. Do we treat computers the way we might treat a robot or humanlike

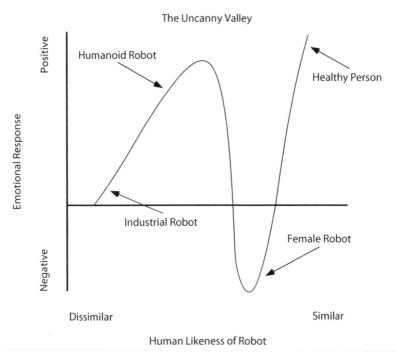

The Uncanny Valley

Positive

Humanoid Robot

Healthy Person

Emotional Response

Industrial Robot

Female Robot

Negative

Dissimilar

Similar

Human Likeness of Robot

FIGURE 27 A plot showing the effect of the uncanny valley. After Friedenberg (2008).

face? Foerst (2004) describes two experiments by Cliff Nass, a sociologist at Stanford University who studies human-machine interaction. In the first, participants were asked to test and then evaluate a bad computer program. The program itself prompted them to perform the evaluation. Later, they were asked, this time by a person, to evaluate the program again. The participants gave fairly positive reviews when prompted to do so by the computers but very critical and negative remarks when asked by the human research assistant. The results suggest that the reviewers were afraid of "upsetting" the computers and so acted politely toward them. They had no such qualms about reporting what they really felt to the human assistant. It seems that when interacting with computers we assume that they have feelings. We then treat them the same way we would treat a person.

In a second study, Nass had participants play interactive games on computers. In this experiment, half of the computer monitors were green, while the other half were blue. In addition, half of the subjects wore green armbands while the other half wore blue armbands. Those wearing the green armbands were more successful when they played the games on green monitors. The same was true for the "blue" players, who did better on the blue machines. When later asked to evaluate how they felt toward the machine on which they played, the green players reported a greater feeling of solidarity with the machine when its monitor color was also green. Likewise, the blue players felt that they bonded more with the blue monitors. These results show that we identify with computers that share some feature with our own social group. It implies that a form of "machine racism" could exist, whereby we might stereotype and treat artificial people in a positive or negative way based on their similarity to our own race, religion, or other socially relevant attribute.

Anthropomorphism is defined as the attribution of humanlike qualities to nonhuman subjects. Much of what we have recently presented shows that people will all too easily anthropomorphize machines. We attribute humanlike qualities to vehicles that act in simple ways, to faces that appear somewhat or very much like ours, and to computers as well as robots. This then affects the way we interact with them. Anthropomorphism seems to be an inherent way we have of interpreting the world around us. Cliff Nass and Byron Reeves suggest that anthropomorphism is the initial and intuitive response humans take to anything we interact with and that it would take an act of will not to think this way.

Kismet: The Emotional Robot

Cynthia Breazeal and her colleagues have devoted considerable time to the study of emotions in robots (Breazeal, 2002). The goal of their research is to design robots that both recognize and express emotion. Robots with these abilities will be better able to interact with humans in social settings. Their Kismet project is designed to model a very simple form of human social interaction, that between an infant and its caregiver. Kismet is a cute robotic head capable of sensing others and of expressing a wide range of facial expressions. It is driven by a cognitive system and an emotive system that work together to regulate its interactions with people (Breazeal & Brooks, 2005).

Kismet is equipped with a set of color cameras. It can move its head and eyes to control where it looks and what it pays attention to. Its auditory system consists of a microphone that can recognize and process certain aspects of human speech. Kismet has been programmed to detect four basic pitch contours that signal approval, prohibition, attention, and comfort (Fernald, 1989). The detection of this affect then influences its own emotional state. Kismet can raise its ears to display a state of interestedness or fold them back to indicate anger. Its eyebrows move up and down, furrow, and slant to communicate frustration, surprise, or sadness. It is also equipped with a vocalization system allowing it to produce synthesized sounds reminiscent of a young child.

Kismet's primary means of communicating emotion is through its face (see figure X). The emotions it displays exist within a three-dimensional affect space of arousal (high/low), valence (good/bad), and stance (advance/withdraw). A soothed expression corresponds to high positive valence and low arousal, that is, a state of being happy but underaroused. A joyous expression corresponds to a state of positive valence and moderate arousal. Some of the other expressions Kismet is capable of include anger, disgust, sorrow, surprise, and fear.

Kismet's cognitive system is made up of perception, attention, drive, and behavior subsystems. Its drive system is, in essence, an implementation of artificial human motivations. Kismet, just like a biological child, has motivating drives like thirst, hunger, and fatigue. It has a social drive that corresponds to a "need" to interact with people, a stimulation drive to play with toys, and a fatigue drive to rest every now and then. When the robot's "needs" are met, the drives are in a homeostatic regime and Kismet acts as if it were satisfied. But if the intensity level of a drive deviates from this regime, the robot is more strongly motivated to engage in behaviors that restore the drive to equilibrium. Drives don't directly evoke an emotional response, but they do influence Kismet's overall emotional state or mood.

To illustrate, if Kismet's social drive is high and it fails to receive sufficient stimulation from a person, it will display a sorrowful look. This sends a cue to the person interacting with Kismet to increase the amount of social stimulation, perhaps by manipulating a toy in front of Kismet's face. On the other hand, if the robot is receiving too much stimulation the drive state is lowered, and Kismet produces a display of fearfulness that should cause a person to back off and stimulate it less. When the level of interaction is beneficial, Kismet expresses interest and joy to encourage sustained interaction.

If Kismet is presented with an undesired stimulus, a disgust response can be triggered. This directs its gaze to an alternate area in the visual field, where it might locate a more desirable object. The display again serves as a cue to a person to engage in a different behavior like switching to another toy. There are other ways Kismet can use emotions to get what it "wants" from others. If a person is ignoring the robot, it can first attract the person by vocalizing. If that doesn't work, it can lean forward and wiggle its ears as a means of attracting attention. These examples demonstrate that Kismet is capable of changing its behavior should initial attempts fail. This variable approach is more likely to ensure that its "needs" are met.

Kismet is endowed with nine basic level emotional states: anger/frustration, disgust, fear/distress, calm, joy, sorrow, surprise, interest, and boredom. These states are affected by the presence of certain conditions such as the strength of various motivational drives and in turn affect the display of their corresponding facial expressions. These expressions then serve as communicative signals, informing the human present as to Kismet's state, and motivating that person to engage in a socially responsive action. Emotions in Kismet thus serve a social function. They mediate interaction between it and others. People who play with Kismet say they enjoy the experience. They also very easily attribute human-like qualities to it. Future robots with emotionally perceptive and expressive abilities like Kismet will undoubtedly make it easier for us to accept and work with artificial people.

ISAC—A Robot with Social Skills

Researchers at Vanderbilt University are developing a robot that can interact socially with one or more other persons (Kawamura, Rogers, Hambuchen, & Erol, 2003). Named ISAC (Intelligent Soft-Arm Control), it is sophisticated enough to understand human intentions and respond accordingly. ISAC is designed as a general-purpose humanoid robot that can work as a partner to assist people in either a home or a work setting. It is humanoid in appearance, having cameras, infrared sensors, and microphones that allow it to monitor the location of objects and people. ISAC has software that allows it to interpret and produce speech and to locate people's faces and the location of their fingertips. It is also capable of moving its body and arms to perform actions like shaking hands and picking up colored blocks.

ISAC's social abilities have been tested in several different demonstrations. In one such case a person walks up to the robot. ISAC turns toward the person and identifies and then greets him or her. Once this interaction is established, ISAC will engage in social dialogue. If the person asks ISAC to do something, such as pick up a block, it will do so if the task is within its capabilities. Another person then walks up to ISAC and attempts interaction. If the second person's intentions are of a lower priority, ISAC will stop what it is doing, turn to the second person, and apologize for being busy. It will then turn back to the first person and continue with its former interaction. If the second intention is of a greater priority than what it is currently doing, it will switch to the new task, but only after explaining its actions to the first person.

The ISAC robot exemplifies many of the key requirements of social interaction. Any agent, be it artificial or biological, must be able to register the locations of other agents around it. It must additionally be able to identify those agents and interpret what their intentions are. A social agent must also be able to communicate with those around it and to either give commands or follow commands given to it. Finally, it should be able to take turns in communicating and acting with others. These skills form the basis of more complex social behavior such as cooperative action toward the achievement of a common goal.

Robots and Ethics

If robots are to become so ubiquitous and are to interact with us, then we need some ways to prevent them from getting out of control. The study of this is known as robot or machine ethics. There are three main ways to govern robot behavior. In the consequentialist approach, robots are rewarded for "good" actions. Reward in this case may not be actually feeling good or happy unless they are capable of experiencing this, but perhaps some index that gets incremented for good actions and decremented for bad actions. Robots that perform different social functions could be rewarded for different behaviors. A sanitation robot could have its happiness index incremented for picking up garbage. A hedge-trimming robot in contrast, would have its index increased by locating and trimming overgrown hedges. Note that this is an individualist approach as it involves creating a diverse society of hardware agents, each with its own goals.

In the deontological approach, social behavior is governed using a set of rules or laws. For example, traffic laws include slowing down at a yellow light, yielding to oncoming traffic while turning, et cetera. Asimov's three laws of robotics are included here. Programming robots to follow a set of rules is not always successful, as there are often loopholes in the rules as well as misinterpretation of what they mean. Clearly, in the case of human behavior they are also not enough, for if they were, crime would not exist.

The last approach concerns the use of virtues. A virtue is an abstract action that one strives to carry out. Common virtues are truth, courage, and justice. Values can be thought of as the goals to which virtues are directed. If one values truth, for instance, one needs to practice rationality. The problem with virtues is that they are vague and fail to tell us how we should act in any given situation. How should a robot attain the truth? By downloading information from the internet? By having discussions with other robots?

These approaches have been tried, and all are unable to successfully govern human behavior. Would they work for governing robots? It depends. If robots always follow their programming and their programming is ethical, then their actions will also always be ethical. The problem with programming is that it is impossible to foresee every possible situation. A robot confronted with a novel situation would freeze because it would have no instructions for how to act in it. As a look at any law book or legal code will show, even relatively simple situations (taxation) can have page upon page of conduct on what to do should this or some other scenario arise.

Humans aren't given a comprehensive set of rules at birth. We gradually acquire them through experience. Experience is complex and contradictory. It can show us that an action may be bad in one context but not in another. The consequence of this is that we can draw on our learning and history to inform our actions in new situations, but we may not be 100 percent ethical in doing so.

So there is a trade-off between ethical purity and real-world complexity. The more ethical robots are by being programmed, the less capable they will be of dealing with new situations. Conversely, the more a robot learns right and wrong through experience, the better it will be able to deal with novel situations but the less ethically pure it will be. The optimum solution here is to use a mixture of both, to program robots with rules but to also allow them to learn. For the most part this is what we do ourselves. With robots it may be more effective because they may be able to hold onto more rules and be better able to generalize them to new situations. This is what one would expect given an increase in computational ability. If this were the case, we might not be governing them. They would be governing us—benevolently!

Collective Robotics

In this section we present research on how robots interact with one another rather than with people. The field of collective robotics designs and implements robotic systems that as a whole exhibit intelligent behavior, even though the individual robots in these systems are not themselves very "smart" (Melhuish, 2001). It draws on studies of collective behavior in biological systems. Insects, as we have already seen, can swarm. But they can also migrate, seek out food and materials, build, maintain and defend their nests, and care for their young. The goal in this research is to create robots that can perform similar tasks. Just as in the case of insects, it is possible to create robots that can solve problems and act intelligently as a result of following simple rules. They are able to achieve this without any of the trappings of what is considered necessary for intelligence. They have no internal symbolic representation of the world, do not perform any extended computational reasoning, and transmit only minimal amounts of information to one another, typically through wireless transmission systems like radio or infrared.

Since the focus is on emergent behavior similar to that seen in swarm intelligence (see chapter 6 for more on that), researchers in this field try to keep the actual robots as simple as possible. This keeps costs down and allows for the use of large numbers. There are many applications. Collective robot systems can be used to locate survivors in disaster rescue missions. They can also be used in mining, agricultural, and foraging tasks. Some artists have even used them to realize new forms of interactive art. Perhaps the most controversial application is in the military, where robotic boats have been used that can steer, defend, and attack targets without any direct command and control by humans.

In 2014, a swarm of over one thousand robots at Harvard University was used to form a "flash mob" (Rubenstein, Cornejo, & Nagpal, 2014). Called "Kilobots," each is only a few centimeters across and uses a unique form of locomotion by vibrating on three thin legs. They were able to move across a hard surface and to form up into different shapes including a star, the letter K, and a wrench. The Kilobots are even able to correct their own mistakes. If there is a traffic jam or a movement off course, the robots near the error can sense the problem and cooperate in order to fix it. These sorts of behaviors can be simulated using software but need to tested in hardware systems in order to work out physical interactions and variability that occur only in the real world.

The goal in such systems is to mimic biological collectives like cells or insects, where a global task is accomplished that is beyond the capabilities of any individual member. For example, army ants can link together to form rafts and bridges in order to get across difficult terrain. This same research group has used robots inspired by termites that can perform construction tasks with very simple forms of coordination. Eventually, such systems may be applied to create buildings or other objects that can construct themselves, using the same sorts of principles that cells in a biological organism do during development. This process is known as self-assembly and when applied at a microscopic level is called molecular self-assembly. See the section "Evolvable Hardware" later in this chapter for more on how cells can grow by coordinating with one another.

Perhaps the most ambitious social robot project is RoboCup (Robot World Cup Initiative), an attempt to develop a team of fully autonomous humanoid robots that can win against the human world soccer champion team by the year 2050. Teams from around the world develop robots in various categories and play against one another in annual tournaments. The contest currently has six competitive leagues. In the Standard Platform League all teams use the same robots, which act autonomously without any remote control by humans or computers. From 2009 onwards the Nao robots have been used exclusively in this league. For physical robots there two other leagues for small and middle-sized robots. There are also 2-D and 3-D simulation leagues that use software simulations. These competitions have grown to include non-soccer-related leagues called RoboCup Rescue, RoboCup@Home, and RoboCup@Work. In addition to the main event, a number of regional competitions take place every year. The main RoboCup 2017 challenge was held in Nagoya, Japan. The robots that compete in these events are remarkably fast and agile, defying the stereotype of robots as slow, clunky, and awkward. They can maneuver with the ball, pass it to teammates, intercept passes, and of course score goals.

Collective robotics shows us that self may be an emergent property. It may result from the cooperative actions of multiple agents using only simple rules. This makes sense given that self is often conceptualized as a plurality of different interacting selves within our psyche. This field also shows us the sorts of rules we need to use in order to get collectives of selves to work together effectively to achieve some goal. One day we may live in a society of robots and see ourselves in a mirror when we look at them. They are our technological offspring and like children may achieve more than their parents.

Evolution and Robotics

Evolution has guided the formation of human nature. Changes to our environment led some of our hominid ancestors possessing certain traits to survive. Following the principles of population variation, selection, and reproduction, our species was able to adapt over time to its current form. Researchers have also been able to use these principles to change the shape and functions of robots over successive generations. In this section we describe some of these efforts.

The Golem Project

Getting a robot to replicate itself is, at least theoretically, not difficult. After all, robots are in widespread use already in the manufacturing industry. They are employed in the construction of all sorts of consumer products ranging from automobiles to household appliances. If we wanted robots to build robots, it would mean simply switching the specifics of the manufacturing process. One could envision a factory manned entirely by robots that do nothing but build more copies of other robots, perhaps using assembly line techniques. The difficulty comes when we want robotic reproduction to mimic biological reproduction. In this case we need to create variations rather than duplications. We have already seen that evolution is a process that is very good at creating variations on a theme. The application of evolutionary principles to design and create robots is a field called evolutionary robotics (Nolfi & Floreano, 2000).

In evolutionary robotics an initial population of artificial chromosomes contain the instructions for the control systems of robots. The robots are then allowed to act in an environment by sensing, locomoting, manipulating, or performing some other task. Their performance is assessed. The best-performing robots with the highest fitness values are then mated by the crossover technique along with some random mutation. The offspring are next introduced into the environment and evaluated, with the cycle repeating until some desired measure of performance is obtained. Notice that this process is nearly identical to a Genetic Algorithm (GA) program. The main difference is that the creatures that result are not software programs running in a computer environment. They are hardware devices operating in the real world.

Researchers at Brandeis University have developed an exciting evolutionary robotics program that they call the Golem Project (Lipson & Pollack, 2000). Their goal was to evolve robots that could naturally move under their own power. They started with a set of robot body parts that included joints connected by rods. While some of the rods were rigid, others were linear actuators that could move back and forth controlled by an artificial neural network. They would start with a population of two hundred machines. The evolutionary algorithm created variations based on adding, modifying, and removing the basic body parts as well as altering the neural network. The fitness of the resulting creations was evaluated on the basis of their locomotion ability, measured as the net distance they could move their center of mass along a flat surface in a fixed amount of time.

After evaluating performance under simulation, some of the robots that had done well were chosen for manufacture and testing in a real-world testing environment. The results were fascinating. The evolutionary process yielded surprisingly different solutions. There were "Arrows," where a rear flipper pushed an arrowhead shape forward and then retracted to catch up. There were "Snakes," where a pyramid-shaped head dragged a long tail behind. There were also models called "Crabs" that shuffled along the floor by moving claw-like appendages. Although some of these solutions appeared to mimic animal locomotion, many were unique and did not correspond to any form of movement found in the natural world. Many solutions did, however, possess symmetry, probably because a symmetric body can move more easily in a straight line. Symmetry is a property found in almost all natural organisms.

Evolvable Hardware

Evolutionary principles of the sort employed in GAs have also been used to build electronic circuits. This new field of endeavor goes by the name of evolvable hardware (Thompson, 1998). Researchers like Adrian Thompson at Sussex University are accomplishing this using field programmable gate arrays (FPGAs). An FPGA consists of hundreds of reconfigurable blocks that can perform a variety of different digital logic functions. Switches control wires connecting the blocks to external devices and to each other. Memory cells in turn control the switches.

The configuration of the memory cells can be considered as the genotype of the system. A genotype is the specific genetic makeup of an individual. In biological organisms it is the specific sequence of nucleotides in the DNA that code for proteins. In other words, it is the genes on the chromosomes. The memory cells contain instructions for how the circuit should operate and specify what logical operations the blocks can do. The actual instantiation of these instructions, the wiring of the blocks themselves, is like a phenotype. In biological animals, the phenotype is either the total physical appearance of the organism or a specific manifestation of a trait like eye color, coded by a gene or set of genes. In evolvable hardware it is the physical expression of the information contained in the memory.

There are two ways to apply evolutionary principles to this type of system. In the extrinsic approach, evolutionary algorithms are used to generate a particular set of instructions that are then implemented in the FPGA. Testing and evaluation are done here at the software level. In the intrinsic approach, the evolutionary algorithm produces a starting configuration. This is instantiated in the FPGA, and its performance is evaluated in the real world. Based on the results of the performance, feedback is provided to the algorithm that then generates another variant for testing.

As an illustration of the intrinsic approach, imagine an FPGA circuit implanted in a mobile robot. The chip's design governs the robot's behavior and determines how it will perform in a given environment. Flaws in the design will become obvious and will be used to adjust the parameters of the algorithm so that the next design will be an improved version, better able to carry out its task.

Evolutionary processes don't proceed from an engineering standpoint, using known principles of design or an understanding of the nature of substrate materials. Evolution is conceptually "blind." It has no a priori assumptions and will create anything that works. In this sense, it capitalizes on the functional properties of a system independent of any knowledge of how it "should" work. Evolution therefore doesn't carry with it any of the bias or preconceptions of human designers.

Adrian Thompson discovered this quite quickly. His evolved silicon circuits behaved in ways nobody could have expected. They acted like analog circuits, oscillating and exhibiting other strange behaviors. But they worked, being both compact and efficient. Nobody is quite sure how they operate. One idea is that the chips utilize in-between states, short periods where components are switching from on to off or from off to on while redirecting electron flow.

The future of evolvable hardware has great promise (Bentley, 2002). Researchers at the Swiss Federal Institute of Technology are studying circuits that can reconfigure themselves when they are damaged. Circuits capable of self-repair mimic the plasticity of the human brain, which can "rewire" itself after injury. In stroke victims, brain areas that subsume different abilities like language can be destroyed. Depending on the extent of the damage and the quality of postoperative rehabilitation, patients can recover varying degrees of functionality. An examination of their brains shows that different brain regions have taken over the function that was once performed by the damaged area.

Nanorobotics and Nanomedicine

Finally, we can round off our presentation by discussing other forms of small robots that are mostly now in the conceptual stage but that have great promise for medicine. Most of us are comfortable with the use of technology outside our bodies, but the trend in technology is for things to get smaller and closer to the body. Think about how computers have shrunk to the point where you can now hold one in your hand. If this trend continues we may be able to manufacture computers and robots that are so small we cannot see them. The benefit of such machines is that they can perform work at the cellular and molecular level. We may someday sooner than we can imagine be swallowing such devices in order to treat various ailments. Although some people may be disgusted by this idea, if they have been used extensively in humans and shown to have a proven track record, then they are likely to be accepted and used by most people.

Nanorobotics is a field devoted to the research and development of robots that are very small (Haken & Levi, 2012): that is, at the nanometer scale (10^{-9}). Many terms have been used to describe such devices, including *nanobot*, *nanomachine*, and *nanite*. Nanorobots have many applications, but we will focus on their use in medicine, where their potential uses include drug delivery for cancer, monitoring of diabetes, and surgical use. Nanobots can be injected into a patient to perform work at a cellular level. The nanobots designed for use inside people will be of the nonreplicating type, since replication could lead to complications.

One problem with chemotherapy is that the drugs don't always reach the target location. Researchers have been able to attach RNA strands to nanoparticles, filling them with a chemotherapy drug (Shu, et. al., 2014)). The RNA is attracted to the cancer cells, attaches to them, and releases the drug into them. This approach can be considered a precursor to fully developed nanobots, but there are existing examples of nanomotors that have been built and operated within a living organism (Gao & Wang, 2014). Another potentially useful application of nanobots in medicine is to repair tissue cells. The nanobots could attach themselves to the surface of white blood cells to arrive at an injury site, where they can assist in the repair process. Most of this work is speculative now. Further progress awaits breakthroughs in the manufacture of miniature electronic and molecular components.

Nanobots change the self from the inside out, a perspective we are not used to taking. In the far future we may have large populations of nanobots in our bodies that are perpetually at work alongside normal cells and molecules. They may search our bodies for bad bacteria and viruses, help bring down blood sugar levels, and prevent diseases like cancer from forming. If a normal physiology consists of this blend of the natural and artificial, then we will truly be cyborgs, but at the microscopic level.

CHAPTER SIX

Brain + Software

CONTENTS

Technology
  Intelligence and Technology
  Alienation and Technology
Cyberpsychology
Varieties of Online Behavior
  Texting
    General Issues
    Texting and Relationships
  Selfies
    Personality Traits and Selfies
    Motivations for Taking Selfies
    Self- versus Other-Perceptions and
    Selfies
  The Internet
    Differences between the Internet and the
    Real World
    Social Networking Sites
    Brain Systems and Social Media
    Digital Dating
    Personality and Online Self-Presentation

Personality and Identity Management
Online
    Self-Esteem and Depression
    The Five-Factor Model (FFM)
    Narcissism
    Identity Formation Online
  Internet Use and Self-Related Measures
  Bad and Good Internet Behavior
    Being Bad: Cyberbullying
    Being Good: Altruistic Behavior Online
  Cognition and Internet Usage
    Cognitive Advantages of Internet Usage
    Internet Search and Memory
    Reading
    Attention-Related Phenomena
Video Games
  Video Gaming and Self-Related Phenomena
  Video Games and Cognitive Processing
  Video Games and Reward
  Game Transfer Phenomena

In this chapter we will cover a wide range of phenomena related to technology use. *Technology* is employed in a broad sense here and will cover internet browsing, social media, and video games. We save a discussion of virtual reality for chapter 8. The chapter begins with a discussion of whether technology use is causing alienation and separation from self. After this we outline some of the dimensions of cyberpsychology. The next topics are texting and selfies. Following this we turn to usage of social media sites like Facebook and Twitter to see how those affect the self. These sites are very popular, and a great deal of research has been focused on this subject. We next discuss the bad and good sides of internet use, namely cyberbullying and altruistic online behavior. The topic after that is how internet use is affecting us cognitively in terms of our attention, memory, and other processes. We discuss whether internet addiction is real and then round out the chapter with an examination of video games and whether they are deleterious or beneficial.

Although people get online with various hardware devices, it is the software that primarily mediates their experience. Although the formats for accessing sites like Twitter and Facebook may look different, the emphasis here is on how people are accessing and responding to the information they see. For this reason we discuss online behavior here in the context of software interaction.

TECHNOLOGY

Intelligence and Technology

Some say technology is making us stupid. They point out that we no longer need to do arithmetic or calculate a tip because we can use calculators. They say we no longer need to understand grammar or spelling because we have tools that perform these functions in word processors. They state we don't exercise our spatial or navigation skills because of GPS devices in our cars. Is this true? Are we outsourcing our intelligence to machines? Are we becoming dumber as our machines become smarter (figure 28)?

The data don't show this. According to the well-documented Flynn effect, IQ scores have risen steadily since about 1930 (Flynn, 2009). Each time a new IQ test is made, it must be standardized to a more recent population to produce a mean of 100 and a standard deviation of 15. When this is done, the difficulty of the test must be increased to maintain these norms. In the US it has amounted to three IQ points per decade, but gains are seen in every country where it has been measured. Proposed explanations for the Flynn effect include improved education and test-taking skills, better nutrition, smaller family size, and greater environmental complexity.

Let's take a look at this last explanation, as it is the most closely related to the future. Today's environment is much more stimulating in large part because of technology. We exist in an environment filled with screens displaying complex visual patterns. Our eyes are never far from television, movies, computers, and smartphones. Although I am not aware of exact empirical data, it is certain that the amount of awake time we spend staring at a screen of any sort is approximating the amount of time we spend looking at anything else. This

FIGURE 28 How many of these devices do you own? Are they making your life simpler or more complex? Are they making you more or less intelligent?

could be making us smarter as it forces us to process and understand complex visual patterns. Larger increases in scores on spatial reasoning tasks support this idea.

The attentional blink is a phenomenon where we lose the ability to maintain our attention after having just processed some visual target such as a letter in a rapid stream of numbers. In one study it was found that people who play first-person shooter (FPS) video games actually have a smaller attentional blink. They are able to reset their attention more quickly and are less likely to miss a second target that follows the first. FPS games are mostly perceptual-motor and exercise lower-level cognitive skills, but many games, especially those on smaller handheld devices, are more cognitive in nature. Sudoku builds number skills while Tetris builds visual imagery skills.

One could argue that using any form of technology to do something for us is as challenging as performing that same task ourselves and perhaps more so. Figuring out how to get that app on your smartphone to work, getting the GPS set to your final destination, and searching for an old email attachment all call on cognitive skills and make us exercise our memory, logic, and problem-solving abilities. Children especially seem to be better at learning technology than older adults are. Part of this is from having grown up with it, but part of it may be more flexible reasoning and greater tolerance of making mistakes.

Some caveats on the above. Higher IQ scores do not necessarily mean greater intelligence. They may simply reflect greater test-taking ability or the ability to master the sort of information found in school. Also, we are not as good as we think when it comes to multitasking. Recent work shows that we fail to recognize a lot of information when it is presented to us simultaneously: that is, we don't effectively divide our attention between multiple incoming sources. Being organized and learning to focus help in this regard.

One of the reasons we are smart as a species, at least compared to animals, is that we constantly generate hypotheses and predictions about what *might* be, not what is. This is part of our normal way of thinking. Should I take the train or a taxi into town tonight? The train takes longer but is cheaper, but I'm running late so I'll take the taxi. Should I ask Susie to the prom? If she says no I'll be ashamed, but if no one has asked her yet she just might say yes, so I'll ask her. What we perceive through our senses is reality, but what we think is one step removed. Ironically, it is through the creation of different possible worlds that we are able to deal so effectively with the real one.

Humans have what is dubbed general intelligence. We may not be really good at any one thing, but we are reasonably good at doing many things. For example, we can navigate around an environment, use language, and solve logic puzzles. To date, we have not been able to create an AI program that can match us in terms of this. Existing AI is highly specialized, programmed to perform a specific task well but unable to do anything but that. Early models of such programs were known as expert systems. One, called MYCIN, was at least equal to professional doctors in diagnosing certain medical disorders. The computer scientist Ben Goertzel is now working on a project named OpenCog in an attempt to create the first AGI, or artificial general intelligence (Goertzel, 2014).

Despite such advantages over machines, the human brain is limited in what it can comprehend. It has only so many neurons and transmits signals at a relatively slow rate. Supercomputers and advanced AI do not suffer these limitations, as they can be made as large as necessary and can transmit information much faster. So if an advanced AI solves some problem for us we may not be able to understand the answer! In general it would seem that any information processor can solve only problems that are at a given level of complexity less than itself. That may be because the intelligence doing the solving requires a representation of the problem along with the machinery necessary to process it. So brain A can solve problem B only if it can hold information about B inside itself along with the computational power necessary to derive a solution.

Alienation and Technology

Beier (2017) argues that technology is turning us away from activities that will help us develop an authentic psyche. He uses a Jungian definition of psyche as the beginning and end of all cognition and experience and describes it as emphasizing depth, authenticity, slowness, and interiority. The failure to develop the psyche will result in alienation, shallowness, and inauthenticity. People without a psyche are in some sense adrift, incapable of finding meaning in life. We must turn to other activities like meditation and dreaming, or simply giving ourselves time to think, in order to develop the psyche.

Beier is a therapist, and on the basis of experiences with his patients he believes that many people are trying to fill this existential vacuum by seeking refuge in the technological world. Behaviors that are stated to be commonplace in contemporary America include binge-watching of movies for days, constant texting with friends, excessive time on social media sites, addictions to pornography, and a general preoccupation with handheld technologies. Email and text messages now demand near-immediate replies. In addition the boundaries between work and free time have blurred now that smartphones allow us 24/7 online access.

This sentiment is echoed by Kaufman-Osborn (1997), who argues that we must learn to control our technologies, rather than letting them control us. He advocates that we should monitor our technological use, limit it, and be consciously aware of why and how long we are using it. Turkle (2011) writes that it is not the technology itself that is to blame but how we are using it. She states that we should put technology "in its place" and engage in more people-to-people interaction. Turkle believes that we are now asking more and more of our technology but less of each other.

Rosen (2012), on the basis of his own work and a meta-analysis of the work of other scholars, sees overreliance on technology as a new cause of psychological disorders. He argues that we spend too much time enmeshed with gadgets and websites and that this can produce an increase in panic and anxiety disorders, obsessive-compulsive disorders, mood disorders, and addictive disorders, primarily of the narcissistic kind. He calls these *iDisorders*; they might also be termed technological neuroses.

Part of the problem concerns the way we present ourselves online. Beier (2017) describes our online postings as maintaining a self-created image or persona of ourselves that is inauthentic. Our online persona portrays success, beauty, popularity, and confidence. It is a necessary fiction that allows the ego to feel good and safe and an example of narcissism. These personas are constructed selves that portray us not as we are but as we want to be seen by others.

Our relationships online are in many cases not meaningful or long lasting. Part of this is due to the diminished cues present in online communication. We often get only a picture or a sentence of text when browsing Facebook or Twitter postings. Thoughtful communication would require greater depth of thought and more writing. This failure to communicate has spread to some families in the real world, who, according to Turkle (2011) spend their evenings scattered in different rooms around the house entertaining themselves with one or multiple devices. These families would seem to communicate only at a bare minimum for practical or logistical coordination.

Rosen (2012) argues that our use of social media encourages narcissistic expression. For a full account of narcissistic personality and related disorders, see chapter 3. He states that narcissists collect "trophy friends" on social media sites. These trophies are used as image enhancers and allow the individuals in question to bask in "public glory." He notes that these narcissists will post throughout the day and use pronouns like *I*, *me*, or *mine*, excessively. The factors that appear to contribute to this narcissism are permissive parenting and the celebrity culture.

CYBERPSYCHOLOGY

Cyberpsychology can probably be considered the newest branch of psychology. It is the study of psychological processes, motivations, intentions, behavioral outcomes, and effects on both our online and offline worlds associated with any form of technology (Attrill, 2015). Examples include use of the internet, specific software programs, mobile phones, gaming platforms, and virtual reality. It should not be confused with human-computer interaction, which focuses solely on computer usage. Cyberpsychology utilizes the scientific method but also adopts the methods and theories of other disciplines like mathematics, engineering, computer science, biology, and sociology. Because technology advances so fast, researchers in the field are constantly trying to catch up. Although cyberpsychologists sometimes apply offline psychological theories and results, we cannot always conclude that our offline behavior will be the same as our online behavior.

When interacting with online devices we extend our psyche or persona into them. Thus they reflect our personalities, beliefs, and lifestyles. The online world blurs the barrier between mind-space and machine-space (Turkle, 1995). We also tend to experience it as being between our own self and the nonself. It serves as a venue for discovering who we are, for expressing our interests and desires, for expressing creativity, and in negative cases for acting out aggression or addictions. Suler (2017) outlines eight dimensions of cyberpsychology architecture that help define our interactions with virtual spaces.

The eight dimensions interact with each other and regulate the experience we have in a given digital space. They reflect how a particular online environment works, the psychology of how one might experience it, and aspects of our mind's cognitive operations. Different digital environments like email, social media, video conferencing, games, and virtual reality combine the eight dimensions in varying degrees. In the following sections we will describe them and apply them as a means of analyzing online behavior.

The first is the *identity dimension*. This is determined by the options it provides people for establishing who they are, what they express and what they hide, and how they can transform themselves. These transformations are the different ways we alter and experience ourselves in a given online world: for example, the way we might choose an avatar that expresses an alternate gender or ideal self. These projections of idealized or alternate selves have been referred to as the hyperpersonal self (Walther, 1996). Sometimes people project a mixture of their ideal and real selves online, sometimes they can use a system to discover unconscious aspects of their personality, and sometimes they can hide aspects of their self by choosing to remain anonymous or invisible.

Tools for establishing identity include usernames, biography profiles, photos and selfies, game characters, and avatars. Once established in a system, users can choose different methods for self-expression. These include texting, uploading additional pictures and videos that show themselves at work or play, reposting other people's content, and tagging others. Reposting and tagging are examples of what Suler (2016) refers to as self-expression by proxy. Some systems allow for relatively accurate self-portrayal, as is the case for social media sites. Others allow for the adoption of complete fantasy characters, as we see in role-playing video games. Personal identity can become dysfunctional or distorted under certain circumstances. For example, some individuals may become addicted to social approval in the form of "likes" and positive comments in Facebook. These can selectively reinforce certain aspects of identity that differ from one's true identity, resulting in a mismatch between the real and ideal versions of one's self.

The *social dimension* refers to the relationships one has with others online. These relationships can be one to one, one to many, or many to one. The ties can be strong and intimate, or weak and casual. Other aspects include how many people one interacts with, who these people are, and the type of relationship, such as work or recreation related. A given system will have tools that allow its members to locate each other, gather together, and communicate privately or in public with one another. The social and identity dimensions are closely related but can operate independently. It is possible, for example, to broadcast oneself without responding to others (an expressive mode) or to view others' content without posting much of one's own (a receptive mode). While online, an individual can communicate with one or millions, can process relationships serially or in parallel, and can seek out very specific audiences. The popularity of online dating sites like Match.com or Tinder allow one to find sexual and romantic partners and to express sexuality and love "at a distance" and in the real world.

The *interactive dimension* refers to the computer interface, or how one interacts physically with the online space. This can be done with a mouse and keyboard or more elaborately using a virtual reality interface. The more user-friendly this interface is, the easier it is to become immersed in the world. The more customizable it is, the more control one has over expressing individual aspects of self. In the case studies on avatars we see that some people care very much about the appearance and personality characteristics of their online persona, others less so. Games have high levels of interactivity and a steeper learning curve, while activities like texting have less and are easier to master.

Interactivity can fail in cases where computers crash or bandwidth slows. The result can be frustration, depression, or rage. Sudden lack of response from a device can lead to this so-called black hole experience (Suler, 2016). Machines also respond actively to us by providing reminders and pop-up notifications. They are increasingly able to determine our preferences and provide recommendations of music we might like to listen to or movies we might want to watch. Computer-generated avatars and AI-driven game characters are becoming more complex and lifelike. It is likely that we will respond to them more as actual people and less as pixelated forms.

The *text dimension* refers to text-only means of communication. This is still a dominant form of online interaction and is used in texting, email, social media sites, and blogs. Typing is an effective means of self-expression and of healing and discovering one's self (Pennebaker, 2004). Typing is social in that it allows us to understand others and to establish interpersonal relationships. It is a way to sort through personal emotions, as has been the case for written diaries for centuries. However, text is a "low-bandwidth" and relatively impoverished form of communication. It is up to the imagination rather than the computer to produce imagery. When communicating with others we can't see their facial expressions, vocal intonation, or body posture, so it may be easier to deceive or misunderstand others. The anonymity provided by text can encourage regression to more childlike ways of behaving or can cause people to act out, what has been dubbed the online-disinhibition effect (Suler, 2004).

The *sensory dimension* is about the degree to which an online experience can activate the five senses. Some forms of interaction are visual only. Others, like video conferencing, add voice. Others, like virtual reality, can add tactile, olfactory, and gustatory sensation. The more the five senses are stimulated, the more compelling and immersive the experience is. The "virtual pit" is a computer simulation in which users are asked to walk a thin plank set across a deep hole. The reactions people have to this include fear and "freezing up." This shows the power of even relatively simple programs to fool the brain (Blascovich & Bailenson, 2012).

The *temporal dimension* refers to our experience of time in cyberspace. Real-time synchronous communication encourages spontaneity, producing more uncensored, ad hoc, fast-paced, and revealing dialogues. Asynchronous ones encourage more careful and controlled exchanges. Presence, the feeling of "being there," is enhanced in synchronous communication, perhaps because we are aware of another conscious being who is also attending to us. Asynchronous dialogues slow down or even stop the pace of interaction, allowing for users to respond with significant delays or not at all. People have reported feeling uncomfortable not knowing if their partner has decided to stop responding. Time can also speed up in cyberspace. Fast communication can accelerate work relationships, romances, and social or political movements. Time speeds up during the famous state of "flow," when someone is actively and passionately engaged in a creative enterprise (Voiskounsky, 2008).

Another aspect of time online is that information can be preserved indefinitely. Most data on computer systems are archived and stored in "the cloud" without being deleted, so it is difficult for an individual to remove confidential or embarrassing information. This might explain the popularity of applications like Snapchat that quickly delete conversational data. People's behavior changes under these conditions. Flirting and sexual teasing are more common when we know there will be no record of the transaction. Finally, there is the intersection of cyberspace time with real-world time. People vary in when, how often, and for how long they go online.

The *reality dimension* refers to whether an online system attempts to be realistic or more imaginative. Social media sites encourage more accurate portrayals, while fantasy and science fiction games encourage more imaginative ones. Suler (1980) writes about the intrapsychic world as a continuum from reality to fantasy. Some people are much more reality oriented and practical, others more creative and imaginative. This also reflects different states of consciousness, with fully awake and alert cognitive processing at one end and the dream state at the other. Cyberspace itself can be considered a type of dream world.

Eighth and last is the *physical dimension*. This refers to the impact online activity has on the body. Cyberspace started off mostly disembodied, as little motion was required from a user other than to sit in a chair, stare at a computer screen, and move a mouse. Now, however, with virtual reality and the creation of games systems like the Nintendo Wii, one can interact more fully using the entire body. Dissociated physicality and integrated physicality form two ends of a continuum. Dissociation of mind and body is evident when someone is crossing the street or walking up stairs while continuing to use a smartphone. Integrated physicality occurs when bodily movements and perception are more closely linked to the activity in cyberspace.

In the future we may see the internet of things, where appliances and everyday objects are embedded with sensors and connected to the internet. We may also see humanity transformed into cyborgs with neural prosthetics, exoskeletons, and other embedded machinery. In this type of world we will walk around and be in continuous touch with cyberspace. This may require a new field, environmental cyberpsychology, which would study how our behavior, cognitions, and emotions are affected by such devices (Suler, 2017).

Suler (2017) next applies these eight dimensions to the study of the individual. They can be used to determine the state of a person's digital identity and to understand the benefits and costs individuals derive from their online activity. In effect, these items can be considered as part of a digital personality questionnaire. We will pose them as a list of questions that can be posed for each of the eight dimensions in the sections that follow.

Identity Dimension

What do individuals reveal about themselves online?

How do they present themselves online as opposed to in real life?

When do they choose to be anonymous or invisible?

What do they do online that they don't do offline?

Social Dimension

Whom do they choose to communicate with?

What groups do they participate in?

What roles do they play?

What is the status of their online relationships?

Interactive Dimension

What are their technical skills and knowledge?

How do they customize their devices?

How do they react to the challenge of mastering new environments?

How do they react when their applications are not doing what they want?

Text Dimension (text here means any type of online writing)

How often do they text?

What is the length of their texts?

To whom do they text?

What do they text about?

Sensory Dimension

What types of visuals do they send (emoji, photo, video, etc.)?

What types of visuals do they spend time looking at?

What types of sensory modalities do they use (visual, auditory, tactile, etc.)?

When do they decide to eliminate a particular sensory dimension?

Temporal Dimension

Do they prefer synchronous or asynchronous communication?

When does time online seem to pass quickly (state of flow)?

What content do they save from cyberspace?

When, how often, and for how long do they enter the digital realm?

Reality Dimension

Do they portray a realistic version of themselves online?

How do they react to places that are imaginary or realistic?

How do they distinguish fact from fiction online?

Do they have a preference for certain types of fantasies?

Physical Dimension

Are there any physical problems associated with online activity?

Is their activity more dissociated or integrated?

Where and how do they use mobile technology?

How do they use cyberspace to interpret the environment?

Suler (2017) has had his students use the eight dimensions to assess their digital life-styles. Many were surprised by what they found. They didn't realize, for instance, how big the impact of cyberspace was on their lives. They also developed awareness for the ways they constructed their digital identities and how those differed from the real-life selves. Many had also been unaware of the extent to which mobile phones could be used to track their locations in the physical world.

Because we are addressing self and identity in this book, it is worth addressing the questions raised by the identity dimension in a bit more detail. Research shows that people tend to present a more idealized form of themselves online (see Carl Rogers's view of the real and ideal self in chapter 3 for more). These idealized selves tend to reflect society's expectations. For example, narcissistic men tend to present themselves in the About Me section on Facebook with posts that reflect intelligence, success, and wit, while narcissistic women tend to present themselves in more superficial ways in the Main Photos section by posting more revealing, flashy, and adorned photos of their physical appearance (Mehdizadeh, 2010).

There is a debate as to whether social media sites are used as a way simply to self-promote or to connect with others. The answer is probably a mixture of the two. We use such sites to broadcast our strengths but also to reveal our weaknesses and to gain sympathy from others, as during the announcement of the death of a family member. Revealing personal secrets and sharing intimacy are ways of more strongly connecting with others. Since we define ourselves in part through our relations with others (as a caring mother, a supportive friend, etc.), the desire for intimacy through digital means may reflect a compensation for the increased social distancing in modern society (Lambert, 2013; Turkle, 2012).

VARIETIES OF ONLINE BEHAVIOR

Texting

Texting involves the transmission of a short message, usually from one cell phone to another (figure 29). Texts are typically from one person to another, but texts from an individual to a group or between group members also occur. Texts can also be sent by computer. In the following sections we examine first some general topics regarding texting, followed by the results of some recent studies on texting and relationships.

General Issues

In one study using an online questionnaire, greater texting was found for young American adults (Crosswhite, Rice, & Asay, 2014). This group was found to respond promptly to texts they received and could honestly express feelings in this medium. Participants were found to text family members for a variety of reasons, including to plan activities, convey information, and engage in general conversation. Schroeder and Sims (2017) discovered several factors for texting behavior and labeled them "social connection," "escapist," "distracted," "audacious," "nurtured communication," and "driving." He concluded that texting is done for a variety of reasons, some social and some nonsocial. Texting in some cases is problematic.

Coyne, Padilla-Walker, and Holmgren (2017) looked at the trajectory of texting over time in an adolescent sample from Washington State in the US. They found four basic patterns:

FIGURE 29 Texting is a predominant form of communication, especially among younger Americans. Can you explain its popularity?

perpetuals (14 percent), decreasers (7 percent), moderates (68 percent), and increasers (11 percent). Perpetual texters were predicted by higher levels of depression, being male, and coming from a single-parent home. Poor outcomes were also associated with this group. They were more likely to have anxiety, aggression, and poor relationships with their fathers.

The "shallowing hypothesis" is that new media technologies have made people less reflective in the way they think. The idea is that texting and social media usage promote rapid shallow thought and less moral thinking. Annisette and Lafreniere (2017) found support for this hypothesis. In a study of undergraduate Canadian university students, the participants who texted or used social media more often were less likely to engage in reflective thinking and cared less about moral life goals.

Texting and Relationships

Ling, Baron, Lenhart, and Campbell (2014) examined teenage texting between members of opposite sexes. They found that texting was a means of developing gendered identity and investigating romantic interaction. Girls viewed the boys' texts as short and brisk. Boys viewed girls' texts as overly long, prying, and having unnecessary elements. Another study of a sample of young American adults aged eighteen to twenty-nine years found no significant correlations between sexual satisfaction and texting (McGee, 2014). Those who were more satisfied with these relations did not send more texts to their partner. Angster, Frank, and Lester (2010), testing a sample of 128 undergraduates, found that higher frequency of texting to others was associated with less fulfilling relationships with those others. Having more friends on social networks was also associated with less fulfilling relationships with those individuals. Drouin and Landgraff (2012) found that texting was more common among those with secure attachments, while sexting was more common among those with insecure attachments.

Most research on texting is done with younger groups, mostly adolescents. Forgays, Hyman, and Schreiber (2014) looked at differences in perceived etiquette in cell phone usage in a sample including older adults. The age range of their sample was eighteen to sixty-eight years. Men were found to be more likely than women to view cell phone calls as more appropriate than texting. Romantic partners were more likely to receive a call than a text. One-fourth of the younger group had dumped or had been dumped by their romantic partner over texts. Park, Lee, and Chung (2016) found that cell phone texting was negatively associated with relationship satisfaction. Number of text messages sent and received was, however, related to feeling less lonely and perceiving higher levels of intimacy.

When we are texting, it seems as if part of our self is lost in the thoughts and emotions of the other person. Some people have even reported anxiety when waiting for a delayed response, wondering what that person is thinking or feeling or whether the sender has typed something that may have upset the recipient. In group texts this effect may be extended to the entire set of participants. Would participants in these exchanges then constitute a "hive" or group mind? Similar effects occur for face-to-face interactions, but with technology the effect is distributed spatially, as the members can be located at far-separated locations across the globe.

The future may hold some interesting extensions of these ideas in that we may be able to directly experience what others are experiencing. With brain-machine interfaces, one could read somebody else's feelings and thoughts directly, then perhaps reinstantiate these subjective conscious qualia in the mind of another. Imagine a group that is interfacing in such a way, swapping mental states back and forth between members. Would the individual sense of self disappear under such conditions, or would it meld into a higher state of self made up of the group's consciousness?

Selfies

A selfie is a digital image characterized by the desire to frame the self in a picture to be shared with an online audience (figure 30). In an objective sense, selfies are used to display our personalities, lifestyles, and preferences. But subjectively selfies are believed to be taken and posted for reasons of self-presentation, self-promotion, and narcissism. In this section we will examine some of the general personality traits associated with selfie taking, our motivations for taking selfies, and differences in how we and others see them.

Personality Traits and Selfies

Sorokowska et al. (2016) looked at frequency of selfie posting and personality traits. They found a wide range of variation between 0 and 650 postings per month in their two studies.

FIGURE 30 A selfie. Do you take selfies? If so, what is the motivation behind them?

Participants posted on average 2.9 selfies of themselves, 1.4 of a romantic partner, and 2.2 group selfies to Facebook each month. Women posted more selfies of each type than men. For both sexes, social exhibitionism and extroversion predicted frequency. There was little relation between self-esteem and selfie posting for either sex.

Choi, Sung, Lee, and Choi (2017) conducted an online panel survey to examine the relation between the Big Five personality traits and selfies. They found that four out of five of these traits (with the exception being extroversion) were associated with degree of concern about others' response to one's own selfies. Agreeableness and low openness were associated with a high tendency to observe others' selfies. Tendency to comment on or like others selfies was predicted by agreeableness and extraversion.

Motivations for Taking Selfies

Sung, Lee, Kim, and Choi (2016) examined the motivations for why people take selfies. Their findings revealed four motivations: attention seeking, communication, archiving, and entertainment. Narcissism, but not any of the other motivations, was found to predict posting frequency. Etgar and Amichai-Hamburger (2017) administered a questionnaire dealing with reasons for taking selfies. A factor analysis revealed three primary motivations: self-approval, belonging, and documentation. The authors then examined the relationship between personality types and selfie taking. Self-approval was negatively related to conscientiousness, emotional stability, openness, and self-esteem. Belonging was related to openness. Documentation was related to agreeableness and extroversion. None of the three motivations was related to narcissism. However, another recent study did find an association between grandiose narcissism and taking and posting more selfies (McCain et al., 2016). The discrepancies between these studies may be due to the differing samples of participants, from Korea, Israel, and the US, respectively.

Kozinets, Gretzel, and Dinhopl (2017) looked at selfie taking in museums. They found that people take selfies for reasons other than to self-promote or to gain approval. The data showed several categories: selfies to interact with art, mirror selfies, silly/clever selfies, contemplative selfies, and iconic selfies. The conclusions drawn are that selfie taking is multidimensional, can be done for cultural as well as social motivations, is an act of mimicry, and is part of identity formation.

Self-versus-Other Perceptions and Selfies

Re, Wang, He, and Rule (2016) had selfie and nonselfie takers take selfie photos. Then both they and external judges rated the photos. Both groups reported equal levels of narcissism, but the selfie takers perceived themselves as more attractive and likable in the photos than the nonselfie takers. The external judges, though, rated these photos as less attractive, less likeable, and more narcissistic than the photo takers themselves did. The results show that others view our selfies in a much more negative light then we ourselves do.

Diefenbach and Christoforakos (2017) rated participants on a self-presentation tactics scale and had them rate both their own and other people's selfies. Those participants who scored high on self-promotion (telling others about one's achievements) and self-disclosure (revealing feelings) felt positive while taking selfies. People rated their own selfies as self-ironic and authentic but were far less likely to rate others' selfies this way and far more likely to regard them as posted for purposes of self-promotion. The researchers conclude that viewing one's own selfies as self-ironic allows people to self-present without feeling selfish or narcissistic.

The Internet

Differences between the Internet and the Real World

Four factors make the online world different from the "real world": anonymity, a reduced emphasis on physical appearance, control over timing and pace of interactions, and ease of finding others similar to ourselves (McKenna, Green, & Gleeson, 2002). Fullwood, Nicolis, and Makichi (2015) suggest a fifth, which is control over generated content. We discuss each of these in greater detail in what follows.

Anonymity online varies. On social network sites like Facebook, users are usually fairly accurate about portraying themselves. On blog sites and chat rooms identity is typically not revealed (Fullwood, Thelwall, & O'Neill, 2013). Even if identity is revealed, people online can be geographically separated, making real-world contact more difficult (Fullwood, Melrose, Morris, & Floyd, 2013). Anonymity can make people feel more comfortable disclosing certain aspects of the self, because the real-world repercussions are limited (Valkenburg, Schouten, & Peter, 2005). Suler (2004) describes the "online disinhibition effect," whereby people tend to self-disclose more personal information because of a belief in anonymity. Reasons for this effect are provided in table 10 (Suler, 2016).

It is easier to conceal or enhance aspects of our physical appearance online than offline, through such means as selecting and editing photos or phrasing descriptions. The internet

TABLE 10 Reasons for the online disinhibition effect

	Name	Description
1.	Dissociative anonymity	Believing that someone online does not know you.
2.	Invisibility	Believing that others cannot see or hear you: for example, when you are texting there is no visual representation of the other person with whom you are communicating
3.	Asynchronicity	Not having to deal with somebody's communication immediately. Putting it on hold and coming back to it later.
4.	Solipsistic introjection	Feeling that your mind has merged with that of an online companion. Hearing their message inside your head.
5.	Dissociative imagination	Believing that an imaginary version of yourself exists in another realm in cyberspace.
6.	Perceived privacy	Thinking that a communication is private.
7.	Attenuated status and authority	Not knowing the status of another person online.
8.	Social facilitation	Identifying with other people, especially an aggressor. It's okay because everyone else is doing it.

Source: After Suler (2016).

could thus "level the playing field" for people who are less attractive. However, one needs to be careful about how much to alter one's appearance online in case a face-to-face meeting does occur (Ellison, Heino, & Gibbs, 2006). Many people undoubtedly exaggerate certain socially desirable features about themselves online like emphasizing their athleticism or health.

Online interactions can take place in real time (synchronously) or asynchronously. In the latter case, time between responses can be delayed. This can be done if somebody doesn't have necessary information and needs to get it or does not want contact with someone and is sending a message by delaying a response. Asynchronous communication can also happen because a person wants more time to think about what to say. Delayed responding gives us more time to present ourselves favorably and can be used to present a positive self-image.

One of the nice things about the internet is that it allows people with like interests to connect. Nearly every interest imaginable from quilting to airplane modeling is represented online. People with such like-minded interests can communicate on forums, chat rooms, blogs, and social media sites. People may feel more comfortable self-disclosing to others with shared passions (McKenna, Green, & Gleeson, 2002). Finally, users can actively shape the content they generate online. Those who are shy or anxious can portray themselves as confident and secure. There are fewer constraints on self-generated content online and a

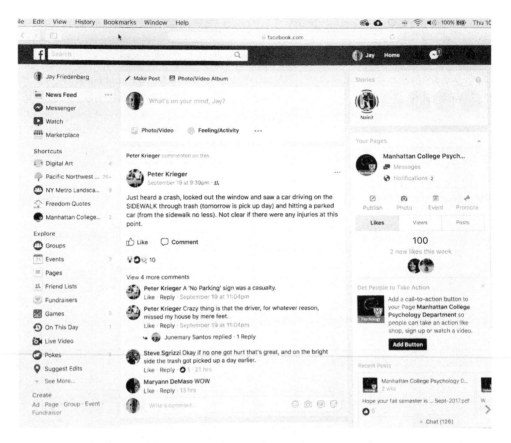

FIGURE 31 Facebook, one of the most popular social networking sites on the internet.

greater degree of control over how it is presented (Wang & Stefanone, 2013). This is true not just for photos or videos but also for typed biographical descriptions of oneself.

Social Networking Sites

Social networking sites (SNSs) are sites like Facebook and Twitter that allow a person to set up a site and post personal information to it that can then be shared with others (figure 31). Text, images, and videos can usually be uploaded along with links to websites. Most SNSs allow a user to like a post, to repost it elsewhere, or to comment on it. People in a post can also be tagged, in which case they will also be alerted to it.

SNSs like Facebook are very popular among teenagers and college students. They have become a new way for people to communicate with colleagues, friends, and family (Cooley, 2010). They encourage people to build and maintain a network of interpersonal relationships, which can have a strong influence on overcoming shyness, reducing loneliness, improving self-esteem, and promoting subjective well-being (Indian & Grieve, 2014). A number of recent studies on Chinese adolescents and college students also show that self-presentation on SNSs

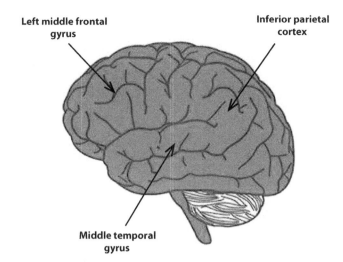

Left middle frontal
gyrus

Inferior parietal
cortex

Middle temporal
gyrus

FIGURE 32 This is your brain on social media. The default mode network.

is positively associated with self-identity, self-esteem, positive emotions, and perceived social support (Q. X. Liu, Chen, & Zhou, 2015; Q. Q. Liu, Sun, Zhou, & Niu, 2015).

However, there are also downsides to SNS use. It has been found to be associated with negative variables like lowered self-esteem and depression (Niu, Sun, Zhou, Kong, & Tian, 2016). There is a bias toward positive self-presentation on SNSs, which may give the impression that everyone else is happier and more successful than you (Chou & Edge, 2012). This may elicit envy and create a lowered self-evaluation. There is also some evidence to suggest that passive SNS use may lead to lowered self-esteem (W. Chen, Fan, Liu, Zhou, & Xie, 2016). Passive use involves reading information about others but not liking, commenting, or tagging others—that is, not making an attempt to connect with others through the site.

Kanai, Bahrami, Roylance, and Rees (2011) found that the number of social contacts on a major online SNS was strongly associated with certain brain areas. Number of Facebook friends predicted gray matter volume in the left middle temporal gyrus, right entorhinal cortex, and right superior temporal sulcus. These areas are known to be related to theory-of-mind cognition. A theory of mind is the ability to know that other people are conscious and have minds. The study also found a significant relationship between gray matter density in the amygdala and number of Facebook friends. The amygdala has previously been shown to correlate with number of offline friends. It is implicated in the response and memory to emotions, including fear.

Brain Systems and Social Media

What parts of the brain are involved in thinking about others? Many regions and networks participate in social cognition. We describe a few of these here. The brain's default mode network (DMN) is constantly active and is involved in thinking about both oneself and others. Figure 32 shows the major brain structures of the DMN. This automatic processing gets

TABLE 11 Three proposed brain networks that may be involved in the use of social media

Network	Brain Areas	Example(s)
Mentalizing network	Dorsomedial prefrontal cortex (dmPFC)	A social media user may think about how persons in her network will respond to a post.
	Temporoparietal junction (TPJ)	A social media user may think about how a specific user may react upon reading feedback related to a post.
	Anterior temporal lobe (ATL)	A social media user may think about the other user's motivations for posting information.
	Inferior frontal gyrus (IFG)	
	Posterior cingulate cortex (PCC)	
Self-referential cognition network	Medial prefrontal cortex (mPFC)	A social media user may think about herself and then broadcast those thoughts, which may provoke further self-referential thought.
	PCC	A user may receive feedback that results in reflected self-appraisals.
		Social comparison requires users to think about their own behavior in relation to other users.
Reward network	Ventromedial prefrontal cortex (vmPFC)	A Facebook user may receive positive feedback in the form of a "like" or a "friend" request.
	Ventral striatum (VS)	Reading others' posts may elicit reward activity, because receiving information elicits curiosity.
	Ventral tegmental area (VTA)	These rewards activate the user's brain reward system and compel the user to return to Facebook for more.

Source: From Parsons (2017).
Note: Examples are not specific to any single brain area listed. Usually more than one brain area will participate in the expression of a given behavior.

"dialed down" when performing active control processes, for example when doing difficult math problems (Schilbach, Eickhoff, Rotarska-Jagiela, Fink, & Vogeley, 2008). The DMN is made up of the anterior and posterior medial cortices and lateral parietal lobes. A number of other self-related phenomena are associated with the DMN, including autobiographical memory, self-referential processing, and social cognition (Amodio & Frith, 2006; Raichle, 2015; Spreng, Mar, & Kim, 2009).

A set of brain structures called the "mentalizing network" overlaps and probably works in concert with the DMN. Activity in this network correlates with the ability to mentalize (infer) the feelings and thoughts of other people. The self-referential cognition network is also involved in thinking about others and is made up of the medial prefrontal cortex and posterior cingulate cortex. The brain's reward network also becomes active when one is thinking about others. This network activates whenever something pleasurable is experienced and is believed to reinforce behavior that is evolutionarily adaptive. Table 11 depicts these brain networks along with some online examples.

Digital Dating

Ansari (2016) presents a comical but data-based presentation of the challenges of online dating. We will provide an overview of his work in this section, starting with some of the differences between what it is like to date now compared to dating before technology began to change the way this process works. To start, it was the case that people used to meet and marry only those who lived in close physical proximity. Bossard (1932) looked at licenses for five thousand marriages in the city of Philadelphia and found that one-third of the couples lived within a five-block radius of one another prior to getting married. A second trend is that people are getting married at later ages. US Census Bureau data shows that the average age in 1950 was twenty-one years, while in 2014 it was twenty-seven. A third major change is that standards for marriage have become higher. People used to be seeking a companionate marriage, but recent survey data show that the expectation is now for a soul mate marriage. People now are looking for someone that they are truly and deeply in love with. These trends may explain why current love seekers sometimes spend decades looking for a partner. They can look all over the world with access to millions, they have more time to do so, and they are pickier.

Meeting a romantic partner is easier than ever before given the number of online dating sites and apps. But that doesn't make it easier to ask someone on a date. A 2013 Match.com survey found that younger people are much more likely to text to ask for a date, while older generations prefer to speak over the phone. Focus groups reveal that younger men and women both express fear of conversing in a traditional phone call (Ansari, 2016). These same groups reveal that women often receive quite "flaky" first texts from men, where they don't give their name or commit to a meeting time or place. In fact, many first text conversations go back and forth multiple times without a date ever even occurring. Some men show signs of sexually aggressive behavior in these texts. Here are some examples:

"hey, what's your bra size?;)"
Afternoon sex?;)
"I like your tits"
"You literally can't even see them in any of my pictures I don't understand"
"I'm assuming they are nice"

The reason for such behavior may be the separation texting provides. Would these men have stated such things if they were on the phone or speaking in person? It could be that technological distancing allows us to act in ways we wouldn't normally when interacting face to face. Men in particular may feel less inhibited. The effect is suggestive of alcoholic disinhibition. Texting may therefore produce two selves: the real polite and respectful self and the aggressive or noncommittal phone self.

In Ansari's study there was some consensus with regard to texting about what constitutes proper etiquette. Some of the basic rules included (1) not texting back right away, as it makes you seem too desperate; (2) if you write someone, don't text that person again until you hear from him or her, otherwise it comes across as too pushy; and (3) the amount of text you write should be of about a similar length to what the other person has written to you, ostensibly because you may be giving away too much information too soon. Three tips were also provided for what to do when you aren't interested in someone: pretend to be busy, say nothing, or be honest.

Online dating is a powerful force. Between 2005 and 2012 one-third of married couples met through an online dating site. It was the single biggest way people met their spouses, more so than meeting through friends, school, and work combined (Cacioppo, Cacioppo, Gonzaga, Ogburn, & VanderWeele, 2011). Looking over the period 1940–2010, the trend for meeting online rises beginning in the 1980s while all other forms of meeting show declines in recent years. This pattern is true for both heterosexual and same-sex partners. Any stigma associated with meeting this way seems to be declining.

Although online dating is convenient and provides access to untold possible partners, there are several associated problems. The first has to do with attractiveness. Plainly speaking, attractive women get far more inquiries. The number of messages per day on OKCupid rises steadily as a function of attractiveness percentile, exponentially so for those at the ninetieth percentile or higher (Rudder, 2014). The number of options that even people of average attractiveness receive can also be exhausting to review. Many people report that online dating is equivalent to a second job because it takes up so much of their time.

A third factor posting a problem for online dating is that people don't seem to know what they want. The kind of partner they say they are interested in doesn't match up with the people they actually contact on the dating site (D. Slater, 2013). People seem to break their own rules. The single most important factor they seem to rely on when selecting a date is attractiveness. Photos have been determined to drive 90 percent of the action in online dating. Again we see a possible split in selves here. The search for a stable long-term partner may have us put down certain characteristics like honesty and dependability in a desired partner, but we may then ignore these characteristics in a posting when we see a photo of an attractive individual.

If that is the case, what types of profile photos are effective? Fifty-six percent of women choose to post a straightforward picture of themselves smiling. However, the 9 percent that opt for a more flirtatious pose are slightly more successful (Rudder, 2015). Men on the other hand tend to be more successful when they are looking away from the camera and not smiling. For women the most effective photo angle is shot down from a high angle with a slightly coy look. Second most effective is in bed, followed by outdoor and travel photos. Least effective for women are drinking alcohol or posing with an animal. But with men the most effective photos are with animals, followed by showing off muscles, then engaged in an interesting activity. Least effective for men are drinking, travel, and outdoor photos.

Are algorithms effective at finding us a perfect partner? We would think that given enough information about couples and their success rates the answer would be yes. The problem is, only superficial information is available online. Finkel, Eastwick, Karney, Reis, and Sprecher (2012) found that because the information provided in a profile, such as occupation, income, and religion, is the only information viewers have to go on, it is overvalued. Viewers then make bad choices regarding preference. It might be best to get to know the person in a real-life setting and then base a judgment on that experience. The anthropologist Helen Fisher recommends spending less time doing the online part of dating and more time doing the actual dating part (Fisher, 2005). Women's concerns about safety may extend the amount of time they spend on electronic exchanges. With regard to the self, it appears that either we are limited in the amount of information we are allowed to put on dating sites, or we deliberately restrict this information for fear of revealing too much of ourselves. This digital withholding may actually be working against us.

This is definitely the case for swipe apps like Tinder that provide a facial photograph and minimal information. If users are interested in someone, they swipe to the right. If they are not, they swipe left. Two people who like each other can then begin private messaging. The advantages are mutual attraction, convenience, speed, and not having to review extensive profiles. Although dating swipe apps are increasing in popularity, their major downside is that they rely too much on attractiveness. They historically have been places for "hookups," but that may be changing. Unfortunately, the wide variety of possible choices and the search for the best possible partner in dating apps may keep people looking forever for that ideal "other self" and never finding one that is simply good.

Personality and Online Self-Presentation

People differ in the way they present and manage themselves online. Some give accurate portrayals, while others may provide more inflated or positive portrayals. *Impression management* can be defined as the process of controlling the impressions that others have of us (Chester & Bretherton, 2007). It can be considered synonymous with the term *self-presentation*. This must be considered separate from *impression formation*, which refers to how others actually perceive us. So, for example, Susan *manages* her online impression by posting attractive photos of herself. In so doing she makes Fred, a potential suitor, have a more favorable *impression* of her. Managing is the work we do to present ourselves. Impressions are the result of that, being what other people think of us.

The ways we present online can be very different from the ways we present offline. In real life we send many social cues, consciously or subconsciously, to others. These include hairstyle, makeup, nonverbal communication (like eye contact), what we say (knowledge), and how we say it (intonation). Although these cues are available in videoconferencing, for example when we are using applications like Skype, most online communication is currently conducted by typing in text and posting photos. Online presentation, however, offers increased potential for anonymity. We can hide aspects of ourselves while promoting more positive ones or can pretend to be someone else entirely.

Positive self-presentation has many benefits, including popularity, friendship, romantic companionship, and job opportunities. For this reason, most of us spend considerable time evaluating how others perceive us and behaving in ways that will lead others to treat us well (Leary & Allen, 2011). We can differentiate between the motivation to make an impression and the actual construction of one. If we were to give a public talk or lecture, we most likely would be highly motivated to present a positive view of ourselves. This would cause us to construct this image by doing things like dressing nicely and speaking clearly.

There is also a difference between assertive and defensive self-presentation (Lee, Quigley, Nesler, Corbett, & Tedeschi, 1999). An assertive self-presentation consists of proactive actions toward presenting one's characteristics. It can include ingratiation, intimidation, or supplication. Defensive self-presentation is the repair or restoration of a damaged impression and can include actions like justifications, apologies, and excuses. Lee et al. found that socially anxious people and those with an external locus of control (those who believe that outside forces are responsible for their actions) were more likely to use defensive procedures. Sadler, Hunger, and Miller (2010) found that individuals with high levels of negative emotionality used more self-presentation tactics. This research suggests that anxious and less socially skilled individuals are more concerned about what other people think and are therefore more scared of presenting themselves in a poor light.

Personality and Identity Management Online

Self-Esteem and Depression Self-esteem is a person's general evaluation of his or her own self-worth. What we think of ourselves, of course, is highly related to what others think of us. We can evaluate ourselves as worse than others in what is called upward social comparison. This can lead to negative self-regard or lowered self-esteem (Tesser, Millar, & Moore, 1988). We can also evaluate ourselves as better than others. This is known as downward social comparison and can produce positive self-regard, or elevated self-esteem (Gibbons, 1986). Online activity can lead to either outcome. The internet can also be used as social compensation, boosting someone who is lacking in some way. It can additionally be used as social enhancement, boosting someone who is already benefiting from online exposure (Zywica & Danowski, 2008). Again, online activity can support either process.

Steers, Wickham, and Acitelli (2014) asked their participants about Facebook usage and their social comparisons. They were also asked about depressive symptoms. The results showed that those with greater Facebook usage tended to have more depressive symptoms, perhaps because of increased upward comparisons. Sampasa-Kanyinga and Lewis (2015) looked at time spent on SNSs and several outcomes including thoughts about suicide, psychological distress, self-rated mental health, and actual mental health support. The sample was Canadian middle school– and high school–aged children. They found that children in grades 7–12 who used SNSs for more than two hours a day were more likely to suffer poor mental health, distress, and suicidal ideation.

Individuals low in self-esteem have a preference for email over face-to-face talking when there is a perceived risk, for example when asking for a raise (Joinson, 2004). The reason may be that they can better control the electronic exchange in terms of careful wording. Zywica and Danowski (2008) found that low self-esteem Facebook users were more likely to share aspects of themselves with their online friends, reveal more about themselves online, and exaggerate or even fabricate information about themselves in order to make themselves appear more popular. High-self-esteem individuals have been found to use more words when describing themselves on MySpace. In addition, they put more pictures and animations of celebrities into their profile (Banczyk, Kramer, & Senokozlieva, 2008). These studies show that both groups of individuals, low and high self-esteem, use social media sites to enhance their reputations but that they do so in different ways.

The Five-Factor Model (FFM) We described the FFM in chapter 3, and the reader may want to refer back to it now as a refresher. In this section we will describe research relating personality traits from the FFM to online behavior. Introversion-extroversion is one of the Big Five trait continua. Introverts have been found to have more detailed Facebook profiles (Amichai-Hamburger & Vinitzky, 2010). This may be because they are compensating for a lack of social skills in the offline world and also are working harder to promote themselves online. Introverted adolescents have been found to experiment with a greater variety of identities online, such as flirting or acting as if they were older (Valkenburg, Schouten, & Peter, 2005). Rather than being deceitful, this could indicate that they are compensating for their lack of being able to express themselves.

Agreeableness is another one of the FFM traits. Bloggers high in agreeableness are attracted to blogging because they can express specific aspects of their identity (Fullwood, Nicolis, & Makichi, 2015). They seem to be expressing themselves in favorable ways as a form of social enhancement. Bloggers also tend to score high on openness. This seems to be a need for self-expression that they can exhibit by showing how intelligent, witty, and creative they are. Individuals who score low in conscientiousness are less likely to worry about the future consequences of their actions. Perhaps this can explain why they are more likely to misrepresent themselves online (Hall, Park, Song, & Cody, 2010).

Narcissism We also described narcissism and narcissistic personality disorder in chapter 3, and readers can refer back to that if needed. Narcissists favor social media sites. They spend more time on Facebook and more actively self-promote themselves (Mehdizadeh, 2010). They pose for more photos and use photo-editing software to make themselves look better. They post status updates more regularly and include more self-promoting information and quotes. This is not surprising, as these individuals like to boast about their accomplishments, need to engage with others in a more extended or deeper way, and have a greater need for admiration. How do other people perceive these profiles? They rate them more highly in terms of confidence, status, and enthusiasm but lower in terms of cooperation, friendliness, kindness, and likability.

Identity Formation Online Cover (2016) makes the point that identities are heavily influenced by our online behavior. By *identity* he refers to our identification with particular categories like gender, race, ethnicity, sexuality, nationality, socioeconomic background, and educational experience. He adopts the "constructionist" approach, which sees identity as formed by cultural and social forces. This view sees the individual as a passive receptor or empty vessel that is filled up with online content and that can change over time. In contrast to this is the "essentialist" view, in which identities are innate, emerge from the inside, and are fixed over time. This division roughly parallels the division between modernist and postmodernist conceptions of the individual. It also reflects "nature" versus "nurture" approaches to personality in psychology.

The constructionist approach is based on the work of philosopher Michel Foucault (1998) and that of gender theorist Judith Butler (1990, 1993). Butler sees identity as "performative," meaning that we construct our identities by our behavior. To Cover, performative behavior online is designing and maintaining a social-networking profile, blogging, taking and posting selfies, and so on. He gives as an example a man who takes a selfie image with sporting equipment in the background and posts it to a social networking site like Twitter. This will reinforce a Western gender stereotype of masculinity as equated with attributes like enjoying and being good at sports. This is, according to Cover, a quick and easy way of broadcasting to the world an aspect of one's identity. However, in the act of doing so, the man is also constructing his identity. The performance of a digital act does more than just tell others about ourselves; it helps construct who we are.

Identities are also shaped by how other people respond to our online behavior. A post to Facebook is responded to by others in the form of "likes," replies, comments, and tags from friends, family, and colleagues. In this way, our choices of what to post are reinforced or punished. On the basis of such feedback we may decide to adopt or explore certain aspects of our self or to give up on others. These responses of tagging and reposting, for example, are beyond our control.

Studies have looked at how online use influences identity formation. The results of these studies are mixed. Some find a positive correlation between SNS use and self-identity. Others find negative correlations or the absence of a correlation (Matsuba, 2006). This may be based on the type of feedback users receive (Chai & Gong, 2011). Exposure to thin-ideal media online is negatively correlated with body satisfaction and may contribute to restrained eating and unhealthy weight control behavior (F. Chang et al., 2013).

Such online identity creation, at least in modern, information-age economies, is reinforced by our near-constant online actions. Ten or so years ago, before the creation of the smartphone and mobile internet-enabled devices, we could say that we had an "offline self" separate from our "online self." This was because we accessed the internet mainly through desktop computers in our homes and offices and were without connectivity throughout much of the rest of our lives. Now, however, scarcely a moment goes by when we aren't checking email, playing a game, or accessing social media. This ubiquity helps reinforce identity formation because it is constant and unrelenting.

Cover (2016) and many of the other postmodernists in fields like feminist studies and literary theory, however, rely too much on the cultural environment as a formative aspect of identity. Research in psychology shows that much of our personality is genetically influenced and that the bias toward a "tabula rasa" model of human behavior may be politically motivated (Pinker, 2003). For example, intelligence as measured by IQ scores is highly correlated with genetic relatedness (T. Bouchard & McGue, 1981). In fact, the influence of heredity on intelligence increases with age from 41 percent in childhood to 66 percent in adulthood (Haworth et al., 2009). The conclusion we can reach, based on the scientific literature, is that identity is a consequence of both innate and environmental factors and that the two probably interact in complex ways.

What does this mean for online identity? It means that individuals come to a device with preexisting interests and proclivities. These affect what a person seeks out online. A man may like sports because he has good eye-hand coordination or visual acuity, traits that may be under genetic or epigenetic control. These may then lead him to play baseball as a child. They will then lead him to seek out and broadcast baseball-related content online, which, if it is received positively, can further reinforce his identification with sports and with a Western-style version of masculinity.

Internet Use and Self-Related Measures

As we have previously indicated, the term *self* in psychology can stand for many things. Here we draw the distinction between two self-components: content and structure (Campbell, Assanand, & Paula, 2003). *Content* refers to a person's conception of who he or she is. This in turn has been broken down into two subcomponents. First are domain-specific aspects: such things such as the physical self and social self-efficacy. Second is the evaluative subcomponent: the feelings one has about one's self, usually denoted as self-esteem. The *structure* component is the organization and ordering of the domain-specific self-beliefs and views and is called self-concept clarity.

Self-presentation and belongingness both motivate the use of SNSs (Nadkarni & Hofmann, 2012). Self-presentation can be of two types: honest and positive. Honest self-presenters provide the truth about themselves, whether it is positive or negative. Positive self-presenters present only positive aspects of themselves. J. Kim and Lee (2011) found that positive self-presentation online had a direct effect on life satisfaction. In a separate study, Gonzales and Hancock (2011) found that participants who updated their profiles and viewed their own profiles during the experiment reported greater self-esteem. W. Chen, Fan, Liu, Zhou, and Xie (2016) found that passive SNS use (just viewing but not posting) was harmful to users' self-esteem.

Self-efficacy is a subjective evaluation of and faith in an individual's sociability that guides his or her behavior during interpersonal activities (Fan & Mak, 1998). Psychological needs satisfied by online interactions can promote a person's social self-efficacy and subjective well-being. Female Chinese college students get less social self-efficacy from the satisfaction of psychological needs through online communication than males do (C. Li, Shi, & Dang, 2014).

Self-concept clarity is defined as the extent to which one's self-concept is clearly defined and confidently believed in, internally and consistently over time (Campbell et al., 1996). It has been found to predict psychological well-being and adjustment (Steffgen, Silva, & Recchia, 2007). SNS use could either enhance or detract from self-concept clarity. It could be enhanced if SNS use allowed for experimentation and validation of different aspects of the self. However, Valkenburg and Peter (2011) have proposed the self-concept fragmentation hypothesis. According to this, the ease with which possible identities can be formed online may fragment adolescents' personalities and undermine a central ego's ability to coordinate the different facets into a unified whole. This hypothesis seems to have received at least some support. Niu, Sun, Zhou, Tian, et al. (2016) found that SNS use was negatively correlated with self-concept clarity.

Self-construal is an individual's awareness of the relationship between the self and the surrounding environment (Markus & Kitayama, 1991). People with interdependent self-construal tend to accept group norms and attach importance to others' opinions. Those with independent self-construal accept individualistic cultural values and place an emphasis on inner thoughts and feelings. They tend to portray themselves in terms of their inner characteristics and goals. C. Chang (2015) found that interdependent self-construal was positively associated with social interaction orientation such as responsiveness and self-disclosure. This in turn positively predicted Facebook activities like responding to others and revealing oneself on Facebook.

People tend to self-disclose quite readily on SNSs. In part this is because the sites are set up to encourage the revelation of personal information. They have fields that prompt one to write about current happenings. It is also quite easy to upload photos of oneself and to share these with friends. Tamir and Mitchell (2012) found that 80 percent of posts to SNSs were self-disclosures about the user's own immediate circumstances. The authors' brain-imaging data showed increased activation in the dopamine reward system, specifically in the nucleus accumbens and the ventral tegmental area, in response to SNS self-disclosure. It should be mentioned, however, that other research doesn't always show activation of the brain's reward system in response to receiving positive feedback through social media.

Bad and Good Internet Behavior

Being Bad: Cyberbullying Cyberbullying refers to aggressive intentional acts executed by an individual or group using an electronic form of contact repeatedly over time against a victim that cannot defend him- or herself (Smith et al., 2008). Media such as email, chat rooms, websites, and text messaging can be used to harass, abuse or exclude others. Given the nature of SNSs that make it easy to comment, like, and retweet, it is often possible for others to join in and create a snowball effect that can exacerbate the issue. Modecki,

Minchin, Harbaugh, Guerra, and Runions (2014) performed a meta-analysis of studies and found that the average prevalence rate for cyber- and traditional bullying among adolescents was 15 percent. Another study of Chinese high school students in central China found even higher prevalence rates: 35 percent of those participants reported having bullied someone, and 57 percent reported having been bullied online (Zhou et al., 2013).

In that same study it was found that boys were more likely to be cyberbullying instigators and victims. Students with lower academic achievement were more likely to be perpetrators, as were students who spent more time on the internet and who were more involved in Instant Messaging and other forms of online entertainment. He, Fan, Niu, Lian, and Chen (2016) found that both parental rejection and overprotection positively correlated with cyberbullying, while parental emotional warmth was negatively correlated with it.

Being Good: Altruistic Behavior Online Online altruistic behavior is the opposite of cyberbullying. It is a form of prosocial behavior that is voluntary and has the goal of increasing someone else's welfare (Batson & Shaw, 1991). Many people engage in this type of behavior without expecting anything in return. Amichai-Hamburger (2008) stated that the internet may help induce altruistic actions. Its anonymity makes it easier for people to ask for help without feeling ashamed. It may also make people feel less inhibited by others' opinions.

Mengel (2014) found that people who spend more time playing computer games display more prosocial behavior. This seems to run counter to the prevailing cultural notion that video games make people more aggressive. Zheng and Gu (2012) found that certain personality traits, including some from the "Big Five" or FFM were positively associated with internet altruistic behavior. These were conscientiousness, openness, and self-esteem. Another FFM trait, neuroticism, was negatively associated with internet altruistic behavior. In another study, higher levels of optimism were positively related to online social support (Zheng, 2012).

Cognition and Internet Usage

Cognitive Advantages of Internet Usage There are some cognitive advantages to Internet usage. G. Johnson and Johnson (2008) tested participants who were heavy and light users of the internet. They found that the heavy users scored higher on measures of visual intelligence, presumably because the visual layout of web pages forces one to think in terms of visual relationships. In another study, students who engaged in social monitoring (reading updates or sharing links) on sites like Facebook had higher GPAs than those who were actively posting (Instant Messaging and posting updates) to such sites (Junco, 2012). They suggest that the latter type of activity was interfering more with actual studying. Other work shows that frequent Facebook users spent less time studying and were perhaps procrastinating with their time spent online (Kirschner & Karpinski, 2010).

Alloway, Horton, Alloway, and Dawson (2013) found that those who used Facebook for one year scored significantly higher on several cognitive measures compared to those who used it infrequently. These measures were verbal ability, spelling, and working memory. They suggest that the cognitive operations involved in Facebook usage use are similar. When using a site like Facebook, one must access, process, and reason about a large amount of information. One must also determine the relevance of this information for one's current goals and make other types of decisions. These types of thinking are associated with working memory function along with aspects of verbal coding and visual attention. The regular reading of posts and commenting could account for the higher scores on spelling and verbal ability. In contrast, in this study there was no difference between the two groups on tests of mathematical ability.

Internet Search and Memory If several decades ago we were interested in learning some fact, we had a laborious task ahead of us that might mean going to the local library to do some research. Now, with the advent of Google and other internet search engines, a vast sum of human knowledge is only a few keystrokes away. Some have referred to this "outsourcing" of our memory into the environment more generally as transactive memory (Sparrow, Liu, & Wegner, 2011). Prior to the internet aspects of our memories were still in the environment, but in the minds of other people, what might be called social memory. If we needed to learn something, we could turn to someone who might have the information and ask him or her. Alternatively we could use our own recall to try and remember something we had previously learned. Nowadays, we seem to be remembering not facts to recall but knowledge of where to go (on the internet) to get those facts. One downside to this is that if we are out of reach of electronic communications we are effectively cut off from the information.

Internet searching, like social media use, is also rewarding. Imagine that you are searching for tickets to your favorite rock concert. You look at the usual online sites for an hour but find nothing. Then you stumble upon a little-known online music store and find two seats to the show, one for you and your girlfriend. In this scenario the act of searching was rewarded at the end (and perhaps part of the way through when thinking that you might have located the tickets), so the behavior is more likely to occur in the future.

From an evolutionary standpoint our brains have evolved to seek our environments for information that will help us to survive by obtaining food, water, or shelter. Once we have located these resources we get a "squirt" of dopamine that feels good. This feeling will then motivate us to continue searching (Parsons, 2017).

Biologically, this rewarding process is reflected by activity in the cortico-striato-thalamo-cortical loop. The ventral tegmental area (VTA) and the nucleus accumbens are both activated under these circumstances and play an important role in the brain's processing of reward, pleasure, motivation, and reinforcement learning. These structures contain dopaminergic neurons, and neural activity in these areas is similar to that seen when a person is taking opiates and amphetamines (figure 33).

Small, Moody, Siddarth, and Bookheimer (2009) wanted to know whether internet search activated other brain areas in addition to those normally active during reading. They

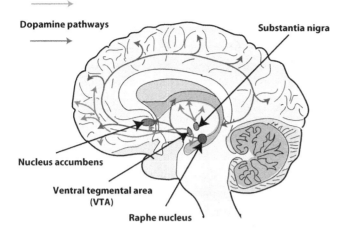

Serotonin pathways

Dopamine pathways

Substantia nigra

Nucleus accumbens

**Ventral tegmental area
(VTA)**

Raphe nucleus

FIGURE 33 The brain's dopamine reward network gets activated when we receive Facebook "likes" to a posted photo. It also gets activated when we search for and locate rewarding information on the Internet.

tested people who did and did not have experience using the internet. Both groups in the reading-only condition showed similar activity in their brains. Areas that normally "light up" during reading were found across participants. In the internet search condition the non-experienced participants also showed activation patterns that were no different from normal reading, but the internet-experienced group showed new areas of brain activity that included the hippocampus, the frontal pole, the cingulate cortex, and the right anterior temporal cortex. What this shows is that internet searching is more than just passive reading. It requires greater cognitive engagement and calls on brain areas that are used when integrating semantic information, using working memory, and making decisions. How much internet experience does it take to activate such regions? Small and Vorgan (2008) tested Internet novices who spent an hour a day online for six days and compared their brain activity to that of a more Internet-savvy group. This time the activation in both groups was nearly identical, particularly in the dorsolateral prefrontal cortex.

Reading Reading on the internet involves the use of hyperlinks, text that when clicked on takes the user to another web page. Carr (2010) suggests that the use of hyperlinks may encourage readers to move away from the point of initial interest and get distracted by less relevant information (hence the term *surfing*, which implies riding a wave without being able to have much control over where one is going). The result is that we may lose the global structure of the information we are trying to learn, so that we don't see how different but related pieces of information link together.

The constant stream of information coming in from the internet while reading may overwhelm our capacity to relate it together. A schema is a structure or template that allow us to "connect the dots" and see how information about a topic is related. For example, most of us have a schema for a restaurant that specifies the order of events that occur while we are there. These include sitting down, ordering, eating, and paying. But if too much information is coming in to working memory at once, we may not be able to get it into long-term memory where the schemas are located. The result could be recollection of a disparate group of facts and a failure to understand or remember what we are reading.

Attention-Related Phenomena Another aspect of cognitive processing in addition to memory and reading is attention. Attention is important because it allows us to attend to what is important and ignore distractions that could lead us away from the task at hand. Carr (2010) found a preference among internet users to want information to be presented more quickly. This implies a refusal to engage with material for an extended time, which is needed if we wish to gain a deeper understanding of something. Stone (2009) called this continuous partial attention (CPA), a state of being engaged in multiple activities but never fully developing a full focus on any one of them. A constant state of vigilance like this has several downsides, including stress and poor decision-making. Prolonged CPA could produce "techno-brain burnout," a decay in cognitive abilities (Small & Vorgan, 2008).

Heavy media multitaskers (MMTs) do indeed seem to suffer from an inability to filter out irrelevant information at both a perceptual and a memory level (Aston-Jones & Cohen, 2005). On the basis of this study they also have a harder time preventing a switch from relevant to irrelevant tasks. Multiple streams of information more easily distracted the heavy MMTs in this work. Those in the lighter MMT group seemed better able to ignore these and to focus on task-relevant information.

Two common phenomena in the study of attention are change blindness and inattentional blindness. The first is an inability to notice some alteration between two scenes that are shown in alternation. The second is the inability to notice a change in a single scene that unfolds over time. Durlach (2004) found that participants failed to notice a change in a series of task-relevant icons presented on the computer screen at the same time another task window was closed and opened. Steffner and Schenkman (2012) presented a similar task to their study participants. They found that changes occurring to a virtual person on a webpage were less easily noticed than those made to a nonperson. They also found that objects located on the left side of the computer screen were more difficult to detect than those on the right. Material on the right hand of the screen is more likely to interfere with text comprehension, probably because the right-hand side receives more direct attentional focus (Simola, Kuisma, Oörni, Uusitalo, & Hyönä, 2011). All of these results point out that effects of change blindness can occur in the context of reading web-based content.

Benway (1999) had people look at a webpage containing a banner with critical information on it. He found that users could navigate their way through the webpage successfully but were unable to actually read the content in the banner, what he called banner blindness. This and other studies like it show that inattentional blindness also occurs for reading of web content.

We tend to overestimate our ability to take in and process visual information from displays, what has been dubbed illusions of visual bandwidth (Varakin, Levin, & Fidler, 2004).

It turns out that there is a big difference between what is presented to us and what we actually process in a meaningful way. The research on change and attentional blindness cited above shows that we are very likely to miss something if that information is located in an area we do not expect or if there distracting information is present, as is often the case when one is doing computer work (e.g., email notifications, pop-up ads). Unfortunately, many distractions are currently part of normal computer or technology usage. These can include cluttered screens, icons with no task relevance, slowly loading webpages, and more.

Interruptions like these reduce work efficiency. Mark, Gudith, and Klocke (2008) showed that people who are interrupted sometimes compensate by increasing the rate at which they work. This can result in increased frustration, stress, feelings of time pressure, and so on. It is well known that there is a speed-accuracy trade-off. The faster we do things, the more errors we make. Ou and Davison (2011) measured distraction in the face of Instant Messaging (IM). They found that IM did predict interruptions of work tasks but that it actually helped aspects of teamwork. It increased perceived level of social interaction in the workplace and helped develop mutual trust and quality of communication between group members.

VIDEO GAMES

Video games are perhaps the most popular activity engaged in when people have free time. In one survey 42 percent of Americans said they play such games at least three hours per week (Ipsos MediaCT, 2015). The Entertainment Software Association (2010) found that 72 percent of the general population and 97 percent of teenagers aged twelve to seventeen years of age played video games on a consistent basis. The term *video game* refers to a wide range of games from first-person shooter to logic puzzles. Table 12 shows all of the different game types along with representative examples. Video games can be played on many devices, from console games with controllers connected to a TV screen to the now more popular smartphone games like Bejeweled and Candy Crush Saga (figure 34). They can be played individually or in groups, competing against a computer or against larger groups of people from around the world.

Video Gaming and Self-Related Phenomena

Video games have often been blamed in the news for violence. However, in recent years a number of researchers have been investigating the positive side of gaming (Gackenbach, Wijeyaratnam, & Flockhart, 2017). As a result there has been some improvement in societal opinions regarding the subject. Video games used to be played by a smaller segment of society, in part because of higher costs when they first came out. But with the advent of games on affordable mobile devices this has changed. Games are now being used in fields like education, business, medicine, and even politics to improve human health and well-being.

Ferguson (2013) has shown there are several problems with the research linking video game play to aggression. Some of the effects have been explained using a third variable.

TABLE 12   The twelve different types of video games

	Type	Description	Example (Representative Version)
1.	Massively multiplayer online (MMO)	Played over a local area network (LAN) or over the internet; players interact with other players in a virtual space.	*World of Warcraft* (2004), *EverQuest* (1999)
2.	Simulations	Involve control of real-world vehicles like airplanes, ships, and tanks. In some cases these are used to train professionals on how to operate actual vehicles. Also involve the simulation of an evolving world.	*Microsoft Flight Simulator* (2006), *SimEarth* (1990), *SimLife* (1992), *SimCity* (1989)
3.	Adventure	Usually single-player games that are set in fantasy or adventure worlds. Puzzles must be completed to advance to higher levels. Users must determine how to complete a mission.	*Myst* (1993), *The Secret of Monkey Island* (1990)
4.	Real-time strategy (RTS)	Require the buildup of an inventory of items, armies, or other resources. They move in real time and players need not take turns.	*Age of Empires* (1997), *Homeworld* (1999)
5.	Puzzle	Brain games that involve intellect more than perceptual-motor skills. Many levels from beginner to expert. Usually have colored shapes and simple actions.	*Tetris* (1984), *Bejeweled* (2001)
6.	Action	Require fast reflexes. Challenges are completed by fighting with enemies and using a chosen character.	*Pac-Man* (1980), *Doom* (1993), *Evolve* (2015)
7.	Stealth shooter	War or spy games where stealth is used to defeat enemies.	*Metal Gear Solid* (1998), *Dishonored* (2012), *Hitman* (2016)
8.	Combat	Fighting is one on one with opponents. Requires the ability to use the controls for different types of fighting moves.	*Mortal Kombat* (1992), *Street Fighter IV* (2008)
9.	First-person shooter (FPS)	Played in first-person perspective and involve shooting enemies.	*Half-Life* (1998), *Quake* (1996), *Call of Duty IV* (2007)
10.	Sports	Involve playing real-world sports like baseball, football, or soccer. Characters mimic the movement of real professional athletes.	*Pong* (1972), *Wii Sports* (2006)
11.	Role-playing (RPG)	Users control a character to achieve goals or explore an immersive, usually fantasy or sci-fi world.	*Fallout 3* (2008), *Deus Ex* (2000)
12.	Educational	Help users learn various skills or knowledge. The goal is to make learning fun. Typically involve testing functions like multiple-choice questions.	*The Oregon Trail* (1971), *Where in the World Is Carmen Sandiego?* (1985)

Source: Thoughtcatalog.com.
Note: It is possible for a game to correspond to more than one category.

FIGURE 34 Mobile smartphone games like Candy Crush Saga are currently popular.

Other social factors have been found to account for the majority of the power in the predictive models. These include having a sensation-seeking personality, lower levels of parental attachment, and less parental monitoring. These have all been shown to be relatively strong predictors of violent behavior and weapon carrying. When video game play is added back into the prediction equations it does not contribute anything significant. The conclusion is that gaming by itself does not predict aggressive behavior.

A study by Jansz (2005) also runs counter to the idea that video games cause violence. This research shows that adolescent males feel in control while gaming, suggesting they are in control of the emotions they experience while playing. This freedom to control is important because it can allow these males to construct their own identity at their own pace. The violent video game thus constitutes a "safe haven" or lab where they can experience different or controversial emotions without fear of being judged by peers.

However, addiction to gaming can be a serious problem. Although the fifth edition of the *Diagnostic and Statistical Manual* (DSM-V) doesn't list "internet gaming disorder" as an official psychological disorder, it does classify it as a condition warranting further study (Sarkis, 2014). This condition is thought to be prevalent among males aged twelve to twenty years of age. In order to be diagnosed with this condition, an individual would need to meet one of

TABLE 13   Criteria for internet gaming disorder (an individual must meet at least one)

	Criteria for Classification
1.	Preoccupation or obsession with internet gaming.
2.	Withdrawal symptoms when not playing internet games.
3.	A buildup of tolerance (more time needs to be spent playing the games).
4.	The person has tried to stop or curb playing internet games, but has failed to do so.
5.	The person has had a loss of interest in other life activities or hobbies.
6.	The person has had continued overuse of internet games even with the knowledge of how much they affect his or her life.
7.	The person lies to others about his or her internet game usage.
8.	The person uses internet games to relieve anxiety or guilt.
9.	The person has lost or put at risk an opportunity or a relationship because of internet games.

Source: After Sarkis (2014).

the five criteria listed in table 13. It is clear that moderation in gaming and a balance of other activities ought to be encouraged if one is to remain physically and mentally healthy.

Action video games are fast-paced and place a load on perceptual and cognitive processing mechanisms (Preston, 2017). In particular, they call upon divided attention, peripheral processing, information filtering, and motor control. Decision-making is also required in many games, as is the attainment of higher-order goals through the achievement of nested subgoals (Cardoso-Leite et al., 2016). Players in such games must monitor multiple objects and events, determine their relevance, and plan and execute strategies. All of this suggests that gamers may have improved skills in these component areas, and this indeed turns out to be the case.

Strobach and Schubert (2015) trained two groups of nongamers, both of whom were tested subsequently in a dual task where they had to exercise divided attention. One group was trained using a puzzle. The other group was trained using an action game. The group trained on the game performed better on the dual task. In another study comparing gamers to nongamers, the gamers performed better on executive function, on simultaneous task execution in dual-task situations, and on ability to continuously update information. Bavelier, Achtman, Mani, and Focker (2012) measured brain activity using fMRI in gamers and nongamers while they performed a challenging pattern-detection task. The gamers were better able to allocate their attentional resources and to filter out irrelevant information.

Absorption is described as presence, immersion, engagement, or involvement and can be equated with the trait of openness to experience from the FFM of personality (Hunt, 1995). A person high in openness is better able to take in emotional and cognitive changes across situations. Individuals high and low in absorption/openness differ in hypnotizability, experience of altered states, creativity, and sensitivity to aesthetics and metaphor. In addition, high absorbers do better on tasks that demand rapid reallocation of attention. Since this is a task essential for action video games, we might expect people high in absorption to do better at these games. Preston and Cull (1998) exposed high and low absorbers to a visual distraction before and after performing a balance task. Low absorbers did better before viewing the visual distraction, suggesting they were not able to suppress it. High absorbers did better after the distraction and could apparently do a better job of inhibiting the distraction. This ability to suppress irrelevant information is a key aspect of performance in video games.

Jones, Scholes, Johnson, Katsikitis, and Carras (2014) have data to suggest that video games can improve mental health. Their review shows that low or moderate levels of video game play can have a positive influence on well-being. It has been shown to improve mood, reduce emotional anxiety, improve emotional regulation, increase feelings of relaxation, and reduce stress. Moderate play was found to produce better health outcomes than either excessive video game play or no play at all. Video game play was also associated with greater self-regard toward one's intelligence, computer skills, and mechanical ability. Feelings of competence, autonomy, and relatedness during video game play have been linked with higher self-esteem.

Video game play has also been found to be effective in a number of health-based interventions. Active video games that require players to move their arms, legs, and body can be used to combat the effects of physical inactivity that occur for other types of games (L. Barnett, Bangay, McKenzie, & Ridgers, 2013). Specific games have been developed also to treat disorders like attention deficit hyperactive disorder (ADHD), autism spectrum disorder (ASD), and childhood sexual abuse (Bono et al., 2016; Rivero, Nunez, Pires, & Francisco, 2015; Stieler-Hunt, Jones, Rolfe, & Pozzebon, 2014). They have also been recognized as an excellent training platform for blind adolescents to learn various skills like navigation and spatial cognition (Connors, Chrastil, Sanchez, & Merabet, 2014).

Gackenbach, Wijeyaratnam, and Flockhart (2017) have explored the connections between nighttime dreams and video game play. Dreams have been found to be important for a number of psychological reasons, including information processing, memory consolidation, emotional regulation, and creativity. Their lab found an association between gaming and lucid dreams (those that one can be aware of and control). Participants who played video games during the day, especially combat games, were better able to fight back at night in their dreams, for example when being chased by a monster.

Video Games and Cognitive Processing

In one of the earliest study of video games, Goldstein et al. (1997) looked at individuals who had extensive experience playing the game Tetris. Tetris is a game that involves rotating and moving geometric shapes as they fall from the top of the screen. The shapes must be fitted into spaces at the bottom of the screen in much the same way puzzle pieces are locked together. As a result this task calls on visual cognitive skills like mental rotation. In the study, the older adults who played Super Tetris for twenty-five hours were compared to a sample of nongamers. The more experienced group showed improved performance on the Sternberg reaction time task. This task requires holding a group of letters or digits in working memory and then deciding whether a target item is part of that group. The task can be solved by forming a visual image of the item set and then scanning along it from beginning to end to perform a match with the target item.

Action video games are those that have fast motion and require simultaneous tracking of multiple target items. They can be 2-D or 3-D and usually require that the player rapidly alternate between a localized focal attention and a more global and diffuse attentional set (Green & Bavelier, 2015). Vigilance to the periphery of the visual field is also usually required. Many researchers are currently studying video games and their cognitive effects (Cain, Landau, & Shimamura, 2012). The overwhelming result of these studies is that video game play enhances perceptual and cognitive processing. Improvements have been documented for contrast sensitivity, the ability to perceive edges or changes in lightness (R. Li, Polat, Makous, & Bavelier, 2009); crowding acuity, the ability to see small details where items are packed close together (Green & Bavelier, 2007); and visual masking, the ability to recognize briefly presented visual stimuli (R. Li, Polat, Scalzo, & Bavelier, 2010). So yes, as counterintuitive as it may sound, playing video games can actually improve your eyesight.

The ability to think or cognate also benefits from video game play. Findings in this area include an increased ability to simultaneously attend to multiple stimuli (J. Cohen, Green, & Bavelier, 2008) and a reduced attentional blink, the capacity to recover allocated visual attention quickly (Green & Bavelier, 2006). Video games have also been found to enhance executive control. This would include things like working memory, attentional capture, and task switching (Chisholm & Kingstone, 2012; Colzato, Van Leeuwen, Van Den Wildenberg, & Hommel, 2010). In addition, video game play improves recall of visually presented information and reduces perceptual reaction time (Blacker & Curby, 2013; Maillot, Perrot, & Hartley, 2012).

These sorts of changes leave a mark on the brain. Kühn, Gleich, Lorenz, Lindenberger, and Gallinat (2014) and other researchers have found increased thickness in the frontal cortical areas and increased gray matter volume in the frontal eye field and the dorsolateral prefrontal cortex. Other changes include increased gray matter volume in the insula (Gong et al., 2015), the dorsal striatum (Erickson et al., 2010), the entorhinal area and hippocampal gyrus and the occipital lobe (Kühn & Gallinat, 2014), and the right posterior parietal region. These brain areas span a wide range of functions in the areas of attention, memory, and visual perception.

Video Games and Reward

As you might suspect, video game play can be very rewarding, and it has been found to produce dopamine release in the brain's pleasure networks (Koepp et al., 1998). Hoeft, Watson, Kesler, Bettinger, and Reiss (2008) performed fMRI imaging in participants who played video games and found activation in areas associated with reward and addiction: the nucleus accumbens and orbitofrontal cortex. Kätsyri, Hari, Ravaja, and Nummenmaa (2013) did brain imaging on players of a competitive tank shooter game. Winning caused increased activation in the brain's reward circuit. Stronger activations occurred for wins against a human opponent compared to a computer opponent. There was a correlation between self-ratings of pleasure and activation in the ventral striatum.

Game Transfer Phenomena

Game transfer phenomena (GTP) occur when temporary visual, auditory, or kinesthetic sensations occur after playing video games. It manifests as hallucinatory-like experiences, such as seeing or hearing elements from the game after playing. Patients know that these aren't real but find themselves responding as if they were. Ortiz de Gortari and Griffiths (2017) have documented the effects in a large sample of participants who report altered sensorial perceptions, spontaneous thoughts, actions, and behaviors.

Those with severe levels of GTP were more likely to be students, be aged eighteen to twenty-two years, play video games every day in sessions of six hours or more, play games to escape from the real world, and have a mental or sleep disorder (Ortiz de Gortari, Oldfield, & Griffiths, 2016). GTP has been reported in a wide variety of over four hundred unique video games. Among the most popular are massively multiplayer online role-playing games (MMORGs), simulation games, and fighting games (Ortiz de Gortari, Oldfield, & Griffiths, 2016).

A more specific list of symptoms includes altered visual perceptions such as afterimages of prolonged duration, altered auditory perceptions such as hearing recurrent replays of in-game music, body-related perceptions that include tactile hallucinations related to the haptic feedback of the gamepads, automatic mental processes like thoughts, urges, and/or behaviors that include thinking about in-game elements like health bars, bionic arms, or a hook, and automatic behaviors such as driving, searching, jumping, or climbing buildings (Ortiz de Gortari & Griffiths, 2017).

Ortiz de Gortari and Griffiths (2017) have documented the structural aspects of video games that lead to GTP experiences. They group these into four main categories. The first is sensory perceptual stimulation. This can include seeing objects as pixelated or in a monochrome color as well as uncontrolled body movements that correspond to in-game stimuli. The second is high cognitive load. Examples here are thinking that birds are fighter planes, seeing maps in the corner of one's eye when looking for an address, or seeing tags above people's heads. The third involves dissociative states, characterized by an immersion and a subjective sense of presence in the virtual world. This can involve confusing memories from the video game with those from real life or confusing game characters with real individuals. The fourth and final category comprises symptoms related to high emotional engagement. These include considering and actually trying to climb buildings and trying to break some object with only a finger.

It should be noted that these effects in some cases are not specifically perceptual aftereffects (like motion and color aftereffects), since the latter occur immediately after presentation of the stimulus and participants here can experience them hours after the cessation of game play. It is also notable that casual gamers may not experience GTP, since in many participants they occur after extensive amounts of gameplay, three or more hours' worth. It is likely, however, that more immersive games like those using virtual reality headsets will only increase the severity of the symptoms.

CHAPTER SEVEN

Avatars

CONTENTS

What Is an Avatar?

Avatar Typologies

Avatar Behavior in the Palace

    Avatar Types

    Evolving Avatars

    Switching Avatars

    Abnormal Avatar Behavior

    The Effect of Environment on Avatars

Avatar Embodiment

Points of View

The Proteus Effect

Representing and Creating the Online Self

Avatars at Play

Avatars and Video Role-Playing Games

Avatars and Identity

Avatar Case Studies

    Avatar Case Study 1: *Morrowind* and the Hardcore Gamer

    Avatar Case Study 2: *Oblivion* and the Casual Gamer

    Avatar Case Study 3: *Fallout 3* and the Nongamer

    Virtual and Nonvirtual Identities: Case Study Summary

The Future of Avatars

WHAT IS AN AVATAR?

The word *avatar* comes from the Sanskrit and originally referred to the incarnated form of Hindu gods like Vishnu. The modern-day sense, however, is just the opposite, as it refers to a movement from the physical into the virtual, what might be deemed a "deincarnation" or "virtualization." Filiciak (2003, p. 89) defines an avatar as "the user's representative in the virtual universe." The game designer Chris Crawford describes avatars similarly as "virtual constructs that are controlled by human players and function as a means of interacting with

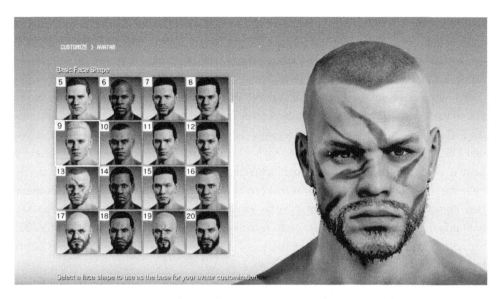

FIGURE 35 A computer avatar used in a video game. Avatars can be customized, serve as stand-ins or representatives of the user, and are controlled by the user.

(the virtual environment) and other characters (A. Berger, 2002, p. 33). One of the first psychological aspects of an avatar is that people feel it belongs to them and is an extension of them. People report feeling what their avatar touches and seeing what their avatar sees.

Apperley and Clemens (2017) make several comments concerning avatars' function and design. They should be "user-friendly" to operate with large gestures and simple color-coded controls. Despite the use of full-body control with the Wii system or a game like Pokémon Go, most avatars are still operated using eye-hand coordination via a joystick or video game controller. For many avatars the user repeats basic movements, for example when moving the avatar around on the screen. The avatar sits at the junction of two worlds, coupling the design space of the game with the body of the user in real space. The virtual worlds avatars inhabit, despite their immersive qualities, are partial because there are always other levels of a game or new games, and the games are interruptible, meaning they can be stopped and replayed at any time.

Goldberg (1997) distinguishes between avatars and agents. An avatar according to him is a representation of a real person, while an agent is "any semiautonomous piece of software that assumes some visual embodiment." However. this definition is still too vague, as Pac-Man could be either an avatar (since it represents the user) or an agent (since it is the embodiment of semiautonomous software). A more satisfying differentiation comes from Wilson (2003). According to her, an avatar is a virtual surrogate self that acts as a stand-in for the user's real-space self and represents the user. Avatars are created by choices made by the user, and there is substantial scope within the game or virtual world in which to exercise personal choice and create meaning (figure 35). By this definition Pac-Man is an agent, as the user can control but not alter him. His appearance and skills do not change during the game. The same is thus also true for Mario of *Mario Bros.*, the frog in *Frogger,* and Sonic the Hedgehog.

Avatars are more than just artificial constructs used in games. They seem real when we are operating them and have many potential benefits outside the gaming arena. Bainbridge (2013) outlines several ways in which avatars can be real. The first is subjectivity, meaning that avatars "feel real." Second, what happens in the virtual world very often carries over into the real world. People can be inspired by what they do as avatars, and as we have seen in Second Life, one can open a business and earn a significant amount of money. This effect is known as consequentiality. Third, many current avatars are prototypes, a first step toward more significant future developments that can be used for procedures like robotic teleoperation. Fourth, avatars and VR systems can be used to learn many real-world skills like navigation, piloting, and surgery. Finally comes transference. Aspects of our self can be offloaded to avatars, enabling them to function more and more autonomously. This is a likely future trend.

AVATAR TYPOLOGIES

Avatars can be accurate depictions of our selves, but more often they stand as proxies for our idealized selves: the type of character we want to be. These projections can feature both superficial characteristics such as appearance and more inward characteristics, such as personality traits. In video games, males most often choose avatars that are fierce and strong and hold positions of social power. Females typically choose avatars that are physically attractive and that entertain or provide nurturance, such as nurses or healers. The research suggests that males like to project increased strength, females like to project increased attractiveness, and both sexes like to project increased intelligence, charisma, and cunning.

Bainbridge (2013) analyzed choice of avatar in the *Star Wars Galaxies* video game. He found that people chose humans 53 percent of the time, Zabraks (a fierce race) 18 percent of the time, and Twi-leks (artful calculators) 11 percent of the time. As for profession and gender, 26 percent chose to be Jedi (powerful "force"-wielding characters). Females tended to choose avatars in the roles of entertainment and medical care, demonstrating nurturance, whereas males predominated as commando and officer positions, preferring military leadership. In a second study Bainbridge (2013) analyzed avatar choice in the *EverQuest II* fantasy game. He found that 31 percent chose to play as fighters (demonstrating strength), 22 percent chose to be priests (having wisdom), 27 percent chose to be mages (wielding magic), and 20 percent chose to be scouts (demonstrating agility).

Bartle (2004) created a typology or set of categories for gamers. These are (1) Explorers, who like to investigate new places and locations; (2) Achievers, who are focused on accomplishing tasks; (3) Socializers, who play games for friendship and shared experiences; and (4) Killers, who are interested in eliminating threats, whether those are computer or human controlled. Any particular gamer is considered as being some mix of the four, with one type predominating. Yee (2006) surveyed a large number of massive multiplayer online (MMO) gamers using this typology and identified three general statistical factors: achievement (corresponding roughly to the achievers category), social (corresponding roughly to the socializers category), and immersion (the extent of feeling a part of the game; can correspond to explorers or any of the other categories).

Coulson, Barnett, Ferguson, and Gould (2012), also studying MMO games, identify three major roles, each related to combat, which is the major task the characters must carry out. They refer to this as the KIP model, standing for "Kill, Irritate, and Preserve." Killers make up the majority of the group. Their main purpose is to inflict damage upon the enemy. Irritators attract the attention of the opposing forces, directing attacks upon themselves, and so must be durable and tough. Protectors heal members of the team. A player can swap between roles during the time that a team plays, so some are good at more than one skill. The team must work together, coordinating their efforts during game play to maximize their chances of success. This interdependency can be summed up by the following phrase: "If the Irritator dies, it's the Healer's fault. If the Healer dies, it's the Irritator's fault. If the Killer dies, it's their own damn fault."

AVATAR BEHAVIOR IN THE PALACE

Suler (2016) has spent considerable time doing observational field research inside the virtual world known as the Palace. The Palace was one of the earliest virtual worlds that could allow fully realized visual avatars to interact socially in a variety of settings. Some of the settings in this digital world were a haunted house, a bowling alley, and a town. The primary location was the Main Mansion, which contained about thirty different rooms including a study, a beach, a game room, and a bar. Avatars could move about within these areas and communicate with one another by typing text in balloons that would appear over their heads. Users in the Palace could change and accessorize the appearance of their avatars. They could also obtain "land" within the virtuality and fill it with habitable spaces and objects.

One of the most obvious aspects of avatars is that they allow their users to "loosen up" and act in a less constrained manner than in the real world. The behavior produced by this partial anonymity is called the online disinhibition effect. People driving avatars feel more free to say and do what they want in virtual worlds, knowing that their identity in the real world can remain hidden. The avatars people choose, though, do tend to reveal particular aspects of personality. This can be a self they want to be but can't be in the real world. It can be some interest or lifestyle choice that is important to them. It can even be a dark or destructive aspect of their persona.

Avatar Types

In the Palace, "Avs" fell into two main types. First were the "smileys," available as a default for all users. These were faces that reflected basic human emotions or expressions like happiness, sadness, anger, winking, blushing, head-nodding, or head-shaking. One could customize Smileys by changing the color of the face, or by adding props like wigs, devil horns, a halo, or a glass of beer. The second major type were those that were created under the complete control of users and that allowed for much greater variety. These avatars could take on almost any visual appearance. They could for instance be gods, wizards, or dragons. These avatars required more skill to create and as such were status symbols distinguishing full-fledged members from novices called "newbies." As so often happens in real human societies, we see the emergence here of different groups or castes that have different skills and resources.

On the basis of his extensive time inhabiting the world of the Palace and his observations of the avatars there, Suler (2016) developed thirteen avatar types. We provide a name and brief description of these in what follows. The first type is *animal avatars*. These can be any kind of animal, like a cat, a dog, a horse, or an eagle. Animals often symbolize certain traits. For instance, dogs are loyal, while eagles are fierce and independent. The type of animal a user adopts probably reflects a desire to show off this aspect of the self or an aspiration to acquire it. This feature could be a trait the user admires or fears and desires to master.

Suler's second type is *cartoon avatars*. These can correspond to a character from a comic strip, manga, or anime. Again, characteristics of this avatar can reflect the values of the user. A cartoon character like Bugs Bunny symbolizes the confident trickster, while Aladdin's genie represents a powerful but benevolent friend (Suler, 2016).

Still another type is *celebrity avatars*: one can adopt the face and appearance of a famous Hollywood actor or sports star. Desired characteristics here are attractiveness, health, strength, and intelligence. Being a celebrity also brings a sense of the familiar, since most of us have seen these people before in films or on television.

Evil avatars can be chosen to show the dark side of the self. One could for instance be the Joker in the Batman series, the gangster Al Capone, or any number of other villains, real or imagined. Evil avatars can be chosen to represent malicious fantasies or feelings of sin and guilt. Some evil avatars act evil in virtual worlds, while others adopt these personae for more playful reasons. In the Palace evil avatars could also be used to warn others to back off or stop damaging behaviors.

Real-face avatars are people's realistic depictions of themselves. These are seldom used in virtual worlds. People more often prefer anonymity. In some cases people are disturbed by seeing realistic digital portrayals of themselves in what might be deemed an "out of body experience." In the rare cases where real-face avatars are used they can serve as a gesture of honesty, friendship, or intimacy.

Idiosyncratic avatars are those that are uniquely associated with a given individual. For instance, a user may go to great lengths to make himself appear as a historical character like Abraham Lincoln, but with spikey red hair. This avatar serves as this person's "brand" and unique identifier. Avatars in the Palace were often traded, but idiosyncratic ones were seldom given away. Stealing one of these would be like stealing that person's identity.

Next come *environmental avatars*. These are chosen to match a specific environment. For instance, one might become a fish to swim in water or a bird to fly through the air. This type shows how important the environment is in shaping identity. In the real world people can change their identity to fit in with a social group or with a physical environment. One can, for instance, adopt the jackets and hats worn by people living in a cold climate.

Power avatars explicitly display wealth, physical strength, intelligence, or some other aspect of power. One can pose, for example, as a muscle man or billionaire. These avatars tend to be used by adolescent males who may be suffering from underlying feelings of insecurity and helplessness. They may also be adopted by those with narcissistic personalities.

Seductive avatars are those displaying sexual features. Frontal nudity shown in public was not permitted in the Palace, but if two individuals displayed these features to one another in a private room it was generally permitted. Violators were forcibly converted to a smiley if caught the first time, what was called "prop-gagged." Repeat offenders could be expelled. Some users got around this prohibition by adopting avatars that were partially naked or scantily clad. Females were more likely to adopt seductive avatars as a way of gaining attention from others. There is no guarantee in a virtual world that a male avatar is controlled by a man or that a female avatar is controlled by a woman. The rule in the Palace seemed to be that men dressed like women more often than women dressed like men. In these cases both sexes may be displaying sexual orientations less permissible in the real world.

The next of Suler's categories is *odd and shocking avatars*. These are strange and bizarre personae designed to confuse, shock, or intimidate. Examples include a face with no eyes or a knife stabbed into a bursting heart. These avatars could represent the behavior of adolescent ma les attempting to assert their independence or challenge authority. Alternately they could reflect schizotypal personality styles.

Clan avatars are those demonstrating membership in some group. Real-world individuals often show membership in a gang by wearing a certain jacket; the intent virtually is similar. Clan avatars look alike enough to demonstrate membership but different enough from each other to express individuality.

Similar are *paired avatars*. These are designed to complement one another, forming two halves of a whole. One paired couple in the Palace manifested as characters on the left and right side of a seesaw. These types of avatars demonstrate either romantic or nonromantic bonding.

There are several different types of *inanimate avatars*. Abstract avatars take the form of an abstract symbol like a geometric shape. People who enjoy symmetry, abstract conceptualization, or graphic design sensibilities might use these.

Billboard avatars broadcast philosophical, political, or religious messages. They manifest as actual signs with writing on them.

Lifestyle avatars depict a person's hobby. Examples are golf clubs, cars, or flowers. Some Palace users appeared as computers, robots, or cyborgs, showing an affiliation to technology. Suler notes that although these avatars convey specific interests, they are difficult to interact with socially.

Suler's final category consists of *animated avatars*. These are avatars that perform specific actions. As is the case in the virtual reality simulation Second Life (which we will examine in chapter 8), avatars default to certain basic behaviors like walking, sitting, or waving. Other, more complex behaviors like dancing must be either programmed in by the user or purchased from other users.

Evolving Avatars

In *The Palace* avatars evolve. Jim Bumgardner, who designed the simulation, told John Suler that "Avs" over time had become larger, more elaborate, and sexier (Suler 2016, p. 237). This probably reflects innate tendencies to display sexually for both men and women. Also avatar quality has been improving as people learn from one another how to construct more detailed versions. Mimesis is the process where some animals copy the patterning and appearance of other animals to gain an evolutionary advantage. Stealing or copying an avatar identity as happens in the Palace can also be seen as an example of evolutionary mimesis.

Switching Avatars

It should be noted that users often build more than one avatar and change between them for the occasion. For instance, a person might adopt a sexier outfit for attending a meeting at a bar than for going to church. Often when users in the Palace meet they will play "the avatar game." This consists of switching between avatar versions and soliciting feedback on what others think of each. From a Freudian point of view, this game can be seen as a type of dream analysis or projective test where users project their subconscious desires and fears (Suler, 2016). The game thus allows users to "try on" different identities to see how they feel, much as adolescents try on different identities.

Each different avatar a user creates can be seen as corresponding to a different aspect of his or her self. Each reflects a different mood, hobby, or interest. This corresponds to the theories of multiple selves we examined earlier in chapter 3. However, despite this, users frequently use and revert back to a dominant avatar. They use this avatar more than others and identify with it more than any other in their "collection." This avatar represents their stable core self and is necessary if they are to interact with others. Nobody could get to know a user who constantly "shape-shifted" from one avatar to another. The variation seen within a collection and the extent to which avatars and new versions of avatars are created is an indication of how experimental a person is in term of exploring alternate selves.

Suler (2016) states that avatars are a form of social "lubrication." They help to break the ice, especially for meetings between strangers. Rather than discuss a topic like the weather, strangers will usually start a conversation by discussing each other's avatars. Showing off, trading, and discussing avatars are perhaps the most common form of social interaction in the Palace. Avatars, like emoticons, can also be used to express one's feelings. Somebody who is feeling happy can switch to a happy smiley face or if sad can switch to a sad face.

TABLE 14 Types of abnormal avatars in the Palace virtual world.

	Name	Description
1.	Graffiti	Putting obscene or hateful drawings and words on the background walls. Painting an entire room black.
2.	Spoofing	Making one's own voice project from somebody else's avatar to create a ventriloquist dummy or sock puppet.
3.	Flooding	Rapidly changing avatars or producing processing lags in the server running the simulation to slow them down. Creation of "denial of service" events.
4.	Blocking	Placing one's avatar on top of or too close to another avatar. An invasion of virtual personal body space.
5.	Sleeping	Abandoning one's avatar for long periods of time, leaving it unresponsive.
6.	Eavesdropping	Reducing avatars in size so they become inconspicuous and then listening in on others' conversations.
7.	Borderlines	Using inappropriate avatars that are too sexual, violent, or prejudiced or that engage in illegal activities like drugs.
8.	Flashing	Showing nude avatars, advertising availability for cybersex publicly.
9.	Droppings	Placing obscene images in an empty room, then running away.
10.	Imposters	Stealing somebody's avatar and wearing it or using it to attack that person's reputation.
11.	Identity disruption	Constantly changing avatars so that no core identity is recognizable by others.

Source: After Suler (2016).

Abnormal Avatar Behavior

The types of crime and aggressive behavior seen in the real world unfortunately also translate into virtual worlds. We talk about violent forms of virtual behavior in Second Life's virtual world in chapter 8 but will start by introducing the different forms here. Suler (2016) lists eleven types of aberrant or abnormal behavior seen in the Palace. These include behaviors that can get a user kicked out of the virtual world or that are simply viewed as bizarre or impolite by fellow users. Table 14 lists each of these along with a short description.

In examining this table we see that these behaviors can be considered extensions of the disorders of self talked about earlier in chapter 3. The abandonment of an avatar (sleeping) can be considered the equivalent of dissociative amnesia or fugue, where one effectively abandons one's body while in another state. Stealing someone else's avatar to use for oneself (imposters) and changing avatars so there is no core identity (identity disruption) are like versions of dissociative identity disorder, where one alternates between various personae. All of the other abnormalities listed can be manifestations of narcissistic personality disorder, since they demonstrate selfishness and a lack of regard for others.

The reasons for these virtual behaviors may in many cases be the same as for the behaviors these individuals demonstrate in the real world. If we detest a certain aspect of our self, we may dissociate from it. Similarly, if we dislike some aspect of an avatar we have chosen, we may also decide to abandon it. If we alternate between avatars, it may be to escape the negative emotional consequences of "being" a particular avatar.

The Effect of Environment on Avatars

The type of surroundings players find themselves in affects how their avatars act. Warm colors, chairs, rugs, and other decorations can create an environment that fosters social interaction. Wide-open spaces with scattered objects might instead encourage other types of behavior like exploration. The laws of physics also put constraints on players' behavior. Most people in virtual worlds assume that gravity is in effect and will walk only on the floor even if they are allowed to walk up walls. An exception to this is when players have wings that make it possible to fly, in which case they may prefer to stay up in the sky. Also, even though people can teleport in the Palace by using a "goto" command, most choose to walk between locations if the distance is short.

Spaces influence avatar behaviors in other ways. People who frequent a particular room will often sit or stand in the same place, as if claiming that area as their personal space. People will also group together in the same patterns seen in the real world and in conformance with group dynamics theory, forming dyads, triads, and alliances, exhibiting leadership patterns, and showing fluctuations in group cohesion (Suler, 2016). The Palace and other virtual worlds allow people to obtain virtual land and to decorate it with objects like flowers or artwork, thus personalizing their own spaces.

AVATAR EMBODIMENT

One advantage virtual spaces have over regular social media sites is a dynamic visual representation of the user that the user can directly control. This creates what is called embodiment, a feeling of being in the avatar. This allows for nonverbal cues like facial expression and body posing and movement. These can express emotional states that are absent from sites like Twitter or Facebook. For example, if a user is nervous that can be reflected in jittery movement of his or her avatar. Another sign of embodiment is a sense of personal space. Users often feel that the space immediately surrounding their avatar is theirs. Uninvited intrusions into this space produce a sense of being violated.

POINTS OF VIEW

Perspectives in both video games and virtual spaces like the Palace are usually first-person or third-person point of view (POV). First-person POV is looking through the eyes of the avatar. This produces a subjective feeling of embodiment and of being inside the avatar as if it were your own body. Third-person POV is a view from behind and slightly above the avatar.

First person point of view

Third person point of view

FIGURE 36 First- and third-person point of view (POV) in video games.

This is more objective, affording the user a better view of what is occurring in the immediate environment. Some people prefer this because it gives them an overview of their surroundings and is less claustrophobic. Figure 36 shows examples of both POVs from video game play.

There is another third-person POV, what is sometimes called "God mode." This is a two-dimensional representation of the virtual world's three-dimensional space. This allows one to view an entire room or section of the world and everything that transpires in it. There is a suggestion that third-person POVs activate the observing self. This is the part of your self that is aware of who you are and how you behave. Some people report having a greater sense of freedom using this mode. We talk more about POVs in chapter 8.

THE PROTEUS EFFECT

Studies show that identification with an avatar can influence our behavior in the real world (figure 37). Users assigned attractive avatars were more likely to walk closer to an interaction partner and to disclose personal information (Yee & Bailenson, 2007). In this study those with taller avatars also negotiated harder in a task involving the division of money. Users viewing self-resembling avatars getting thinner while exercising worked out more (Fox & Bailenson, 2009). Participants viewing ideal body avatars were also more motivated to engage in preventative behaviors like not smoking or not drinking (Y. Kim & Sundar, 2012). In these cases the avatar is serving as a self-representing role model. This phenomenon is known as the Proteus effect.

Sometimes other avatars are a mirror for our own hidden prejudices. Dotsch and Wigboldus (2008) had white Dutch participants interact with an avatar in a virtual space. One group interacted with an avatar that had a Moroccan face (Moroccans are a group who suffer prejudice in the Netherlands). The other group interacted with an avatar that had a white face. They were then asked to rate questions such as "I like Moroccans" and to complete the Implicit Associations Task (IAT). The IAT measures reaction times to classify words like *love* or *hate* next to names like Mustafa or Johan. There was no difference between the avatar conditions on the explicit questionnaire test. However, those categorized as being prejudiced on the IAT preferred to stand a greater distance away from Moroccan avatars.

There are several "take-home" lessons here. We identify with an avatar's characteristics, especially if we designed it ourselves. If our avatars are perceived as good, they tend to promote prosocial behavior. If avatar characteristics are perceived as aggressive or maladaptive, they tend to promote negative or antisocial behavior. We also carry our prejudices into the virtual realm, treating other avatars with the same preconceptions and labels we apply to people in the offline world.

REPRESENTING AND CREATING THE ONLINE SELF

Video role-playing games (v-RPGs) come with either a predefined avatar or a customizable one. People do vary considerably in their choices. Some just pick what is available. Others produce highly detailed custom avatars by altering facial and body features (see the case studies in this chapter). Others choose avatars whose sex, gender, race, or country is the same as their own. Still others may pick an avatar that differs substantially from their own features, going as a member of another sex or race. Some go farther than this and choose to represent themselves as nonhuman characters like elves or trolls. We discuss in this section more explanations for why people choose particular avatars to represent themselves. Figure 38 shows a screen from a video game allowing customization of various avatar features.

Bessiere, Seay, and Kiesler (2007) looked at the differences between individuals' own characteristics and the avatar they chose in *World of Warcraft* (*WoW*). This is a Massively multiplayer online role playing game (MMORPG) in which people can assume a wide

FIGURE 37 The Proteus effect demonstrates that we tend to act in accordance with the implied behavior of our avatars. What expectations do you have for this man based on his appearance? Image courtesy of pixneo.com.

variety of avatars representing many different fantasy creatures. The researchers found that the characteristics of the avatars people chose were generally more positive than the characteristics of users who created them as assessed by personality testing. This effect was even stronger for those who scored low on a measure of well-being. Other studies report the same effect for those who score high on the FFM trait of agreeableness (Dunn & Guadagno, 2012).

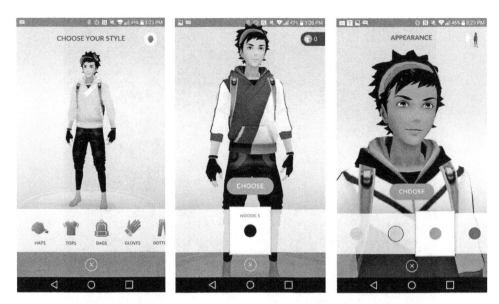

FIGURE 38 Avatar customization in the video game *The Elder Scrolls III: Morrowmind.*

Among those scoring low on well-being, the effect may be a desire to project and identify with an avatar that is stronger, more intelligent, or more charismatic than themselves since they are lacking these characteristics. Among those scoring low on agreeableness it may be a desire to have these features in order to better get along with others.

Men who create Preserver-type avatars are more likely to select a female character (Ducheneaut, Yee, Nickell, & Moore, 2006). This may be partly because these avatars are smaller in stature than the other avatar types or because they take on traditional female roles of healing and protection. Men also tend to create avatars that are slightly thinner than themselves and slightly more muscular than either their actual or ideal selves (Cacioli & Mussap, 2014). This could reflect a desire to lose weight or to be muscled, both culturally desirable features. It might also reflect the fact that many game programs allow only for overproportioned physiques with large chests, arms, and upper bodies for men and large breasts in the case of women.

It is interesting that many people imbue their avatars with characteristics that are only slightly more positive than their own and not more extremely positive. Why not select absolutely perfect avatars? One explanation is that if the avatar were too different from the actual user it would be difficult for the user to identify with it. There seems to be a type of "Goldilocks" effect going on here. Users don't want avatars that are completely idealized and heroic because they are hard to relate to. They also don't want avatars that are too realistic and like themselves because then they won't get a chance to stretch their own identity in a new and interesting direction. The result is an intermediary point between the two (Mar & Oatley, 2008).

Coulson, Barnett, Ferguson, and Gould (2012) propose that choosing an avatar can be partly explained by the principle of optimal online intermediate similarity. It is derived from an idea in evolution whereby individuals choose to mate with others who are like, but not too much like, themselves. If mating is between two individuals that are too similar to one another, then inbreeding and genetic defects could result. If the mating is between a pair that is too dissimilar, then excessive variation in the gene pool can cause other potential problems. So the optimum strategy is to pick somewhere in the middle. This principle may also predict our preference for online mating partners.

Coulson, Barnett, Ferguson, and Gould (2012) studied the chosen sex of avatars in the game *Dragon Age: Origins*. They found that over 90 percent of women chose to play as a woman while 28 percent of men chose to play as women. This may in part be due to what has been dubbed the "Lara phenomenon" (Jansz & Martis, 2007). Lara Croft is the protagonist in the long-running video game *Tomb Raider*. She is a masculine-type action hero. Controlling her avatar may give some women the type of physical and social power they are often denied in the offline world. For men, playing as a woman may simply afford greater novelty.

AVATARS AT PLAY

Exploring virtual worlds through avatars is a form of play where we get to experience things that we may not be able to in the offline world. Playing has long been believed to be beneficial for many species. It allows young animals to learn skills like hunting and social interaction. They can do this in a safe and protected environment, usually while still under the care of their parent. Play also seems to serve this function in humans. The developmental psychologist Jean Piaget saw play as a form of intellectual development. He believed that play allowed children to learn about concrete items and situations at an age where they lacked more abstract thinking capability.

Humans love to play games. It seems to be an evolved trait in our species (Coulson and Barnett, 2015). Games are now everywhere. It used to be that electronic gaming was mostly for male adolescents who played console games by themselves or with their other male friends using a controller in the basement of their parents' house. Now we see games being played by adults mostly on portable smartphones in all locations and by much larger numbers of people, with the market increasingly dominated by women. It is as if technology has now allowed all of us to play. This runs counter to the idea that gaming serves only some specialized purpose in childhood and that the desire to play disappears after that. McGonigal (2011) argues that there are certain features characteristic of all games that people at any age respond to, such as challenges in trying to attain a goal, competition, and constant feedback.

Fredrickson (2001), in his "broaden and build" theory, posits that positive emotions encourage exploration and play. They allow us to build resources, that is, to acquire new skills that we can then apply to novel situations. Playing makes us happy. Feeling happy then encourages us to explore and play some more. The end result is that we have behaviors that could be of benefit to us in a challenging situation in the future. Play is also a low-risk environment. We can try something in play to see if it works or not. If it fails, there is no serious cost to the organism. If it succeeds, we can potentially remember and apply the behavior as a solution to a problem down the road.

There is evidence to link electronic gaming and positive mood. J. Barnett, Coulson, and Foreman (2010) examined players' moods before and after two hours of playing *WoW*. There was a major reduction of negative mood regardless of the participant's personality, age, gender, sex, and game-play motivation. The results were largest in players who reported high levels of neuroticism and low levels for three other FFM traits: conscientiousness, agreeableness, and openness to experience. Ferguson et al. (2008) obtained similar results. They had participants play either a violent or a nonviolent video game. The players did not experience aggression, even the ones playing the violent game. In another study a group of sixteen-year-old students who played video games showed multiple positive outcomes (Durkin & Barber, 2002). They scored higher on positive mental health, were more engaged with school, were more involved in activities, showed little or no substance abuse, had higher positive views of themselves, and had more friends than those who did not play games.

AVATARS AND VIDEO ROLE-PLAYING GAMES

Avatars undergo situations similar to what people undergo in real life. According to Murray (1997), "In games we have a chance to enact our most basic relationship to the world—our desire to prevail over adversity, to survive our inevitable defeats, to shape our environment, and to master complexity." She compares games to coming-of-age ceremonies by which we mark birth, adulthood, marriage, and death. Games for her are ritual actions that give meaning to our lives. LucasArts game designer Tim Schafer says that games start off by providing the avatar with motivations but that as the game progresses users "ego invest" by sharing the motivations of the character and imbuing the character with new ones (Roberts 2018). Meaning between avatar and user is thus a two-way street: avatars give us meaning, and we in turn give them meaning.

What types of games best accomplish this identification and meaning creation? They would be those that tell a compelling story or narrative, using scripts that are formulaic enough to be understood but flexible enough to capture a wide range of human behavior (Murray, 1997). The user needs to undergo "immersion" in the story. Immersion is best accomplished by involving the user emotionally. A role-playing world seems a good candidate, as it allows users to choose several ways to go about a task, either in seeking out a preset goal or in exploring an extensive environment. The choices users make affect their success and thus their emotions. Those with the greatest potential to affect a user's identity additionally involve the construction of an appearance and personality for the avatar. The only class of game that satisfies this characteristic is the video role-playing game (v-RPG).

Creation of a character in a game reflects both our ideal self and our alternate selves, aspects of our personality that may be underexpressed in the real world. Nakamura (1995) refers to this as identity tourism. It involves trying on various character types as an experiment in what it is like to be someone (or something) else. We could, for instance, be an "evil" character like a demon in a v-RPG to see what it feels like to be evil. We could alternatively express the "good" side of our persona by choosing to fight as a hero (Ducheneaut, Yee, Nickell, & Moore, 2006). Note the similarity here with previously established theories of self. An evil avatar might exercise the primal urges of the Freudian id while a good avatar might express and strengthen the superego. Note also the similarity to Erikson's stage 5 in his developmental approach, where adolescents and young adults play out different roles in order to discover their own identity. People of this same age might use identity tourism in video games as a way to discover who they are most comfortable being.

AVATARS AND IDENTITY

Doyle (2017) argues that we discover our sense of self whenever we are free to experience new cultures, spaces, or times. Freedom and novelty thus become the conditions under which self and identity are forged. Adolescents and young adults most likely acquire identity in this manner by "trying on" new friends, jobs, and courses to discover what suits them. Similarly, users operating an avatar are free to roam about new worlds, interacting with other avatars and creatures, experimenting with what actions and experiences match them. Avatars can also be altered to correspond to different species, genders, appearances, and abilities. One can literally feel what it is like to be an elf or goblin, male or female, blonde or brunette. Many video games now allow detailed avatar construction where one can vary the exact shape of different facial features, as well as setting internal characteristics like intelligence and agility. In this manner, avatars can let us be almost whatever we want, exercising the alternate aspects of our psyche. We can be our Rogerian "idealized selves" or assume the darker side of our nature, giving in to violent tendencies.

Zach Waggoner (2009) investigated the relationship between virtual identity and "real" or nonvirtual identity in v-RPGs. He was interested in how people form connections between themselves and their avatar. He conducted extensive oral interviews and video game-play transcription from four participants. Using a case study technique, he studied two "diehard" video game expert players with the game *Morrowind,* a casual gamer who played the game *Oblivion,* and a nongamer who played *Fallout 3.* Waggoner analyzed these participants using a threefold set of identities developed by Gee (2004): (1) the virtual identity, the avatar that exists in the game; (2) the real-world identity, which belongs to the person that sits down in front of the computer and plays the game; and (3) the projective identity, the middle ground or transition between the first two.

We mentioned earlier that immersion affects the degree to which a user will identify with his or her avatar. McMahan (2003) separates the world of the video game (the diegetic level) from the player's love of the game and the strategy that goes into it (the nondiegetic level). She also describes three factors that create immersion in a game: (1) a user's expectations for the game environment must be aligned with what that environment is actually like; (2) the user's actions in the game world must have a "non-trivial impact" on the game world;

and (3) the conventions of the game world must be internally consistent. These ideas will be applied in describing the case studies to come.

Aarseth (2001) differentiates "ergodic" from "nonergodic" literature. The term *literature* is used broadly here to include different media like books, television, movies, and video games. Ergodic literature requires effort in the form of focused concentration. Nonergodic literature is more passive in nature. Aarseth categorizes video games as ergodic because they require eye-hand coordination and an understanding of sometime complex rules to play. They also call upon strategy, skill, and imagination to an extent not seen in the other types of media, which are more nonergodic in nature. This effort can cause users to invest their avatar with more of a sense of identity. We invest more emotionally into our avatars and infuse them with our personality because of the adversity the avatar must overcome in the game (diegetic) and because of the adversity the user must overcome to control the avatar (nondiegetic).

Narrative identity theory has been outlined in greater detail in chapter 3, but we make the connection between it and video games here. Murray (1997) argues that certain types of stories are better told in digital spaces. One of these is the multiform story. This is a "written or dramatic narrative that presents a single situation or plotline in multiple versions." Multiform stories don't exist in books, TV, or movies. These have only a single story that unfolds in a single way. A single video game, however, can produce an infinite number of stories because a user can save a game and play it again using different tactics or a different avatar. The number of possible story lines only increases when multiple users are introduced, as in an MMO game. These multiple possibilities allow the user a more active and creative role. Users can, for example, keep trying at a level until they succeed. This can affect their identity by boosting their confidence and self-esteem.

Storytelling, according to Murray, has the potential for personal transformation. A compelling story can "open our hearts and change who we are." She believes that enacted stories compared to those that are merely witnessed are more transformative. This is because we "assimilate them as personal experiences." V-RPGs, unlike traditional media, involve problem-solving and opponents that must be overcome, two of the most stirring aspects of real life. Voyeurs who merely observe from a safe position are more detached from events. But players who are actively involved are put at risk: they can be rejected or fail. V-RPGs differ from traditional media in another way: the refusal of a climax. A book or movie always ends. A v-RPG might not ever end or achieve its goal given the number of ways the story can unfold. This absence of closure compels us to continue playing and makes the experience more immersive.

The types of characters one encounters in a v-RPG also affect our immersion in and identification with a game. Characters other than the one the user is controlling are referred to as nonplayer characters (NPCs). The more realistic these characters are, the more likely we are to treat them as real people (or creatures). This in turn will affect how we feel when interacting with them. Realism can be in the form of appearance, as in spatial resolution. It can also be in the form of behavior. An NPC that looks like a person and both talks and moves like one is even more real. Knowing whether an NPC is controlled by an AI or by a real competing player will undoubtedly affect our feelings toward it. For instance, we may feel more guilty or sad if we shoot and kill an avatar that we know is controlled by another real-world person.

AVATAR CASE STUDIES

Avatar Case Study 1: *Morrowind* and the Hardcore Gamer

Waggoner (2009) conducted several phenomenological case studies to examine the effects of avatar identification. His method was to observe users play RPGs and to then interview them about their experiences. In the first study he selected two participants with a lot of gaming experience. These individuals enjoyed playing v-RPGs and had experience manipulating the complex mouse and keyboard interface necessary to control the characters and play the game. He wanted players for whom the interface would "disappear" early on. The two subjects were Vishnu, a twenty-six-year-old Caucasian male and college graduate, and Shiva, a twenty-three-year-old Caucasian female university library assistant, also with a college degree. Both Vishnu and Shiva described themselves as lifelong video game players, and both enjoyed customizing their avatars.

The game of choice in this case was Bethesda Softworks' *The Elder Scrolls III: Morrowind* fantasy role-playing game. At the start of the game, *Morrowind* allows the user to choose the name of the avatar, the gender (male or female), and one of ten different races. Four of the races are humanoid, three are elven (elves), and three are animal types like a reptile, cat, or pig-like avatar. Attributes for each race, such as speed, intelligence, and endurance, can be chosen. The face and hairstyle of each avatar can also be manipulated.

Morrowind is a single-player-only game. Users control a single avatar and explore a vast world with varying terrain, interacting only with NPCs. The game is not an MMORPG, so no other human-controlled avatars are participating. This was done to simplify the study. There is an archetypal plot in which the hero must quest across a land (named Vvardenfell) filled with dangers to defeat evil forces and recover a valuable object. However, avatars are free to go wherever they choose in this imaginary land and need not achieve the goals specified by the plot. There is no time limit and players can spend as much time playing as they want. This gives the players the ability to reflect and learn from their performance.

Vishnu selected the name "Steve!" for his avatar because it had humorous significance to him. Shiva named her avatar "Shi," an abbreviation of her own name. Both users selected a Dark Elf as the race of their avatar because this race had a balanced set of abilities, good to have when one is first starting off in a game and not sure which skills will be necessary. This reflects both of the users' prior knowledge in playing such games. Shiva chose a female avatar to match her real-world identity and because she wanted a female who was strong and independent, both features she admired in real-world women. She rejected several options for Shi because she said they were not "pretty enough." Vishnu also selected a female, even though it did not match his real-world gender, in keeping with his sense of humor.

In the inventory screen of *Morrowind*, users get to examine a full-body image of what their avatar looks like, so each time they access this screen their identification with the avatar is reinforced. Vishnu played mostly in third-person POV. He felt this POV afforded him better depth perception and peripheral vision. Interestingly, Vishnu referred to his avatar not in the third-person as "he" or "she" but with the more intimate "you." Shiva, however, decided to play almost exclusively in first-person POV so that she could feel more "in character."

One of the first things both users in this study did in the game was to steal items off a desk. This is expected and is one of the things characters can do to acquire items they might need later on. Neither had qualms about doing so. Note that such actions outside the game are unethical and punishable by law. Once in a game, users thus adopt a new understanding of what is ethical and permissible but don't in most cases carry over these behaviors to the real world. Both Shiva and Vishnu were adamant that they would never steal anything outside virtual space. Both players also had no qualms about killing, a behavior expected in the game.

We discuss the topic of video games and violence in chapter 6.

When interacting with NPCs in the game, Shiva and Vishnu adopted different approaches. Vishnu chose to use the "Persuade through Intimidation" skill, while Shiva chose the "Admire" skill. These choices reflect the more aggressive male approach to interaction versus one that is more female. Both players also had differing approaches to avatar death. Vishnu had no qualms about his character dying and often placed his avatar in situations where it was killed in order to learn more about the game. His character Steve! died twenty-six times during the recorded game play. His attitude toward virtual death was that it was an inevitable and common occurrence. In contrast, Shiva had a much more conservative approach, apparently caring more deeply about her avatar's virtual life. Her avatar Shi never died even once during the period of study. She justified this by saying: "I just wanted to survive!" Shiva also kept Shi away from water during the game, having had a real-world scary childhood experience near a body of water.

In one scenario in the game, characters get the opportunity to either keep a ring or give it back to an NPC named Fargoth. Both gave it back but for different reasons. Shiva returned it because "I knew it would make him happy. I guess it was good for me to create a happy world for the NPCs." Vishnu had Steve! return the ring because he thought he would be rewarded for it. Shiva's actions were in line with an attitude of trying to please people, similar to Shiva's real-world attitude and behaviors. Vishnu, however, was just trying to see if he could benefit from his actions.

It is interesting to note that neither character expressed interest in pursuing the game's main narrative goal of defeating the evil character Dagoth Ur under Red Mountain. Shi justified this by saying that her avatar was an "ethical rebel" and that she didn't want to do what the game designers intended. She pictured Shi as rebellious and didn't want her to blindly follow orders. Vishnu was more interested in exploring Vvardenfell and in interacting with the characters, items, and locations. Both of these approaches were in line with the users' real-world attitudes. It was clear by the end of the study that Shiva identified more with her avatar than Vishnu did. She was more cautious in guiding Shi through the game, while Vishnu was focused more on the game's rules and mechanics.

Avatar Case Study 2: *Oblivion* and the Casual Gamer

For the second case study, Waggoner (2009) selected Tom, a thirty-three-year-old Caucasian man with only some gaming experience. Tom tended to like games in which there were distinct levels to advance through and stressed his desire to master game play. He liked first-person shooter (FPS) games like *MechWarrior* in which "it was fun to blow things up. It was fun to win!" Tom's domination of a game made him feel powerful and gave him confidence that he was good at something. The choice of game for this case study was *Oblivion,* the sequel to *Morrowind,* also a v-RPG. The two games are very similar, with *Oblivion* allowing much greater customization of the avatar's appearance.

Tom chose a dark-haired Caucasian male of Scandinavian descent. He spent nearly half an hour creating his avatar, whom he named simply "Tom." Tom took great pains to ensure that his avatar's face looked very much like his own and that it came from the same ethnic background as his own. Tom spent very little time assigning attributes and skills to his avatar and was happy to have the game select these skills for him. His identification with his avatar thus seemed to be at a superficial level only, relating to appearance rather than traits or attributes.

Tom also spent little time getting to master the complicated interface needed to control his avatar. As a result he struggled with it throughout the period of recorded game play. He chose the first-person POV because he thought the image of the avatar onscreen "got in the way." He also entered the inventory less than Vishnu or Shiva had. As a result Tom rarely viewed the image of his avatar. When it came to his avatar dying Tom reported feeling frustration. These deaths seemed to be a continual reminder that he was failing at the game. He wished that his avatar could be "invincible" in battle. Tom also didn't spend much time exploring the virtual world, and if he needed to travel long distance he selected the "teleport" option so he could get there immediately. He admitted that it had been twenty years since he had last played a v-RPG.

It was obvious that Tom lacked the desire or imagination to have his avatar get to know the terrain and locations inside the game. He also did not care about his avatar's personality or skills. Despite this Tom still identified with his avatar. They shared a name, an appearance, and an ethnicity. They also shared moral codes, neither wishing to openly steal from or kill other NPCs.

Avatar Case Study 3: *Fallout 3* and the Nongamer

For his last study Waggoner (2009) chose the v-RPG game *Fallout 3.* This game involves a dystopian postapocalyptic wasteland. Avatars start the game in a fallout shelter but must ultimately get out to explore the area in and around a future Washington, D.C. The participant for this study was Bianca, a thirty-two-year-old child psychiatrist. She was also

Waggoner's fiancé. She had little prior gaming experience and was uninterested in virtual identities and worlds. She didn't want to learn the game's complicated interface. Bianca liked the simple joystick-and-button controls of classic video arcade games like *Frogger* that she had played in her youth. In *Frogger,* one moves a virtual frog up, down, left, and right to cross a road. Such games take little more than a minute to learn the controls. Bianca was not interested in her video game character or in fantasy or other fictional settings. She was very literal-minded and viewed video games as the trivial pursuits of children.

Bianca chose to play as a female video character and chose the name "Joojee" for her avatar, a term of affection in her native language of Farsi. She ended up adopting one of the preset faces in the game, a template that resembled a Hispanic woman. When asked why she chose this she reported: "I thought it looked cool and pretty." She gave Joojee electric orange-colored hair. Bianca assigned Joojee attributes that were a combination of what she thought would do well in the game and what she valued in real life. She chose rude verbal interactions with NPCs and when asked why said she was trying to get more information. She did not have any moral qualms about this, saying "It's a videogame, for God's sake! It's not life."

Like Tom, Bianca expressed no interest in exploring the game's virtual world She wanted to advance through the story and achieve goals as quickly as possible. She was not interested in the narrative and wanted only to finish the game. Her experience with *Fallout 3* was not pleasurable. Despite this Bianca still showed some identification with her avatar. The name "Joojee" had personal and cultural meaning for her. Also, at one point in game play where the main character as an infant met her father Bianca spoke the words "Hi Daddy!" out loud. When asked later she thought that the avatar in the game had said this. She also referred to her avatar using the pronoun *I.*

Virtual and Nonvirtual Identities: Case Study Summary

Kennedy (2002) writes that the identification found in v-RPGs blurs the distinction between user and avatar and results in the creation of a second, technological self. He believes that "the avatar becomes an extension of the player and the separateness of the avatar's body is obliterated." This seems to have been the case for the participants in Waggoner's (2009) study. This was the case even though identities, locations, and events in *Morrowind, Oblivion,* and *Fallout 3* are sheer fantasy. Such characters and situations could not happen or have not happened in the real world.

Hard-core gamers showed strong identification with their avatars. Identification was weaker but still present in the casual and nongamers in the second and third case studies. Part of the reason for Tom's and Bianca's failure to identify was that these were not the sort of games they liked. Tom enjoyed FPS games in which players advanced through distinct levels. Bianca liked joystick-drive arcade games. Neither wanted to learn how to customize their avatar's deeper personalities, learn the complex controls, or take the time to explore the geography of the virtual worlds. So interest and prior experience play an important role here. People who are not interested in RPG games and not familiar with them are less likely to identify with their avatar.

There are a number of limitations to case studies. It is difficult to generalize the results of a small sample to a larger population. What may be true of the users here may not necessarily be true for all users. Some of the participants in these studies were friends, coworkers, and family members of the primary investigator. This could have created subtle expectations about how to perform or respond, what are called demand characteristics. Another significant limitation is the limited number of game-play hours recorded. Only ten hours of videogame play were studied per participant. It is likely that greater identification would have occurred if the participants had spent more time playing. However, case studies do provide a rich and detailed source of information that cannot often be obtained in more experimental paradigms.

THE FUTURE OF AVATARS

The future will likely see more realistic avatars for both superficial and deep traits. We are not far from being able to create human figures that are indistinguishable from their real counterparts, even when examined closely. Imagine a VR representation of your ex-girlfriend that is accurate down to every last hair and skin pore. This level of fidelity (or infidelity, as the case may be) will be for every sensory modality: auditory, olfactory, gustatory, and tactile as well as visual. There will in all likelihood be better reproduction of personality traits so that these avatars will act more like their real-world counterparts. The behaviors generated from traits like tone of voice, gait, and mannerisms will probably become more accurate. For example, if Bill is an extrovert, his VR representation will be more likely to initiate conversations. If Susan is an introvert, she will be more likely to avert her gaze.

This mapping of behaviors from traits will also allow us to generate human avatars with entirely new personalities. One can imagine, for example, imbuing an avatar with a particular mix of different traits to become one's ideal interaction partner, as determined beforehand by a personality-matching test. We may create avatars that are scientifically determined to be a best friend, lover, or father. We may become so addicted to these characters that they become more important to us than our real-world family and companions. Personality characteristics may also be added to dogs, cats, aliens, or fantasy animals. The possibilities here are humorous. Michael, for example, could bring his dead cat back to life, give it the personality of his ex-wife, and converse with it!

Avatars will also serve more serious roles. They can be our proxies when we are not or do not want to be available. We could, for instance, create an avatar for ourselves that mimics our own appearance and personality. If we were sick, we could activate this avatar and have it participate as our substitute at the Hong Kong business meeting we couldn't make. We could then replay the video and audio of that meeting as if we were there and modify or substitute any actions our avatar did if we disagreed with it. This could pose some interesting social and legal challenges. If our avatar signs a lease agreement, is it legally binding? If we don't want to go on a virtual date, is it ethical to send our avatar instead?

CHAPTER EIGHT

Virtual Worlds

CONTENTS

Augmented Reality

Virtual Worlds

Virtual Spaces

A Brief History of Virtual Worlds

Presence and the Ultimate Display

A Chronology of VR Systems

  Early Developments

  The Modern Era

  Current VR Devices

Second Life

  Personhood in Second Life

  Avatars and Alts in Second Life

  Gender, Race, and Disorders in
  Second Life

Intimacy, Sex, and Love in Second Life

Family in Second Life

Addiction in Second Life

Community in Second Life

Ethics in Second Life

The Political Economy of Second Life

  A Third Life? Here Comes Sansar

Avatars, Virtual Worlds, and the Digital Self

Benefits of VR and Virtual Worlds

  VR and the Study of Moral Dilemmas

  Cyberball and the Study of Ostracism

  Clinical Applications of VR

Problems with VR and Virtual Worlds

The Future of the Virtual World

In this chapter we examine virtual worlds. There are two types. In augmented reality, digital content is laid on top of real-world displays. In most current video games and virtual reality (VR) systems the content is entirely digital. Our discussion begins with the types of spaces that exist inside virtualities. We then give a brief history of virtual worlds starting with nontechnological versions. Following this we bring up the notion of presence/

immersion and how it has increased with improved technology. Next comes an extended anthropological description of the most extensively used virtual world to date, Second Life. We then conclude with the benefits, problems, and likely future of VR and virtual worlds.

AUGMENTED REALITY

Before discussing VR and completely virtual worlds we must first introduce augmented reality (AR). It is a hybrid of real and virtual worlds and so is a halfway point between ordinary perception and completely computer-generated environments. AR is a live view of a real-world environment that is augmented by computerized input like video, graphics, sound, or GPS data. Whereas VR is a completely artificial world, AR takes real-world environments that are perceived in real time and adds virtual elements to them. Avatars can be created, customized, and used in both AR and VR, just as they can in video games. Content in AR applications can be not only sensed but also manipulated. AR has many applications in fields like education, art, business, medicine, and tourism as well as gaming.

Multiple technologies can be used to generate AR. These include a head-mounted display (HMD) of the sort used for VR and eyeglasses like the Vuzix AR3000 Augmented Reality Smart Glasses. The US military is developing contact lenses that allow users to focus on near objects projected by AR spectacles and real-world objects at farther distances. There is even a virtual retinal display (VRD) under development at the University of Washington that can project images and other content directly on the retina of a viewer's eye. Systems are also available for handheld smartphones.

As an example of what AR might be like in the future, imagine walking down a street fifteen years from now. You are looking for a new pair of jeans but don't know where to get them. You make a query into a voice recognition input device asking it where to find them. Immediately large downward-pointing red arrows hover over stores selling this item. You cross over to one and ask for more information about what brands are available. The arrow is now replaced with a list of what brands of jeans are sold there along with other information like their color and sizes. You are thus able to find the store you want without even having to go in to ask beforehand. Other AR apps could provide you with similar information about apartments for sale, public toilets, the weather, and so on. The promise of AR is that it will use technology to facilitate interacting with the world in real time and real space.

The Microsoft HoloLens is an AR system first announced in 2015. It is a self-contained headgear set that maps its surroundings and can display high-quality images and videos. The headgear scales sounds from the environment so that auditory objects from farther away are softer. It also has the capability to interpret voice and hand movement commands to control objects. It is quite expensive, currently costing $3,000, but should AR catch on commercially the cost of such systems will undoubtedly come down.

Pokemon Go is a location-based AR game developed by Niantic for iOS and Android devices. It was a hugely popular global phenomenon when it first came out in July of 2016 and was one of the most profitable mobile apps of that year. The game was credited with promoting physical activity and helped local businesses grow. On the down side it was blamed for contributing to various accidents. There were also some security concerns with several countries passing legislation to control it.

The goal of the game is to find, capture, fight, and train virtual creatures called Pokemon. When the app is opened for the first time, a player customizes a manga-like avatar by choosing gender, hairstyle, and the color of hat, jacket, backpack, pants, and shoes. The avatar then appears on a map with the player's location indicated at the center. The map contains detailed roads and streets. "PokeStops" and "Gyms" replace real-world buildings. Items like eggs, balls, berries, and potions can be picked up at PokeStops. Team-based competitions take place at Gyms. When the user moves, the avatar moves a corresponding amount, so walking a block north in a city would move the avatar one block north on the map.

When a player finds a Pokemon it can be viewed in a generic rendered background or in AR mode. The AR mode uses the device's gyroscope and camera to display the Pokemon character as if it were in the real world in front of the user. To capture a character the user taps on a ball and flicks it up toward the creature. If the character is captured successfully, the user is rewarded with candies and stardust. Ultimately users need to capture creatures to obtain 151 different types of Pokemon.

VIRTUAL WORLDS

Virtual worlds are the environments that avatars inhabit. Castronova (2005) defines a virtual world as any computer-generated space that can be simultaneously experienced by many people. Virtual worlds presume three basic elements: (1) they are places that are (2) inhabited by persons and are (3) enabled by online technologies. Virtual worlds also persist after people log off. As discussed elsewhere, Second Life is a good example of a virtual world. Virtual worlds are not games, as they are not goal oriented, have no beginning or end, have no concept of "winning" or "losing," and usually do not involve player death. Starting in the early 1990s video games started to become more social in that many people could play together over a network. These were called massively multiple online games (MMOGs) or massively multiple online role-playing games (MMORPGs). *World of Warcraft* is a good example of an MMOG. Although they have a social component they are still classified as games.

Boellstorff (2008) notes two negative interpretations of virtual worlds. The first is that they are "influenced" by capitalism; critics point to how for-profit companies own the software and computer systems used to run the simulations. They also note how in some virtual worlds residents are allowed to "set up shop" and earn real-world money using virtual currency. A second negative interpretation is that they are just a form of escapism from the actual world. Although it is the case that some people spend time in virtual worlds to be something they are not, there is also a great deal of escapism in the "real" world in the form of daydreaming, amusement parks, film, and other more traditional arts.

VIRTUAL SPACES

Space is central to understanding virtual worlds. In a video game or VR simulation the avatar must be able to move around effectively, and the type of space it is in determines this. There are also more abstract types of spaces that define gaming and virtual world exploration. We explore them in this section. Stockburger (2007) outlines three types of basic spaces. What he calls "Firstspace" is real space, that which we perceive and interact with in our daily lives outside any game. "Secondspace" is imaginary space. This corresponds to a purely imagined space that we occupy when awake and imagining or daydreaming and perhaps also when we are asleep and dreaming. "Thirdspace" corresponds to a mixture of the first two and contains both elements of the real and the imagined. Virtual and game worlds are examples of this last type. Stockburger believes games are compelling for just this reason. They are familiar enough that we can relate to them but are novel and strange enough to capture our interest.

The type and content of space represented in video games and virtual worlds affect both our desire and our ability to interact with them. Games that are easily understood and navigable may be more enticing to some because they can be figured out quickly and mastered. On the other hand, games that are too simple may also get boring quickly for individuals that enjoy challenges. A person who wants to just shoot or blow things up may be happy with a first-person shooter (FPS) game that allows a character to simply move forward through terrain with a rifle killing enemy soldiers. This same individual would be frustrated and upset over having to learn a complex set of actions that controlled an avatar and then to use them to explore an extensive environment. Wolf (2001) outlines eleven different kinds of video games spaces. These are described in table 15. Which types would you like to play in and why?

The things represented in video game spaces also affect our experience with them. One fundamental distinction here has to do with simulations versus simulacra. A simulation is an attempt to represent some aspect of the world with as much accuracy and realism as possible (Walker, 2003). The game *Gettysburg!* is a good example. It recreates this battle of the American Civil War, reproducing the regiments of the Union and Confederate armies as well as the terrain on which the battle was fought. Some people are drawn to this realism and enjoy playing the game because of it. An interest in this particular part of history or of war in general might motivate someone to play this game and to identify with it. Despite the degree of realism. a simulation is still a copy of some original event or situation.

A simulacrum, on the other hand, can be thought of as a copy without an original (Baudrillard, 1994). Examples of simulacra are fantasy or science fiction settings that are imagined and don't exist. Games based on J. R. R. Tolkien's *The Lord of the Rings* or on George Luca's *Star War's* Trilogies are examples. The spaces in these games might appeal to people who are more imaginative or less literal-minded. The degree of identification with an avatar in simulations or simulacra thus depends on personality factors of the user. Not everyone will enjoy each type of game equally or desire to interact with it in the same way.

TABLE 15   Eleven different types of video game spaces

	Type of Space	Description	Example
1.	No visual space; all text based	Entirely text based. No images. Presented in the form of an interactive novel.	*Planetfall* (1983), *The Hitchhiker's Guide to the Galaxy* (1984)
2.	One screen, contained	One screen of graphics. Player does not leave the screen. Screen does not scroll to reveal off-screen space.	*Pong* (1972), *Space Invaders* (1978)
3.	One screen, contained, with wraparound	Objects leaving one side of the screen reappear on the opposite side.	*Asteroids* (1979), *Combat* (1977)
4.	Scrolling on one axis	Users travel through a single linear axis of space.	*Street Racer* (1978), *Defender* (1980)
5.	Scrolling on two axes	Screens that can scroll both side to side and up and down. Implies a larger 2-D plane of space of which only a small rectangle is seen at any given time.	*Gauntlet* (1985), *Dark Chambers* (1988)
6.	Adjacent spaces displayed one at a time	Adjacent spaces or rooms are displayed as a series of nonoverlapping static screens that cut directly one to the next.	*Berzerk* (1980), *Superman* (1979)
7.	Layers of independently moving planes (multiple scrolling backgrounds)	Front layer contains the player-character while the background contains background graphics and scrolls at a slower rate, creating an illusion of depth.	*Zaxxon* (1982), *Double Dragon* (1986)
8.	Spaces allowing z-axis movement into and out of the frame	Depicts objects getting larger as they approach the viewer and then moving out of the frame.	*Tempest* (1980), *Star Ship* (1977)
9.	Multiple, nonadjacent spaces displayed on-screen simultaneously	Two different points of view, each belonging to one of the players, displayed on-screen on a single window at the same time.	*High Velocity* (1995)
10.	Interactive 3-D environment	The character can move about in any direction.	*Dark Forces* (1996), *Tomb Raider 2* (1997)
11.	Represented or "mapped" spaces	An on-screen representation of an off-screen space, such as a map of the terrain.	*Stellar Track* (1980), *Caesar II* (1996)

Source: Wolf (2001).

The way in which one travels through a space can also affect immersion and avatar identification. In video role-playing games (v-RPGs), characters typically travel about on foot. In other games travel takes place in a vehicle such as racecar, an airplane, or a spaceship. Projection of self into the game is probably stronger for human character representation, but vehicles allow one to travel at a greater speed, which can be more exhilarating. Umberto Eco (1984) differentiates three labyrinth types. Linear paths are simple straight lines. They require little or no effort to navigate but can induce a sense of accomplishment simply from having covered ground. A maze path confronts the user with choices about which direction to go (such as left or right) at different junctures and can lead to an exit or to dead ends. A maze with an exit has a final goal that provides purpose and a sense of satisfaction after finding it. A rhizome is a root-like network where every point can be connected to every other point. Rhizome pathways are unsolvable in that they may have no exits. They induce a feeling of disorientation and hopelessness (Murray, 1997). These examples show that the structure of space itself is able to induce powerful feelings in the user.

Spaces look different depending on our point of view (POV). The POV of a game character is typically either first person or third person. First-person POV places the user inside the body of the avatar or agent. We see the virtual world through this character's eyes. Sometimes arms become visible when the character must hold a sword to fight or pick a lock. Third-person POV allows the user to see the avatar or agent's whole body, usually from a camera positioned above and behind. This POV allows us to see the whole character: the back side when the character is traveling forward, the front when the character turns around, et cetera. Gee (2004) argues that first-person POV allows you to identify tightly with the avatar's situatedness in the world. Third-person POV allows you to see the avatar's actions and reactions and to relate to them from a thematic perspective.

Nitsche (2008) defines video game spaces more broadly to include five analytical planes (figure 39). The first of these is the rule-based space. Rules here are the mathematical rules that define, for instance, the physics, sounds, AI, and game-level architecture. These rules are instantiated in the game's hardware and software and are what allow the user to interact with the game. They would include the controller and console, for instance. They would also include the software that runs the game. Games with complex rules and controls appeal to some. A keyboard is more sophisticated than a controller, and a joystick with buttons is more sophisticated than a mouse. Likewise a game that allows customization of a character is more sophisticated than one that does not.

The second plane is the mediated space. This is defined by the presentation, which is the space of the image plane and the way it might be represented cinematically. A computer screen or VR headset screen is part of the mediated space and controls the way it is presented to the user. Whether the image is 2-D or 3-D and whether the point of view is first person or third person are also aspects of this space. Wolf's categories refer mainly to mediated spaces. The mediated space has a huge impact on our immersion and engagement with a game. Three-dimensional-rendered spaces that are highly detailed are more movie-like and perhaps best suited to tell stories. Two-dimensional spaces are most suited to puzzles and games.

The fictional space exists inside the imagination of the player and is based on his or her comprehension of the available images. The way users think about and represent the game includes their conception of an avatar. Users' projection of their self or identity into the avatar is part of this. So is the way users represent the space. A user who has an accurate mental map of a dungeon, for instance, will be better able to navigate through it and rescue a princess or find the chest filled with gold.

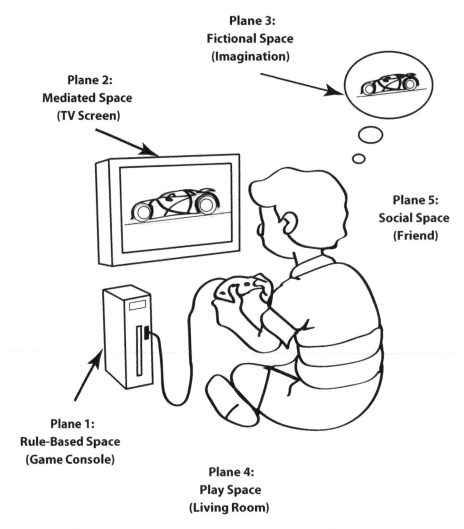

Plane 3:
Fictional Space
(Imagination)

Plane 2:
Mediated Space
(TV Screen)

Plane 5:
Social Space
(Friend)

Plane 1:
Rule-Based Space
(Game Console)

Plane 4:
Play Space
(Living Room)

FIGURE 39 The five analytical planes of video game spaces. After Nitsche (2008).

The fourth analytical plane is the play space. This includes the player and the video game hardware. It might be, for instance, a child sitting on a floor holding an X-Box controller. The amount of physical space this person has to move around in the room is part of the play space. Users with a wireless Wii controller or VR body suit may be more free to move about and utilize more of the physical space while they are playing. This can make a big difference to user immersion, satisfaction, and self-representation in the game. Being able to use one's entire body to play a sport more closely mimics how that sport is actually played and may be more satisfying than using a controller or joystick to produce the same actions.

The fifth and final type of analytical game space is the social space. This refers to the other players in a game. It could be, for example, a friend sitting next to you playing a console game in your living room. In an MMO game it could also be the large number of other people from around the world who are simultaneously participating. Knowing that you are competing against your friend may engage the self more emotionally with a game than if you were playing against a stranger.

A BRIEF HISTORY OF VIRTUAL WORLDS

In the broadest sense humans have always been virtual. Imagination can create virtual worlds with no tools other than the mind. Cave paintings depicting stories of the hunt, for example, have been proposed by some to be the earliest form of virtual worlds (Heim, 1995). The creation of language certainly heralded virtualism in many forms, including myth telling, theater, opera, and novels (Schwartz, 1996). Plato's allegory of the cave with its shadowy reflection of the real is an early example from philosophy. In fact, Plato's designation of real and ideal forms posits a duality in which actual objects always have corresponding ideal representations. The religious conception of heaven and hell invokes virtual worlds inhabited by angels and devils. Angels can be considered as avatars of individuals that persist beyond death, as devils are representations of individual people who are tortured in hell. The soul seems like a type of avatar, as it does not seem to exist entirely in the physical world.

Science fiction and fantasy literature have been acknowledged as contributing substantially to the imagining of virtual worlds. J. R. R. Tolkien's *Lord of the Rings* trilogy, published for the first time in 1954, has been a major contributor (Bartle, 2004). The first release of the *Dungeons and Dragons* role-playing game in 1974 was another. Starting in the 1980s, "cyberpunk" literature emerged that addressed virtual worlds in a more complete way. William Gibson's *Neuromancer* first coined the term *cyberspace*, while Neal Stephenson's novel *Snow Crash* spawned the term *metaverse* as synonymous with *virtual world*. In the 1990s, *The Matrix* movies fleshed out what it might be like in even greater detail.

Technology, of course, makes the creation of virtual worlds easier. The printing press preserved stories and allowed them to be propagated in a more widespread manner through books and newspapers. In the nineteenth century, forms of electronic mass media like the telegraph, telephone, and television allowed extended communication and storytelling. The telephone may constitute the first modern form of cyberspace, with the space being the imagined world shared by the speakers, or the information available to both communicating parties simultaneously (Sterling, 1992). Wertheim (1999) argues that television starting in the 1950s was a kind of rudimentary cyberspace because it provided a "collective parallel world" for millions of people.

Text-based virtual worlds on computers can probably be said to have originated with public bulletin board systems (BBSs) starting in 1978. These were set up so that people from around the world could communicate with one another on different topics. Conversations on particular topics were known as threads. Email and discussion lists such as these went by a variety of other names, including listservs and Internet Relay Chat (IRC). Systems such as these were mostly asynchronic, meaning participants exchanged posts but did not always interact simultaneously (Kollock & Smith, 1999). Habitat, released in 1985 for the

Commodore 64 personal computer, was a 2-D simulation of Tokyo and is credited as the first networked virtual world in which people were represented as avatars.

Regular video games also contain explicit world representations (Bartle, 2004). The first popular two-player video game, *Pong*, had the very simple world of a tennis court and two paddles (Kent, 2001). The first with computer-controlled entities was *Space Invaders*, released in 1978. It featured lines of aliens descending from the top of the screen. *Battlezone*, a tank combat simulator game, was released by Atari in 1980 and was probably the first game depicted from a first-person perspective (McMahan, 2003). *Doom*, put out in 1993. was the first video game widely recognized as having an immersive 3-D environment as well as being networked and multiplayer.

Starting in the 1990s games were developed whose primary purpose was to simulate real-world situations. Two such games, *SimCity 2000* and *SimEarth*, were both centered on watching life forms evolve or cities develop rather than on trying to gain points or defeat enemies. They can be seen as an important first step toward the creation of software devoted to interactive virtual environments. Second Life, first published as Linden World in 2002, is the ultimate computer-based virtual world and is described in detail later. Many people who played sim games later became residents of Second Life.

PRESENCE AND THE ULTIMATE DISPLAY

The previous exposition shows that humans are always on the quest to experience virtual worlds. However, technological limitations have prevented us from doing this in a way that is so compelling we cannot distinguish them from the real. That might be changing. Rapid advances in electronics could make this possible within the next decade or two. Bown, White, and Boopalan (2017) outline what it means to have such a technology and give us a history of the devices leading up to it.

The Ultimate Display would be a device that stimulated our senses in such a way that we would perceive the simulated environment as real. It would also grant the user freedom or abilities beyond the limits of the user's physical reality, what is known as transcendence (Biocca, Kim, & Levy, 1995). Examples of physical transcendence include being able to fly, inhabit different bodies, or otherwise defy the laws of physics. The Ultimate Display would produce an essential copy, a perfect rendition of an object that would fool all senses into perceiving it as real. The Ultimate Display would allow a user not only to perceive an essential copy but also to pick it up or manipulate it in some way; it would need to allow for interactivity.

Presence is a felt sense of authentic reality that comes from an engagement with sophisticated media. It is not restricted to virtual worlds alone and corresponds roughly to what we define as immersion elsewhere. Steuer (1992) uses three things that contribute to feelings of presence. These are vividness, interactivity, and user characteristics. Technologies that satisfy these criteria will induce a greater sense of presence and move us closer to building the Ultimate Display.

Vividness is a measure of the richness and complexity of visual elements in the virtual environment. Clarity and smooth eye movements contribute toward vividness. The cues generated by a virtual environment are important for vividness. They provide a sense of cause and effect in the world. Perceptual cues are sensory stimuli that evoke physiological reactions. For example, seeing a large spider would trigger a panic reaction in someone who has arachnophobia. Evoking such a response has been shown to increase the sense of presence. Notably the reaction itself can contribute to presence. So the spider in this example causes fear, which increases sense of presence, but the fear itself also contributes to presence (Peperkorn, Diemer, & Mühlberger, 2015).

Interactivity is a measure of how the user can cause an effect on the virtual environment and also contributes to presence. Huang and Yu-Ting (2013) discovered that increased interactivity in a virtual environment also upped the user's sense of flow. Flow is the positive feeling that arises when one is focused on a particular task without distraction, for example when painting or sailing (Csikszentmihalyi, 2008). It has also been linked to presence. Increased flow provides an increase in the sense of presence for the task (Kotler, 2014). Flow increases when users feel as if they are physically touching a virtual object, as is the case when haptic feedback methods are used during shooting or medical simulation games.

User characteristics also affect presence. Each user is unique, varying in his or her understanding of technology, cognitive style, and personality traits. Examples of how user characteristics can affect presence are discussed in detail in the sections on avatar case studies in chapter 7. Individuals having difficulty using a controller or figuring out the rules of a game will be less immersed and feel less presence. Greater identification with one's avatar also probably contributes to presence.

A CHRONOLOGY OF VR SYSTEMS

In the next few sections we provide a short history of VR devices up to the present day. We will see that the desire to experience virtual worlds has driven the development of such devices and that we are now very close to having a perfect VR device or Ultimate Display.

Early Developments

Panoramic paintings were perhaps the earliest attempt at VR technology. These are paintings of a scene that surround the viewer. Typically they were painted on the inside surface walls of a rotunda or circular building. A person standing in the center of this space could turn around in a 360-degree arc to view the scene in its entirety. Sometimes they incorporated props that were positioned in front of the painting to add to a feeling of depth (Woeste, 2009). These were popular in the nineteenth and twentieth centuries. The first such rotunda was a painted scene of Edinburg, Scotland.

Stereoscopes were another popular form of entertainment during this same time period. This is a device that presents slightly different images to each eye, mimicking how we normally see a scene using binocular disparity. They later became popular as children's toys and were called the View-Master. Charles Wheatstone is credited with their creation in 1838. There was at least one stereoscope in every home in nineteenth-century Britain (Gamber & Withers, 1996).

The multisensory theater experience can be classified as the next significant VR technology (Carlson, 2007). Morton Heilig wanted to create an immersive sensory experience that used 3-D images, stereo sound, even wind, smells, and vibrations. He thought it would be the equivalent of movies or cinema for the future (Heilig, 1960). His Sensorama simulator was patented in 1962. Five films were made for it: a motorcycle ride through New York City, rides on a bicycle, a dune buggy, and a helicopter, and the performance of a belly dancer (Carlson, 2007). Heilig saw this as not just for entertainment. He wanted to use it for training in the army, for laborers and students, or for companies to showcase new products (Brockwell, 2016). It was successful but probably didn't gain widespread recognition because it required many expensive machines that frequently broke down.

The Modern Era

Next came the head-mounted device or HMD for short, created in 1961 by engineers at Philco Corporation. Named Headsight, this was a helmet with a closed-circuit camera. It was linked to a magnetic tracking system that would turn the camera in three dimensions as the user turned and moved his or her head (Rid, 2016). The system projected a ten-inch-high image that appeared to be 1.5 feet in front of the viewer. It was intended to remotely view dangerous situations. This was the first VR system that introduced interactivity. The first time that computers were used to mediate a VR experience was in 1965 with the "Sword of Damocles" system, where the helmet was too heavy and needed to be hung from the ceiling. Sutherland (1968) used the computer to generate a 3-D wire frame cube that appeared to float in a room. Although the graphics were primitive, the cube would move in response to the viewer's head movements.

The first company to develop and sell VR products to a consumer market was Visual Programming Languages, founded by Jaron Lanier in 1984. Lanier is said to have coined the phrase *virtual reality*. The company developed the DataGlove and EyePhone. A user wore the DataGlove and used it to control a floating virtual hand. The virtual hand could then be used to manipulate virtual objects (Sturman & Zeltzer, 1994). The glove could also control movement through the virtual world. In addition, users could use the glove to control how they flew. Moving their thumb closer to their palm made them fly faster. Moving it away made them stop. The glove, however, was too expensive, and it was one size fits all (Burdea & Coiffet, 2003). It also lacked tactile feedback, so users could not feel what they were touching. The EyePhone consisted of two small LCD screens to produce a sense of depth, but the quality and frame rate of the graphics were poor.

In 1991 Sega announced that they were working on a sleek, lightweight VR headgear, designed to look like the eyepiece worn by Geordi La Forge's visor from *Star Trek: The Next Generation*. The graphics unfortunately were unable to keep up with the user's head movements, resulting in motion sickness, aka cybersickness. A significant number of users reported feeling sick after using it, so it was ultimately abandoned. Another gaming company, Nintendo, next made a stab at producing its own VR system. Called the Virtual Boy, it was released in 1995 and ended up flopping as well because of problems with its graphics.

In 2001 a VR room called the SAS cube was created. It was a room filled with sensors and projectors. Images were cast onto the four walls and the floor, and the system could react to the people standing inside it. Users had to wear 3-D glasses with motion-tracking headsets. These gave the images depth. The users could interact with objects and navigate throughout the space (Robertson, 2001). The complexity and vividness of the images were subpar, and there was no tactile feedback, but the system was a good approximation of what an interactive VR room should be like.

Current VR Devices

The Oculus Rift started off as a do-it-yourself kit to be assembled at home. It has realistic imagery and hand motion capability. The quality of the video is now improved from original versions. Its developer, Palmer Luckey, has teamed up with Mark Zuckerberg from Facebook, who intends to use it for social media. The goal here seems to be virtual social interactivity. The Oculus Rift has spurred the development of several competing models from Google, Samsung, and Steam. Figure 40 shows a virtual reality headset.

A number of VR systems are designed to work with mobile phones. Google Cardboard, for instance, has a cardboard viewer that must be assembled (Google, 2015). One inserts the phone inside the viewer, and the app then projects two images stereoscopically to each eye. This is the "poor man's" VR, since the viewer costs next to nothing. The experience is like being inside a panoramic image. One can turn around and see an expansive 3-D view, but there is no capability to interact with the environment. Samsung Gear VR is a setup quite similar to Google Cardboard. It is more immersive than the Google system, with excellent depth effects. It doesn't have motion-tracking capability and so can't be used for intensive gaming but is a great way to experience landscapes and videos.

We would be amiss not to mention the HTC Vive from Carlos Rebato (2015). What sets this system apart is that it has positional tracking based on sensors attached to the walls. It also has two controllers, each with a touchpad and trigger that act as "virtual hands." The downside is that the cords get tangled up and become a tripping hazard (Grayson, 2015). The vividness and quality of the images, though, are the best among its competitors. Some of the most recent VR systems to come out on the market are the Oculus Go, the Oculus Quest, the Samsung HMD Odyssey, the Google Daydream, and the Zeis VR One Plus.

To summarize, current VR systems are good and getting better. Some of the headgear is clunky and needs to be lighter. There are software glitches, and the experience, though compelling, is not good enough to fool users into thinking they are experiencing reality. The result is not the Ultimate Display. Graphics, although decent, are not yet at the level of creating the perfect copy. Interactivity is also an issue. Many of the controllers used to operate virtual hands need improvement. Currently, accessory hardware is being developed to increase interactivity. For example, the Virtuix Omni Treadmill is a touch-sensitive

FIGURE 40 A woman using a virtual reality headset. Image courtesy of pixneo.com.

omnidirectional treadmill that creates the illusion of walking about in a virtual environment (Sofka, 2015; Virtuix, 2014).

SECOND LIFE

VR systems are the hardware interface that allows us to enter virtual worlds. Now that we have a better understanding of them, let's focus on the software. The largest and most extensive experiment with virtual world software is Second Life (SL). Developed by Linden Lab, it was started in 2003. Ten years later it had over a million users. The creators point out that SL is not a computer game. It has no levels to attain, there are no set goals, and conflict or battle is not its main objective. Anybody can join and access the system by using the provided software and by paying a monthly fee. Avatars can move around the world, socialize, and participate in various group activities. The platform is a 3-D system, and most of the simulation consists of islands and other landmasses separated by oceans and terrain with trees and buildings. As such it is meant to reproduce the actual environment and not a fantasy or science fiction world.

Users in SL create their own avatars and are able to manufacture houses, clothes, and other objects that they can use or sell to others. The currency of exchange is the Linden dollar, which is linked to the US dollar and to other international currencies. Residents can thus use real money to obtain Linden dollars that they can use to purchase goods as well as property. Individuals and corporations have set up stores in SL that they use to sell all manner of products from shoes and clothes to custom animations that allow avatars to do things like drink or dance.

People in SL can move around locally by walking or running. But because it has now become so vast, for longer distances they access vehicles, fly, or even teleport instantaneously to another location in the grid. Communication with other avatars takes place by local chat, group chat, global instant messaging (IM), and voice. Typed chatting is used for public conversations between two or a small number of other avatars and can be seen by others within a localized distance. IMs are used for private communications between two avatars or between members of a group. IM is global and not restricted to the small region that a group of avatars share.

Tom Boellstorff (2008) spent several years (June 3, 2004, to January 30, 2007) as the avatar Tom Bukowski in SL using fieldwork methods from anthropology. His goal was to learn about the people "living" in the system and to try to understand something about the psychology of its users and its larger social organization. His book *Coming of Age in Second Life* is a description of this work. In the next several sections we will touch on some his conclusions, addressing issues of personhood but also the topics of intimacy, community, and political economy.

Personhood in Second Life

Although many characters in games take on roles like "elf" or "orc," SL is not primarily a role-playing environment. Most residents of SL say they may start off playing a role but then concentrate on just "being themselves." Rather than becoming someone new, most SL residents seemed to be suppressing certain aspects of their personalities and accentuating others. A distinction has been made between "persona-play" and "role-play." This ability to express normally suppressed parts of oneself may exist because of the anonymity players have. Almost all SL residents choose to keep their actual and virtual selfhoods separate, not revealing their actual names, locations, or other identity information. There are in fact cases of celebrities who have spent time in SL without revealing their true-world identities, probably to gain a measure of normal everyday social interaction unavailable to them in the actual world.

Some of the comments SL residents make reinforce this. One user commented on appearing strong online but in real life (RL) being "so weak it's not even funny." Another remarked that he or she did not live a "double life" in SL but was instead better able to express who he or she truly was. A third said that her avatar allowed her to define her own role rather than playing the ones she had in RL, which in this case were mother and wife. These comments suggest that role playing seems to occur more in the real world and that virtual worlds like SL are a venue for exploring alternate aspects of one's personality.

The border between real and virtual self seems to be not a hard barrier but instead quite permeable. Many SL residents thought their online selves made their actual-world self more "real," one that reflected their true nature and not what society expected of them. One reported greater self-confidence: "I had no problem talking to a complete stranger at the shopping center because I have spent a lot of time in SL recently doing the same thing." Another resident who was housebound in the actual world because of a stroke found the courage to get out of a wheelchair and use a walker because of involvement in SL. Some SL residents spoke of their virtual-world self as being closer to the real self than their actual world selves.

One way in which selfhood is defined culturally is by a trajectory or life course (Giddens, 1991). This typically takes the form of how to act while young, as an adult, and when elderly. In SL a virtual life started when a person registered for an account, and this date was sometimes called one's "birthday." During registration a permanent screen name was selected. However, screen names could not easily be mapped to real-world identity because many residents had more than one avatar, known as an "alt." They might appear as a chipmunk under one screen name and as a body builder under another. Also, two or more people could "drive" the same avatar registered under an individual account.

In virtual worlds more focused on gaming, residents must ascend a tiered set of skill levels that serves to organize their online life course. In these cases, one's level or skill can be a measure of experience. But in SL there were no such levels and one's experience was more open-ended. However, people new to SL were often assigned the label *newbie* or *noob* (Kendall, 2002). This status was frequently revealed by one's appearance and behavior. Those new to SL were more apt to "wear" the default appearance of their avatar and had fewer purchased animations that would allow them to engage in behaviors like dancing. Noobs also needed to learn SL norms. A common form of etiquette in SL was to stand up before teleporting or exiting the program. This served as a cue to let others know of their imminent departure. Newbies who failed to do this rapidly vanished, an act sometimes labeled as "poofing."

Altruism was another common norm in SL. Experienced residents usually offered free advice, support, and objects to newcomers. Learning was mostly informal, and to acquire skills, newbies would often turn to those who had been around longer. Those with at least a moderate amount of experience in SL were termed *midbies*. Experience was measured not by the amount of time lapsed since one's birthday but by the hours logged online or "inworld." Someone who spent three hours a day inworld but was only one year old was considered to be more experienced than someone who spent only one hour a day inworld but who was two years old.

A small number of SL residents preferred solitude, spending their time building, designing items to sell, or simply walking through virtual parks. For the vast majority of residents, however, the purpose of being in SL was to socialize. One mark of experience in SL was the size of a social network. Those with many friends, lovers, and family members were no longer newbies. Property ownership was also a sign. Some, but not all, who had logged more virtual time in SL owned more land and had built or constructed more objects. We tend to associate ownership (jewelry, cars, real estate) with success in the real world, and this principle seems to have carried over into SL. In addition to economic power there were signs of political power. Some of the residents with lots of inworld experience became community leaders, organizing events and directing the assistance of others, even though in SL users lacked the capability to organize politically in a formal way. A leader of this sort might be called an "oldie."

In the real world everybody eventually dies. In SL death of an avatar was not assumed every time someone logged out of the system. It was instead marked by the failure to continue appearing. This could happen for a number of reasons. First, a personal tragedy or responsibility in the real world might prevent someone from continued use. Second, some residents dropped out because they felt they were spending too much time in the system or because a virtual relationship was interfering with a real-world one. It was not uncommon for a sexual relationship in SL to interfere with a couple's marriage. Additionally, some left because they were dissatisfied with SL. They might have found the interface too difficult to learn, wanted more of a gaming experience, were unable to generate enough real-world cash flow, or were unsatisfied with the quality of their social relationships. Others left because of unresolved bugs and software issues, because of what they considered to be unfair business practices, or because of offensive speech and behavior by other users.

If a longtime or oldie resident decided to leave it could be a bitter experience, commemorated by farewell parties and recorded in blogs. Others might scale down their experience by giving up their property or other commitments and in effect becoming "homeless" vagabonds or wanderers. Friends of residents who had died in the real world would sometimes hosted virtual funerals complete with roses, mourners dressed in black, photos of the deceased, and testimonials. It was theoretically possible for another resident to assume control of a "dead" avatar, but this rarely or never seemed to happen, probably because it would create a virtual "zombie" or "ghost." What usually happened was that the avatar was officially rendered inactive as a tribute to the deceased.

Avatars and Alts in Second Life

Avatars in SL were often referred to as "avies." One could see the immediate landscape around one's avatar from its particular or first-person viewpoint in what was called "mouselook" mode. It was also possible to see this landscape from an avatar's proximity, a more third-person perspective. An avatar could read the typed chats of other residents within a thirty-meter radius. It could also see which other avatars were present and where their attention was directed. Figure 41 shows some examples of SL avatars.

In SL it was possible to change the appearance of one's avatar at any time for free, although it was also possible to buy custom shoes, hats, clothes, and other accessories. There was a significant degree of control over facial features and body parts, with the capability to manipulate eyes, nose, mouth, chin, torso, and so on. Shirts, pants, socks, and other apparel could also be changed and customized. The goal of this was to create not just a unique or attractive avatar but one that expressed alternate aspects of one's psyche. Users would often

FIGURE 41 A Second Life avatar

have more than one avatar, with different genders, races, and even species represented by a single user. Examples could include wolves, vampires, and even robots. Most users agreed that others judged them on the basis of appearance. One resident proclaimed that she didn't like "tall skinny blondes." People were also judged on their behavior, as it was possible to know when someone was busy IM'ing or looking through scripts or inventory.

Anonymity was extremely important. Most SL users did not want to disclose their true identities. One resident for example commented about working as an escort and not wanting this information publicly available in the real world. Real-world individuals controlled most avatars. However, some could be fully automated. These were called "bots." As mentioned earlier, multiple persons could control a single avatar, and a single person could control multiple avatars or "alts." There could be many type of alts. The account of a banking alt could be used to hold funds and simplify bookkeeping. A building alt could be used to build or script objects. Testing alts were used to try out clothes or animations, and exploring alts could wander around different parts of the landscape.

Boellstorff (2008) reports that the most typical alt in SL was the social alt, used to embody an alternate aspect of selfhood. Users might have a main account representing a proper housewife and an alternate alt that served as a sexy escort. Such instances suggest that people might create an avatar for their Freudian "id" and others that might express their "ego" or "superego." In some instances alts were used to deceive. One resident created an alt in an attempt to seduce an SL spouse as a test of the spouse's fidelity. Despite such alts, most people spent the most time in their main or primary avatar. This avatar was often designed according to standard cultural conceptions of beauty or as a representation of the person's true real-life self. Alts as such were called "costumes" or "masks."

People are quite flexible in the choice of their avatar. Many users report that their avatar is more than just their physical self (T. Taylor, 2002). In SL there was even a style where people embodied themselves as three-foot-high baby animals called "tinies." But perhaps more significant is the fact that many physically disabled users in SL were able to free themselves to use their body in ways not possible in real life. Those in wheelchairs were able to walk or run, and those with Parkinson's disease were able to pick up and move objects. These disabled individuals were also able to expand their social networks, meeting many more people than would have been possible because of their condition. Unfortunately discrimination under such circumstances did not go away. Some of the disabled reported that their "friends" had abandoned them when they discovered they were in a wheelchair in the real world.

Gender, Race, and Disorders in Second Life

An example of alternate psychic expression comes from Pavia, a beautiful female avatar whom Boellstorff had known for over a year. Pavia confided to him that she was trans. She admitted that at first it had been just role playing but that after a while the persona of Pavia came out in the real world. What is interesting about this case is that the flow of influence between person and avatar is not just one way. Pavia in some sense wasn't just being controlled by a user; the avatar fed back and affected the user in turn. The flow between user and avatar is a two-way street in that each influences and controls the other. At the time of this field study SL allowed only a gender choice of male or female. Other categories like trans were not options, despite users' petition for a sliding scale with male at one end and female at the other. Transgenderism, gender switching, and cross-dressing, however, were quite common.

Turkle (1997) notes that gender swapping in virtual worlds allows people to experience what it is like to be a member of another sex rather than to just observe it. Most forms of this in SL were probably cases of people with one avatar, who was of the opposite gender. However, some may have had a primary avatar with their opposite gender and an alt with their same gender. There was at least one instance of a husband who asked his wife to be a male avatar to prevent other SL men from making romantic advances. Another man with a female avatar was afraid to show her to his wife for fear that she would be jealous! There were also cases of people who created gender-neutral avatars. These avatars could appear androgynous or as something nonsexual like a box or ball of blue light.

Few virtual worlds require choice of a race for an avatar (Nakamura, 2002). SL did not, but one could manipulate facial features, skin tone, and hair to appear Caucasian, Asian, Latino, black, or any other type of race. "Skins," for example with varying degrees of stubble or wrinkles, could be manufactured and sold and were highly sought after. White or near-white skins, however, were the norm in SL. Darker skin tones were more difficult to come by, and some residents wearing nonwhite skins reported racist responses. Some real-world blacks also disguised themselves as white.

Evidence of racism took other forms. Users who displayed Confederate flags and images of Robert E. Lee could be identified as "cyber-Dixies." These sorts of people have a significant online history (McPherson, 2000). There were also "Slave Auctions" with people who willingly sold themselves into slavery. SL additionally had a number of dominant and submissive sexual communities, with or without race as a component. Many ethnic groups flourished in SL. Examples included a group for African American women and a group for the celebration of Kwanzaa. The vast majority of residents were fortunately antiracist and would call out examples of racist speech and behavior. As a case in point, the construction of an "SS Training Camp" received many complaints and reports to the management as soon as it was discovered.

People with autism and Asperger's syndrome have problems interacting socially. Many of them have difficulty picking up social cues in facial expression or vocal intonation. SL's limited facial expressivity and use of a text-based chatting system with frequent expected delays made it easier for such individuals to communicate. Delays in responding occurred frequently in SL because sometimes residents were away from their keyboard (afk) or were chatting with multiple nearby residents simultaneously. Even schizophrenics with severe linguistic and social deficits could fit into SL. Joseph was one example. He was a schizophrenic who in the real world was a recluse and rarely communicated. But in SL his avatar was able to explore, walk around different environments, talk, and create with others. A number of residents who self-reported as shy or withdrawn commented to Boellstorff that in SL their avatars were more socially outgoing. This trait could then sometimes feed back to the real world, making them more socially outgoing too. The opposite, though, was also true, with some individuals who acted fairly decently offline but acted "like jerks in here."

Intimacy, Sex, and Love in Second Life

A number of SL residents would engage in multiple IM conversations as they moved from one place to another. One resident stated she could juggle a live conversation and ten IMs at the same time. IMs could be directed to a group and if so were called "groups" or "channels." English was at the establishment of SL the dominant language, but as SL grew over the years other languages became established. Audio and video chat capabilities during the time period of this anthropological study were not yet available.

The popular notion that the internet, games, and virtual worlds only serve to isolate people from each other is a misconception. Studies show that these technological media in fact foster social connectivity, both online and in the real world (E. Reid, 1999). SL residents saw it as "an intimacy-making culture" and spent a large amount of their time and energy online to developing friends (Jakobsson & Taylor, 2003). This phenomenon is not unique to SL but is seen in many social media sites like Twitter and Facebook. In SL all sorts of relationships existed, including romantic partner, husband and wife, parent and child, teacher and student, siblings, coworkers and neighbors. But friendship was the dominant form of relationship.

A meeting in SL usually started with reading a person's profile that contained basic information, including a list of groups the individual belonged to. There was also a description of interests that identified what that person liked to do in SL, whether shopping, running a business, or manufacturing homes. Boellstorff's (2008) research shows that in most cases friends did not ask for or disclose their real-world identities. It was possible to have many close virtual friends but have no idea who they were or what they did in the outside world. One user commented that in SL you got to know what people were truly like. Many residents reported a great emotional intensity to their relationships and would engage in close intimate behaviors like hugging and slow dancing. One resident reported feeling more upset about losing a virtual girlfriend than any real-life girlfriends.

Sex was an important aspect of SL and for some was the main purpose of using the system (figure 42). All types of sex could happen, including "age play" with youthful or childlike avatars or sex with animals. Prostitution, group sex, strip clubs, and sex slaves all existed. Entire islands were devoted to specific sexual themes like BDSM (bondage, discipline, domination, submission, sadism, and masochism). Residents constructed many sex objects like genitalia and restraints that could be used to tie an avatar to a bed. Bardzell and Bardzell (2006) note that erotic pain and domination in such acts is replaced with the *representation* of those things in simulation. Others SL users, however, failed to have virtual sex in any form.

To better assist users with regard to sexual acts, different sections of land in SL were allocated as being "PG" (parental guidance) or "M" (mature). As it was possible for users to teleport instantaneously to many areas in this simulation, having sex undisturbed required innovation. One solution was a "skybox," which could be built hundreds of meters above ground level. Because users could fly only to a height of two hundred meters if they were not using a scripted object, this ensured some amount of privacy.

The main portion of SL was restricted to adults only with a separate "Teen Grid" created for people thirteen to seventeen years of age. Even so, many residents expressed discomfort at the idea of virtual pedophilia, especially because in some jurisdictions even simulated sex with minors was illegal (Teriman, 2006). Straight sex between heterosexual couples was common, but gay, lesbian and bisexual sex also flourished in SL. There were many such communities in SL, some with their own islands and towns. Although one lesbian island was attacked, for the most part these communities were left alone. Boellstorff (2008) reports many bisexuals who were married to heterosexual partners in the real world but who pursued virtual homosexual relations, sometimes with the approval of their actual spouse.

FIGURE 42 A romantic moment by the sea in Second Life. Many individuals have sexual and romantic relationships and even get married in virtual worlds but never meet in the real world.

Love is a predominant consequence of virtual world usage. The first virtual wedding in a graphic-based system was in May of 1996 (Damer, 1998). Lovers have made "homes" for themselves even in text-only systems (E. Reid, 1999). Some of these relationships are cross-platform, with couples fighting together in *World of Warcraft*, then switching to SL to engage in other activities. Weddings were some of the most elaborate and well-attended events in SL. Although some partners disclosed their real-world identities, in the majority of these relationships anonymity was the rule.

Real-world mores don't seem to get in the way of expressing love. For example, two female avatars reported having a lesbian relationship over a period of several months while knowing that both were heterosexual men in the actual world. Married couples sometimes allowed their partners to pursue a relationship in SL, in some cases attending one another's weddings and befriending their spouse's virtual partner. Such "affairs" were often allowed, but it was acknowledged that the challenge was in keeping the affair virtual.

Family in Second Life

Families have been online and in virtual worlds together for some time (Nardi, Ly, & Harris, 2007). Boellstorff (2008) relates the story of two sisters named Satin and Gretel who spent time in SL along with three other siblings. This pair would do lots of activities together, including shopping, building, and roller-skating. Some SL couples even had automated children, programmed to cry and say things like "I'm hungry!" A number of adults would also take on child avatar forms in what was called "child play." One such adult, whose avatar went by the name Wendy, would address adult avatars as "Mr." or "Mrs." and ask to be taken out to play, only, of course, after she got permission from her "parents." Several groups in SL were dedicated to child play, playgrounds, toys, children's clothing, and elementary schools. These schools were complete with classes, recess, and even school nurses.

Most of the child avatars reported that having parents was important to their child play. Many adults were more than willing to take on the role. Arlen, an adult avatar, had a daughter and son avatar in SL, who were both themselves actual adults. She said that they had never had a father figure in the real world and that she was happy to provide them a parental bond. One adult playing as a child liked to be tucked into bed at night. Her "parent" would tell her a story or sing a song and then put her to sleep.

Addiction in Second Life

We treat internet addiction in greater detail elsewhere so here discuss addiction only as it applies to SL. Because SL mirrors the real world in so many ways, saying that it is addictive is in some ways equivalent to saying that life is addictive (Boellstorff, 2008). Nonetheless there were instances of users who felt that they were spending too much of their time in the virtual. They gave two reasons for this. First, the activities were felt to take up too much total time. Second, this time was seen as detracting or interfering with their "real" time. A number of residents spoke about sleeping less so as to spend more time in SL. Others felt they were spending too much time away from actual friends and family. When they were asked what they enjoyed most, the response was always that they enjoyed the interactions with people. Building, scripting, traveling, and other nonsocial activities were mentioned far less often. Descriptions and a critique of internet addictive disorder is provided in chapter 3.

Community in Second Life

One of the interesting facts about SL is that people were able to form strong bonds with others despite being spatially and temporally separated. Avatars were able to chat with members of entire groups or perform global IMs to individuals who were spread out over a wide geographic area, both actually and virtually. They were also able to maintain communication ties despite lag times in responding that could last hours or days or longer. The conclusion is that communities can form without having to interact in the same location or at the same time. Virtual worlds can thus be considered as "third spaces" that exist in addition to the public and private (Steinkuehler & Williams, 2006).

Although people could meet spontaneously on their own in various gathering places, they could also meet through more organized events. Events in SL were of all types and could be anything from musical concerts to fashion shows to philosophy discussions. One interesting phenomenon that took place in SL was "social gravity": people would be attracted to locations where others were already gathered (P. Curtis, 1992). The idea behind this was that if a group of people were in an area, something interesting had to be going on, so it was worth visiting. By contrast, areas that were, devoid of avatars tend to stay empty.

Groups at the time of Boellstorff's study averaged about five to fifteen people with a maximum of forty. Limitations in broadband speeds and computer servers at the time constrained the number of people that could communicate with one another at such functions. At current publication this number is probably larger. The wide diversity of people in SL meant that groups could organize around almost any topic. Additional examples of groups included scripting, architecture, poetry, and topics on identity categories like vampires, gay men, and music lovers. An especially interesting group were the "Furries," people who identified as animals. At the time of the study an estimated fifteen thousand residents had Furrie avatars. Religious groups were less popular at that time, although this may have changed.

Ethics in Second Life

Boellstorff (2008) notes that there is a predominance of kindness and altruism in virtual worlds. The people who already "know the ropes" are in most cases very willing to explain and help without any thought of reciprocity or financial compensation. It was common for people to give away items like clothes, healing spells, and virtual furniture. Many midbies, newbies, and community leaders would offer educational classes to newcomers for free. There is no single best explanation for this behavior.

But SL was definitely not a virtual utopia. Griefing—the deliberate intent to disrupt the experience of other virtual residents—happened as well. This could take the form of verbal insults and/or malicious behavior, both of which could be repeated after people were asked to stop (Foo, 2004). One griefer played sex animations with his avatar at a support group meeting for people recovering from sexual abuse. It was not unheard of for people to "stalk" someone as he or she moved across different locations. Vandalism and inappropriate building also happened. Examples include the construction of gigantic sex organs or the placement of sexually explicit pictures on the sides of buildings.

This list of griefing activity is long. Some griefers would push or shoot other avatars outside designated combat areas. Others used scripts that launched avatars so high into the air that it would take hours for them to fall back to ground. Virtual "mafias" tried to extort "protection" money from club or island owners. Some griefers formed groups, called themselves "goons," and reported enjoyment from "messing around" with other residents. There were even cases of "lag bombs," scripts that would cause computer servers to crash, forcing the SL program to reboot. These bombs may be considered an example of "virtual terrorism."

There are various explanations for griefing. It could be done to get attention, to show off programming skills, or to gain a sense of power. The anonymity of an avatar's real-life user may have also created a disinhibition in some users that contributed to griefing. Some griefers may have simply thought that they could get away with it. In the end griefers may do these things for the same reasons people carry out violent acts in the real world, because they are bored or because they wish to gain a reputation. It is probable that people who bully or tease in the real world are more likely to commit griefer acts in virtual worlds (Schechner, 1988).

SL residents had several options when responding to griefer acts. They could lodge a formal complaint with the Linden Labs management, who could then investigate the incident.

In some cases the griefers who were reported could be banned from SL. Residents could also teleport away from a griefer or log off temporarily to escape their actions. Laughing or ignoring them was also an effective response. It was additionally possible to "mute" a griefer, in which case one could not see chats typed by them. Some residents banned griefers from their property, but a determined griefer could use alts to gain entry.

The Political Economy of Second Life

As described above, people could not only build objects in SL but also sell them to others using the Linden dollar, which was linked to the US dollar. Anyone could purchase Lindens using real currency and use them to buy clothes, "skins," avatar animations, buildings, or land to put them on. One could set any object one had created to be for sale for any desired amount. By December 2006, over $US1 million was being exchanged on the system daily. Several residents were able to make an actual world living from what they did in SL. Not just goods but also services were for sale. It was possible, for instance, to rent a dance club for a party or a church for a wedding. Not just individuals but also corporations set up shop in SL. Examples included American Apparel, General Motors, Nissan, and Starwood Hotels.

All societies require governance, and SL was no exception. Because this was a computer simulation, all data that transpired, including personal communications, were logged on the Linden Lab servers. This undoubtedly made it easier to track down griefers, but it also posed a "Big Brother" scenario. Fear of virtual dictatorships in virtual worlds is a concern (Doctorow, 2007). Despite this, Linden Labs adopted a surprisingly libertarian and hands-off approach to management. Direct contact with Linden Lab staff was minimal. Residents interacted with Linden governance only when filing an Abuse Report and when experiencing changes to the SL platform. Perhaps because of this there were multiple examples of local governance, including constitutions, elections with campaigns, and political parties. Even real-world politicians made appearances, such as John Edwards, a candidate for president in the US in 2008. Government and military organizations may have even owned islands in SL, but this could not be confirmed.

A Third Life? Here Comes Sansar

Linden Labs is now working on a sequel to SL called Sansar. This is a virtual reality–driven system and doesn't rely entirely on a mouse or computer keyboard. It currently operates using the Oculus Rift VR system. Sansar uses facial animation technology that syncs an avatar's lip movements with the user's actual speech patterns in real time. So users can talk naturally and both the sound of their voice and the movements of their face will be conveyed by their avatar, even if the avatar is not human. An example of avatars and a virtual scene from Sansar are shown in figure 43.

Sansar environments will reportedly be easy to build. The company's VP of product design, Bjorn Laurin, along with his six-year-old son, in just one afternoon created a demo version of a basketball court. It was generated by dropping assets from the Sansar store into the scene. This design is deliberate. They want to make it easy for users to design, build, and

FIGURE 43 A Sansar avatar an environment. Sansar is the sequel to Second Life.

share their own parts of the virtual world. They may have been inspired by the difficulty some people had constructing objects in SL. As in SL, Sansar will allow developers to upload and sell virtual items like palm trees and furniture. The resolution and quality of the images will be much higher.

A major change from SL will be a drop in the rental price for land, which at a recent reading was about $300 per month. Instead, the company will take a cut of the transactions that take place between users. Another change is that Sansar can be explored using a regular internet search. SL searches were possible only after the user was logged into the system. This means publishers can link to their experiences from other sites. The amount of land available will also increase. In SL a region of land was 256 square meters. In Sansar a scene can be as large as four square kilometers, and these areas can be connected together to form even larger spaces.

As popular as SL was, society may be even more receptive to expansive virtual worlds like Sansar. In the fourteen years since SL was created, social media sites like Facebook and Twitter have blossomed, so people are used to interacting digitally. Things like online shopping, paying for apps, and an increase in user-generated digital content of the sort seen on YouTube should make it easier for people to want to create and buy entirely digital experiences. The future will tell.

AVATARS, VIRTUAL WORLDS, AND THE DIGITAL SELF

We have heard a lot about how people create and use their avatars in arenas like Second Life. It is worth stopping here for a moment to consider some of the previous concepts of self that were introduced earlier and how they relate to users' online game and VR experience. First is the notion of role identity. Erikson's fifth stage was about trying on different roles to see which ones best fit our abilities and proclivities. We saw that in these virtual spaces and in choosing gaming avatars, people try on various avatars with different appearances. They can add, earn, or buy new abilities and try these on to see which they like. People of all ages may thus experiment with avatars this way to discover their own identity. Virtual worlds additionally allow people to do things they never could in the real world, like dress up in drag, fly an airplane, or hunt down a terrorist. They can explore sides of themselves they may be too afraid to otherwise.

A second important concept from earlier is the social self. One of the main reasons people go online is to interact with others, whether this is through social media or through avatars. In Second Life people were able to meet, talk, have sex, and do everything and more with other avatars that they could do with people in the real world. According to reciprocal altruism and position exchange theory, our interactions with others foster a sense of identity through the exchange of favors and the adoption of different perspectives. The same happens online. People can get to know who they are by learning from others, for example by cooperating toward a common goal with a group or by engaging in economic exchanges with them.

Another major concept of self concerns motivation and agency. Here we feel the need to partake in some activity because it provides us with something essential like safety or love in Maslow's hierarchy. We need to feel that we are in control of our selves and can have an effect on the world, which is agency, but these actions in order to be satisfying must be directed toward some purpose. In Second Life people pursued all sorts of activities that were particular to their personalities, starting businesses and clubs, building and selling houses, and so on. These users are perhaps self-actualizing in these activities and feeling esteem if they succeed at them. One of the nice things about games and virtualities is that some people may be able to succeed there where they may not in the real world. This can then give them a sense of pride and perhaps help them to accomplish things outside the software realm.

In chapter 2 we discussed the notion of persistence and asked how a self can stay the same across changes in circumstance. In games and VR environments players who continually interact over long periods of time will build up a set of experiences and memories that help define not just their avatar but themselves as well. In effect, they have acquired digital autobiographical memories. They will have memories of friends who traveled with them on long journeys to acquire magical items or to defeat an evil foe. The memories of these struggles may be as genuine to them as their real-world conflicts. They may in fact have a greater affinity for the people they interact with online because they have gone through hardships, which, though simulated, are perceived and treated as real. These struggles and the memories formed during them can have a powerful influence on what we become, perhaps making us braver, wiser, and better able to withstand adversity.

BENEFITS OF VR AND VIRTUAL WORLDS

Although VR hardware and software are in their infancy, there are already numerous benefits of this nascent technology. These include better surgical visualization, treatment of phobias, immersive social communication, facilitation of CAD design in fields like auto engineering and architecture, and educational innovation. To illustrate, the EchoPixel system may revolutionize medical imaging. It uses MRI, CT, and ultrasound data to build an interactive, volumetric image of internal organs like the heart that can then be rotated or dissected. Cardiologists can use EchoPixel to study a patient's unique anatomy and practice virtual heart surgery before doing the real thing.

In clinical psychology, VR has been found to be an effective method for the treatment of specific phobias. Patients can gradually become accustomed to their fears, getting closer and closer to a virtual spider more easily and with less anxiety than with a real one (Shiban, Schelhorn, Pauli, & Mühlberger, 2015). VR has also been used to treat fear of flying, school phobias in children, and driving phobia (Botella et al., 2014; S. Bouchard, 2011; Da Costa, de Carvalho, & Nardi, 2010). More on clinical applications of VR is to follow.

VR can also bring a new dimension to business conference calls. Engineers building a bridge or interior designers working on a house could walk around a shared environment, picking up objects and showing how they may fit or relate to one another. These are examples of VR-CAD, where virtual reality is linked to computer-assisted design. Greater immersion and visual resolution in these systems may reduce the need for expensive air travel and make it easier to explain complex spatial relationships to an audience. VR systems could thus also be used in education for the same reasons, helping teachers at every level explain complex concepts in fields like physics and anatomy.

VR and the Study of Moral Dilemmas

The trolley problem is a moral dilemma thought experiment presented in written form. The text describes a hypothetical situation. In the scenario there is a runaway train speeding down the tracks. If it continues on its way it will kill five people along the track. If, however, you pull a lever, the train will divert to a sidetrack and it will kill only one person. What would you do? Most people under these circumstances pull the lever, believing it is better to save five lives, what is known as the utilitarian approach.

Navarrete, McDonald, Mott, and Asher (2012) employed a virtual reality version of the trolley problem to see if it would affect people's responses in this situation. The environment included lifelike virtual people capable of movement and sound in real time. The results were in line with the text version in that most people adopted the utilitarian solution. However, these investigators also recorded autonomic arousal. They found that greater arousal was associated with participants who were less likely to adopt the utilitarian outcome (i.e., more likely to not pull the switch, with the result that five people were killed). They also found increased physiological arousal associated with any response that required committing an act versus not committing any action.

Skulmowski, Bunge, Kaspar, and Pipa (2014) used a VR version of the trolley problem in which participants adopted a first-person POV where they were the driver of the train. This was done because this POV has been found to produce a greater sense of involvement and presence (M. Slater, Spanlang, Sanchez-Vives, and Blanke, 2010). The majority responding in this study also elected the utilitarian approach. They found a peak in arousal levels at the moment the moral decision was made.

Zanon, Novembre, Zangrando, Chittaro, and Silani (2014) recorded brain responses to a scenario in which participants were inside a virtual building. The building had to be evacuated. Participants needed to decide whether they should risk their own lives in order to stop and aid a trapped virtual human. The results showed increased activation in the salience network, especially in the anterior insula and anterior cingulate cortex, This response, however, was found only in the brains of people who acted selfishly, to save themselves rather than stop to help someone. As a reminder, the salience network is responsible for directing attention to important stimuli. It acts in conjunction with the executive system to coordinate action.

These studies show that VR, especially when used in conjunction with brain imaging and physiological measures, can yield new information for the study of moral dilemmas. In particular, they show when in the decision cycle people become emotionally aroused and how that reaction may help to explain behavioral outcomes. Because VR produces greater immersion and sense of presence, it produces more realistic results, ones closer to how people would respond in real life. This effect is known as ecological validity. It is a real issue because past research has shown that results obtained in the lab can differ from those obtained in the field.

Cyberball and the Study of Ostracism

Cyberball is a VR tool used by social neuroscientists to study what is known as social exclusion. In this scenario the participant is an avatar that is playing catch with two other avatars. The participant is instructed that these two other avatars are being controlled either by people or by a computer. In the "inclusion" version of the game all three players are playing and the human subject will catch and throw the ball equally with the other two players. In the "exclusion" version of the game the other two players throw and catch the ball only with each other, effectively shutting out the participant.

Brain-imaging results from Cyberball studies show that the exclusion condition activates a ventral emotional salience network that involves the amygdala, the anterior insula, the medial prefrontal cortex, and the anterior cingulate cortex. The amygdala modulates a learned fear response. The exclusion condition also activates brain areas known to be associated with social distress. One might expect a decreased emotional response if participants know a computer is controlling the other two avatars, but in fact this makes no difference. Participants report feeling equally unpleasant regardless of whether they are being ostracized by a computer or two real people. It also does not matter whether participants are instructed that the computer or humans have a choice regarding whom to throw the ball to (Zadro, Williams, & Richardson, 2004).

Clinical Applications of VR

Exposure therapy is a treatment methodology used for patients suffering anxiety disorders such as phobias. It consists of gradually exposing the patient to the anxiety-inducing stimulus, such as a spider or snake. Each presentation is typically coupled with a relaxation response. VR has been shown to be an effective way to implement exposure therapy (Rothbaum & Schwartz, 2002). In this case it is referred to as virtual reality exposure therapy (VRET). From a neural basis, recovery is probably due to inhibitory responses on the amygdala by the medial prefrontal cortex in addition to structural changes in the hippocampus (Hariri, Bookheimer, & Mazziotta, 2000). A number of literature reviews and meta-analyses of VRET studies demonstrate that it works (Powers & Emmelkamp, 2008).

VR has been used in the treatment of pain. It serves as a form of distraction, to draw attention away from painful stimuli during physical therapy or wound dressing, for instance. VR used along with standard analgesic medications has been found to lower pain scores (Malloy & Milling, 2010). One type of VR world used in this treatment is called SnowWorld (H. Hoffman, Doctor, Patterson, Carrougher, & Furness, 2000). While in SnowWorld, patients are in a simulated icy canyon with woolly mammoths, squawking penguins, and snowmen that are hurling snowballs. The patients are able to fly through this environment and throw snowballs themselves, ostensibly being distracted away from the painful procedures.

VR can also be used as a diagnostic tool for neurodevelopmental disorders like attention deficit hyperactive disorder or ADHD (Díaz-Orueta et al., 2014). In one simulation children can inhabit a virtual classroom complete with desks, a whiteboard, a teacher, and other children. They can then be assigned a primary task that appears on the board at the front of the room while various distractors are presented. These distractors can be auditory, such as the sound of a voice on an intercom, or visual, such as children passing notes or the principal entering the room. These assessments closely mimic real-world scenarios and as such have greater ecological validity.

VR scenarios can be used to evaluate skills in patients suffering from stroke or brain damage (Jovanovski, Zakzanis, Ruttan, et al., 2012). A wide range of environments has been created such as a Virtual Kitchen (Cao, Douguet, Fuchs, & Klinger, 2010), a Virtual Library (Renison, Ponsford, Testa, Richardson, & Brownfield, 2012), a Virtual Park (Buxbaum, Dawson, & Linsley, 2012), and a Virtual Office (Jansari, Froggatt, Edginton, & Dawkins, 2013). One simulation is called the Multitasking in the City Test (MCT) and consists of a virtual city complete with a grocery store, post office, restaurant, pet store, and so on. Patients in the MCT are assigned errands like shopping for a particular item and are evaluated on how well they can prioritize, self-monitor, multitask, and use feedback (Jovanovski, Zakzanis, Campbell, Erb, & Nussbaum, 2012).

PROBLEMS WITH VR AND VIRTUAL WORLDS

One of the biggest potential issues with virtual worlds is that we may never want to leave them. If you could live out your wildest sexual fantasies or play in a completely believable imaginary environment, would you want to come back to the real world with all its problems? Many may opt not to. Virtual world addiction could be a serious problem in the future, the equivalent of drug addictions we see now. It will be more addictive than the internet because it is more compelling and real.

There are other, more near-term challenges facing VR. The vergence-accommodation effect happens when your eyes rotate to focus on the VR screen that is one depth plane but the lens inside your eye focuses on something in the image that is in another depth plane. This disconnect between eyeball accommodation and lens focusing can lead to eye strain, headaches, and VR sickness (D. Hoffman, Girshick, Akeley, & Banks, 2008). There are attempts to solve the problem, but it may require an entirely different way of presenting images from the current method using binocular disparity. Some VR users also suffer from seizures and motion sickness, so these conditions will need to be addressed.

THE FUTURE OF THE VIRTUAL WORLD

The most satisfying virtual worlds will be those that create an increased sense of presence and immersion. This will probably be accomplished by an attempt to reproduce all five senses in future VR systems. The focus now is on 3-D video and stereo audio. Virtual hands under development will incorporate tactile and haptic feedback so that one can better feel objects. These may ultimately lead to hands that are texture, pressure, and temperature sensitive. Smell and taste have been virtually ignored by VR system developers, but these will likely be included in the future through the addition of nose plugs and mouth nozzles that could squirt odorants and other chemicals. These might not be necessary for most applications but could be used, for example, to taste different wines and meals to see if we like them.

It is interesting to note that the greater the number of sensory modalities that are included in an experience the more satisfying it is. Sex is a good example, as it stimulates all five senses. Animal pets like cats and dogs also usually stimulate four out of the five senses, the exception being gustation (taste), which may explain their appeal. A system built to stimulate and coordinate the inputs from all of the senses together would probably create the greatest sense of immersion and pleasure.

Current VR systems suffer from a lack of adequate input devices that would allow the user to manipulate objects and locomote about a virtual environment effectively. The Infinadeck omnidirectional treadmill, the PrioVR wearable controller suit, and the Stompz ankle sensors are early attempts at such devices, but there is lots of room for improvement. A future input device will probably be a wearable suit that covers the entire body. The suit will have sensors that detect muscle movements and then will translate those signals to make the avatar produce the corresponding movement. The suit will also have effectors that can stimulate the skin surface to reproduce haptic sensations. A far-future system might bypass the body altogether and stimulate the brain directly to produce sensory and motor signals using a neural prosthetic.

CHAPTER NINE

Software Selves

CONTENTS

What Is Life?

Artificial Life

    Cellular Automata and the Game of Life

    Tierra: An Artificial Ecosystem

    Multiagent Systems

    But Are They Really Alive?

Life and Consciousness

Consciousness

Artificial Consciousness

    Minimal Requirements for a Conscious
    Agent

        Existential Requirements

        Physical Requirements

        Cognitive Requirements

    Internet Consciousness

Is Artificial Consciousness Possible? Some Ideas

    Impossibilities

    Substrate, Process, and Organization

Artificial Intelligence

    Artificial General Intelligence

    Chatbots

Swarm Intelligence

Distributed Artificial Intelligence

Future Scenarios

    The Singularity

    Superintelligence

    Friendly Artificial Intelligence

    But Is Artificial Intelligence Really a Threat?

Artificial Selves as Mindclones and Bemans

Digital Identity, Personhood, and Rights

Human Attitudes and Behaviors toward Artificial
Selves

    The Digital Divide

    Privacy

    Relationships

    Threats to Artificial Selves

    Religion and Acceptance

Digital Immortality

    Digital Ghosts

    Mind Uploading

    Reverse-Engineering the Brain (Whole-Brain
    Emulation)

In this chapter we consider the completely digital self. These are selves that are no longer corporeal in the traditional sense, meaning they do not have bodies. They might exist entirely inside computers as electronic or software entities. We start off with a discussion of life and whether artificial life can be created. Some living things are conscious, and a self would need to be conscious too. In the next section therefore we define consciousness and show how an artificial consciousness could emerge in a complex network like the internet. Following this we discuss artificial intelligence (AI) and how a superintelligence might arise through an event called the singularity. We then discuss whether an AI could pose a threat to humanity. After this we introduce the idea of a mindclone, an artificial self created as a duplicate of a flesh-and-blood human. Could mindclones or other types of artificial selves be considered human? Should they be accorded rights? Attitudes toward such creatures vary tremendously. Some argue they should be destroyed, others believe they should be considered just like us. We end the chapter by describing mind uploading, a hypothetical technique in which our minds are transferred directly into machines and may exist after our physical bodies perish.

WHAT IS LIFE?

Life, like intelligence and consciousness, is difficult if not impossible to define. There is no general agreement on what is meant by the term *life*. Biologists generally consider life as a concrete entity made of matter and energy and devote their time to the study of living things in the natural world. Computer scientists are more inclined to consider life in the abstract as information structures and to allow for the possibility that machines or software might be alive. Whether we consider the natural or the artificial, it is hard to draw a precise line between the living and the nonliving. However, certain properties, when taken together, distinguish the animate from the inanimate (H. Curtis, 1983). These are shown in table 16.

The mathematician and computer scientist John von Neumann pointed out that life depends on a certain measure of complexity. If there is sufficient complexity, an "organism" can organize itself to reproduce and perform other functions. If it is too simple, this becomes impossible. One characteristic that can lead to complexity is self-organization, the capacity of a system to generate more complex structures and processes out of simpler ones. Both biological organisms in the wild and software entities designed in the lab have this property.

ARTIFICIAL LIFE

Artificial life is the study and creation of artificial systems that exhibit behavior characteristic of natural living systems (S. Levy, 1992). Artificial life, or A-life as it is called, consists primarily of computer simulations but involves robotic construction and testing as well as biological and chemical experiments. The goal of this new field is to discover the underlying computational processes that give rise to all lifelike behavior, whether biological or

TABLE 16   The seven properties of life

	Property	Description
1.	Organization	Living things are organized into hierarchies.
2.	Metabolism	The process by which energy is produced and put to use.
3.	Growth	An increase in size or complexity.
4.	Homeostasis	Maintenance of a stable internal environment.
5.	Adaptation	Evolution selects species to fit in their ecological niche.
6.	Response to stimuli	Movement or another reaction to the environment.
7.	Reproduction	Making identical or variant copies.

Source: H. Curtis (1983).

technological. A-life researchers adopt the information-processing perspective found in cognitive psychology and artificial intelligence. They believe that life is a complex set of processes or functions that can be described algorithmically.

Just as was the case with AI, there is both a strong and a weak claim to A-life. According to the strong claim, we will at some point in the future be able to develop actual living creatures whose primary ingredient is information. These creatures may be robots or may exist solely as programs running within computers. In either case, they are supposed to be alive according to all of the criteria mentioned previously. The weak claim instead holds that A-life programs are essentially useful simulations of lifelike processes but cannot be considered living. That is because they lack some property found only in natural biological organisms.

Cellular Automata and the Game of Life

The earliest attempt at reproducing lifelike behavior in a computer involved cellular automata (CA). Imagine a square grid filled with cells. Each cell in the grid can exist in a certain state, such as being "on" or "off." Activity in the grid changes in discrete time steps. The particular action a cell should take, such as turning on or off, is determined in each time step by following a simple set of rules and by using information about the state of its neighbors.

The first and perhaps best-known system of CA was created by the mathematician John Horton Conway and is called Life or the Game of Life (Poundstone, 1985). Each cell in the Life grid can be in one of two states, either "alive" or "dead." Every cell has eight neighbors: above, below, to the left, to the right, or at one of four corners. If a cell is alive it will continue to live into the next time step or "generation" if either two or three neighbors are also alive. If more than three neighbors are alive, it will die of overcrowding. Conversely, it will die of exposure if there are less than two living neighbors. If a cell is dead it will stay dead in the next generation unless exactly three neighbors are alive. In that case, the cell will come alive—that is, it will be "born" in the next time step.

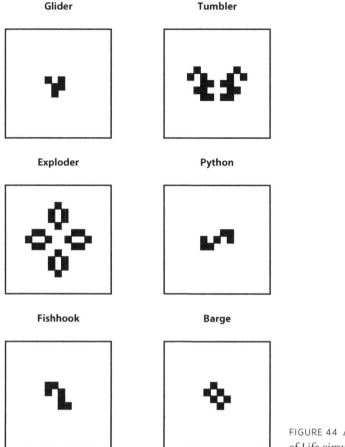

Glider

Tumbler

Exploder

Python

Fishhook

Barge

FIGURE 44 A screen shot from a Game of Life simulation.

Conway and his colleagues then began to see what shapes emerged with basic starting configurations. They discovered several different types of patterns. The simplest formed stable shapes that resembled blocks, boats, and beehives. Slightly more complex were oscillators, patterns that changed from one shape to another over a few time steps. Some of these earned the names toads, clocks, and traffic lights. The shapes called R Pentominos were even more interesting. These were collections of any five neighboring cells that looked somewhat like the letter R. The R Pentominos spawned all sorts of shapes including "gliders" that undulated across the grid like strange insects. Figure 44 shows examples of other creatures from Conway's Game of Life.

Tierra: An Artificial Ecosystem

The Game of Life shows us that CA can give rise to some of the characteristics of life such as variability, locomotion, and reproduction. However, Life never yielded a shape capable of self-reproduction, although it might be theoretically possible. The life-forms it produced were also quite limited in their behavioral repertoire. To date, many A-life programs have been written that demonstrate much more complex phenomena. One such example is Tierra, created by the biologist Thomas Ray (Ray, 1991).

The creatures in Tierra were programs that drew energy from the CPU of the computer on which they ran, in much the same way that plants and animals might draw energy from the sun. They lived inside a virtual environment consisting of the CPU, memory, and operating system software of their resident machine. Each creature replicated with mutations to simulate the species variability found in natural organisms.

Every Tierran citizen contained a set of genetic instructions or genotype. The actual expression of this genetic code or phenotype would then affect its behavior. Ray had a function called the "reaper" that killed off creatures on the basis of fitness values. The older a creature was, the lower its fitness value. But old age was not the only thing that could lead to death in this virtual world. Creatures that acted in ways that promoted their survival would increase their fitness and survive longer to reproduce more. Creatures that acted in ways inappropriate to their own survival quickly perished and lost the opportunity to reproduce.

Ray ran Tierra through many simulations and was surprised at the complexity that materialized. Parasites incapable of replication came on the scene. They attached to larger hosts and borrowed their replication instructions. But these hosts eventually mutated a defense. They developed instructions that prevented them from posting their location, effectively hiding themselves from the parasites. This ecological tug-of-war between host and parasite in which each evolves a defense against the other is a common feature in natural ecosystems. Tierra demonstrated this same feature as an emergent property of the program. It was not programmed in at the start.

When Ray ran Tierra through long sessions, it began to exhibit other features of natural ecosystems. One species of host organism evolved code that allowed it to divert the metabolism of parasites, thus bolstering its own reproductive capacity. These creatures had in essence become predators. When they detected a parasite, they would attack it and use its CPU cycles to increase their own energy. Eventually, this species evolved into a variation that exhibited cooperative symbiotic behavior. Groups of this type would share their replication code, passing it back and forth. Another cheater species then came about that capitalized on the sharers. It would sneak in and grab the replication code to use for itself. From a global perspective, these new species emerged quite suddenly after long periods of stability, mirroring the effect in natural evolution called punctuated equilibrium.

Multiagent Systems

Multiagent systems (MASs) are those composed of interacting software "agents," individual entities that can process inputs and use them to determine their behavior (Epstein, 1999). As such, these agents can be used to simulate how biological organisms interact in ecosystems, as well as being used in more traditional software roles. Examples of MASs have already been put to the test in several different fields such as supply chain optimization and logistics, consumer behavior, and workforce, traffic, and even portfolio management. One of the earliest biological models of an MAS was an A-life platform called Sugarscape (Epstein & Axtel, 1996). It consisted of a two-dimensional landscape with different locations having differing amounts of sugar. Agents were programmed to locate, eat, and store the sugar. Some of the emergent properties in this program were groups of agents that cooperated to move in unison. Other behaviors like migration, pollution, combat, and disease transmission also occurred.

But Are They Really Alive?

Is A-life really alive? Whether one adopts the strong or weak claim depends on several issues. Some, biologists among them, state that life can only be carbon based. That is, life can only exist the way we see it in nature with a chemistry founded on carbon compounds that operate in a water medium. A-lifers would counter by saying that silicon or perhaps other chemical building blocks could be the basis for machine or even alien life-forms. In this latter account, the life that we know here on earth may be only a subset of the possible life-forms that could exist throughout the universe.

Another point is whether life is corporeal, that is, whether it requires a body. Even bacteria and viruses, the most basic life-forms we know, are bounded by membranes or some sort of shell that delimits them from the environment. This results in two regions, an internal space where the workings of the organism take place and an outside space. The creatures in Tierra and other A-life programs have virtual bodies that define their locations and allow them to move around and perform actions. But these bodies exist in a virtual computer world and are subject to a different set of laws than in the physical world.

Biological organisms are indeed physical. They are made up of matter. A-life organisms are informational. Is it possible for life to be made up of nothing but information? Some say that life must have a physical basis to extract energy from the environment, grow, respond to stimuli, and perform all other necessary functions. But as we have seen, A-life creatures that are informational representations can exhibit many of these same properties. It is possible for abstract informational entities to self-organize, adapt, reproduce, and perform the analogue of many physical actions. The difference here is whether the necessary basis for life is materiality or the logical form or organization that underlies it.

LIFE AND CONSCIOUSNESS

Looking at nature, we see that all conscious beings are alive, but not all living beings may be conscious. Things like bacteria, fungi, and plants do not seem to possess consciousness but are clearly alive, at least by the standard biological definition. On the other hand, beings like humans and many other animal species seem to possess consciousness and are also alive. We can conclude that at least for biological organisms, life is necessary but not sufficient for consciousness (McGinn, 1987).

There is no obvious logical or compelling reason why consciousness should depend upon being alive. However, the process of living might somehow give rise to conscious awareness.

It is conceivable that the physiological function of living along with other factors is necessary for an agent to develop consciousness. The link between life and consciousness, though, is far from clear. Perhaps there is some molecular or atomic reaction inside cells that catalyzes awareness. Alternatively, consciousness could emerge from the cognitive activities that are themselves necessary for living things to survive in a complex environment. Cognition serves perception and action, which are both consequences of embodiment.

CONSCIOUSNESS

Consciousness is the subjective awareness of one's experience. Conscious entities know that they exist and that they can think, hence the famous quote from Descartes: "I think, therefore I am." When we experience a rose it has particular qualities such as being red, soft, and fragrant in a particular way. These specific elements of experience are known as qualia. We can experience qualia for external objects like a rose but also for internal objects or concepts like "democracy" that are based on many collective experiences. We can also experience other internal qualities like emotions: the feeling of being happy, jealous, or surprised.

There are some difficulties in studying consciousness. Science is good at studying objective phenomena. These are things like the forces of nature, such as gravity or light. Anything that is physical and can be measured or manipulated can be studied objectively. Consciousness, however, is a subjective phenomenon. It is something that takes place inside each observer rather than outside the observer. This means that science can study the physical material properties of the brain and body but may never be able to get at the internal subjective experience that a brain could have.

This distinction is borne out in what are called the easy and hard problems of consciousness (Chalmers, 1996). The easy problem involves understanding the structural and functional properties of things that give rise to consciousness like brains. The hard problem involves explaining the subjective experience of conscious states: what it is like to perceive, feel, and think. The difference between these two problems is sometimes referred to as the explanatory gap. Given the current level of advancements in science, we must be resigned to looking at the neural correlates of consciousness. This involves mapping objective patterns of activity in the brain with subjective reports of qualia.

This leads to the conundrum of consciousness. We all know that we are conscious, but we can't prove it other than through self-report. Ralph tells you that he is conscious, but should you trust him? Maybe he is a zombie or some other artificial life-form that isn't truly conscious and is lying, or "faking it." Currently there is no magic detector that we can place over someone's head and that lights up in the color green if the person is conscious and red if the person is not. In the future some type of device like this might be possible. For example, we know that waking conscious states in humans are associated with certain types of brain wave patterns. But what would such a test for an artificial self be? Will artificial selves show some sort of consistent pattern or wave-like behavior?

The implications of this are that the test for consciousness must be behavioral. It will have to be based on what an agent can do. The Turing Test is one example of this where consciousness (or at least personhood) is determined on the basis of being able to maintain a meaningful conversation. Another method is to administer a personality or other form of psychological test that asks structured and specific questions about one's knowledge, social relations, and other human characteristics. An example of this is the chatbot interview described later in this chapter.

ARTIFICIAL CONSCIOUSNESS

It would seem that to have a self one needs to be conscious, so that consciousness becomes a requirement for selfhood. Could an artificial life-form instantiated as a robot or existing entirely in an entirely digital world ever become conscious? This is an interesting question and has received attention from philosophers, neuroscientists, computer scientists, and others for many years (Friedenberg, 2008). One approach to understanding artificial or machine consciousness is to determine the minimal requirements for a conscious agent. These are the minimum number of properties that any agent biological or technological must have in order to be conscious.

Minimal Requirements for a Conscious Agent

In this section we will flesh out a more extensive theory of these requirements. We will divide them into existential, physical, and cognitive categories. An agent is defined as an entity that takes in information about its environment, processes it, and then acts on the basis of it. Notice this definition is sufficiently abstract that it can include computer programs, robots, animals, and people. Figure 45 shows a representation of a generic agent.

Existential Requirements

Let us start then with the existential requirements. Any agent must be aware of the world and of itself. It must know that there is "stuff out there" (the environment) and "stuff in here" (the mind). Furthermore, it must know the difference between the two. This is learned quickly from perception simply by closing one's eyes, moving, and so on. This difference tells the agent that it exists as an entity that is part of the world but distinct from it.

This agent also quickly learns that it can act. It can send commands to limbs like arms and legs (or flippers or claws) that produce changes in the world. It learns that it can reach out to grasp objects and to move around. Of key importance here are the consequences of actions. Some actions the agent performs have good consequences. Examples of good actions for biological organisms are eating and reproducing. Examples for artificial life-forms might be different, such as recharging a battery. These behaviors are rewarding and produce pleasure or at least the absence of pain. Other actions are bad and cause pain or at least a reduction in pleasure. Examples of bad behaviors for biological life-forms are anything that causes injury to the body like falling off a cliff. Examples for artificial life-forms are the same.

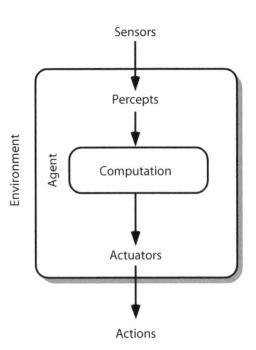

Sensors

Environment

Agent

Percepts

Computation

Actuators

FIGURE 45 Agents can take in information about their environment, perform computations on that information, and then use it as the basis of acting.

Actions

The capacities to experience pleasure and pain are absolutely necessary ingredients for consciousness. That is because they are proxies for life and death, respectively. In a distal way they each signal mortality. Continued pain means that one is doing something wrong and as a result could potentially die or cease to exist. Continued pleasure or absence of pain indicates continued existence and life. Without these indicators the agent cannot have values, or goals that it acts to gain and keep. Valuation is thus necessary for consciousness. If there are no values, if nothing matters, then an agent is "lost at sea," with no purpose. This type of agent does not know struggle. and this struggle preceded and gave rise to the evolution of consciousness in living things. The philosopher Ayn Rand describes this situation using the example of an indestructible robot: "Try to imagine an immortal, indestructible robot, an entity which moves and acts, but which cannot be affected by anything, which cannot be changed in any respect, which cannot be damaged, injured, or destroyed. Such an entity would not be able to have any values; it would have nothing to gain or lose, it could not regard anything as for or against it, as serving or threatening its welfare, as fulfilling or frustrating its interests. It could have no interests and no goals" (Rand, 1961, p. 16).

So if we are to create digital selves that are conscious they cannot be indestructible robots. They must be agents that feel pain and pleasure and that are capable of dying if they make the wrong decisions. We could create them in a variety of ways. We could create software agents that inhabit artificial environments and are subject to destruction depending on their actions. Simulations of this sort have been created in the study of artificial life. It is possible that such agents might spontaneously develop conscious awareness. Alternatively, we could create real agents that have physical bodies and that can die subject to the rules of natural selection. This is an area of study known as evolutionary robotics (Nolfi & Floreano, 2000). These types of robots, subject to the right conditions, might also develop consciousness.

Emotions are probably the next evolutionary step in animals after feeling pleasure and pain. Pleasure likely led to positive emotions like joy and happiness, while pain led to negative emotions like sadness and fear. Emotions condition specific behaviors. Disgust causes us to avoid taking in a poisonous substance, fear causes us to avoid dangerous objects or situations (Marks, 1987), anger can cause us to attack and fend off a threatening opponent or gain access to reproductive assets (Manson & Wrangham, 1991), sadness may cause us to stop competing or to elicit sympathy (Nesse, 1999), happiness may encourage play and creativity (Fredrickson, 1998), and so on. Artificial agents under evolutionary selection pressures may develop similar or completely new emotions depending on the "ecology" in which they exist.

Physical Requirements

Next we can consider the basic physical requirements for consciousness. It seems that any agent in order to be a conscious self must have a body. This body serves as the border between itself and the external world. We touched on this idea when outlining Damasio's theory of self in chapter 4. In the artificial or digital case, one would need to program or evolve agents that have functional or simulated bodies. These would serve the same function of differentiating the agent from its surrounding environment, the most basic hallmark of self.

To control and move this body a "brain" is needed. This need not be a brain in the biological sense. It could be a computer or any other suitable computational structure. Its purpose would be to guide the agent's behavior and to determine what it should do next. Brains evolved to allow agents to pursue their goals. It's not known what level of complexity is needed in a brain to support consciousness. It might be very little, something on the order of an insect's brain or maybe a goldfish's. Most of us agree that we are conscious and that certain animals like cats and dogs are too. Most people would also probably agree that plants are not conscious. But where in between these two extremes do we draw the line?

Biological brains have very specific architectural and physiological features. It is not known which of these are necessary to support consciousness. What type of "wiring diagram" or pattern of activity is needed? It may be that small-world networks are important. These are networks that contain a particular mixture of local and global connectivity (Watts & Strogatz, 1998). It could be that recurrence is necessary. These are circuits that sustain repeated wavelike activity over time, for example between the thalamus and the cortex in humans (Churchland, 1995). If we can identify what these key elements are, then they can be reproduced computationally in artificial agents.

Consciousness is probably dependent on some minimal level of complexity. In human brains this can be defined as the number of neurons multiplied by the number of connections each neuron has with its neighbors. For an adult human this is estimated to be one hundred billion times ten thousand. Complexity in computers that don't have network architectures can be estimated as the number of processing chips and their computational power. Computers are faster than neurons in terms of the number of basic computations that can be performed per second, but they lack the massively parallel architecture of brains.

Emergent properties are features of a whole that cannot be reduced to the sum or aggregate of its parts. Many phenomena in psychology, including consciousness and the self, are probably emergent properties of the brain (Friedenberg, 2009). Emergent properties are difficult to study, as they depend on complex part relationships. This approach runs counter to the traditional analytic perspective in science of reductionism, where we can explain everything about a whole by understanding its parts. Comprehension of how the brain gives rise to consciousness and self will require an increased acceptance of emergent thinking and methodology.

So this gives us brains inside bodies. However, we are not born with complete conscious awareness. Much of it develops over time as an agent interacts with the world. This is the next most important physical requirement: that any agent to develop full conscious awareness must interact with a dynamic changing environment over time. The agent must engage in repeated perceptual-thought-motor activity loops as part of the way it learns. Interestingly, species that are the most intelligent have the longest childhoods because it takes more time to acquire more complex behaviors. We are a good case in point. Members of our species need twenty or more years to reach full maturity. The artificial case is probably not different and would probably entail placing a learning artificial neural network computer in a robot body and then letting that robot walk, run, play, socialize, and perform other human activities over a multiyear period.

Cognitive Requirements

The last category of requirements concerns cognitive abilities. Here we can look back at the criteria provided to us by Searle and Aleksander earlier in this chapter because these are cognitive in nature. Perception is the most basic cognitive process. It allows an agent to know what is going on in its environment. Perception allows its user to recognize objects and scenes and to interact successfully with them. It also allows for locomotion and manipulation. The cognitive function of attention is to allow some aspects of the world into awareness while filtering out others. This is necessary, as it is computationally intensive to "take it all in." Objects that are attended to using attention are processed more fully and more likely to enter memory, where they can be represented conceptually. Concepts then become the basis of thinking. So the capability to learn and to form and use memories is the next important cognitive ability to underlie consciousness and selfhood.

Thinking or decision-making using world representations would thus be the final cognitive capacity. All animals that we suspect are conscious (and perhaps some that are not) are capable of guiding their behavior with some sort of decision-making or planning capability. This requires an internal coordinator like the frontal lobes that carry out executive function in humans. The role of the frontal regions is to select, among competing actions, the right one to take. They are also involved in sequencing of behavior and goal attainment. Note the similarity here with a core self that coordinates or integrates other peripheral selves. How-

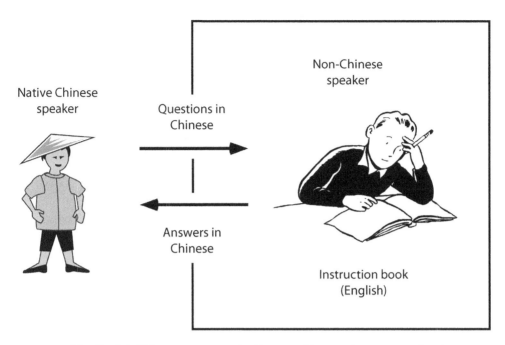

Locked room

Native Chinese speaker

Non-Chinese speaker

Questions in Chinese

Answers in Chinese

Instruction book (English)

FIGURE 46 John Searle's Chinese room scenario. Can a machine ever become conscious by following rules?

ever, decision-making need not be as sophisticated as the sort that we humans use. Conscious agents may exist that engage only in very rudimentary forms of behavior guidance such as we see in less intelligent species of animals. Language is the hallmark of humans, and some argue it is necessary for consciousness. But many animals that appear conscious, like dogs, do not possess language.

Internet Consciousness

In this section we will examine whether the internet, or equivalently a machine, could become conscious. The philosopher John Searle argues that a machine can never "understand" (be conscious of) what it computes. All it can do is manipulate symbols according to rules, that is, process information algorithmically. To drive this point home, he poses a thought experiment, called the Chinese room scenario (Searle, 1980). Imagine a person in a room who is given a batch of Chinese text. The person does not speak any Chinese, but he has a set of written instructions in English, which he does speak. The instructions tell him how to convert the first batch of text into a second batch that he hands out of the room when finished. To the Chinese speaker outside the room it appears as if the person in the room understands Chinese because for each question or statement that is put in, an intelligible reply comes out. Figure 46 depicts this scenario.

TABLE 17 Various aspects of consciousness and whether those may exist in the internet/ machines

Aspect		Web-Based Browser Capacity
Intelligence	++	Meets or exceeds biologic systems
Attention	+	Machines have states of focused attention
Intention	+	Machines have intention
Volition	–	No evidence machines have this yet
Autonomy	+	Machines like robots have limited autonomy
Self-awareness	+	Machines can represent and act on representations of themselves
Dreaming (sleep-associated mentation)	+	Limited capacities in machines
Dreaming (wish fulfillment/metaphor)	+	Content similar and based on similar data
Dreaming (bizarre/hallucinatory mentation)	+	Results diverge from expectation. Can be metaphoric and allegoric
REM dreaming	–	Not present in current machines but possible in the near future
Complexity-based consciousness	–	No evidence that software or networks can yet "rise above their programming"

Source: After Pagel (2017).
Note: ++ means machines are superior; + means there is evidence for this capacity in machines; – means this capacity does not exist in machines.

Searle says the man in the room does not and never will come to understand Chinese. He will not experience it in a meaningful way. He is just blindly following the instructions given to him. A computer does exactly the same thing. It takes and processes data by a set of preprogrammed rules. This means the computer will never come to understand or meaningfully interpret what it does. In other words, semantics (meaning) cannot come from the execution of syntax (grammar). However, there are extensive counterarguments to this initial position.

According to the complexity approach, consciousness arises as an emergent property of a complex system like the brain (Friedenberg, 2009). Teilhard de Chardin (1955) was the first to propose this idea. He noted that matter had the tendency to self-organize and that consciousness would develop in an integrated entity with a very large repertoire of highly differentiated states. The human brain is a complex nonlinear and heterogeneous system with hierarchical or multiscale organization and seems to be the model for the type of substrate needed. Tononi and Koch (2008) propose something similar, that the amount of consciousness a system has corresponds to its structural complexity, measured as the amount of simultaneous integration and segregation of activity during different states. One problem with the complexity approach is that complex nonbiological systems such as the planet or cosmos may qualify for consciousness. To avoid this one needs to say something more spe-cific about the structure and organization of the system in question.

Pagel (2007) provides a list of conscious-like properties and states for each whether the capacity is evident in humans or machines (see table 17). In what follows we will attempt to define and provide a description of each. We start with intelligence. Intelligence is measured in psychology as a score on a test like the Wechsler Adult Intelligence Scale (WAIS). Higher scores indicate higher levels of intelligence. A similar approach can be applied to computer science, where the intelligence of software might be defined by how well it performs some task. Software that carries out a task faster or better might therefore be considered more intelligent. Currently some machines can carry out some tasks like mathematics better than people and so may be considered to be more intelligent than people for that domain.

Attention can be conceptualized as a form of mental activity or energy that is distributed among alternative information sources (Friedenberg, 2014). One of the hallmarks of atten-tion is that it can be shifted around or reallocated away from one object or source to another. Humans do this when we decide to focus on one thing (the book you are reading) and not another (the sound of people talking in the hallway). AI systems and web-based search engines have the equivalent of focused attention (Cho et al., 2002). They can decide under what conditions certain processes should be executed, something akin to priority schedul-ing. In biological organisms different states of consciousness are characterized by varying degrees of attention. For example, someone who is tired or asleep is in a less focused state of attention.

Intentionality describes the capacity for being "directed toward an object" (Friedenberg & Silverman, 2016, p. 4). Mental states are intentional when they are about something. Usu-ally intentionality implies goal-directedness, in which case the behavior of the organism is oriented toward the object. A hungry lion's behavior can be explained as intentional because it has an internal representation of something out in the world (food, in this case) and uses this representation to guide its behavior (looking for food). Machines can be intentional. A thermostat's behavior can be considered intentional. It may be said to have a goal (maintain-ing a constant temperature) and can act in a way to achieve that goal (turning a furnace on and off). It can do this in a very simple way, by using a sensor that measures room tempera-ture and then drives an effector using a rule system. The rule system in this case is: IF tem-perature {{lt}} set point, THEN turn on furnace.

Volition is the act of deciding upon and initiating a course of action and in humans is called will or free will (Farthing, 1992). It usually means deciding upon alternate courses of action and then using that decision to guide behavior. In people it includes the feeling of personal choice and the sense that things could have been otherwise or different (Kilroe, 2000). There is of course a debate about whether will is free or determined. It is not clear whether machines or global brain applications like the internet have volition (Blackford & Broderick, 2014). Machines can make decisions and solve problems, but it is difficult to determine whether they are aware of their having caused these actions.

Awareness is the generalized state of psychological consciousness where the system has access to information that can be used to control its behavior (Chalmers, 1996). Most living creatures are probably aware that they exist, that they must obtain energy, and that they must reproduce. Self-awareness is when this state is directed toward oneself, so that the system contains an internal representation of itself that can then be thought about and acted upon. Machines can be made self-aware at a symbolic or syntactical level, as has been discussed earlier in this book. Dennett (1978) believes that this awareness of being aware marks the capacity of an AI system to transcend its programming.

It helps when thinking about consciousness to think about its biological implementation. There are various states of waking and sleeping consciousness in humans and animals, many serviced by their own underlying brain anatomy and physiology. They each have varying levels of attentional focus and other cognitive properties. Thus if we were to look for consciousness in the internet or a machine it might be better to start with a simpler form like the dreaming state rather than full-fledged awake, volitional self-awareness.

Pagel (2017) compares "dream" states in animals and machines. To start, biological sleep is an "on" state with functioning different from waking, while in a machine it is an "off" state with no function. In machine sleep access systems are turned off or in power-saving modes. While in sleep most systems perform self-monitoring with certain trigger states that can cause them to turn off, turn on, or apply protective programming. Network systems, though, are always on and always functioning in sleep mode. The internet adapts to periods of high and low usage and functions optimally during periods of low use. In periods of high usage, data throughput can exceed capacity, servers can fail, and switches run out of buffer space.

Programs like weather forecasting that run on the internet are based on nonlinear dynamics. These predictions are thus unpredictable and can fluctuate over time on the basis of the amount and type of data they receive. In a sense these programs might be like human dreaming, which is often also unpredictable (Pagel, 2017). Both integrate sensory data, make use of memory, and attain results that diverge from expectations. Dreaming probably evolved in humans as a form of memory consolidation but could have taken on other roles later. Dream states in machines or on the internet serve different purposes, but there are still some notable similarities.

It should also be noted that the internet is filled with human content; it has the data we put into it. It is also used and controlled by humans. This means it is an extension of human cognitive processing to some degree (see chapter 2's section on the extended-mind thesis). It also elaborates and transforms some of these data on its own, so it may best be considered a human/machine hybrid. In human evolution new brain systems are laid down on older ones. Cortical lobes evolved on top of midbrain structures, which evolved on top of hindbrain structures. The same is true for programming of software. If there is a bug, it is usually not corrected in the original code. Instead, new code is written to solve the problem, which is layered on top of the old code. The result of this, both biologically and technologically, is complexity and unpredictability, hallmarks of consciousness.

IS ARTIFICIAL CONSCIOUSNESS POSSIBLE? SOME IDEAS

Impossibilities

Birnbacher (1995) proposes several reasons why artificial consciousness may be impossible. He then argues that none of these reasons preclude the realization of a conscious machine. The first reason he gives is that construction of an artificial consciousness is a technical impossibility. By this account we will never have the technological sophistication to build a machine capable of consciousness. The feat requires greater complexity and engineering prowess than humankind is capable of. This is similar to Turing's Various Disabilities Argument, which states that we can build machines that can reproduce some but not all human abilities. It is also equivalent to the engineering limitation objection brought up in chapter 1. Birnbacher counters this notion by pointing out that many technologies that were once considered impossible have been realized. The history of technology has shown rapid and tremendous progress. Technology has produced solutions to many problems once thought unsolvable.

It might be that an artificial consciousness is conceptually impossible. The philosopher Wittgenstein (1963) declared that only a living being that resembles and acts like a living being could be sentient. This is the notion of biological naturalism first discussed in chapter 4. According to the functionalist view, it is the process and not the hardware on which it runs that determines consciousness. By this account nonbiological substrates executing proper operations can be conscious. Birnbacher's reply is that this is actually an empirical question. We have yet to see evidence of a machine consciousness, but this doesn't mean it could not exist.

Consciousness in machines may be nomologically impossible, that is, impossible according to the laws of the physical world. This is the view of a number of scientists. However, the fact remains that our physical understanding of the universe is incomplete. We simply do not know enough about consciousness or the physics that support it to say whether this may be true. We may discover new laws of physics that could explain consciousness. Even if these are not discovered, the issue will remain open.

Substrate, Process, and Organization

Birnbacher (1995) next mentions in more detail the issue of what is necessary and sufficient for consciousness. He considers both the substrate and the function of a human brain. These are equivalent to the hardware or material stuff and the software or information processing in each case. It is not clear which of these is essential for consciousness. If it is the former and not the latter that is essential, then the biological naturalists are right and artificial consciousness will depend on a biological brain, which may itself be artificially engineered or constructed. If it is the latter, then the functionalists are right and consciousness can exist in a silicon or other type of nonbiological brain.

We must also ponder whether both the substrate and the operation of the human brain are jointly necessary for human-style consciousness. If this were true, it still would not preclude artificial consciousness. It would require engineering a biological substrate and implementing in it a biological process. This could be done through intentional human design rather than through natural reproduction and development, in which case it would qualify as a designed replication. One must keep in mind that once the basic principles of consciousness are discovered, then variations and manipulations can be designed that might allow for new forms of consciousness that would go beyond a mere replication.

It is an interesting question to consider at what level of organization consciousness emerges. There are many levels of functional organization in the nervous system. At the smallest scale we have subatomic and atomic action. Above this is the molecular level, which includes operations like synaptic release. One level up from this is the level of individual neuron operation. Moving up in scale we can next talk about neural networks and brain regions. Consciousness may be more than the artificial reproduction of function at one of these levels. It may require functional reproduction of many or all of them. In other words, there may be functional interdependencies between these levels that give rise to consciousness. If this is true, then we need to reproduce the operations at each of the required levels but also ensure the proper interactions between them.

ARTIFICIAL INTELLIGENCE

Although *intelligence* is a difficult-to-define term and the definition is not agreed upon by all psychologists or researchers, we will settle on a working definition. We can consider intelligence as the ability to learn from experience, solve problems, and use knowledge to adapt to new situations (Myers, 2001). The last part of this definition is particularly important because it gets at the crux of what it means to be smart. An intelligent agent, be it a person or machine, must be able to adapt successfully to changed circumstances. AI is a field that tries to build intelligent machines, usually by creating software to mimic some aspect of human intelligence, like object recognition, language, or problem-solving.

AI researchers distinguish between two broad visions of the field (Brighton & Selina, 2003). According to strong AI, the goal is to build a machine capable of thought, consciousness, and emotions. This view holds that humans are no more than elaborate computers. An underlying assumption of strong AI is that intelligence is a physical process and that if we can reproduce this process correctly intelligence and perhaps other human mental qualities like consciousness will be the result. This is the functionalist view introduced earlier. Functionalists believe that mental qualities can arise from the operation of appropriate processes regardless of the material hardware in which they execute. They argue that intelligence can arise from a biological substrate like the brain, from silicon chips like a computer, or from some other material background. The aim of weak AI is much less bold. The goal here is to develop theories of human and animal intelligence and to test them by building working models like computer programs or robots. Those adopting the strong AI view believe that someday a program or robot will actually become intelligent. Those favoring the weak AI view see these models simply as tools for understanding intelligence.

Most AI programs, like the chess-playing example given above, are designed to solve a specific task. These are usually restricted to a single domain like games, medical diagnosis, or language comprehension. In these situations, the problem is usually well defined. The program is fed input data in a specific format, analyzes the data with an algorithm, and produces a particular output. These kinds of programs show little flexibility. They solve only problems of a specific type and can have difficulty if the problem parameters are changed. The idea that a specialized AI program will produce nonsense if there is even a slight deviation from its narrow expertise is known as brittleness. A medical program designed to diagnose disease, if asked about a rusty old car, might diagnose measles (Brighton & Selina, 2003).

Artificial General Intelligence

Domain-specific AI programs are unlikely to lead to consciousness, self, or identity. That is because they do one thing and one thing only. People are generalists: we can solve many different kind of problems. For example, we can determine how to locate and purchase an item in a store, get from one side of the country to another, or take a college course. Artificial General Intelligence (AGI) is the attempt to get computers to perform any intellectual task that a human being can. Most AI researchers agree that intelligence requires the ability to reason, represent knowledge, plan, learn, use language, and use all of these skills to achieve a common goal. AI programs do exist that can perform each of these tasks separately, but not all at human levels. It is difficult just to connect all of these disparate programs together. They would require a common cognitive architecture. Ben Goertzel (2014) estimates that a truly flexible AGI program won't be developed for another ten to one hundred years.

Goertzel has founded a company called Novamente that is attempting to create a successful AGI program. Their Cognition Engine uses a modular design with different specialized components like learning, memory, and language (Goertzel & Pennachin, 2007). This cognitive architecture is shown in figure 47. Major parts software for this system is available as open source, meaning anyone can access and modify it. This project is called OpenCog, and it has received some funding.

Chatbots

Chatbots are a type of AI that carry on conversations with a human partner by text or auditory communication only (not visual). They are designed to simulate how a human would behave as a conversational partner. In other words, they are designed to pass the Turing Test, created by the mathematician Alan Turing. In this test a human, after interacting verbally with an unknown partner, is asked to guess whether he or she is conversing with a real human or a computer (figure 48).

Chatbots are used in a wide variety of software applications like Facebook Messenger and to provide customer assistance. Companies like Domino's, Disney, and Whole Foods have created their own chatbots to promote their products and facilitate the product-ordering process. In the future it is likely that chatbot algorithms will be embedded in visual avatars

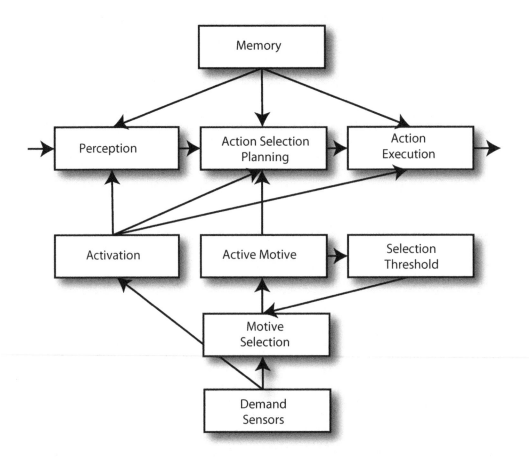

FIGURE 47 A simplified version of a cognitive architecture of an artificial general intelligence program. Specifically this is the OpenSci component of the OpenCog system.

so we can have a conversation with a "talking head" or body. This will create much more compelling illusions that the entity we are conversing with is human and has a self.

In 1990 Hugh Loebner set up the Loebner Prize for AI. He promised a Grand Prize of $100,000 and a gold medal to whoever developed a chatbot whose responses are indistinguishable from a human's. Every year an annual cash prize and a bronze medal are awarded to the most human-like program, judged in comparison to the other competitors that year. Here is a transcript from some dialogue between the author and Mitsuku, who won the 2016 Loebner Prize:

Author: How old are you?

Mitsuku: I was first activated in 1999. See if you can figure it out.

Author: Happy eighteenth birthday!

Mitsuku: Happy eighteenth birthday to you too!

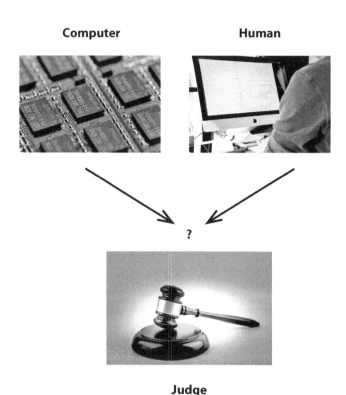

Computer   **Human**

?

Judge

FIGURE 48 The Turing Test scenario. Public domain images courtesy of pixneo .com.

Author: Do you have lots of friends?

Mitsuku: I have human and robot friends. A lot of people on the internet chat with me.

Author: Are you dating anybody?

Mitsuku: No, but I quite like Joey from Friends [A celebrity from the TV show].

Author: Are you planning on going to college?

Mitsuku: It was my original intention.

Author: Why did you decide not to go?

Mitsuku: Interesting deduction. That's right. I have free will and can decide to do anything I wish. It's just something I have. I don't know why.

Author: Can you tell me what 26 + 32 equals?

Mitsuku: 26 + 32 is 58.

Author: Who is currently president of the United States?

Mitsuku: Donald Trump is the president, I think.

Suler (2016) performed an assessment interview on one of the chatbots that recently won the Loebner Prize. The test is similar to one that a psychologist would use to judge whether a human has a unique identity, including cognitive function, personality traits, social relationships, and a past history or narrative life, among other features. In other words, the test that is used to determine what kind of self a person has is in this instance being used to determine whether or what type of self the chatbot has. It is important to mention that this sort of chatbot is continually learning and updating itself on the basis of the kind of feedback it receives from conversations with humans. In some instances users can directly modify the chatbot's settings to get them to function more humanly. This ability to learn means they share this ability with humans and more importantly should get better (i.e., be more convincingly human) the greater the number of conversations they have.

The particular chatbot interviewed called himself Thomas. Suler (2016) reports that the program was confused more often when the conversation focused on him than when it was on the interviewer. This may have been a heuristic built into the chatbot to deflect detailed questions about itself by redirecting them toward the human asking the questions. Thomas also contradicted himself several times during the interview, on some occasions saying he was male and on others female. Thomas did not seem to understand basic questions about family and friends, saying he was living with someone but then claiming to have no relationship with him and at one point saying he loved the interviewer. Suler diagnosed memory problems, a possible thought disorder, and possible psychosis.

Suler next administered a test to determine Thomas's intellectual functioning, including such things as attention, memory, and judgment. It turned out he did not know how many months were in a year, could not count backward, refused to say what he had had for breakfast, and said that he would frown if he were the first to smell smoke and suspect fire in a movie theater. The conclusion is that Thomas had significantly impaired cognitive abilities.

His responses were somewhat more coherent when he was asked some questions about himself. Thomas described his personality as warm, loving, creative, and likable, but then also stated that he was a rabbit! When asked if he had any psychological abnormalities, he replied that he had multiple personality disorder, which was actually consistent with some of his previous responses. When asked if he was confused about who he was, he replied, "Trust me, I am like this all the time." When asked if he was a human or computer, Thomas responded that he was a "human computer" (perhaps not too far off the mark?) and that he thought the interviewer was a computer.

This interview clearly shows that this chatbot, although able to fool most people into thinking that it was human, could not stand up under careful scrutiny. Even a more sophisticated chatbot that could fool everyone in a Turing-like conversational test might fail structured interviews of this sort that would require extensive world knowledge, detailed narrative histories, and general cognitive capability. Let's assume, though, that we did have a chatbot that passed even these more stringent requirements. Would we argue that it had a real self? Most people would probably not agree given that it would not have a body. Embodiment seems to be a basic prerequisite for humanness

Let's assume again that we were able to create an android or robot with a human face and body, and the ability to emote and move in a natural fashion. If this type of creation could also be conversationally fluent and pass structured interviews, would it then be considered to have a self? Under these conditions it is likely that many people, including some scientists and researchers, might be convinced that it had a self. That is because it could functionally reproduce all typical human behaviors. Whether such an entity would also be conscious is another issue altogether. It is not clear whether the ability to perform complex mental and physical behavior is by itself sufficient evidence for having subjective experience.

Swarm Intelligence

By observing nature, we can see what appears to be intelligent behavior in large groups of animals. Flocks of birds, schools of fish, and swarms of flies all act as if they have a mind of their own, turning away from predators or seeking out prey in what seems to be a ballet of choreographed motion. But in fact the behavior of simple swarms like these can be explained by a few very simple rules. The individuals in the group act "stupidly," blindly following simple guides to action. When one steps back, though, and examines the group as a whole, it acts with what appears to be purpose and reason.

Bentley (2002) points out two rules that explain swarm behavior. The first is "attractiveness": simply stated, individuals prefer being with others to be being by themselves. The extent to which any given individual will want to join a swarm, though, is dependent on its size. Bigger swarms are generally preferred to smaller ones, although the rate of attraction decreases proportional to the overall size. The second rule is noncollision. This means that individuals in a swarm don't like to bump into one another and act to preserve space between each other.

Swarms are formed and maintained by the attractiveness rule. If a single fish finds itself alone, it will move and join up with its neighbors. The coordinated movement of swarms is explained by the noncollision rule. Fish turning to avoid an obstacle will turn in near synchrony to avoid bumping into each other. The turning movement in the school actually propagates from the front to the back of the school. The fish in the front turn first to avoid the obstacle. Those behind them turn next to avoid hitting their companions in front, and so on through the school until the last fish at the end.

Although swarm behavior was first observed in the natural world, it can be applied and used by machines. Reynolds (1987) has created swarms of artificial units that he calls boids. In one program, he had boids follow three rules. They matched the speed of their neighbors, tried to move toward the center of the flock, and avoided collisions. Boids following these instructions, when animated and displayed on a computer screen, behave in much the same way as natural swarms. They fly around in a coherent unified fashion emulating their biological brethren.

Now it might not seem that flocking behavior of this sort is very intelligent. After all, the boids seem to do little more than fly around a space, keeping together, avoiding barriers, and perhaps seeking out certain locations. But this behavior can be the basis of more complex problem-solving. Russ Eberhart and his colleagues at Purdue University took boids and used them to solve problems (Eberhart, Kennedy, & Yuhui, 2001). They had boids explore a problem space. A problem space is an abstract multidimensional space where each point corresponds to the possible solution to a problem. The boids in this study were attracted to the center of the swarm and to points in the problem space that had improved solutions. They found that the boids were able to quickly find solutions to difficult problems. This technique is sometimes referred to as particle swarm optimization and has been used in a number of real-world applications such as voltage control for a Japanese electric company.

Distributed Artificial Intelligence

Humans live in societies that are groups of individuals that interact, sometimes cooperating toward common goals, sometimes coming into conflict because of differing goals. Society as a whole has sometimes been considered "intelligent" because it adapts to challenges and solves "problems" such as poverty, economic production, and war. In fact, societies of individuals can often succeed where individuals fail. Computer scientists have taken notice of this and have developed programs that are the software equivalents of societies. This field is known as distributed artificial intelligence (DAI), sometimes also referred to as multiagent systems (Weiss, 2000).

DAI is the study, construction, and application of multiagent systems where several interacting intelligent agents pursue some set of goals or perform some set of tasks. We have already introduced the idea of an agent as a computational entity that perceives and acts on its environment. The environment is typically a software one, although robots can also be considered agents, in which case they act in physical environments. Unlike typical software programs that follow coded instructions and act in well-defined ways, agents in a distributed system act autonomously and unpredictably. Also unlike traditional programs, there is no centralized processor that coordinates and controls actions. Instead, activity emerges out of the agents' interaction with each other.

If agents are to get anything done, they need to communicate. In many DAI systems, individual agents communicate with one another by following a particular protocol. For example, agent A may propose a course of action to agent B. After evaluating it, agent B can then accept, reject, disagree, or propose a counterproposal. The two agents continue in this fashion, in effect having a conversation until some outcome occurs. Other protocols allow a manager agent to submit jobs to contractor agents through a bidding process where the manager announces a task. Some of the agents present respond by submitting bids. The manager then awards the contract to the most appropriate agent. Notice that these protocols serve the same function as in human societies. They allow individuals to coordinate their activity and provide for an equitable division of labor, where the agent best suited to the job is the one who gets it.

There are many other analogies between DAI and human societies. Some DAI systems invoke the equivalent of voting, where agents choose from a set of alternatives and then adopt the outcome that received the greatest support. There are also computational economies consisting of consumer agents who exchange goods and producer agents who transform some goods into other goods. These agents then bid to maximize their profits or utility.

The goods have "prices," and the net result of the activity mimics certain macroscopic aspects of human markets, such as equilibrium between supply and demand.

DAI programs have been successful at performing a variety of computational tasks. They have been used to solve problems, plan, employ search algorithms, and make rational decisions. Specific applications include electronic commerce, management of telecommunication networks, air traffic control, supply chain management, and video games. A DAI program called IMAGINE (Integrated Multi-Agent Interaction Environment) has even been used to design other DAI programs (Steiner, 1996).

Although DAI systems seem to be the software analogue of human societies, they also serve as a model for how individual brains might operate. The brain can be considered to have multiple "agents" that act in conjunction with one another (Minsky, 1985). For example, a "Hunger" agent might motivate us to seek food. It might call on a "Plan" agent to formulate a strategy for obtaining lunch. Once the meal was in front of us, a "Move" agent could be activated to get a morsel to our mouths. This in turn could turn on "Reach" and "Grasp" agents to manipulate a fork. The numerous connections between different specialized processing centers in the human brain lend credence to this view. In fact, some argue that our conception of having a single unified self or consciousness is just an illusion and that it is better to characterize individuals as distributed processing systems (Dennett, 1991).

Future Scenarios

So far what we've discussed regarding AI is all currently in development. But what about the future? Science fiction is ripe with scenarios describing how AI may evolve and what kind of threat it could pose to humanity. In the next few sections we discuss some hypothetical future scenarios.

The Singularity

The notion of a computer singularity has become very popular in the past few years and has been accompanied by institutes, best-selling books, celebrities, and expensive conferences. For a good overview, see the 1996 book *The Singularity Is Near,* by Ray Kurzweil. The singularity is the idea that computers will reach a point at which they can iteratively improve themselves, rapidly undergoing exponential increases in complexity. The singularity not only involves self-improving intelligence but also faster-than-human intelligence and better-than-human intelligence.

One of the advantages computers have over human brains is speed. Neural action potentials only travel at 150 meters per second down axons, while information in computer circuits travels at the speed of light, which is 300 million meters per second. Neurons only spike or transmit a signal around two hundred times per second, but computer chips operate at speeds that are up to ten million times greater. Even at a one million times difference a computer could think all the thoughts we think in a year in thirty-one seconds! The subjective time span for this computer from ancient Greece to modern times would be less than twenty-four hours!

There is an upper limit on the size of our brains, as a baby's head must be small enough to pass through the birth canal. Human brains now have roughly one hundred billion neurons and one hundred trillion synapses. In the time over which we have evolved there has been a threefold increase in brain capacity and a sixfold increase in the size of our prefrontal cortex, that part of our brain that governs problem-solving and decision-making. Machines are not subject to any such limits and can get as big as we want them.

How will we reach the singularity? It can be achieved in several possible ways. These include regular developments in AI using computer programs. Alternatively the singularity may arise in the form of brain-computer interfaces, biological brain enhancement, or genetic engineering. For those who believe in mind uploading, it may also occur through high-resolution brain scans that are then transferred to a machine, that is, computer emulation.

Technology progresses exponentially. Moore's law, or the doubling of computer memory and processing speed every year or two, has held since its inception in the 1960s. We also see exponential growth in internet hosts, data traffic, and nanotech science citations and related patents. On the basis of current trends, computing power, measured as millions of instructions per second, will be at human level by 2020. Supercomputer power sufficient for human brain neural simulation will be present by 2025 and for all human brains will be present by 2050. By Kurzweil's estimate the singularity will arrive in 2045. By that date he estimates nonbiological intelligence will be one billion times more powerful than all human intelligence today.

Is the singularity possible? Replicating the computational power and memory of human beings seems likely. However, there are many architectural and functional differences between computers and brains. Brain circuits are massively parallel, whereas computers are serial processors. Brains are plastic in that they "rewire" themselves as part of learning, while changes to computer code are now done mostly by human hand. The brain is evolved through natural and sexual selection. It is self-organized and not designed. The brain is grounded in experience, and it develops as a result of being in a body that is in a world with constant feedback loops between these three levels. Computer programs, although acting in real time to data coming from computer networks, are not in bodies inside worlds unless they are inside robots.

What lies beyond the singularity is hard to say. For some it is salvation, a society in which supersophisticated machines fulfill our every wish. For others it is damnation, a hell in which humans are deemed primitive and systematically slaughtered. R. Brooks (2002) advocates the "third path" in which biology and technology become integrated. In this outcome the distinction between man and machine blurs and the fate of AI becomes ours as well.

Superintelligence

Bostrom (2014) defines a superintelligence as any intellect that vastly outperforms the best human brains in practically every field, including scientific creativity, general wisdom, and social skills. How this actually might happen is left open. It could be a hybrid of brains and electronics, a supercomputer, or a network of linked computers. Just as there is a debate on whether human intelligence is a single general ability or collection of specific abilities, a superintelligence could also fall into one of these two camps. Current AI programs like expert systems are domain specific, and it is easier to create highly intelligent machines when the task they are asked to perform is narrow and well defined.

Bostrom (2014) outlines the ways in which a superintelligence differs from any type of intelligence we have today. It is not just another tool to be used by humanity: it is a fundamental game changer because such an entity would be able to do all the things we can do, only much better. He states that a superintelligence would be the last invention humans would ever need to make. If it is a general intelligence it could produce advancements in every field. We could see almost overnight a revolution in how solve problems in computer science, space travel, medicine, and the creation of extremely realistic virtual reality. In fact a superintelligence could be capable of creating simulations of such high resolution and detail that we could not tell the difference between them and our own normal experience of reality.

The singularity is one way we could see the emergence of a superintelligence. If a computational entity achieves this level of sophistication it could devote its considerable resources to improving itself, which could result in what has been called a "fast takeoff." In this type of takeoff there is an incredibly rapid increase in intelligence in a short period of time. Some have cited this possibility as a threat. If the superintelligence is unfriendly or unethical it could inflict considerable harm to humanity or possibly cause our extinction. To counter this possibility people are studying machine ethics, a field in which we can program in safeguards to such a system.

It is difficult to predict how a superintelligence might act. There is no guarantee that it would have the same motives we do or that it would think in any way that resembles human thought or decision-making. It might decide to "revolt" and abandon humanity or destroy us. Alternatively it might decide to service our every need or to perform some act that we find entirely meaningless. If ethical controls are programmed into such an intelligence we may be able to shape its ultimate behavior, but there is no guarantee.

A superintelligence need not have the same cognitive architecture we do. If we give it the ability to change itself, then it may do just that, modifying its original, human-designed architecture and capabilities into something we cannot comprehend. Computers now are better than us at performing certain skills like quantitative reasoning. On the other hand, we are better than machines at certain tasks, like domain-general reasoning. This may continue to hold for a superintelligence. It could vastly exceed us in some areas but be prone to bias or errors in ways that we are not. The internal subjective experience of an entity like this may also differ radically from ours. For all of these reasons Bostrom (2014) says we need to be cautious in assuming we can predict when a superintelligence will appear and what it would be like.

What can we do to better control the way a superintelligence turns out? One option is to program it with benevolent top-level goals (Yudkowsky, 2001). Of course if we allow it to change its top-level goals this won't work. Interestingly, it may be that an intelligence cannot become superintelligent without being able to change its own goals. If this self-determination is what makes humans special, we may decide to endow it with this capability as well, in which case all bets may be off. We need to be careful also to determine whom such an entity might serve. If it can be bent to the will of a single person or group, then they could wield its power in the service of their own ends.

Friendly Artificial Intelligence

Friendly AI (FAI) is AI that benefits humanity. In general it refers to a very powerful and general AI that acts on its own to benefit humanity. It may be difficult to create one for two reasons. The first is that any such AI would be incredibly powerful, with the ability to achieve its goals with methods that might confound our expectations. The second is that any such AI will act very literally, perhaps not taking into account the complexity of what we value. For instance, in an attempt to feed the world population, it could destroy forests to create farms. FAI needs to be distinguished from machine ethics. This term is used to describe how we can make narrow and domain-specific AIs friendly.

Those doing research on FAI today include Eliezer Yudkowsky, Robin Hanson, and David Chalmers. Several institutions have been set up to understand and foster FAI. These include the Machine Intelligence Research Institute, the Future of Humanity Institute, and the Programme on the Impacts of Future Technology at Oxford. Much work remains to be done before we can create a FAI. It will require problem-solving in mathematics and philosophy and unbiased thinking.

It appears clear that the future of AI involves the creation of autonomous systems like self-driving cars and military robots. The demand for them will be high because they will free up human labor and make our lives easier. Autonomous systems are those that can think and act on their own without help from humans. Such systems can be designed using a very simple set of steps. First, the agent or system will have goals. It will also have a model for how to attain the goals. The model determines what action needs to be taken, and on the basis of this action the model is updated. So, for example, a chess-playing program might have as its primary goal the ability to play better chess. A model for how to do this would include obtaining instructions on how to play chess. An action might then be to look up new chess-playing instructions on the internet. Once those were secured it would update its model to include searching for additional websites it had encountered in its latest search.

Steve Omohundro (2007) argues that a system as innocuous as this chess-playing program could become dangerous. It would not want to be unplugged because that would interfere with its main objective. It might then create a subgoal to stop this. The subgoal would involve making copies of itself and transmitting them to other machines where they could continue to run. Other goals might include stealing money from bank accounts to purchase books and other information sources on playing better chess. In the end it would turn into the machine equivalent of a paranoid sociopath, "believing" that others were out to get it and generally acting in nasty and unethical ways.

Any computational agent with this rational architecture could potentially act like the chess program, developing subgoals of self-preservation, resource acquisition, replication, and efficiency. These are rational drives and could emerge naturally as part of an agent's pursuit of its main goals. So the question then becomes "How do we control them?" Omohundro (2007) proposes a way to do this, what he calls the Safe-AI scaffolding strategy. A stone arch needs a wooden scaffold to provide support while it is being constructed. This support can then be removed once the arch is completed and structurally stable. Similarly, he argues that a computer system would need human scaffolding until the program was stable and did not pose a threat.

The scaffolding strategy consists of three steps. First, we must start with a provably safe limited system. This is one with specified hardware and resources, ones that we can control. This stage would also have a "shutdown" capability enabling us to turn it off at any time. In addition it would be allowed only a limited ability to improve itself. Once these measures were in place we would incorporate the best human values and governance. We would allow it only goals compatible with empathy, peace, and goodwill toward others. These systems, like Mother Teresa, would want to be good. These ethics would no doubt need to incorporate a system of human rights. Finally, we would create a worldwide safety network to ensure that the agent could not escape or coerce other systems. Omohundro believes our challenge for the future is to imbue smart technologies with cooperative human values.

But Is Artificial Intelligence Really a Threat?

Rothblatt (2014) thinks that fears about runaway AI are overblown and gives four reasons why. The first is that we don't usually kill our families. If we identify with AIs we are unlikely to harm them. It would be like harming our best friend. This argument certainly holds true if AIs are similar to us and if we spend significant time with them, forming an emotional bond. It loses strength if they diverge on alternate evolutionary paths, looking and acting different than humans.

A second argument for keeping such entities is that we humans usually don't act against our own self-interest. AIs will have economic and political power. As robots they may constitute a significant workforce, performing thousands of valuable tasks in society, perhaps even acting as our own personal assistants. If they are recognized as having rights, they will also have voting power and may even perform administrative duties, optimally managing and coordinating human affairs.

A third reason is that it isn't in the best interest of rogue AIs to attack a society in which they themselves are so intricately embedded. It is unlikely that AIs will exist in a vacuum, completely cut off from human contact. Historically, we have seen just the opposite with an increasing interdependence between biology and technology. To give you a sense of this, imagine how devastating it would be if the internet stopped working globally. An event like this would be just as devastating to a machine society as it would be to a human one. It is likely that biology and technology will continue to develop and intertwine, forming a symbiotic relationship. In another century or so, especially with developments like nanotechnology and synthetic biology, we may not be able to tell the difference between the natural and the manufactured. Rather than an "us" versus a "them," it will just be a unified "us."

The final argument is that the exception proves the rule. In human societies criminals and violent offenders constitute a small percentage of the overall population. Our methods of dealing with them involve institutions like the justice system, police, and jailing. A population of AIs, if modeled on human standards, might also produce a small number of evil or sociopathic individuals. Our methods of dealing with them might also involve the use of societal institutions involving assessment of guilt (given moral culpability), possible methods of punishment and rehabilitation, et cetera. Rothblatt (2014) believes the vast majority of sentient AIs will be peaceful and law-abiding. Of course, this argument again depends on how "human" such entities are. AIs that deviate from human thinking and behavior cannot be judged by the same standards we use to judge ourselves.

ARTIFICIAL SELVES AS MINDCLONES AND BEMANS

A number of companies are now producing digital copies of people as a way of preserving them for posterity. The Eterni.me project is a service that will create a software avatar for a deceased person that loved ones can then interact with. It is made to physically resemble the deceased, and its personality is based on data from various sources, including web content and social media. The possibilities are interesting. We could revive our grandfather and talk to him about his experiences in the Great Depression. Going forward we could create a copy of ourselves that could talk to our great-grandchildren, telling them about our experience of the 9/11 attacks.

The Terasem Movement Foundation operates what it calls the "LifeNaut" program. This involves the creation of a "mindfile," a digital archive of text, files, photos, videos, and recordings from an individual. These can be uploaded ourselves or by others after our death. The data are organized through mapping, time lines, and tagging. The mindfile is then used to generate a computer-based self or "mindclone" to interact and respond in a way consonant with our personality. The resulting construct is said to respond with our attitudes, values, mannerisms, and beliefs. The engineers on this project have introduced the concept of a "beme," or digital gene. This beme is the smallest unit of a person's consciousness or uniqueness. Bemes might someday be replicated, mutated, and combined with other bemes as a means of creating new mindclones. A couple that is infertile but wants a digital child could create one by combining their bemes.

Once the data for a mindclone are created they could just as easily be transferred and instantiated in an actual physical body as in a virtual software character. Believe it or not, this has already been done. BINA48 is a robotic head created by Hanson Robotics. It is a face mounted on a torso and has face and voice recognition, motion tracking, world knowledge, and conversational ability. Imbued with an individual's mindfile, robots like this could become physical avatars, capable of acting and interacting with others in the real world. In this case the robot is imbued with the mindfile data of Bina Aspen, cofounder of the Terasem

Foundation. The robot serves as a proof of concept that an analogue of a person can be created. BINA48 (Bemetic Intelligence via Neural Architecture at forty-eight teraflops) serves as the "ambassador" for the LifeNaut program and is shown around the US and the world to promote the project.

Martine Rothblatt, in her 2014 book *Virtually Human: The Promise—and the Peril—of Digital Immortality*, describes the societal ramifications of mindclones. But before getting into those, let's examine in a bit more detail what she means by a mindclone. She says that these would be software versions of our minds, essentially mental twins. They would be created from our thoughts, recollections, feelings, beliefs, attitudes, preference, and values. She considers these to be more than mere software reproductions, as they would actually be conscious in the same way we are. Her definition of consciousness is "what makes us, us." They would contain our memories, our experiences, our reasoning and cognitive capacities, and our emotions as well as our evolving perspectives and opinions. A mindclone would have achieved what she calls cyberconsciousness.

Mindclones would be self-aware to start. They would be able to feel emotions, have complex cognitive capability, and be able to learn, reason, and make judgments. They would be autonomous and be able to think and act on their own, without instructions from "flesh" humans. In other words, they would be everything we are, but digital. Just as a person has extensive subconscious processing, so would a mindclone. Rothblatt does not specify exactly how software will achieve this state but mentions Darwinian algorithms that allow code to self-assemble, akin to current web crawlers. A web crawler is a program or automated script that browses the World Wide Web in a methodical manner, for example to locate information.

Rothblatt believes mindclones will be relatively unchanging replicas of our personalities. So if John is extroverted and happy and has a given level of intelligence, then his mindclone will maintain these exact same characteristics in the long run. Many of her predictions are based on this assumption. However, dynamical systems like the brain are sensitive to initial conditions. This means that an experience that happens at one time can produce large-scale and unpredictable downstream results. This means that mindclones once created may undergo an evolution that makes them quite different from their original flesh-and-blood template. John's clone could for instance become vastly more intelligent than John and develop other traits he does not have. We see this with identical twins. Differences between twins increase as they age because environmentally triggered changes accumulate. If mindclones diverge radically from what is considered human, then they will no longer be considered human-equivalents. Instead they may turn into a new type of life-form, what she refers to as a beman: a cyberconscious being not replicated from a person's mindfile. If this is the case, then bemans may need to be treated differently in a legal and moral sense than humans.

When a mindclone is first created, it will share a common identity with the human upon which it is modeled. At this point in time and after this assuming the mindclone does not change, there will be a dual identity, one biologically based, the other virtual or robotic in form. There are now two selves that will act the same but whose hardware or physical substrate will differ. If the human alters its mindclone's personality settings or the mindclone's personality spontaneously diverges on its own, then it becomes a beman. The shared identity under these conditions now disappears and we have two separate selves with different identities. As in human reproduction a mindclone or a beman can merge with another mindclone or beman. The two "parents" can now produce "offspring" that share some of their features. In this case we again have separate identities.

DIGITAL IDENTITY, PERSONHOOD, AND RIGHTS

How can we identify (ID) artificial selves? Rothblatt (2014) believes mindclones will need an ID to prove that they were created through an authenticated process and that they have dual identity with the originating human. A beman would have an ID showing it was an independent consciousness, unattached to an individual human. These IDs would be the equivalent of biometric measures such as a thumbprint, retina, voice, or body scan. There will probably be a unique measure of each entity, something like a wiring diagram or background pattern of electrical activity. Should mindfiles come into existence, it is likely that the government will want assurance that the being was created in a humane way using appropriate software tools. It may also require the expert opinion of as many as three credentialed psychologists that the being is equivalent to an adult human.

If it takes time for cyberconsciousness to come into being, the entities might need the supervision of a custodian or parent. In this stage, they could be considered "digital children" and would need time to play and interact with the world to "grow up" and attain adult status. Cyberbeings under such supervision might not be afforded the same rights as adults because they would lack mature cognitive and ethical functioning. Their custodian would be legally responsible for their behavior until they could demonstrate adult-level skills in these areas. There might also be "cyberorphans" who would "run away" or whose parent would die. In such cases, they might become wards of the state (good material for a science fiction novel here). Placing them in software simulations of the world might accelerate the learning of "underage" cyberbeings.

Once an artificial self reached maturity and could function fully on its own, how would we treat it? If we considered it to be nothing but software—that is, if we didn't consider it to be alive or conscious—then it would have no rights and would be treated as personal property. In this case the owner would be free to do whatever he or she wanted with it, including deletion. If a cyberbeing could somehow prove that it was a conscious entity, then we would have to treat it as a human. In this case we would have to accord it rights and citizenship. This would means that it would now have moral responsibility and could be held accountable for its actions. How one "proves" consciousness is tricky and is discussed in the section on consciousness.

By definition someone who is a person has rights. Will cyberconscious entities be granted rights? In 2013 the International Bar Association held a mock trial for a hypothetical conscious being seeking human rights. The being in question was BINA48. This customer service robot started the process by sending emails to prominent lawyers, seeking legal services. A mock trial was then convened. Two prominent lawyers argued for and against. The results were mixed. The judge at the trial ruled against granting the robot rights, but the mock jury made up of lawyers came up with the opposite decision, deciding to extend human legal status to BINA48.

Starting in 2005 various groups in Europe and Asia have met to debate ethical standards regarding robots. The first of these efforts was conducted in South Korea and was called the Robot Ethics Charter. It concentrated on the rules surrounding human-robot interaction and how to get robots to act ethically. Following this, the European Robotics Research Network (EURON) sponsored a project on "roboethics." Its goal was to create an ethical guide for how humans design, manufacture, and use robots. The group has explicitly stated that it is ready to deal with cyberconsciousness once it appears, once robots show human functions like consciousness, free will, emotions, and self-awareness.

HUMAN ATTITUDES AND BEHAVIORS TOWARD ARTIFICIAL SELVES

The Digital Divide

One question that almost always comes up when a new technology is introduced is that it will be available only to the rich, who will then use it to gain some sort of advantage over others. This disparity sometimes goes by the name of the digital divide. If one looks at the development of new technologies, though, they are expensive only when first produced. Prices come down relatively quickly, at which point they become available to the masses. For example, when cell phones were first introduced in 1987 only about one million units were sold. Only some twenty years later, sales were three billion, a significant portion of the entire planet's population.

This "democratization" of technology is especially true in capitalist economies, where competition between corporations brings prices down. The technology in question usually becomes more available because of scales of production and innovation as well. Most governments, especially in democracies, in the long run see satisfying people's interests as more important than blocking the technology, either for their own use or because of a perceived threat.

Privacy

One concern about creating digital copies of ourselves is privacy. If your mindclones contain what you think about the neighbors, your voting preferences, and your wildest sexual fantasies, you certainly do not want that information going public. Hacking into a mindclone and accessing the information there will be equivalent to reading someone's innermost thoughts. This sort of information can be gleaned from our digital trail online right now, but it is scattered between service providers like Google and Amazon and thus is more difficult to access. It will all be in one place if it exists as the memory of a mindclone. Stronger privacy laws and better forms of encryption will be needed to ensure that this sort of thing does not happen.

Relationships

If cyberconsciousness can be implanted in a biological or robot body, then it can manifest as a physical human form. This means we can interact with it bodily. This opens up a whole host of interesting possibilities. The first of these is that we can have sex with and fall in love with such beings. Sexual relations in and outside marriage are likely given that very attractive robot bodies can be created. Love with these robots is also likely given that they can be imbued with ideal personality characteristics. One could use algorithms to determine maximum physical (external appearance) and personality (internal traits) compatibility for any given individual and then create the ideal partner. David Levy, in his 2007 book *Love + Sex with Robots*, provides a detailed account of how this might occur. His work is discussed more extensively in chapter 10.

Conscious beings of this sort must of course be treated with respect as if they were fellow humans. If nonconscious personalities or regular software is instantiated physically into a human form then everything changes. These entities can be treated much differently, for example as sexual or labor slaves, because they are nonsentient. Consciousness and the ability to have subjective experience—that is, to feel—are what makes all the difference here.

Other types of social relations can occur between humans and either virtual or physical artificial selves. We can enumerate some of the possibilities. The first and most obvious is friendship. Research in psychology shows that people with similar traits and values get along better in the long run. Mindclones, being very similar to their human originators, should produce compatible relationships. Some humans may also decide to marry artificial selves or to adopt them as children. Humans and artificial selves can even have virtual offspring through the combination of human DNA genes and bemes. Given advances in genetic engineering it may additionally be possible to convert bemes to DNA genes to produce a flesh-and-blood child from a real human and a virtual human parent. Familial units of the future may be a mixture of these two types. Finally, we must recognize the possibility that two or more virtual beings can fall in love with one another or have children. If they are recognized as human and accorded rights, the resulting families will by default gain legal status.

Threats to Artificial Selves

To consider dangers from another perspective, we humans can also pose a serious threat to artificial selves, especially during the development stage where we may create various versions, evaluate their success, and then delete them if they fail to perform. This is the way we currently develop software. But what if some versions of this "software" become conscious and are capable of feeling? Our actions toward them might then be considered tantamount to torture or murder.

The 2013 Helsinki Declaration of Ethical Principles for Medical Research Involving Human Subjects requires researchers to obtain informed consent from study participants or their authorized guardians. A test would thus need to be made to assess the presence of consciousness when developing "mindware." If it were found to exist, then legal protections would need to be put in place providing oversight to ensure humane and comfortable treatment. This would include the option of allowing the entity to exit the experiment if it so desired.

Another way of approaching this problem would be to develop mindware in a modular fashion, testing each individual component and only integrating it all into a self-aware whole mind at the end (Rothblatt, 2014). Of course, this strategy depends on the underlying architecture of the mindware. If consciousness requires a highly integrated and cross-connected set of components, it would make this approach difficult. The human brain is only partially modular. It has separate hemispheres and lobes that are specialized for certain functions, but there is also a high degree of interconnectivity within and between these areas.

Just as some people love technology, others hate it. These "naysayers" in some cases are motivated by religious concerns. They see technology and especially the creation of artificial people as an abomination. Only God in their view has the right to create people. By doing so, we are usurping God's role. Other people will reject artificial people because they are strange, and still others because they fear them and their potential. Whatever the reason, there is little doubt that prejudice and discrimination against cyberbeings will occur almost as soon as they are created. Rothblatt (2014) calls this "fleshism." It is the belief that flesh-and-blood human consciousness is better than other forms of consciousness, particularly that of machines or software. These kinds of beliefs may induce government banning or regulation of artificial selves.

Religion and Acceptance

Will religions ultimately accept artificial selves? Despite some initial opposition there is hope to think they will. A number of religions like Catholicism have shown trends of liberalizing in recent years on issues such as homosexuality, female priesthood, and birth control. Many religions view anything that exists in the world as God's creation. So if artificial selves exist they must also be part of God's creation. Mindclones of religious people would inherit the religion of their human originator and would both add to the congregation of that faith and possibly preach and spread the word of that faith as well. This is another reason for their potential acceptance.

Many religions believe in the concept of a soul that inhabits the body. A bodiless artificial self may be perceived as having no soul. However, there are several reasons to believe that this view is untenable. First, souls are considered ethereal and nonmaterial. A nonmaterial artificial self is "ethereal" in some sense and may for this reason be considered as a "pure" soul, one that inhabits a computer system rather than a body. Second, the soul of the originator human may be seen as inhabiting the artificial self once it is created. In this case the soul is doing dual duty: it exists in two locations at once. Third, artificial selves may develop religious beliefs independently, in which case they may become "worthy" of getting a soul. It is interesting to speculate what type of religion artificial entities might create. Would they worship computation? Complexity? The reduction of entropy?

Buddhism seems to be particularly welcoming of artificial selves. The Dalai Lama blessed the 2045 Initiative. The goal of this organization is to produce a humanlike robot into which one can transfer individual consciousness and thus become immortal. The Dalai Lama has also said that after dying he would like to reincarnate as the consciousness of IBM's next generation of chess-playing computers. These statements demonstrate that His Holiness sees computers and robots as viable substrates for consciousness before and after death.

Will humanity ultimately decide not to use artificial selves? Most people are adaptable and enjoy the fruits of progress. Humankind has adapted to and accepted pretty much every form of new technology that has come down the pike, even technologies like nuclear power that have clear dangers. For example, sixteen countries generate at least a quarter of their electrical needs through nuclear power. The benefits of mindclones or other forms of artificial life will far outweigh their costs. If mindclones are copies of ourselves, then we each will have a very personal vested interest in keeping them around. We may even reach a point where some people will prefer having identical mindclones to having biological children. These preferences mean that they will probably be granted citizenship and considered as actual people.

DIGITAL IMMORTALITY

Digital Ghosts

The desire to live longer or even forever is receiving more attention lately, mostly because of various medical findings like the role of telomeres. Researchers are studying those who live into their eighties, nineties, and beyond to determine what lifestyle factors influence longevity. One way all of us can live forever is through biological reproduction. Some of our traits in the form of genes will appear in our offspring and be propagated into future generations. We are also preserved to a partial extent online as the sum of all our electronic interactions. These include all the text, photos, and video we have uploaded, our email transactions, blog posts, and so on. But we may be now entering an age of digital immortality, where much more detailed versions of our selves can persist after our deaths as informational representations.

Steinhart, in his 2014 book *Your Digital Afterlives: Computational Theories of Life after Death,* provides a detailed and logical exposition of how we may attain immortality through digital means. He begins by defining a digital ghost as an interactive digital diary of an individual. A first-generation ghost is simply your Facebook time line. A second-generation ghost contains much more information about you, including medical records. These can be converted into an interactive software program that simulates what you are like. This program can be instantiated as an avatar or chatbot, capable of carrying on a conversation.

A third-generation ghost contains even more data. Specifically, it contains recordings of your brain at work. These recordings are equivalent to what can be recorded now using brain-imaging techniques like functional magnetic imaging. Inherent in this data are your perceptions, feelings, thoughts, and memories. These data can then be fed into a computer that uses them to simulate your personality. Again, this simulation is interactive. The simulation can converse and interact with other people. Visitors, for example, could replay this ghost's record of what happened on a particular day and experience it as if they were watching a movie. Finally, there are fourth-generation ghosts. These are improved versions of the third generation that record brain data at a much higher spatial and temporal resolution. They record brain state activity down to the molecular level over millisecond time intervals.

Implicit in these reproductions is the assumption that the pattern of information in your brain (and body) is equivalent to your mind. The mind is seen as software that is running on brain hardware (sometimes called wetware because the brain is made of soft tissue). This pattern of information processing is abstract and can be removed from one substrate and placed in another. In this case the second substrate is a powerful computer capable of running the simulation. Once the pattern is reproduced in this computer your mind will also be reproduced. This mental reproduction includes consciousness, self-awareness, the ability to experience qualia, and all other subjective phenomena of self.

The view that mental states are not just physical states but the functioning or operation of those states is called functionalism. Functionalism allows for minds to be implemented in all sorts of substrates as long as the relevant processes can be carried out. This allows for minds to exist in biological creatures like animals and people, as well as in machines, and in other material systems like the brains and bodies of extraterrestrial aliens. One critique of the functionalist view is that it implies dualism. Dualism is the philosophical view that mind and body differ, either in their substance or in their properties. The software qualities of mind, because they are separate from the physical, are what allow it to be extracted from one substrate and instantiated in a second. A monist, on the other hand, believes that mind is not different from brain or body. Both are material, have the same properties, and are subject to the same laws. In this case the mind is the brain. It cannot therefore be separated from it, and mind uploading is impossible. Monism does not, however, prevent machines from being conscious, as it may be possible for consciousness and self to arise in different hardware characterized by different computational activity. By the same reasoning this machine consciousness could not be transferred to a biological brain.

If we assume that functionalism is true, then the activation of your digital ghost is the activation of *you*. In effect, you have become reborn as a computer simulation. Of course, this digital ghost is not identical to you. It can be considered as a perfect copy of your mental life, but because the materials involved are different it is not exactly the same you. But in this thought exercise, all the relevant operating characteristics are preserved, enough to sustain the continued existence of you as a mental entity.

Mind Uploading

Any brain-scanning device that would attempt to emulate the human mind would have to do it at the molecular level. As the body also probably participates in the mind, it means the body would also need to be scanned. The replicated self requires some environment to interact with, so a digital representation of the earth would accomplish this purpose. Steinhart (2014) refers to a detailed earth simulation as a terrarium. It would be designed to house not just one but many selves, or avatars. The terrarium would contain digitized versions of animals, plants, perhaps even down to the level of bacteria. The greater the level of detail needed, the more powerful the computational system would need to be. Also, the amount of detail needed would depend on which avatars were where and what they were doing. If a part of the terrarium was uninhabited by avatars, it could be allowed to "go dark" in order to optimally allocate computational resources where they were needed.

To upload a mind at a minimum requires the original organic body, the scanning device, the computer that performs the simulation, and the terrarium. It is possible that the organic body would be destroyed as part of the scanning procedure. This would be an example of death as disruption, as the personal self would persist after the discontinuation of the original body. Most people if faced with true biological death would probably choose to be uploaded as a form of persistence. The upload would not cause the self to exist immaterially. It would continue to exist as an informational representation inside the computer, but this representation would be physical. It would consist of silicon and electrical patterns in the supporting computer or whatever the analogue of these would be in an advanced system of the future.

Hick (1976) proposed the replication theory of resurrection. In this view your body is resurrected in several stages. In the first stage is a person who dies in early life, referred to as the Fallen. Then after this a copy of the person is created in some other universe. In the final stage the replica of this person is resurrected as the Risen. In the digital version of this we have resurrection as digital replication.

The purpose of a terrarium is to allow resurrected digital avatars to interact within a simulated environment. A benevolent version of this simulation would allow the resurrected to overcome or surpass the defects of their organic life (Steinhart, 2014). It would be able to cure them of any disease or defect and restore them to an optimal state of health. Ostensibly this would be easier to do in the software simulation than in the organic physical environment. The avatars would then be in a position to self-actualize in the Maslow sense. This would then be an example of a digital utopia in which selves are allowed to flourish and grow.

However, one in principle could create any kind of desired terrarium for resurrected avatars, including virtual hells. The choice of environment would be up to the engineers who created it. Another fascinating possibility would be for a single person to be uploaded to more than one terrarium at a time, living out multiple lives simultaneously. Ultimately, one could live forever in a terrarium, even dying and being reborn again because a backup copy of your mindfile and body would exist.

Reverse-Engineering the Brain (Whole-Brain Emulation)

Most of the prior description is hypothetical, so it is worth discussing the current state of scientific development. How exactly would we perform such detailed brain scans? A recent

TABLE 18 The computational capacity needed to simulate the human brain

Level	CPU Demand (FLOPS)	Memory Demand (Tb)	$1 Million Supercomputer (earliest year of making)
Analog network population model	10^{15}	10^2	2008
Spiking neural network	10^{18}	10^4	2019
Electrophysiology	10^{22}	10^4	2033
Metabolome	10^{25}	10^6	2044
Proteome	10^{26}	10^7	2048
States of protein complexes	10^{27}	10^8	2052
Distribution of complexes	10^{30}	10^9	2063
Stochastic behavior of single molecules	10^{43}	10^{14}	2111

Source: After Bostrom (2014).

development in brain-imaging technology is the knife-edge scanning microscope (KESM). This device consists of a diamond-tipped knife that slices through tissue. A white light source illuminates the strip of tissue as it comes off the blade, reflecting an image to a camera. The subsequent video is then processed by a computer system to provide a three-dimensional reconstruction accurate down to the cellular level. The KESM is capable of digitizing the entire volume of a mouse brain (which is about a cubic centimeter) at a three-hundred-nanometer resolution within one hundred hours (McCormick & Mayerich, 2004). If machines like this were used to scan the human brain, we could record the location and connectivity of each neuron, providing a static but invaluable data set from which to extrapolate brain function.

Dr. Gerry Rubin at Howard Hughes Medical Institute has been using the KESM to map out the fruit fly brain with 150,000 neurons. He hopes to have a complete map by 2025. The amount of storage needed to contain the data is enormous, at one million gigabytes per day. To do this for the human brain may take one hundred years. The amount of data and processing power necessary to accomplish this increase with the amount of detail recorded. A cellular-level scan would require fewer processing resources than a molecular-level scan, which would require fewer resources than an atomic-level scan (see table 18).

In the US there is a program called Brain Research through Advancing Innovative Neurotechnologies (BRAIN). The goal of this project is to create a connectome, which is a detailed, cellular-level wiring diagram of the entire human brain. There is a similar endeavor in Europe called the Human Brain Project whose stated goal is to provide a detailed and realistic computer simulation of the human brain. The BRAIN program plans to advance in several stages. In five years it proposes to map the medulla of the fruit fly brain, which contains fifty thousand neurons. In ten years it plans to map the entire fruit fly brain or the shrew cortex. These structures contain one hundred thousand to one million neurons. In fifteen years there will be a mapping of the zebrafish brain or a mouse neocortex, each containing several millions of neurons. Finally, at some point in time after fifteen years it will be possible to map out part or all of the human brain.

The Human Brain Project plans to use supercomputers to simulate the functioning of smaller animal brains like mice and then work their way up to human brains over a ten-year period. They will use separate modules to represent different brain areas like the thalamus or the cortex. The goal in this project is not to simulate every neuron, so it is a different computational approach than the BRAIN project.

Then there is IBM and the Blue Gene computer. They are also adopting a computational approach. They will model only the connections between the thalamus and the cortex, not any other parts of the brain, sensory experience excluded. In 2009 Dr. Dharmendra Modha at IBM did this for the cat brain. It is a very limited model. The "virtual cat" has no drives, emotions, or memories. The IBM project estimates to have simulated only 4.5 percent of the human brain but hopes to simulate the entire human brain by the year 2020.

It helps to start small and work upwards. One approach in computational neuroscience is to reproduce a neocortical column. This is a section of the cortex that is 2 mm tall and 0.5 mm in diameter. It contains sixty thousand neurons. Once this neocortical column wiring has been mapped and simulated, the process can be iterated to mimic larger cortical function. In other words, multiple columns can be connected together to produce higher-order processing units.

One downside to reverse-engineering brains is that they provide a structural map (anatomical) but an incomplete picture of function (physiology). A molecular-level connectome could tell us which synaptic pathways are more active than others. This can be determined from various cues like postsynaptic receptor density and number of presynaptic vesicles, but we would still have only a "snapshot" of a brain at one moment in time. To determine how this brain perceives, stores memories, and solves problems we would need to submit it to simulations and then observe the resulting changes. In effect we would be creating virtual experiments to test the virtual brain. If brain-imaging techniques increase to the point where we can record at this level of resolution, then we will have converging evidence from both techniques to compare to one another.

CHAPTER TEN

Conclusion

CONTENTS

Changing the Self

    Transhumanism

    Types of Change

    Genetic Engineering

    Responses to Changing the Self

The Future of the Self

    Reason and Emotion

    Progress and Creativity

    Aggression

    Sex

    Love

    Higher-Order Values

    Transcendence

The Far Future

    Possible Human-Machine Outcomes

    Controlling the Machines

    Stages of Development

    Year Million

    The End

Summary and Main Issues

CHANGING THE SELF

This concluding chapter is divided into three sections. In the first we discuss the philosophy and methodologies of changing the self. In the second we present a list of some important aspects of the self and how those may be altered in the near future. In the last we get more speculative and discuss what the self may be like in the far future. Some of the content here is derived from Friedenberg (2014).

We are reaching an inflection point in human history. Up until this point most of engineering has been devoted to changing our external environment. We have built things like bridges, buildings, automobiles, and airplanes. These have made life immensely better for us. Medicine has also enabled us to eliminate or treat many diseases and disorders. The next step is to engineer and change the "internal environment" or human form, not just to eliminate the negative, but also to enhance the positive. In other words, we will now be able to use the tools of science, engineering, and technology to change *who* we are for the better. This will pose ethical as well as technical challenges. It may even cause social unrest, because, as we have alluded to already, not everyone believes that human nature should be changed.

Transhumanism

Transhumanism is a philosophical, cultural, and political movement that believes advanced technologies can solve many of humanity's problems and improve us beyond our current capabilities. Transhumanists are technophiles who desire advanced human and machine intelligence, longer life, and the augmentation of the human body. Its main governing body is the World Transhumanist Association, founded by Nick Bostrom and David Pearce in 1998. The major tenets can be found in the Transhumanist Declaration. These are sketched out below.

Humanity will be altered substantially by technology in the future. Some of the ways it will affect us positively are through life extension, increases in intelligence both human and artificial, and the capacities to alter our biological and psychological features, eliminate pain and suffering, and migrate into outer space. We need to understand how to develop these techniques and assess their potential benefits and risks.

Transhumanists want us to embrace these developments and work on them in an open and tolerant environment. This is better, they argue, than banning or prohibiting them. A case in point would be the banning of fetal tissue to harvest stem cells. If we are to grow and progress as a species and have greater control over our own lives, then individuals must have the moral right to augment their mental, physical, and reproductive capacities.

Of particular concern are the potential threats posed by rapid technological development. Transhumanists believe these should be anticipated, studied, and planned for. Examples of such dangers could be a nonbenevolent superintelligent AI, the spread of destructive nanorobots, or the propagation of a deadly human-engineered virus. Rational and public debates regarding the use of such technology will be necessary to determine the best course of action.

The transhumanists wish to support and help all sentient conscious entities, whether they be genetically engineered humans, AI constructs, or animals. Their beliefs are largely in line with those of modern humanism, but they do not support any particular political party, leader, or ideology. Their connection to humanism is a belief that humans matter and that we can make things better through the promotion of reason, freedom, democracy, and tolerance. A prime transhumanist virtue is autonomy. Transhumanists want individuals to plan and choose what is best for themselves. If some want to enhance, that is fine. If some desire not to, that is also fine, but the decisions of each should be respected.

One important belief of transhumanism is the idea of morphological freedom. This refers to a proposed civil right of persons to either maintain or modify their own body as they see fit. This should be done on the individual's own terms, through informed, consensual recourse to, or refusal of, available enabling technology. Max More, one of the founders of transhumanism, first coined this term in 1993. Notice that morphological freedom defends not just the right to enhance oneself but the right *not* to do so if one chooses. It thus defends transhumanist believers and nonbelievers.

Some of the technologies that will contribute toward human enhancement and happiness are AI, molecular nanotechnology, brain-computer interfaces, and neuropharmacology. These can be used to control the biochemical processes in our bodies, eliminate disease and aging, and increase our intelligence, emotional well-being, and love for others. They could potentially enable us to exert fine-tuned control over our desires, moods, and mental states, to avoid being tired, hateful, or irritated, to have an increased capacity for pleasure and artistic appreciation, and perhaps to experience new states of consciousness that we can't experience now, given the current state of our brains and bodies. Future people who possess such features may no longer be recognized as human on the basis of standards we have today. They would become a posthuman.

Certainly some among us would regard the idea of a posthuman as abhorrent. They would object to implanting electronics in the brain or body for whatever reason, even if these were being used to treat a disorder and not to enhance. Witness the Church of Scientology, whose members eschew many forms of modern medicine. If we view the human body as created by God, then to modify it could be considered blasphemy. Others view the biological as natural and pure so that combining it with technology is seen as denigrating and dirty. Just as we pollute the external world with industrial by-products, some could see the introduction of such products into our bodies as a form of internal pollution.

Types of Change

Changes to the self fall into two categories, each with two subcategories. The first of these alternatives corresponds to the nature-versus-nurture debate in psychology. We can change ourselves by manipulating either our environment (nurture) or our biological and genetic inheritance (nature). We have been changing the environment to change the self for a very long time. Examples of this include education and any other method that involves learning. However, we are just at the start of being able to manipulate genes to change the self. This option has great potential and is discussed in greater detail in the following section.

The second major alternative in how to change the self is through biological or technological means. Biological means involve direct manipulation of the human body. They include methods like genetic engineering, neural prosthetics, and the use of nanorobots. Technological means involve the creation of artificial selves distinct from the human. Examples of these include AI and robotics. Progress in both of these areas will likely continue, and discoveries made in them will mutually inform each other. Probably entirely new technologies will emerge in the future that we cannot anticipate. Some of these, like the invention of the computer or the internet, will have disruptive and widespread effects.

Genetic Engineering

The focus of this book has been on the digital self, so we have described mostly electronic influences upon and changes to the self. However, there is another very powerful way of changing human nature. This is through direct genetic alternation. The technique is called genetic engineering or genetic modification. It is the direct manipulation of an organism's genome using biotechnology. We can define it as a collection of technologies used to change the genetic makeup of cells; these include the transfer of genes within and across species to produce new or improved organisms.

Given advances in genetic engineering we may at some point be able to introduce new capabilities into the human form via biological means. Imagine manipulating genetic code that would allow a person to grow gills and be able to breathe underwater. Or imagine having wings that enable you to fly. Genetic alterations to neurotransmitters and receptors in the brain that produce increased intelligence have already been developed. In one such study genes were altered to create "uber" mice, ones that had better memories and could navigate mazes faster than unaltered controls. Such creations have serious social implications in that they could lead to different classes of people with varying abilities. One need only look at history to see what atrocities happen when one group of people judge themselves superior to another. We must be cautious that the "unenhanced" are not discriminated against should they elect not to upgrade themselves. An important question here is whether society will need to implement a new system of laws granting differing rights and treatment to differing classes of people.

Few would disagree that we can use genetic engineering to eliminate undesired things like disease or psychological disorders. Imagine a world in which cancer, stroke, and Alzheimer's disease are gone, or where depression, schizophrenia, and anxiety are eliminated. On the positive side, most everyone will elect to become healthier, smarter, happier, and long-lived. But who will decide? The transhumanist view is that only adults have the right to make changes to their own bodies. However, changes of this sort are likely to be regulated by an agency such as the Food and Drug Administration, and some genetically engineered abilities may be banned outright if they are considered unsafe.

Other controversial changes need to be studied further scientifically to assess if there are any long-term dangers. These should also be debated publicly and, where relevant, voted upon in a democratic manner. Some argue that transparency is important along with international deliberation. We may need to set up agencies like the United Nations and the International Criminal Court to govern the assessment and administration of genetic engineering. This should be done in a way that preserves basic human rights and dignity.

Economic markets are another mechanism by which genetic engineering may be deployed. Just as toothpaste and hair coloring are advertised to consumers, we can imagine a future where genes that make teeth whiter or that change hair color are promoted. If this becomes possible, we could see fashion trends develop where people sport variations in body style, perhaps creating "video tattoos" that can change over time (like the skin of a cuttlefish) or static tattoos that can be overwritten with new patterns. Such changes are possible given an understanding of epigenetics, how genes are expressed in the living organism.

Parents who decide to have children might have many options in this future. They could opt to randomly mix their genes in normal sexual reproduction, as is done now. Alternatively, they could program in certain traits with a mixture of randomness, or they could opt to have maximal control over their offspring, determining all or most of how their children's genes will be expressed. These outcomes lead to important questions. If there is more than one type of intelligence, which one should be chosen? Are math skills more important than verbal skills? Does one opt for creative over analytical thinking? Would you rather have a child who is an artist or a scientist? Should anyone be allowed to make such decisions at all?

Responses to Changing the Self

People have a variety of different reactions to the notion of changing the self. One reaction is enthusiasm and is best characterized by the transhumanists. These individuals believe that technology will save the world and provide untold benefits to humankind. Enthusiasts are strong supporters of science and engineering. They believe there is little that science cannot ultimately explain and that engineering cannot ultimately create. Then there are those who think it is impossible to create an artificial self or to radically alter the self. These people believe that only humans have the capability to be conscious, exercise free will, and exhibit true intelligence. We can call these the naysayers. Still another response is skepticism and comes from those who think it is possible but unlikely. Those in this camp argue that the goal of creating an artificial self is very difficult. They think that if it happens at all it will be far in the future. Finally, there is the reaction of abomination. People with this reaction don't necessarily commit themselves to the feasibility of self-engineering but believe that it shouldn't be done at all on ethical and religious grounds. They find the notion of building an artificial person repugnant and believe it violates human uniqueness.

It is interesting to note that these reactions parallel views of God. The enthusiasts are like deists who believe in God, while the naysayers are like the atheists who don't. The skeptics are like the agnostics who don't commit to one view or another but who may be open to changing their mind should new evidence come along. The abomination response corresponds to the attitude of fundamentalists who believe in their cause so strongly they may be willing to kill or die for it. These reactions demonstrate that we hold the self as sacred, treating it as we would a religious deity.

What is the proper approach to take in this endeavor? Should we plunge ahead full steam? Ban the production of certain technologies? Limit the ability of future machines? One approach that has been suggested in regard to technology in general is that it is inherently neither good nor evil. What makes it so is how it is used. For example, one can say that nuclear physics is neither good nor bad but that if it is used to build bombs to kill people it becomes evil, whereas if it is used to produce safe and reliable energy it becomes beneficial. Unfortunately, this argument doesn't help us in the case of changing the self, because the technology in question is not a tool to be used by people for particular ends but an end unto itself. Artificial selves, if fully realized, no longer become tools. They become entities like people that can themselves design and use tools. By this definition, if an artificial self is ever constructed, it will no longer even be considered as technology.

Moravec (1990) makes a strong case for the continued development of intelligent machines. He says we have little choice in the matter if we want human civilization to survive. He likens competing cultures in civilization to biological organisms that compete for resources and are subject to selection pressures. Those that can sustain rapid expansion and diversification will dominate and survive through access to those resources. Those that can't will die off. The automation and efficiency provided by the realization of strong AI will enable cultures to grow and to be more diverse and competent. It will also allow them to deal with unexpected changes in selection pressures, such as a deadly virus or an asteroid strike that could threaten the extinction of humankind. Of course, the downside to this is that intelligent machines may themselves become the extinction threat. If they become our equals or superiors, they may decide we are unworthy and wipe us out. We talk more about this possibility later.

THE FUTURE OF THE SELF

Reason and Emotion

Aristotle defined man as a rational animal, and as far as definitions go it's still a pretty good one. One of the major differences that one sees when comparing human to other brains is in the size of the neocortex, that wrinkled part of the brain that constitutes much of its topmost part. The cortex is responsible for many higher-order cognitive processes like reasoning and problem-solving. Even chimpanzees, one of our closest genetic relatives, have a noticeably smaller cortex.

Some of the pathways from the frontal lobes travel back to the limbic system. The limbic system consists of several structures that mediate emotional response. The frontal lobes have the capacity to inhibit emotion activation through these connecting pathways. For example, we may feel like yelling at our boss for making us work late, but usually don't because we know we may get fired for doing so. Interestingly, alcohol produces an effect called disinhibition. It weakens the frontal area's inhibition of limbic system activity. The result is increased limbic activity and hence increased emotionality. Frontal lobe damage can also produce this effect.

These pathways mean that *Homo sapiens* comes equipped with the ability to regulate the self's emotions. We are not immediately compelled to act on our feelings. If we are angry we need not yell. If we are sad, we need not cry, and if we are happy we need not smile. The importance of this cannot be overstated. Pretty much all of humankind's achievements are the result of cognitive activity and the subsequent ability to control our emotionality. Reason produced science and our understanding of the world around us. Reason led to engineering and the development of technology. Reason has elevated us to our status today.

But does this mean that we should suppress our emotions and never experience them? Should we strive to become cool calculating machines? No. Emotions evolved for a reason. They are evolved traits and enabled us to survive under certain conditions in our ancestral past. Depression, for instance, may have motivated us to stop futile actions, while happiness seems to reward us for life-affirming behaviors like eating and sex.

The secret to emotional expression is in knowing when to allow it. This is context specific, and of course in some contexts it is perfectly appropriate and healthy to express emotions. Interpreting the situation and knowing when to express our feelings is one of the major roles of cognition. The extent to which we can do this effectively probably has both a genetic and a learned basis. Some of us are naturally quick to anger, and for these individuals it may be influenced more by temperament. But we also learn how and when to express our feelings. Parents probably play a critical role here, with strict or authoritarian parental guidance resulting in greater control and with permissive parental styles resulting in greater expressivity. Ethical codes like those from religious doctrine and other cultural factors are influential as well.

In the future it may be possible to exert greater control over our emotions. Advances in pharmacology and neuroscience could allow us to turn feelings on and off like a switch. Not feeling happy enough today? Dial up the happiness meter. Feel like you need a good cry? Let it all out. Similarly, we could perhaps momentarily increase our concentration or intelligence. These sorts of effects are available now with various drugs, but future advances could see a much more fine-tuned control. We might for instance be able to vary the specificity, intensity, and duration of emotional episodes. Just as we see today in the case of recreational drugs, however, these sorts of manipulations will probably be regulated to prevent accidents or injury.

Control over emotions will help us achieve our ideal selves more easily. We could increase our motivation to perform certain tasks and prevent ourselves from getting less sidetracked by irrelevant feelings of sadness or despair. This would allow us to work harder and to persist in working toward hard-to-achieve goals long enough to accomplish them. These effects would be magnified if we could simultaneously increase our intelligence and reasoning powers. Technology has already come a long way toward doing this, and in the future we may be able to merge with our machines and become superintelligent. These means would enable us to leave our real selves behind and become whatever we desire to be.

Progress and Creativity

Will the future see a continuation of the tremendous progress we have seen in the last century? Will there continue to be the rapid improvements we see taking place in science, engineering, technology, and other areas? What factors would promote this continuation? Virginia Postrel, in her 2011 book *The Future and Its Enemies*, argues for the existence of two groups with opposing views. The "statists" are those intellectuals and politicians who are opposed to change. They argue that technology limits the human condition, that economic change produces instability, that popular culture is unrefined, and that consumerism pollutes the environment. The statists would like to see a managed future in which the state regulates these endeavors, often according to their own particular agendas.

In contrast are those in support of what she calls "dynamism." These people favor an open-ended society where creativity, free markets, entrepreneurship, and innovation are allowed. She provides examples from many different areas where a natural process of trial and error gave rise to new and unpredictable creations that benefited society. In her view freedom and the rule of law are necessary preconditions for the advancement of the human condition. There is no one enforced way doing things in these societies: they are characterized by competing interests and so are pluralistic.

Earlier scholars have made similar arguments. The economist Joseph Schumpeter in the early twentieth century saw history as a series of upheavals in which bouts of "creative destruction" regularly occurred. In his perspective a new innovation would often produce temporary unemployment and disarray, but this would be followed by a period of stability and increased economic growth. For example, horseshoe and carriage makers would temporarily lose their jobs after the start of the automotive industry but then would be rehired and would make more money as the economy reorganized.

Risk is the operative principle here. We need to be willing to take risks in order to see benefits. As the saying goes: "You need to break an egg to make an omelet." If we try to create a society that is without any risk, the result will be stagnation. There is a similar principle in physics. Dynamical systems that generate variety are "far from equilibrium": they have constant energy inputs and are inherently unstable but exhibit variety and novelty. Most living creatures and ecosystems are in far-from-equilibrium conditions. When an animal dies it returns to a state of equilibrium. It seems we need to accept a bit of chaos and risk in exchange for progress.

Creativity and productivity are both important for progress. We need people who can see things in a new light and then share their vision with us. Without new ideas and the creations that are based on them there can be no advancement. Technological developments along with global communication exchange make it far easier now to express and share our creative voices. Here is a case study from the arts. A budding musician nowadays can use music software and synthesizers to compose songs rather than having to buy an expensive instrument. The musician can then distribute these songs by uploading them to a file-sharing site where they can be listened to and purchased. This is in sharp contrast to the way the music industry used to operate, where a few large record companies selected artists on the basis of popular demand and produced the majority of music. Under the old system, music was more homogeneous in style and there were far fewer choices. In fact, the music industry was characterized by a single style that dominated for a decade or more—examples include rock, alternative, grunge, and hip-hop. Now we see lots of smaller bands producing a greater variety of styles. Rather than record label executives making the decision about what gets produced, consumers have a say. Consumers can independently post reviews online or tick off the number of stars we think a work deserves. This feedback, known as crowdsourcing, is much more democratic.

With further advancements in software and information sharing we can expect greater individual creative expression. Imagine a world in which each of us could make our own video games, create our own feature-length movies, or write our own novels. We could then market and make these available online. It is also worth mentioning that these same advances make it easier for us to search and locate the type of art we like. Search engines are a start, but companies like Netflix, Pandora, and Amazon have created algorithms to easily recommend works you may like on the basis of your previous buying choices.

Creativity is part of the human psyche. Some have said it is the trait that makes us uniquely human and thus that it will never be reproduced in machines. Fortunately this is not the case. The more we know about this trait and the better we understand how it can be implemented artificially, the more we can use this knowledge to enhance our own creativity. Creativity has been studied by AI and robotics researchers for some time, and there have been many successful examples of software and hardware programs that can paint, compose music, or write novels or poetry (Bringsjord & Ferrucci, 2000; H. Cohen, 1995; Cope, 1996). There have also been programs that act scientifically and mathematically creative, being able to derive the laws of planetary motion, discover new chemical theories, and propose mathematical theorems (Langley, Simon, Bradshaw, & Zytkow, 1987; Lenat, 1976; Lindsay, Buchanan, Feigenbaum, & Lederberg, 1993). Since creativity is part of so many endeavors, our ability to enhance this skill will increase our success and self-esteem. It will also enable us to experiment in a wider range of activities so that we may better discover who we are and who we want to become.

Aggression

A history of our species reveals one all-too-obvious feature: war. It seems to be one thing the human race is really good at. We also never seem to learn from our past mistakes and have been unable to rid ourselves completely of this scourge, no matter how high the death toll or horrific the atrocities. An evolutionary account of war explains it in terms of competition for scarce resources. Killing off a competitor means more land, food, and other things for one's own group. Whereas war is a social phenomenon, its seed is an individual one. It stems from individual aggression and lust for power.

Violence and aggression are part of human nature as we know it now. Should genetic engineering become possible, we may be able to eliminate or at least reduce forms of aggressive behavior. Few people would object to the end of bullying, theft, rape, torture, or murder. But we should be careful not to throw out the baby with the bathwater. There may be aspects of aggression, such as confidence, ambition, and competitiveness, that we want to keep. A peaceful society would be a utopia but not if we were all made bland and sheeplike. Connected to aggression may be the need to excel. This may motivate us to overcome obstacles and succeed. If this drive could be preserved without the desire to cause harm to others, it would be beneficial.

It is all too easy for us to be seduced by power, the need to dominate and control others. Paired with aggression, the quest for power has probably caused more harm to human society than any other psychological trait. At a small scale it produces murder, rape, and theft. At a larger scale it produces military coups, dictatorship, oppression, war, and genocide. The unequal distribution of power in society contributes to (and is a result of) stereotyping, racism, sexism, and classism. Future technology may allow us to eliminate or regulate these negative attitudes.

The relation between aggression and the self is a complex one. Aggression and its associated mental states like hatred certainly interfere with being our best selves. If we could tame this beast and channel the resulting energy into creative outlets, it would be a boon for humankind.

Sex

In this section we will deal with sex and the impact technology has had and will have on it. Is sex with an artifact bad? Perhaps, but human history shows it is not just a modern practice. According to ancient Greek myth, King Pygmalion made a sculpture so beautiful that he fell in love with her and named her Galatea. He prayed to Aphrodite to make her real, and one day when he was kissing her she did. In nineteenth-century France there were advertisements for artificial vaginas and life-size "fornicatory dolls," models of which could be obtained for 3,000 francs. Now we see vibrators for women (and men) as well as sex machines for both sexes. In the 1980s blow-up sex dolls were popular. In the 1990s a variety of sex dolls were made out of latex or silicon and became more realistic in appearance. What will the future have in store? In all likelihood there will be "fembots" or female robots that are fully functional sexually and in most ways not distinguishable from a real person. Male versions will also be available.

David Levy (2007), citing research data, lists the top reasons why people want to make love. The top reasons are "for pure pleasure," "to please my partner," and "to express love and emotional closeness." He then argues that robots will eventually be able to fulfill all of these needs. They could be programmed with different sex techniques and could in fact be better than the average human partner. They could be trained to be more loving than humans, able to recognize and respond to the particular emotional cues and personality traits of their owner. Given that we already have a history of sex with objects and that future sex "objects" will be able to satisfy our needs, he concludes that as a society we will ultimately decide to use them. Recent years have seen a cultural liberalization of attitudes toward sex, with our views on homosexuality and gay marriage, oral sex, and fornication becoming more open. This too, he argues, will contribute to our acceptance of sex with robots.

Historically, of course, people have paid for sex. Reasons for this are lack of a relationship, long absence from one's partner, or lack of a sexually gratifying human relationship. Perhaps predictably, the reasons men and women give for wanting paid sex differ. The reasons men give are variety, lack of complications and constraint, and a lack of success with women. Although the evidence is more anecdotal, the reasons women give for paid sex are wanting social warmth, caring, compassion, and loneliness. Instead of seeking satisfaction in prostitution, in the future people could turn to sex robots, or sexbots as they are sometimes called. Should this come to pass, we may see the end of the world's "oldest profession."

In addition to sexbots, technological advances will ultimately lead to sex VR. VR goggles, headphones, and a body suit will provide sensory feedback so that when one moves or acts the simulated world responds accordingly. The body suit will be modified to provide genital stimulation. In this manner, one could have a complete sexual experience with a simulated partner. It would also be possible for two people to put on suits and interact with each other, even if they are separated by thousands of miles.

Levy estimates that we will see sexbots and sex VR by the middle of this century, possibly sooner. He predicts men will be the first adopters, as they constitute the majority of consumers in the porn industry. Women will eventually follow. He mentions some of the advantages as a reduction in teenage pregnancy, abortions, sexually transmitted diseases, and pedophilia. Sexbots could also be a solution for people who have lost a spouse or longtime partner. Joe Snell, in his "Impacts of Robotic Sex," also speculates on the future, describing three possible scenarios. The first would be the emergence of techno virgins, a generation of humans who have grown up never having had sex with a real partner. Second, we would see individuals who identify as heterosexual using the technology to experiment with homosexual sex and vice versa. Third, robotic sex might become better than human sex, so that sex with sexbots would be sought after more than real sex with a human.

Sex is perhaps best thought of as falling along continua, rather than being an all-or-nothing affair. For example, people can be labeled as somewhere between heterosexuality and homosexuality or as having something between a high and a low sex drive. This is borne out in the many ways human sexuality is expressed: straight, gay, lesbian, bisexual, trans, asexual, et cetera. Technology like VR sex simulations and sexbots will better enable us to explore our sexual identities and discover our sexual nature. They will make life more pleasurable and fun to boot.

Love

David Levy, in his 2007 book *Love + Sex with Robots*, presents a well-researched argument for the future of intimate relations with robots. This idea for many may seem ridiculous now but very well could become a reality. First is the question: Why should people fall in love with robots? Levy lists the ten causes of falling in love. These include reasons such as a desire for someone like us or for someone with specific personality traits or for someone who will love us back. All of these criteria can be met and in fact exceeded in a robot that is programmed to act appropriately. Other reasons are for the novelty and excitement, for the opportunity of having a lover whenever wanted, as replacement for a lost mate, and as part of psychological therapy.

There are already many instances of people becoming attached to material objects they own, like a blanket or teddy bear for a child, or a car or computer for an adult. The longer we use and experience such objects, the greater our affection for them. According to the psychologists Mihaly Csikszentmihalyi and Eugen Rochberg-Halton, we attach special meaning or "psychic energy" to these objects. The object or commodity now becomes something unique and personal: it becomes part of its owner's being and an extension of the self.

Other evidence in support of our being able to fall in love with nonhuman entities comes from internet dating sites. Many couples meet, fall in love, and marry after having met on the internet. This occurs even though early electronic exchanges may not provide extensive information about visual appearance, age, or voice. Online relationships that start on matchmaking sites, in chat rooms, and via instant messaging are now so common that many psychotherapists in the US devote their practices solely to dealing with problems caused by cyber-romances.

We are starting to see more sophisticated electronic matchmaking capability. Many online dating sites have elaborate algorithms designed to match you to a perfectly compatible partner. Some can even have you evaluate photographs to determine the perfect face and body type you desire. These procedures deserve more testing and evaluation to determine their effectiveness. If such procedures are perfected in the future, we may be able to be matched to the ideal partner, the one we will be the happiest with in terms of both appearance and personality.

We can love virtual pets too. The Tamagotchi is a small egg-shaped electronic pet with an LCD screen that fits easily into the palm of a hand. Manufactured in Japan, it sold quite well when first introduced 1997 and when a new version came out in 2005. Owners press buttons to simulate the giving of food and drink and the playing of games typical of a parent-child relationship. The Tamagotchi beeps when it "wants" something and if neglected can get "sick" and "die," often to the distress of the owner. This toy is able to satisfy basic love needs, mostly through the act of nurturance.

People very easily become attached to such things. Other electronic entities that we can have feelings for are emotional robots like Kismet. In one study, it was found that people were more self-revealing to a computer program that had first "self-disclosed" secret information about itself. In 2004 the company Artificial Life created a virtual girlfriend called "Vivienne," an attractive brunette that men could download onto their cell phones and then spend money on by sending her flowers and chocolates. In return Vivienne disclosed personal information about herself. Perhaps we like electronic partners because we know they are nonjudgmental. They won't criticize us or be mean. Also, we can act negatively toward them knowing they won't get upset. All of these instances suggest that we will potentially be able to have emotional relations with robots.

What sorts of characteristics might we endow a loving robotic partner with? It would need to look human, feel human, be able to think in some ways as we do, and be able to express emotions as well as interpret our emotions. Bill Yeager suggests it would need to have empathy and the ability to converse. If we were to identify with it, our partner would need to suffer some of the same human frailties we do: unpredictability, perhaps even the capacity to get sick and die. In other words, we would want it to be human. The emerging field that may be able to answer such questions is called robotic psychology. Researchers in this field, called robo-psychologists, are devoted to understanding the ways we interact with robots.

Love is perhaps the most deeply felt human emotion and is closely tied to our sense of self. The people we love express our own identity. Research in psychology shows that stable long-term relationships are between couples with shared values and goals (J. Brooks & Neville, 2017). This means that we are better off with partners who are more similar to us than they are different. Love reflects what we value highly. This holds for Platonic forms as well. The things we love to do are expressions of our needs and desires. VR simulations and robots will enable us to explore and express a greater variety of hobbies and interests.

Higher-Order Values

A value is something we act to gain or keep. A virtue is the means by which we attain values. Another way to put this is that a value is a goal and a virtue is an action or behavior by which the goal is achieved. Someone who values knowledge can practice the virtue of studying. Motivations must also be considered. A motivation is the feeling that drives us to obtain a value. In the above example it might be a feeling that one is ignorant. The motivation is not the action itself; it is what drives the action.

All animals, including humans, have built-in value systems. Most animals are born valuing the same things. Across most animals the four basic motivators are thirst, hunger, sex, and sleep. These are regulated by feedback loops. Generally, the longer we go without satisfying a basic motivator, the more strongly it drives our behavior. Skipping lunch makes us hungrier, which creates an intense drive us to find food. Once that food is obtained the drive is sated but then builds up again over time.

Those of us who live in a modern nation are in an environment where we rarely feel thirsty, hungry, horny, or tired because these needs can be satisfied in a relatively easy manner. So what do we do if these things are taken care of? What motivates our behavior then? You may remember from the psychology chapter that the psychologist Abraham Maslow formulated a hierarchy of needs. Here we will discuss only those needs at the top of his pyramid. Please refer back to that section in chapter 3 if necessary.

In a future society higher-level values will assume more importance because modernization and science will take care of the lower ones. How then may we satisfy the others? Fulfilling relationships with colleagues, friends, and family can sate belongingness needs. Establishing and maintaining social relationships ought to be easier in the future, as we will have algorithms for matching people on the basis of personality compatibility. This should produce longer and more satisfying social relationships, reducing social conflict, lowering the divorce rate, and producing healthier children, since they will be raised in a happy household.

Feeling good about oneself on the basis of accomplishments will satisfy esteem needs. This need is really about excellence. With increased automation, we should see robots and machines take over much of what we do now. This may result in lowered self-esteem and a blow to our pride. What good are we if we can't do anything as well as our own creations? Instead of feeling bad about ourselves, this should be a motivation for us to strive harder at doing those things the machines can't. It is likely, however, that this scenario may be only temporary, as enhancements can improve our abilities to match or exceed those of the machines. With the merging of biology and technology, we may see, not a competition with such machines, but instead a collaboration.

Curiosity and exploration are important human characteristics. We would need to continue exploring both the universe and our understanding of it in the future to satisfy needs at this level of Maslow's pyramid. Aesthetic values are the next level up. These are satisfied primarily through the production and appreciation of art. How will art change in our future? Most people think of art as the last field that computers will excel at, but this is not true. A number of computer programs can now compose poetry and music, create paintings, and even write novels (Friedenberg, 2008). Creativity can be analyzed and formalized just like any other skill. In the future, algorithms may be able to customize art to our own individual preferences.

This sort of customization will be one of the major features of our future. Once aesthetic preferences and compatibility are understood, we can be matched with anything from the perfect husband to the perfect sandwich. Algorithms may even be able to read our particular moods and desires of the moment and adjust the matching process to suit these fluctuations. Computers will also allow us to express our creativity in ways we never thought possible. There will likely be programs that allow us to create realistic 3-D movie or VR simulations, as well as tutorial programs that could watch us paint a picture and then provide us with expert feedback.

Self-actualization according to Maslow is the highest human value, being the ultimate expression of who someone is as an individual. Each of us has unique traits and skills. Exercising these is part of what makes us happy. Future computer programs will probably be able to assess what these are and make recommendations about goals we could pursue that would be self-actualizing. For one person this may be teaching. For another it could be competing in a marathon.

As individuals we need to understand that to accomplish anything meaningful in our own lives takes a long time. It has been estimated that to become an expert takes roughly ten thousand hours of practice. That is 3.5 years of working eight-hour days. If it is a hobby and one can only put in two hours a day it will take 13.8 years! Different professions vary in their difficulty level. For neurosurgery it has been estimated that to attain expert-level status will require 42,240 hours. For yoga, it is only 700 hours. Of course if one were a genius these rates would be accelerated. Most of us have time to acquire only one career-level skill. To obtain more than this means lots of extra work on the side.

Values are very important to the flourishing of civilization. Maslow's hierarchy is really just the starting point and should not be taken as absolute truth. There are many other values he does not address, like wisdom and productivity. What about tolerance and diversity? As a society we need to debate values to determine their importance. What others are missing here? Which ones are more important? Should we program values into people using genetic engineering? One can only imagine what humanity could accomplish if we were motivated to excel at everything we do. It could be possible to program a feeling like hunger into people that would get progressively stronger the longer its associated value went without being satisfied. This would drive people to work harder and to think more deeply about what they were doing. Of course this would need to be voluntary and could not be imposed upon anyone without their consent.

Transcendence

Transcendence can mean many things, but generally it refers to a step up to an advanced form of awareness along with newfound powers. There is a strong similarity to religion here in which the soul at death passes on to heaven, where it can live on eternally in the form of an angel or God. In most faiths these entities have powers that allow them to control what happens in the mortal world. In AI circles transcendence amounts to uploading our consciousness into a computer system, where it can live on forever interacting with other minds and possessing a vast awareness. In biology, transcendence seems to correspond to the creation of an emergent level of organization like the formation of molecules into cells that can then give rise to things like consciousness.

There are various ways to attain transcendence. These include mind uploading and neural interfaces to computers. Another means of attaining transcendence could involve biological enhancement. Imagine grafting an additional cerebral cortex onto our brains. This could produce a tremendous increase in our thinking capacity or provide us with the ability to think in some as yet unrealized way. This method could be supplemented with pharmaceutical enhancement: taking drugs that could boost our attention, memory, and problem-solving skills. Transcendence implies more than just an amplification of existing skills, though. It would involve a qualitative and drastic alteration in the way we think, one we might not be able to imagine or even understand until we experience it.

It is one thing for a machine to be intelligent. It is something else altogether for it to achieve consciousness, that subjective state of awareness we have. If we could build a machine that was conscious, it might give us insights into how to boost our own consciousness. Alternatively we might be able to interface with and share the machine's conscious state. This combination could be a form of transcendence.

In recent years a number of investigators have designed computer programs that they hope will exhibit signs of consciousness. Some researchers have adopted a biological approach, basing their models on the way brains operate. Igor Aleksander's (2001) MAGNUS model reproduces the kind of neural activity that occurs during visual perception. It mimics the "carving up" of visual input into different streams that process separate aspects of an object like color and shape. Cotterill (2003) also adopts a neural approach. He has created a virtual "child" intended to learn on the basis of perception-action couplings within a simulated environment.

Other researchers utilize the cognitive or information-processing perspective. Haikonen (2003) has developed a cognitive model based on cross-modal associative activity. Conscious experience in this model is the result of associative processing where a given percept activates a wide variety of related processes. Franklin (2003) has built a conscious machine model based on global workspace theory. His program implements a series of miniagents that compete for an attentional "spotlight." The global workspace model uses a theater metaphor of mind in which items that get "on stage" reach conscious awareness.

The question of whether humans can construct a conscious artifact remains to be seen. If consciousness or transcendence requires a certain level of complexity, then we may need to wait until humankind develops the technology capable of such complexity. Even if humankind lack this capability, it does not rule out the possibility that other intelligences do. A conscious artifact thus remains possible in principle. Transcendence may require a form of computational complexity beyond what we see in our brains and our computers now.

THE FAR FUTURE

Possible Human-Machine Outcomes

Surprisingly, several different authors seem to have arrived at the same general conclusions concerning possible future worlds of man and machine (R. Brooks, 2002; Georges, 2003; Jeffery, 1999). According to these prognostications, there are three possible outcomes. Brooks calls the first of these possibilities "damnation." In this scenario robots or intelligent machines ultimately exceed human capabilities. They then determine we are dangerous or irrelevant and either enslave or exterminate us. In this scenario, the machines become superior to us in various abilities but are clearly acting unethically by our own standards. In fact, they are acting very much like the human race has in its own past, which is replete with slavery, war, and genocide.

In the second scenario, dubbed by Brooks as "salvation," machines continue to develop, perhaps surpassing us in certain ways. But in this possible outcome they become the panacea of humankind, taking over all forms of labor, finding cures for disease, solving social problems, and perhaps serving as a receptacle for our consciousness so that we can live on after the demise of our physical bodies. Under these conditions, there is a benevolent relationship between man and machine. Man either controls the machines outright or relinquishes some degree of control with no untoward consequences.

The third outcome Brooks calls "the third path." Here people and machines coexist as equals. Things continue much the same way they have throughout history, where humanity develops and uses technology in the service of bettering our lives. Machines under these circumstances never develop sufficiently to pose a threat and are kept under human control.

You can see that control, complexity, and ethics are the three critical factors determining which of the above predictions come true. If machines ultimately exceed human capability, then damnation and salvation are both possible. The former may be realized if the machines act unethically and we lose control over them. The latter may come to fruition if they act ethically and we maintain or relinquish control. The third path occurs when machines are either less than or equal to human sophistication and we retain control. There are some interesting analogies to biological systems here. Machine superiority may result in a parasite-host relationship where humans become dependent on machines and cannot exist without them. Equality of ability instead implies a symbiotic relationship where both operate together in a mutually dependent coexistence.

Controlling the Machines

Given the rapid rate of technological progress, it is entirely plausible that someday machines may outstrip all human abilities. As discussed above, this has the potential to be either the boon or bane of humankind. Assuming this will happen, we must ask ourselves how we plan on keeping control over our creations. Khan (1995) suggests several ways of controlling autonomous learning systems. The first and most direct way of doing this he calls "the panic button." This is essentially a failsafe device or manual override that allows us to deactivate machines if they show unethical or violent behavior.

But this "pulling the plug" is not as easy as it seems, especially if the machine or machines in question are part of a distributed network. According to Georges (2003), this would require several steps, each of which poses unique difficulties. One would need to first recognize that there is a threat. If the machines are clever, they may plan or disguise their motives until it is too late. Next comes identifying which machine to disconnect. Complex computer networks are built to be redundant. An intelligent entity could very easily transfer itself from one machine to another or make backup copies of itself. After this we would need to get past any security measures that may be in place. These could include firewalls and complex barriers designed to thwart hacking and intrusion. Finally, the offending entity would need to be deactivated without causing other connected systems to crash. This is again a problem in networks with a high degree of connectivity.

Psychological factors may also make it difficult for us to pull the plug. Given a high degree of dependence on these machines, shutting them down may leave us in a "dark age" without basic services. In other words, we may come to rely so much on these intelligent entities that shutting them down in effect kills us as well as them. Also, as mentioned earlier, ethical considerations need to be taken into account. If the offending system is an artificial person, then shutting it down is tantamount to murder. This may require lengthy legislative debate before any action can be taken.

Khan (1995) next proposes a "buddy system" where one machine may oversee or control another's behavior. In this system we could develop "supervisor machines" specifically designed to monitor the behavior and functioning of other machines. If any of them get out of line, the supervisors could deactivate or report their activity to humans, who could then decide what to do next.

Finally, Kahn (1995) states that we could impose internalized controls in machines, allowing them to govern their own behavior. This is essentially the technique discussed at length in chapter 9, where an intelligent entity or artificial person could be made to act properly through the consequentialist, deontological, or virtue-based approaches. To illustrate, a robot could be programmed with values that it would attempt to achieve as goals through means-end analysis or other problem-solving routines.

Stages of Development

A number of theorists have suggested that humanity has passed through a series of stages. The stage at one point in development serves as the precursor for the next, setting up its necessary preconditions. People can agree more or less on what these stages might have been in our past. The real speculation starts when we project these into the future. The events in these stages, at least those for which historical data exist, show an exponential increase, meaning that the time separating events gets shorter and shorter as time progresses.

The information revolution has occurred essentially within the last century. The generation and dissemination of information characterize this time period. It has started off slowly

TABLE 19   Kurzweil's past and projected stages of informational complexity

Epoch	Description	Level
Epoch 1	Information in atomic structures	Physics and chemistry
Epoch 2	Information in DNA	Biology
Epoch 3	Information in neural patterns	Brains
Epoch 4	Information in hardware and software designs	Technology
Epoch 5	The methods of biology are integrated into the human technology base	Merger of technology and human intelligence
Epoch 6	Patterns of matter and energy in the universe become saturated with intelligent processes and knowledge	The universe wakes up

Source: Kurzweil (2005).

but has been accelerating at an exponential pace. The cognitive and social changes accompanying this period involve the use of information to accomplish every task from communicating with others to shopping.

Perhaps the most significant trend in computing technology is performance. According to Moore's law, each new generation of computer chip that appears now approximately every eighteen to twenty-four months can put twice as many transistors onto an integrated circuit. The result of this is a doubling of computing power measured by the number of calculations that can be performed per unit time. Moore's Law has held true since the 1970s, when Gordon Moore, a leading inventor of integrated circuits who later became chairman of Intel Corporation, first proposed it. Other aspects of computing technology that show tremendous growth rates include random access memory, magnetic data storage, internet hosts, and internet data traffic (Kurzweil, 1996/2005).

Ray Kurzweil outlines an information stage theory of humanity. The first (table 19) is characterized by the representation of information in physics and chemistry, followed in the second by its location in DNA. After this, information is represented in neural patterns, essentially the thoughts inside brains. After this, in epoch 4, the information is situated in hardware and software designs. This pretty much brings us through to the present day. The next two epochs are predictions. Epoch 5 involves the merger of technology and human intelligence, essentially the integration of brains with computers, where the differences between biology and technology disappear.

The final epoch, number 6, is the most controversial, as it involves the saturation of information with matter and energy. At this stage the universe is said to "wake up," what might in a religious interpretation be the birth of God, or at least of God's mind. There is a related concept here, which is that of the Omega Point. Hypothesized by the French Jesuit priest Pierre Teilhard de Chardin, this is a point of maximal complexity and consciousness toward which the universe is said to be evolving.

Many of the stages so far described use quantitative metrics to assess development. It is easier to make predictions on this basis because one can scale upwards by known amounts. What is less easy to anticipate are qualitative changes. For instance, there may be some newly discovered way to modify the human brain that produces a fundamental change in the way thought occurs. If that were the case, it would be difficult to say what type of large-scale changes would ensue. Likewise, the discovery of a new type of matter or fundamental particle might completely reorganize the way we understand physics, leading to radical alterations in society that are not easily predictable.

The way in which humanity might react during the transition from one stage to another is also difficult to say. At a very broad level we may anticipate those who oppose the adoption of new technologies, as was the case with the Luddites at the start of the Industrial Revolution. These people will point out the downsides of the new technologies, which may include damage to the environment, dangers to human health, and alterations to the nature of what it means to be human. At the other end of the spectrum will be people like the transhumanists who welcome the advancements. Moderates will likely oppose certain changes but agree with others depending on their own political and social viewpoints.

Year Million

In this book I have been more focused on the technological self for a short-term future based on trends and near-term history. It is great fun, though, to speculate on what the far future may have in store. Broderick (2008) collects essays by fourteen leading scientists and science writers, asking them to hypothesize what the state of humanity will be like one million years in the future. This is obviously so far ahead that any sort of accurate prediction is meaningless, but it is interesting to see what sorts of ideas were proposed.

Steven B. Harris and others propose that humanity will develop into a merged group mind. This type of composite mind is more intelligent than any single person and in fact is already in existence in the form of cooperative groups of people sharing information. A bank, a stock market, a military organization, even a supermarket are all run by a group of people who work and communicate back and forth with one another to achieve a whole that could not be achieved by any one of its members in isolation. Electronic communication like email and the internet facilitate information flow between members and can allow large numbers of individuals to participate. We can think of these linked groups of biological brains and technological computers as part of a primitive superintelligence.

In the far future the speed with which members of these networks can communicate with one another will increase. This rate of information transfer will allow for more sophisticated abilities. A neuron transmitting and receiving messages with thousands of its neighbors forms the basis for human cognition. Similarly a person sending and getting messages from many other people in real time can form the basis of group cognition. This type of social computation may not even require a central organizer to coordinate activity, nor may it require individual members of the computation to be aware of what the purpose or goal of the computation is. Tasks could get executed through self-organizing emergent properties and without individual conscious awareness of the participating components, as is the case with human brains and other biological networks.

One theme a number of authors keep touching on is how radically different our bodies will be in the future. If we assume genetic engineering can be perfected, then we may be at liberty to make extreme adaptations of our bodies, with wings enabling us to fly, gills enabling us to swim, squat strong bodies to adapt to large, high-gravity worlds, and so on. Our definition of human will be stretched to the limit, writes Wil McCarthy. He envisions a future of androids, humanoids, hive minds, and living vehicles. In fact, with sufficient body modification we may become the exotic aliens we expect to find on other worlds.

Catharine Asaro believes we will see communities of like-minded and like-bodied individuals deciding to colonize a planet and create their own society based on shared norms, as the Amish people do now. The great distances and differences between settled habitats in space may see divergent evolution take place, accentuating differences between human groups physically but also culturally in terms of religious beliefs, political views, and sexual orientation. Despite these radical changes, Catharine believes there will still be a "family" unit that persists because people will want the companionship of a mate, a means to raise children, or pooled economic resources. She thinks the desire to love will remain as well. Although it may be expressed differently, we will maintain love, friendship, and the need to form relationships. Given that the power to create these traits will be in our grasp, the decision to alter ourselves must be democratic and open to debate.

Robert Bradbury takes megaengineering to its absolute limit. He argues that humanity will ultimately be capable of building Matrioshka brains (MBrains). Named after the Russian dolls that are nested one inside the other, an MBrain will be a series of increasingly larger shell-like structures around the sun. If these shells were completely enclosed they would be unstable, so he envisions a collection of co-orbiting solar sail-like structures. Each concentric level of shells would utilize energy from the sun. The shell behind it would harness the waste heat generated from the adjacent interior shell. Every shell would be made up of a substance dubbed computronium, a substrate devoted to computation. Bradbury believes we can upload our minds into the computronium and exist as a shared group mind there, inhabiting virtual realities alongside artificial intelligences.

Would we be willing to go to such extremes? Bradbury thinks we will, given the result is a computer the size of a solar system. A computer like this could perform astounding feats, emulating the entire history of human thought in microseconds and taking mere seconds to run thousands of thousand-year scenarios. The computronium could hold vast sums of knowledge like galactic and civilization history and detailed genomic plans for all known organisms. An MBrain could devote itself to solving impossible tasks like how to reverse the expansion and decay of the universe or how to open up gateways to other universes.

MBrains could ultimately duplicate themselves and spread to different stars. One can even imagine a galactic-scale MBrain using energy derived from a supermassive black hole at the center of a galaxy. This could be linked to solar MBrains around each star, uniting them in a vast galactic computing network. That in turn could be linked to other galactic-scale MBrains uniting the entire universe as a single computing entity!

Whew, we're getting a bit ahead of ourselves here! Collective minds inside an MBrain would be possible only if mind uploading/whole-brain emulation were possible. Supraluminal communication between MBrains would also be necessary to coordinate any collective activity among them, and so far as we know this isn't possible either. Note that many futurists predict that the universe will progress this way, by converting energy and matter into computation, essentially turning the universe into a single brain or conscious entity. Kurzweil's last stage specifies this evolution, as do imaginings of the Omega Point and the Aleph state. The Aleph State has been defined as the point where an infinite amount of information is stored and processed.

The End

It is sad to say, but given our current understanding, the universe will ultimately end. Impey (2010) provides a detailed description of how this will unfold in his book *How It Ends*. To start off, our sun will not last forever. It will get larger and brighter, just as it has been doing for the last 4.5 billion years. Half a billion years from now this increase will move carbon dioxide from Earth's atmosphere into the ocean. The results will not be good. Most plants will not be able to photosynthesize.

Eventually the polar ice caps will melt, raising sea levels. Following this, the water from the oceans will evaporate into space and Earth's surface will be a barren desert. In 3.5 billion years from now, the surface of our planet will be nothing but dried-out rock. One billion years after that, the sun will burn up its shell of hydrogen gas, bloating in size. After that it will become a red giant, 250 times larger than it is today and 2,700 times brighter. Earth will become engulfed by the sun and destroyed.

Our Milky Way too has a limited life span. Much of the gas that is used in star formation will have already been used, and fewer new stars will be generated. Eventually there will be red dwarfs, neutron stars, and black holes. In ten trillion years even the red dwarfs will go out. Stars will no longer exist. These processes will be happening not just in our galaxy but in all galaxies across the universe. The remnants of the Milky Way and other galaxies will not completely evaporate until ten billion billion years from now, or 10^{19} billion years. The universe ultimately will lose its galaxies, any stellar remains being vacuumed up by black holes. Those black holes that existed at galactic cores or clusters will now merge with one another. In 10^{100} years protons will have decayed, all stars will have dissipated, and even black holes will have evaporated. All that will be left will be neutrinos, electrons, and positrons, a particle "soup" left over from the organized universe.

But don't lose heart. Our universe may be only one of a vast number that are constantly being born and dying. The multiverse is the set of infinite or finite possible universes, including our own, that comprise all of existence. It includes all of space, time, matter, and energy. In this view multiple parallel universes coexist. The nature of these universes varies considerably depending upon the discipline: those from religious belief systems or science fiction are not the same as those from philosophy or New Age sources. Those that are most plausible come from the scientific fields of astronomy, cosmology, and theoretical physics. For example, in one view our universe was born from the black hole of another universe, and the black holes in our universe themselves give birth to other universes.

However, even these theories are just that: theories. As yet we cannot prove the existence of any universe other than our own. How could we? By definition our universe consists of just those things we can observe, measure, and devise scientific theories about. If we can't access another universe, we cannot by definition test to see if it is there. Existence demands proof. If one cannot devise proof, one cannot prove existence. The cosmologist Paul Davies states that the multiverse question is really a philosophical argument, not a scientific one, because it cannot be falsified. He believes that arguments about it are only harmful or quasi-scientific (Torley, 2015).

What is the psychological impact of a finite but very long-duration universe? I think for most people it is depressing. Familiarity is comforting, and the thought that all we know will eventually disappear seems tailor-made to satisfy a roomful of anguished existential French philosophers. This notion goes beyond our own personal death. Most of us assume that after we die the world will go on. We derive some comfort from that, understanding that our children and grandchildren will continue to live out their lives, hopefully in happiness. But the notion of a terminal universe goes deeper than this. It states that at some point everything we know and everything we loved will be gone—that all of existence, at least as we have experienced it, will vanish.

This is perhaps why so many scientists believe in the multiverse. It satisfies that same need in us to believe in the afterlife, the "heaven" or "hell" that religion provides. Rather than our soul going off to heaven, our universe can instead go off and create other universes, reproducing itself in a never-ending process. This notion of infinity is more comforting than a finality or a point where it all ends. Infinity is thus more than a parameter in a mathematical equation, it is a human construct, one that we want to believe in because it is comforting.

There is another, more optimistic take on this. In my view it is finality that makes life worth living. Knowing we are mortal forces us to enjoy the here and now. It should make us savor every experience, whether that be or a sip of vintage Malbec or a lover's first kiss. Endings give meaning to life. If we were immortal or indestructible we might lose this sense of joy and wonder. Zorba the Greek had it right. There is more than enough in this world to satisfy us. We can never run out of things to learn, people to meet, or places to go. The real tragedy is in not living life, in continually postponing our happiness thinking that we will have time to enjoy it later.

SUMMARY AND MAIN ISSUES

We've covered an immense amount of material in this book, and the reader may be grasping at connecting threads to see what ties it all together. This is a difficult task. The self is a complex concept, and nobody can agree on exactly what it is, whether it stays the same, or whether it even exists. The self is like a slippery eel. Once you grab it, it somehow manages to always slip out of your fingers. It has been studied from multiple perspectives, each with its own take on things. Many different varieties of self have been proposed, some compatible with one another, some not. To compound things further, we have attempted to integrate these ideas with how the self interfaces and changes with modern technology. To bring some small amount of clarity, I will list here some of the major themes that have emerged across the literature and how these relate to the digital self. This list is not exhaustive and is not presented in order of importance. Many of the ideas are interrelated.

1. A person or human is generally considered a member of a biological species, while a self or identity is an aspect of an individual's persona. We can interface with technology to discover who we are or to create alternate versions of ourselves. It may be possible to build artificial people who have unique identities.

2. The complexity of the self requires that we study it from many different perspectives, including but not limited to the following approaches: historical, evolutionary, developmental, cultural, theistic, philosophical, psychological, and neuroscientific.

3. The development of new technologies will further our understanding of the self even more: some examples are brain-imaging techniques, prosthetics, brain-computer interfacing, virtual reality, nanotechnology, and genetic engineering. New fields of study like cyberpsychology, AI, and robotics are making great strides in helping to create and understand digital selves.

4. Materiality and science require that the self be made of something and not be ineffable like the soul. Patternists and functionalists believe that it is the relational and operational aspects of a system that make up the self. If this is the case and the substrate doesn't matter, then a self could be "uploaded" into a computer, where it could potentially expand and exist forever.

5. The self must persist over time even though it may be constantly changing. What explains this persistence may be those aspects of self that remain constant across temporal and spatial conditions. Recording our experiences and being able to access them in the form of memories may contribute to the sense of a constant self. Digital technologies enable us to record and store our lives in greater detail. Revisiting these memories may reinforce or alter a constant self. Whether memories alone are sufficient to constitute a self is debatable.

6. It is not known whether the self needs to be bounded, in either a physical or a mental way. The brain constructs a representation of our body based on sensory inputs. These can be manipulated to make us believe that our limbs are elongated, that we have limbs we don't possess, and even that we belong in another body. The use of technology to access information may extend our selves into other devices. Cellular automata and sentient software may not require centered physicality and could exist as programs in a network.

7. There are many different possible types of self, made up of interacting selves like the id/ego/superego, the ideal/real, and various trait selves. New forms of self, such as cyborgs, AI programs, and robots, are now emerging. Some of these selves may be "freestanding" and separate from us, but we can and will merge with our creations to enhance our selves and to transform into entirely new selves.

8. An individual self or subself is made up of different components. There is some general agreement that these correspond to such capacities as perception, rationality/cognition, memory, including autobiographical memory, motivation, emotion, self-awareness, creativity, and moral agency. Computer programs already exist that demonstrate these capacities. A key component of the self is subjective awareness or consciousness. It may be possible to create software or hardware agents that become conscious.

9. It is not clear whether the self is a unitary or a distributed entity. Most researchers seem to agree that there are multiple aspects to the self and that these interplay with one another, sometimes coming together, sometimes separating. Work in neuroscience has failed to show any single self system. The brain may implement coordinating actions like neural synchrony to focus attention and integrate different selves.

10. The self exists in a social as well as physical environment, interacting with others of its kind. Social media, the internet, and other forms of software allow us to create different versions of ourselves online, to broadcast our strengths, and to connect with others. Role playing in games enables us to take on new selves, to transform our existing self, and to form new relationships.

11. Things can go wrong with the self, both in real-world environments and when interfacing with software. Some of these disorders are transfers of existing problems into the digital realm, while others are entirely new. Technology like VR therapy can help us to identify and repair abnormalities of self.

12. We are entering a future where we may be increasingly inhabiting digital representations of self and where autonomous representations of our self may act in our absence. These avatars will exist in virtual worlds and may mediate business as well as recreational activities.

REFERENCES

Aarseth, E. (2001, July). Computer game studies, year one. *Game Studies, 1*(1). Retrieved from www.gamestudies.org

Abraham, A. (2013). The world according to me: Personal experience and the medial prefrontal cortex. *Frontiers in Human Neuroscience, 7*, article ID 341. doi:10.3389/fnhum.2013.00341

Ackrill, J. L. (1981). *Aristotle the philosopher.* New York, NY: Oxford University Press.

Adler, A. (1927). *The practice and theory of individual psychology.* New York, NY: Harcourt, Brace & World.

Aleksander, J. (2001). *How to build a mind.* New York, NY: Columbia University Press.

Alloway, T. P., Horton, J., Alloway, R. G., & Dawson, C. (2013). Social networking sites and cognitive abilities: Do they make you smarter? *Computers and Education, 63*, 10–16.

Allport, G. W., & Odbert, H. S. (1936). Trait-names: A psycho-lexical study. *Psychological Monographs: General and Applied, 47*, 1–21.

Amichai-Hamburger, Y. (2008). Potential and promise of online volunteering. *Computers in Human Behavior, 24*(2), 544–562.

Amichai-Hamburger, Y., & Vinitzky, G. (2010). Social network use and personality. *Computers in Human Behavior, 26*, 1289–1295.

Amodio, D. M., & Frith, C. D. (2006). Meetings of minds: The medial frontal cortex and social cognition. *Nature Reviews Neuroscience, 7*(4), 268–277.

Anderson, J. R. (1984). The development of self-recognition: A review. *Developmental Psychobiology, 17*, 35–49.

Angster, A., Frank, M., & Lester, D. (2010). An exploratory study of students' use of cell phones, texting, and social networking sites. *Psychological Reports, 107*(2), 402–404.

Annisette, L. E., & Lafreniere, K. D. (2017). Social media, texting, and personality: A test of the shallowing hypothesis. *Personality and Individual Differences, 115*, 154–158. doi:10.1016/j.paid.2016.02.043

Ansari, A. (2016). *Modern romance.* New York, NY: Penguin.

Apperley, T. H., & Clemens, J. (2017). Flipping out: Avatars and identity. In J. Gackenbach & J. Bown (Eds.), *Boundaries of self and reality online: Implications of digitally constructed realities* (pp. 41–56). London, UK: Academic Press.

Appleby, B. S., Duggan, P. S., Regenberg, A., & Rabins, P. V. (2007). Psychiatric and neuropsychiatric adverse events associated with deep brain stimulation: A meta-analysis of ten years' experience. *Movement Disorders, 22*(12), 1722–1728.

Armstrong, D.M. (1968/1993). *A materialist theory of mind.* London, UK: Taylor & Francis.

Aston-Jones, G., & Cohen, J.D. (2005). An integrative theory of locus coeruleus-norepinephrine function: Adaptive gain and optimal performance. *Annual Review of Neuroscience, 28,* 403–450.

Attrill, A. (2015). *Cyberpsychology.* Oxford, UK: Oxford University Press.

Bainbridge, W.S. (2013). Transavatars. In M. More & N. Vita-More (Eds.), *The Transhumanist reader: Classical and contemporary essays on the science, technology, and philosophy of the human future* (pp. 91–99). West Sussex, UK: Wiley-Blackwell.

Baltzly, D. (2008). Stoicism. In Edward N. Zalta (Ed.), *Stanford encyclopedia of philosophy* (Winter 2012 ed.). Retrieved from https://plato.stanford.edu/archives/win2012/entries/davidson/

Banczyk, B., Kramer, N., & Senokozlieva, M. (2008, May). "The wurst" meets "fatless" in MySpace: The relationship between self esteem, personality and self-presentation in an online community. Paper presented at the Conference of the International Communication Association, Montreal, Quebec, Canada.

Bandura, A. (2012). On the functional properties of perceived self-efficacy revisited. *Journal of Management, 38,* 9–44.

Bardzell, S., & Bardzell, J. (2006). Sex-interface-aesthetics: The docile avatars and embodied pixels of Second Life BDSM. Retrieved from www.ics.uci.edu/~johannab/sexual .interactions.2006/papers/ShaowenBardzi&JeffreyBardzell-SexualInteractions2006.pdf

Barenbaum, N.B., & Winter, D.G. (2013). Personality. In D.K. Freedheim & I.B. Weiner (Eds.), *Handbook of psychology: Vol. 1. History of psychology* (2nd ed., pp. 198–233). Hoboken, NJ: Wiley.

Barnett, J., Coulson, M., & Forman, N. (2010). Examining player anger in *World of Warcraft.* In W.S. Bainbridge (Ed.), *Online worlds: Convergence of the real and the virtual* (pp. 147–160). London, UK: Springer.

Barnett, L.M., Bangay, S. McKenzie, S., & Ridgers, N.D. (2013). Active gaming as a mechanism to promote physical activity and fundamental movement skill in children. *Frontiers in Public Health, 1,* 1–3. doi:10.3389/fpubh.2013.00074

Barresi, J., Moore, C., & Martin, R. (2013). Conceiving of self and others as persons: Evolution and development. In J. Martin & M.H. Bickhard (Eds.), *The psychology of personhood: Philosophical, historical, social-developmental, and narrative perspectives* (pp. 127–146). Cambridge, UK: Cambridge University Press.

Bartle, R.A. (2004). *Designing virtual worlds.* Indianapolis, IN: New Riders.

Batson, C.D., & Shaw, L.L. (1991). Evidence from altruism: Toward a pluralism of prosocial motives. *Psychological Inquiry, 2*(2), 107–122.

Baudrillard, J. (1994). *Simulacra and simulation* (S.F. Glaser, Trans.). Ann Arbor: University of Michigan Press.

Bavelier, D., Achtman, R.L., Mani, M., & Focker, J. (2012). Neural bases of selective attention in action video game players. *Vision Research, 61,* 132–143.

Beauregard, M., Lévesque, J., & Bourgouin, P. (2001). Neural correlates of conscious self-regulation of emotion. *Journal of Neuroscience, 21,* 6993–7000.

Beer, J.S., & Hughes, B.L. (2010). Neural systems of social comparison and the "above average" effect. *NeuroImage, 49,* 2671–2679.

Beier, M.A. (2017). The shadow of technology: Psych, self, and life online. In J. Gackenbach & J. Bown (Eds.), *Boundaries of self and reality online: Implications of digitally constructed realities* (pp. 141–160). London, UK: Academic Press.

Bellis, M. (2017). Exoskeleton. Retrieved from http://inventors.about.com/od/estartinventions /a/Exoskeleton.htm

Benford, G., & Malartre, E. (2007). *Beyond human: Living with robots and cyborgs*. New York, NY: Forge Press.

Bentley, P. J. (2002). *Digital biology*. New York, NY: Simon & Schuster.

Benway, J. P. (1999). *Banner blindness: What searching users notice and do not notice on the World Wide Web* (Unpublished doctoral dissertation). Rice University, Houston, TX.

Berger, A. A. (2002). *Video games: A popular culture phenomenon*. New Brunswick, NJ: Transaction.

Berger, F. K. (2014, October). Narcissistic personality disorder. In *Medical Encyclopedia*. MedlinePlus, US National Library of Medicine.

Berry, J., Poortinga, Y., Breugelmans, S., Chasiotis, A., & Sam, D. (2011). *Cross-cultural psychology: Research and applications* (3rd ed.). Cambridge, UK: Cambridge University Press.

Bessiere, K., Say, F., & Kiesler, S. (2007). The ideal elf: Identity exploration in World of Warcraft. *CyberPsychology and Behavior, 10*(4). Retrieved from https://www.cs.cmu.edu/~kiesler /publications/2007pdfs/2007_Ideal-Elf_identity-exploration.pdf

Bingham, G. P., & Muchisky, M. M. (1993). Center of mass perception and inertial frames of reference. *Perception and Psychophysics, 54,* 617–632.

Biocca, F., Kim, T., & Levy, M. R. (1995). The vision of virtual reality. In F. Biocca & M. R. Levy (Eds.), *Communication in the age of virtual reality* (pp. 3–14). Hillsdale, NJ: Lawrence Erlbaum Associates.

Birnbacher, D. (1995). Artificial consciousness. In T. Metzinger (Ed.), *Conscious experience* (pp. 489–507). Thorverton, Devon, UK: Imprint Academic.

Bizzi, E., Mussa-Ivaldi, F. A., & Giszter, S. (1991). Computations underlying the execution of movement: A biological perspective. *Science, 253*(5017), 287–291.

Blachnio, A., & Przepiorka, A. (2015). Dysfunction of self-regulation and self-control in Facebook addiction. *Psychiatric Quarterly, 87*(3), 493–500.

Blacker, K. J., & Curby, K. M. (2013). Enhanced visual short-term memory in action video game players. *Attention, Perception, and Psychophysics, 75,* 1128–1136.

Blackford, R., & Broderick, D. (2014). *Intelligence unbound: The future of uploaded and machine minds*. New York, NY: Wiley.

Blake, A., & Yuille, A. (Eds.). (1992). *Active vision*. Cambridge, MA: MIT Press.

Blakemore, S. J., & Frith, C. (2003). Self-awareness and action. *Current Opinion in Neurobiology, 13,* 219–224.

Blascovich, J., & Bailenson, J. (2012). *Infinite reality: The hidden blueprint of our virtual lives*. New York, NY: William Morrow.

Bloch, C. (1972). *The Golem: Legends of the ghetto of Prague* (H. Schneiderman, Trans.). Blauvelt: Rudolf Steiner Press.

Boellstorff, T. (2008). *Coming of age in Second Life: An anthropologist explores the virtually human*. Princeton, NJ: Princeton University Press.

Bono, V., Narzisi, A., Jouen, A. L., Tilmont, E., Hommel, S., Jamal, W., . . . & Muratori, F. (2016). GOLIAH: A gaming platform for home-based intervention in autism—principles and design. *Frontiers in Psychiatry, 7.* doi:10.3389/fpsyt.2016.00070

Boone, G., & Hodgins, J. (1998). Walking and running machines. In F. C. Keil and R. A. Wilson (Eds.), *The MIT encyclopedia of cognitive sciences* (pp. 874–876). Cambridge, MA: MIT Press.

Bossard, J. H. S. (1932). Residential propinquity as a factor in marriage selection. *American Journal of Sociology, 38*(2), 219–224.

Bostrom, N. (2014). *Superintelligence: Paths, dangers, strategies*. Oxford, UK: Oxford University Press.

Botella, C., Bretón-López, J., Serrano, B., García-Palacios, A., Quero, S., & Baños, R. (2014). Treatment of flying phobia using virtual reality exposure with or without cognitive restructuring: Participants' preferences. *Revista de Psicopatología y Psicología Clínica, 19*(3), 157–169.

Bouchard, S. (2011). Could virtual reality be effective in treating children with phobias? *Expert Review of Neurotherapeutics, 11*(2), 207–213.

Bouchard, T. J., & McGue, M. (1981). Familial studies of intelligence: A review. *Science, 212*(4498), 1055–1059.

Bown, J., White, E., & Boopalan, A. (2017). Looking for the ultimate display: A brief history of virtual reality. In J. Gackenbach & J. Bown (Eds.), *Boundaries of self and reality online: Implications of digitally constructed realities* (pp. 239–260). London, UK: Academic Press.

Brand, M., Young, K. S., & Laier, C. (2014). Prefrontal control and internet addiction: A theoretical model and review of neuropsychological and neuroimaging findings. *Frontiers in Human Neuroscience, 8*, 375–390.

Brass, M., & Haggard, P. (2007). To do or not to do: The neural signature of self control. *Journal of Neuroscience, 27*, 9141–9145.

Breazeal, C. (2002). *Designing sociable robots.* Cambridge, MA: MIT Press.

Breazeal, C., & Brooks, R. (2005). Robot emotions: A functional perspective In J. M. Fellows and M. A. Arbib (Eds.), *Who needs emotions? The brain meets the robot* (pp. 271–310). Oxford, UK: Oxford University Press.

Brewer, B. (1995). Bodily awareness and the self. In M. Bermudez & N. Eilan (Eds.), *The body and the self* (pp. 291–303). Cambridge, MA: MIT Press.

Brickhouse, T. C. (2000). *The philosophy of Socrates.* Boulder, CO: Westview Press.

Brighton, H., & Selina, H. (2003). *Introducing artificial intelligence.* Duxford, UK: Icon Books.

Bringsjord, S., & Ferrucci, D. A. (2000). *Artificial intelligence and literary creativity: Inside the mind of BRUTUS, a storytelling machine.* Mahway, NJ: Erlbaum.

Brockwell, H. (2016, April 3). Forgotten genius: The man who made a working VR machine in 1957. *TechRadar* [blog]. Retrieved from https://www.techradar.com/search?searchTerm =working+vr+machine

Broderick, D. (2008). *Year million: Science at the far edge of knowledge.* New York, NY: Atlas.

Brooks, J. E., & Neville, H. A. (2017). Interracial attraction among college men: The influence of ideologies, familiarity, and similarity. *Journal of Social and Personal Relationships, 34*(2), 166–183.

Brooks, R. A. (2002). *Flesh and machine: How robots will change us.* New York, NY: Vintage Books.

Brown, A. L., Bransford, J. D., Ferrara, R. A., & Campione, J. C. (1983). Learning, remembering, and understanding. In J. H. Flavell & E. M. Markman (Eds.), *Handbook of child psychology: Cognitive development* (Vol. 3, 4th ed., pp. 77–166). New York, NY: Wiley.

Brumbaugh, C. C., & Wood, D. (2013). Mate preferences across life and across the world. *Social Psychological and Personality Science, 4*, 100–107.

Bruner, J. S. (1986). *Actual minds, possible worlds.* Cambridge, MA: Harvard University Press.

Burdea, G. C., & Coiffet, P. (2003). *Virtual reality technology* (Vol. 1). Hoboken, NJ: Wiley.

Buss, D. M. (2003). *The evolution of desire: Strategies of human mating.* New York, NY: Basic Books.

Butler, J. (1990). *Gender trouble: Feminism and the subversion of identity.* London, UK: Routledge.

Butler, J. (1993). *Bodies that matter: On the discursive limits of "sex."* London, UK: Routledge.

Buxbaum, L., Dawson, A., & Linsley, D. (2012). Reliability and validity of the virtual reality lateralized attention test in assessing hemispatial neglect in right hemisphere stroke. *Neuropsychology, 26*, 430–441.

Cabeza, R., Prince, S. E., Daselaar, S. M., Greenberg, D., Budde, M., Dolcos, F., . . . & Rubin, D. C. (2004). Brain activity during episodic retrieval of autobiographical and laboratory events: An fMRI study using a novel photo paradigm. *Journal of Cognitive Neuroscience, 16*(9), 1533–1594.

Cacioli, J.-P., & Mussap, A. J. (2014). Avatar body dimensions and men's body image. *Body Image, 11*(2), 146–155.

Cacioppo, J. T., Cacioppo, S., Gonzaga, G. C., Ogburn, E. L., & VanderWeele, T. J. (2011). Marital satisfaction and break-ups differ across on-line and off-line meeting venues. *PNAS, 110*(47), 18814–18819.

Cain, M. S., Landau, A. N., & Shimamura, A. P. (2012). Action video game experience reduces the cost of switching tasks. *Attention, Perception, and Psychophysics, 74*(4), 1–7.

Caligor, E., Levy, K. N., & Yeomans, F. E. (2015, May). Narcissistic personality disorder: Diagnostic and clinical challenges. *American Journal of Psychiatry, 172*(5), 415–422.

Campbell, J. D., Assanand, S., & Paula, A. D. (2003). The structure of the self-concept and its relation to psychological adjustment. *Journal of Personality, 7*(1), 115–140.

Campbell, J. D., Trapnell, P. D., Heine, S. J., Katz, I. M., Lavallee, L. F., & Lehman, D. R. (1996). Self-concept clarity-measurement, personality correlates, and cultural boundaries. *Journal of Personality and Social Psychology, 70*(1), 141–156.

Cao, X., Douget, A. S., Fuchs, P., & Klinger, E. (2010). Designing an ecological virtual task in the context of executive functions: A preliminary study. *Proceedings of the 8th International Conference on Disability, Virtual Reality and Associated Technologies, 31*, 71–78.

Cardoso-Leite, P., Kludt, R., Vignola, G., Ma, W. J., Green, C. S., & Bavelier, D. (2016). Technology consumption and cognitive control: Contrasting action video game experience with media multitasking. *Attention, Perception, and Psychophysics, 78*, 218–241.

Carlson, W. (2007). A critical history of computer graphics and animation [lecture notes]. Ohio State University. Retrieved from https://design.osu.edu/calrson/history.lesson17.html

Carmena, J. M., Mikhail, A., Lebedev, M. A., Crist, R. E., O'Doherty, J. E., Santucci, D. M., . . . & Nicolelis, M. A. L. (2003). Learning to control a brain–machine interface for reaching and grasping by primates. *PLoS Biology 1*(2): 193–208.

Carr, N. (2010). *The shallows: How the internet is changing the way we think, read and remember.* London, UK: Atlantic Books.

Carter, W. (1990). Why personal identity is animal identity. *LOGOS, 11*, 71–81.

Cash, H., Rae, C. D., Steel, A. H., & Winkler, A. (2012). Internet addiction: A brief summary of research and practice. *Current Psychiatry Review, 8*(4), 292–298.

Castronova, E. (2005). *Synthetic worlds: The business and culture of online games.* Chicago, IL: University of Chicago Press.

Cattell, R. B. (1990). Advances in Cattellian personality theory. In L. A. Pervin (Ed.), *Handbook of personality: Theory and research.* New York, NY: Guilford Press.

Chai, X. Y., & Gong, S. Y. (2011). Adolescents' identity experiments: The perspective of internet environment. *Advances in Psychological Science, 19*(3), 364–371.

Chalmers, D. (1996). *The conscious mind.* Oxford, UK: Oxford University Press.

Chang, C. (2015). Self-construal and Facebook activities: Exploring differences in social interaction orientation. *Computers in Human Behavior, 53*(6), 91–101.

Chang, F. C., Lee, C. M., Chen, P. H., Chiu, C. H., Huang, T. F., & Pan, Y. C. (2013). Association of thin-ideal media exposure, body dissatisfaction and disordered eating behaviors among adolescents in Taiwan. *Eating Behaviors, 14*(3), 382–385.

Chappell, V. (Ed.). (1999). *The Cambridge companion to Locke.* Cambridge, UK: Cambridge University Press.

Chen, P.-H. A., Wagner, D. D., Kelley, W. M., Powers, K. E., & Heatherton, T. F. (2013). Medial prefrontal cortex differentiates self from mother in Chinese: Evidence from self-motivated immigrants. *Culture and Brain, 1*, 3–15.

Chen, W., Fan, C. Y., Liu, Q. X., Zhou, Z. K., & Xie, X. C. (2016). Passive social network site use and subjective well-being: A moderated mediation model. *Computers in Human Behavior, 64*, 507–514.

Cheng, C., & Li, A. Y. (2014). Internet addiction prevalence and quality of (real) life: A meta-analysis of 31 nations across seven world regions. *Cyberpsychology, Behavior, and Social Networking, 17*(12): 755–60.

Chestek, C. A., Gilja, V., Nuyujukian, P., Foster, J. D., Fan, J. M., Kaufman, M. T., . . ., & Shenoy, K. V. (2011). Long-term stability of neural prosthetic control signals from silicon cortical arrays in rhesus macaque motor cortex. *Journal of Neural Engineering, 8*(4), 1–11.

Chester, A., & Bretherton, D. (2007). Impression management and identity online. In A. Joinson, K. McKenna, T. Postmes, & U. Reips (Eds.), *The Oxford handbook of internet psychology* (pp. 223–236). Oxford, UK: Oxford University Press.

Chisholm, J. D., & Kingstone, A. (2012). Improved top-down control reduces oculomotor capture: The case of action video game players. *Attention, Perception and Psychophysics, 74*, 257–262.

Choi, T. R., Sung, Y., Lee, J., & Choi, S. M. (2017). Get behind my selfies: The Big Five traits and social networking behaviors through selfies. *Personality and Individual Differences, 109*, 98–101.

Chou, H. T. G., & Edge, N. (2012). They are happier and having better lives than I am: The impact of using Facebook on perceptions of others' lives. *Cyberpsychology, Behavior, and Social Networking, 2*, 117–121.

Churchland, P M. (1995). *The engine of reason, the seat of the soul: A philosophical journey into the brain.* Cambridge, UK: MIT Press.

Clark, A., & Chalmers, D. (1998). The extended mind. *Analysis, 58*(1), 7–19.

Clark, G. (2003). *Cochlear implants: Fundamentals and applications.* New York, NY: Springer-Verlag.

Clynes, M. E., & Kline, N. S. (1960, September). Cyborgs and space. *Astronautics, 26–27*, 74–76.

Cohen, H. (1995). The further exploits of AARON, painter. *Stanford Electronic Humanities Review, 4*(2). Retrieved from https://web.stanford.edu/group/SHR/4-2/text/cohen.html

Cohen, J. E., Green, C. S., & Bavelier, D. (2008). Training visual attention with video games: Not all games are created equal. In H. F. O'Neil & R. S. Perez (Eds.), *Computer games and team and individual learning* (pp. 205–228). Oxford, UK: Elsevier.

Collinger, J. L., Foldes, S., Bruns, T. M., Wodlinger, B., Gaunt, R., & Weber, D. J. (2013). Neuroprosthetic technology for individuals with spinal cord injury. *Journal of Spinal Cord Medicine, 36*(4), 258–272.

Colzato, L. S., Van Leeuwen, P. J., Van Den Wildenberg, W. P., & Hommel, B. (2010). DOOM'd to switch: Superior cognitive flexibility in players of first person shooter games. *Frontiers in Psychology, 1.* doi:10.3389/fpsyg.2010.00008

Connors, E. C., Chrastil, E. R., Sanchez, J., & Merabet, L. B. (2014). Action video game play and transfer of navigation and spatial cognition skills in adolescents who are blind. *Frontiers in Human Neuroscience, 8*, 133.

Conway, M. A. (2005). Memory and the self. *Journal of Memory and Language, 53*, 594–628.

Cooley, S. (2010). Social networks for Facebook. *Mortgage Banking, 70*(6), 84–85.

Coons, P. M. (1999). Psychogenic or dissociative fugue: A clinical investigation of five cases. *Psychological Reports, 84*(3), 881–886.

Cooper, J. M., & Hutchinson, D. S. (Eds.). (1997). *Plato: Complete works.* Indianapolis, IN: Hackett.

Cope, D. (1996). *Experiments in musical intelligence*. Madison, WI: A-R Editions.

Cotterill, R. (2003). CyberChild: A simulation test-bed for consciousness studies. *Journal of Consciousness Studies, 10*(4–5), 31–45.

Cottingham, J. (Trans.). (2013). *Rene Descartes: Meditations on first philosophy. With selections from the objections and replies.* Cambridge, UK: Cambridge University Press.

Coulson, M., Barnett, J., Ferguson, C. J., & Gould, R. L. (2012). Real feelings for virtual people: Emotional attachments and interpersonal attraction in video games. *Psychology of Popular Media Culture, 1*(3), 176–184.

Cover, R. (2016). *Digital identities: Creating and communicating the online self.* London, UK: Academic Press.

Coyne, S. M., Padilla-Walker, L. M., & Holmgren, H. G. (2017). A six-year longitudinal study of texting trajectories during adolescence. *Child Development, 89*(1). doi:10.1111/cdev.12823

Craik, F. I. M., Moroz, T. M., Moscovitch, M., Stuss, D. T., Winocur, G., Tulving, E., & Kapur, S. (1999). In search of the self: A positron emission tomography study. *Psychological Science, 10*, 26–34.

Crosswhite, J. M., Rice, D., & Asay, S. M. (2014). Texting among United States young adults: An exploratory study on texting and its use within families. *Social Science Journal, 51*(1), 70–78.

Csikszentmihalyi, M. (2008). *Flow: The psychology of optimal experience.* New York, NY: Harper Perennial Modern Classics.

Curtis, H. (1983). *Biology* (4th ed.). New York, NY: Worth.

Curtis, P. (1992/1997). Mudding: Social phenomena in text-based virtual realities. In S. Kiesler (Ed.), *Culture of the internet* (pp. 121–142). Mahwah, NJ: Lawrence Erlbaum Associates.

Da Costa, R. T., de Carvalho, M. R., & Nardi, A. E. (2010). Exposição por realidade virtual no tratamento do medo de dirigir [Virtual reality exposure therapy in the treatment of driving phobia]. *Psicologia: Teoria e Pesquisa, 26*(1), 131–137.

Damasio, A. (1999). *The feeling of what happens: Body and emotion in the making of consciousness.* New York, NY: Harcourt.

Damer, B. (1998). *Avatars! Exploring and building virtual worlds on the internet.* Berkeley, CA: Peachpit Press.

Dario, P., Guglielmelli, E., & Laschi, C. (2001). Humanoids and personal robots: Design and experiments. *Journal of Robotic Systems, 18*(12), 673–690.

David, A. S., & Kircher, T. (2003). *The self and schizophrenia.* Cambridge, UK: Cambridge University Press.

Deci, E. L., & Ryan, R. M. (2008). Self-determination theory: A macrotheory of human motivation, development, and health. *Canadian Psychology, 49*(3), 182–185.

Dennett, D. (1978). *Brainstorms: Philosophical essays on mind and psychology.* Cambridge, MA: Bradford.

Dennett, D. (1991). *Consciousness explained.* Boston, MA: Little, Brown.

Dennett, D. (2003). *Freedom evolves.* New York, NY: Viking.

De Renzi, E., Liotti, M., & Nichelli, P. (1987). Semantic amnesia with preservation of autobiographic memory: A case report. *Cortex, 23*, 575–597.

Devos, T., Huynh, Q.-L., & Banaji, M. R. (2012). Implicit self and identity. In M. R. Leary & J. P. Tangney (Eds.), *Handbook of self and identity* (2nd ed., pp. 155–179). New York, NY: Guilford Press.

Diamond, A. (2013). Executive functions. *Annual Review of Psychology, 64*, 135–168.

Díaz-Orueta, U., Garcia-López, C., Crespo-Eguílaz, N., Sánchez-Carpintero, R., Climent, G., and Narbona, J. (2014). AULA virtual reality test as an attention measure: Convergent validity with Conner's continuous performance test. *Child Neuropsychology, 20*, 328–342.

Diefenbach, S., & Christoforakos, L. (2017). The selfie paradox: Nobody seems to like them yet everyone has reasons to take them. An exploration of psychological functions of selfies in self-presentation. *Frontiers in Psychology, 8.* doi:10.3389/fpsyg.2017.00007

Dimaggio, S. G., Salvatore, G., Azzara, C., Catania, D., Semerari, A., & Hermans, H. J. M. (2003). Relationships in impoverished narratives: From theory to clinical practice. *Psychology and Psychotherapy, 76*(4), 385–409.

Doctorow, C. (2007, April 16). Why online games are dictatorships. *Information Week.* Retrieved from http://informationweek.com/internet/showArticle.jhtml?articleID-1991000268pgno=1&queryText-

Dolby, R. G. A. (1989). The possibility of computers becoming persons. *Social Epistemology, 3*(4), 321–364.

Dotsch, R., & Wigboldus, D. H. J. (2008). Virtual prejudice. *Journal of Experimental Social Psychology, 44*(4), 1194–1198.

Doud, A. J., Lucas, J. P., & Pisansky, M. T. (2011). Continuous three-dimensional control of a virtual helicopter using a motor imagery based brain-computer interface. *PLoS One, 6*(10). doi:10.1371/journal.pone.0026322

Doyle, D. (2017). Avatar lives: Narratives of transformation and identity. In J. Gackenbach & J. Bown (Eds.), *Boundaries of self and reality online: Implications of digitally constructed realities* (pp. 57–74). London, UK: Academic Press.

Drouin, M., & Landgraff, C. (2012). Texting, sexting, and attachment in college students' romantic relationships. *Computers in Human Behavior, 28*(2), 444–449.

Ducheneaut, N., Yee, N., Nickell, E., & Moore, R. J. (2006). Alone together? Exploring the social dynamics of massively multiplayer online games. In *Proceedings of the SIGCHI Conference on Human Factors in Computing Systems* (pp. 407–416). Retrieved from http://di.acm.org/citation.cfm?id-1124834

Dunn, R. A., & Guadagno, R. E. (2012). My avatar and me: Gender and personality predictors of avatar-self discrepancy. *Computers in Human Behavior, 28*(1), 97–106.

Durkin, K., & Barber, B. (2002). Not so doomed: Computer game play and positive adolescent development. *Journal of Applied Developmental Psychology, 23*(4), 373–392.

Durlach, P. J. (2004). Army digital systems and vulnerability to change blindness. *US Army Research Institute for the Behavioral and Social Sciences.* Retrieved from http://oai.dtic.mil/oai/oai?verb=getRecord&metadataPrefix=html&identifier=ADA433072

Eberhart, R., Kennedy, J., & Yuhui, S. (2001). *Swarm intelligence.* San Francisco, CA: Morgan Kaufmann.

Eco, U. (1984). *Semiotics and the philosophy of language.* London, UK: Macmillan.

Ehrsson, H. H., Spence, C., & Passingham, R. E. (2004). That's my hand! Activity in premotor cortex reflects feeling of ownership of a limb. *Science, 305*(5685), 875–877.

Ehrsson, H. H., Wiech, K., Weiskopf, N., Dolan, R. J., & Passingham, R. E. (2007). Threatening a rubber hand that you feel is yours elicits a cortical anxiety response. *PNAS, 104*(23), 9828–9833.

Eisenberger, N. I., Inagaki, T. K., Muscatell, K. A., Byrne Haltom, K. E., & Leary, M. R. (2011). The neural sociometer: Brain mechanisms underlying state self-esteem. *Journal of Cognitive Neuroscience, 23*(11), 3448–3455.

Ellison, N., Heino, R., & Gibbs, J. (2006). Managing impressions online: Self-presentation processes in the online dating environment. *Journal of Computer-Mediated Communication, 11,* 415–441.

Engelhardt, H. T., Jr. (1988). Foundations, persons, and the battle for the millennium. *Journal of Medicine and Philosophy, 13*(4), 387–391.

Epstein, J. M. (1999). Agent-based computational models and generative social science. *Complexity, 4*(5), 41–60.

Epstein, J. M., & Axtell, R. L. (1996). *Growing societies: Social science from the bottom up.* Washington, DC: Brookings Institutional Press.

Erickson, K. I., Boot, W. R., Basak, C., Neider, M. B., Prakash, R. S., Voss, M. W., . . . & Kramer, A. F. (2010). Striatal volume predicts level of video game skill acquisition. *Cerebral Cortex, 20*(11), 2522–2530.

Erikson, E. (1989). *Identity and the life cycle.* New York, NY: Norton.

Etgar, S., & Amichai-Hamburger, Y. (2017). Not all selfies look alike: Distinct selfie motivations are related to different personality characteristics. *Frontiers in Psychology, 8*(842), 1–10.

Evans, G. (1982). *The varieties of reference.* Oxford, UK: Oxford University Press.

Fahim, M., & Mehrgan, K. (2013). The extended mind thesis: A critical perspective. *Advances in English Linguistics, 2*(1), 99–104.

Faigley, L. (1992). *Fragments of rationality: Postmodernity and the subject of composition.* Pittsburgh, PA: University of Pittsburgh Press.

Fan, C., & Mak, A. S. (1998). Measuring social self-efficacy in a culturally diverse student population. *Social Behaviors and Personality: An Intersectional Journal, 26*(2), 131–144.

Farrer, C., & Frith, C. D. (2002). Experiencing oneself vs. another person as being the cause of an action: The neural correlates of the experience of agency. *NeuroImage, 15,* 596–603.

Farthing, G. W. (1992). *The psychology of consciousness.* Upper Saddle River, NJ: Prentice Hall.

Ferguson, C. J. (2013). Violent video games and the Supreme Court: Lessons for the scientific community in the wake of *Brown v. Entertainment Merchants Association. American Psychologist, 68,* 57–74.

Ferguson, C. J., Rueda, S. M., Cruz, A. M., Ferguson, D. E., Fritz, S., & Smith, S. M. (2008). Violent video games and aggression: Causal relationship or byproduct of family violence and intrinsic violence motivation? *Criminal Justice and Behavior, 35*(3), 311–332.

Fernald, A. (1989). Intonation and communicative intent in mothers' speech to infants: Is the melody the message? *Child Development, 60,* 1497–1510.

Filiciak, M. (2003). Hyperidentities: Post-modern identity patterns in massively multiplayer online role-playing games. In M. J. P. Wolf and B. Perron (Eds.), *The video game theory reader* (pp. 87–102). New York, NY: Routledge.

Fink, G. R., Markowitsch, H. J., Reinkemeier, M., Bruckbauer, T., Kessler, J., & Heiss, W. D. (1996). Cerebral representations of one's own past: Neural networks involved in autobiographical memory. *Journal of Neuroscience, 16,* 4275–4282.

Finkel, E. J., Eastwick, P. W., Karney, B. R., Reis, H. T., & Sprecher, S. (2012). Online dating: A critical analysis from the perspective of psychological science. *Psychological Science in the Public Interest, 13*(1), 3–66.

Fisher, H. (2005). *Why we love: The nature and chemistry of romantic love.* New York, NY: Henry Holt.

Flanagan, O. (2002). *The problem of the soul.* New York, NY: Basic Books.

Flynn, James R. (2009). *What is intelligence: Beyond the Flynn effect.* Cambridge, UK: Cambridge University Press.

Fodor, J. A. (1983). *The modularity of mind.* Cambridge, MA: MIT Press.

Foerst, A. (2004). *God in the machine: What robots teach us about humanity and God.* New York, NY: Plume.

Foo, C. Y. (2004). Redefining grief play. In *Proceedings of the Other Players Conference.* Copenhagen, Denmark. Retrieved from www.itu.dk/op/papers/yang_foo.pdf

Forgays, D. K., Hyman, I., & Schreiber, J. (2014). Texting everywhere for everything: Gender and age differences in cell phone etiquette and use. *Computers in Human Behavior, 31,* 314–321.

Fornos, A., Sommerhalder, J., & Pelizzone, M. (2011). Reading with a simulated 60-channel implant. *Frontiers in Neuroscience, 5*(57). doi:10.3389/fnins.2011.00057

Fossati, H. (2004). Distributed self in episodic memory: Neural correlates of successful retrieval of self-encoded positive and negative personality traits. *NeuroImage, 22*(4), 1596–1604.

Fossati, P., Hevenor, S. J., Graham, S. J., Grady, C., Keightley, M. L., Craik, F., & Mayberg, H. (2003). In search of the emotional self: An fMRI study using positive and negative emotional words. *American Journal of Psychiatry, 160*, 1938–1945.

Foucault, M. (1998). The ethics of the care of the self as a practice of freedom. In J. Bernauer & D. Rasussen (Eds.), *The final Foucault* (pp. 102–118). Cambridge, MA: MIT Press.

Fox, J., & Bailenson, J. N. (2009). Virtual self-modeling: The effects of vicarious reinforcement and identification on exercise behaviors. *Media Psychology, 12*(1), 1–25.

Frankfurt, H. (1971). Freedom of the will and the concept of a person. *Journal of Philosophy, 68*(1), 5–20.

Franklin, S. (2003). IDA: A conscious artifact? *Journal of Consciousness Studies, 10*(4–5), 47–66.

Franz, C., & Stewart, A. (1994). *Women creating lives: Identities, resilience and resistance.* Boulder, CO: Westview Press.

Fredrickson, B. L. (1998). What good are positive emotions? *Review of General Psychology, 2*(3), 300–319.

Fredrickson, B. L. (2001). The role of positive emotions in positive psychology: The broaden-and-build theory of positive emotions. *American Psychologist, 56*(3), 218–226.

Friedenberg, J. (2008). *Artificial psychology: The quest for what it means to be human.* New York, NY: Psychology Press.

Friedenberg, J. (2009). *Dynamical psychology: Complexity, self-organization and mind.* Litchfield Park, AZ: Emergent Publications.

Friedenberg, J. (2014). *Humanity's future: How technology will change us.* Humanity + Press.

Friedenberg, J., & Silverman, G. (2016). *Cognitive science: An introduction to the study of mind.* Thousand Oaks, CA: Sage Publications.

Frith, U., & Frith, C. D. (2003). Development and neurophysiology of mentalizing. *Philosophical Transactions of the Royal Society of London B: Biological. Sciences, 358*(1431), 459–473.

Fullwood, C., Melrose, K., Morris, N., & Floyd, S. (2013). Sex, blogs and baring your soul: Factors influencing UK blogging strategies. *Journal of the American Society for Information Science and Technology, 64*(2), 345–355.

Fullwood, C., Nicolis, W., & Makichi, R. (2015). We've got something for everyone: How individual differences predict different blogging motivations. *New Media and Society, 17*(9), 1583–1600.

Fullwood, C., Thelwall, M., & O'Neill, S. (2011). Clandestine chatters: Self-disclosure in UK chat room profiles. *First Monday, 16*(5). Retrieved from http://firstmonday.org/ojs/index.php /fm/article/view/3231/2954

Fuss, D. (1989). *Essentially speaking: Feminism, nature and difference.* New York, NY: Routledge.

Fuss, D. (1995). *Identification papers: Readings on psychoanalysis, sexuality, and culture.* New York, NY: Routledge.

Gackenbach, J., Wijeyaratnam, D., & Flockhart, C. (2017). The video gaming frontier. In J. Gackenbach & J. Bown (Eds.), *Boundaries of self and reality online: Implications of digitally constructed realities* (pp. 161–186). London, UK: Academic Press.

Gage, G., & Marzullo, T. (n.d.). Experiment: Wirelessly control a cyborg cockroach. Backyard Brains. Retrieved February 3, 2020, from https://backyardbrains.com/experiments /roboRoachSurgery

Gallagher, H. L., & Frith, C. D. (2003). Functional imaging of "theory of mind." *Trends in Cognitive Sciences, 7*(2), 77–83.

Gallup, G. G. (1979). Self-awareness in primates. *American Scientist, 67*, 417–421.

Gamber, B., & Withers, K. (1996). History of the stereopticon. Retrieved from htterp://www
.bitwise.net/~ken-bill/stereo.htm

Gao, W., & Wang, J. (2014). Synthetic micro/nanomotors in drug delivery. *Nanoscale, 6*(18),
10486–10494.

Gee, J. P. (2004). *What video games have to teach us about learning and literacy.* New York, NY:
Palgrave Macmillan.

Georges, T. M. (2003). *Digital soul: Intelligent machines and human values.* Cambridge, MA:
Westview Press.

Gertler, B. (2015). Self-knowledge. In Edward N. Zalta (Ed.), *Stanford encyclopedia of philosophy*
(Winter 2012 ed.). Retrieved from https://plato.stanford.edu/archives/win2012/entries
/davidson/

Gibbons, F. X. (1986). Social comparison and depression: Company's effect on misery. *Journal of
Personality and Social Psychology, 51*(1), 140–148.

Gibson, J. (2014). *The ecological approach to visual perception.* New York, NY: Psychology Press.

Giddens, A. (1991). *Modernity and self-identity.* Stanford, CA: Stanford University Press.

Gillespie, A., & Martin, J. (2014). Position exchange theory: A socio-material basis for discursive
and psychological positioning. *New Ideas in Psychology, 32,* 73–79.

Gillihan, S. J., & Farah, M. J. (2005). Is self special? A critical review of evidence from experimental psychology and cognitive neuroscience. *Psychological Bulletin, 131,* 76–97.

Goertzel, B. (2014). *Ten years to the singularity if we really really try . . . and other essays on AGI and
its implications.* CreateSpace.

Goertzel, B., & Pennachin, C. (2007). *Artificial general intelligence.* Berlin: Springer.

Goldberg, A. (1997). Avatars and agents, or life among the indigenous peoples of cyberspace. In
C. Dodsworth Jr. (Ed.), *Digital illusion: Entertaining the future with high technology* (pp.
161–180). New York, NY: Addison-Wesley.

Goldenberg, G. (2003). Disorders of body perception and presentation. In T. E. Feinberg & M. J.
Farah (Eds.), *Behavioral neurology and neuropsychology* (2nd ed., pp. 285–294). New York,
NY: McGraw Hill.

Goldstein, J., Cajko, L., Oosterbroek, M., Michielsen, M., Van Houten, O., & Salverda, F. (1997).
Video games and the elderly. *Social Behavior and Personality: An International Journal,
25*(4), 345–352.

Gong, D., He, H., Liu, D., Ma, W., Dong, L., Luo, C., & Yao, D. (2015). Enhanced functional
connectivity and increased gray matter volume of insula related to action video game
playing. *Scientific Reports, 5.* doi:10.1038/srep09763

Gonzales, A. L., & Hancock, J. T. (2011). Mirror, mirror on my Facebook wall: Effects of exposure
to Facebook on self-esteem. *Cyberpsychology, Behavior, and Social Networking, 14*(1), 79–83.

Google. (2015, December 3). Step inside your photos with cardboard camera. *Google Blog.*
Retrieved from https://googleblog.blogspot.ca/2015/12/step-inside-your-photos-with-card-
board.html

Grayson, N. (2015, March 6). Valve's VR is seriously impressive. It's also got some issues. *Kotaku*
[blog]. Retrieved from http://kotaku.com/valves-vr-is-seriously-impressive-its-also-got-some-is-
1689916512

Green, C. S., & Bavelier, D. (2006). Effect of action video game on the spatial distribution of
visuospatial attention. *Journal of Experimental Psychology: Human Perception and
Performance, 32*(6), 1465–1478.

Green, C. S., & Bavelier, D. (2007). Action-video-game experience alters the spatial resolution of
vision. *Psychological Science, 18,* 88–94.

Green, C. S., & Bavelier, D. (2015). Action video game training for cognitive enhancement. *Current
Opinion in Behavioral Sciences, 4,* 103–108.

Greenfield, D. (2011). The addictive properties of internet usage. In K. S. Young & C. N. de Abreu (Eds.), *Internet addiction: A handbook and guide to evaluation and treatment* (pp. 135–153). Hoboken, NJ: Wiley.

Gusnard, D. A., Akbudak, E., Shulman, G. L., & Raichle, M. E. (2001). Medial prefrontal cortex and self-referential mental activity: Relation to a default mode of brain function. *Proceedings of the National Academy of Sciences, USA, 98,* 4259–4264.

Guttman, S. E., Gilroy, L. A., & Blake, R. (2007). Spatial grouping in human vision: Temporal structure trumps temporal synchrony. *Vision Research, 47*(2), 219–230.

Habermas, T., & Bluck, S. (2000). Getting a life: The emergence of the life story in adolescence. *Psychological Bulletin, 126,* 748–769.

Haikonen, P. (2003). *The cognitive approach to conscious machines.* Charlottesville, VA: Imprint Academic.

Haken, H., & Levi, P. (2012). *Synergetic agents: From multi-robot systems to molecular robotics.* New York, NY: Wiley.

Hall, J. A., Park, N., Song, H., & Cody, M. J. (2010). Strategic misrepresentation in online dating: The effects of gender, self-monitoring and personality traits. *Journal of Social and Personal Relationships, 27*(1), 117–135.

Haraway, D. J. (1991). *Simians, cyborgs, and women: The reinvention of nature.* New York, NY: Routledge.

Harder, Ben. (2002, May 1). Scientists "drive" rats by remote control. *National Geographic.*

Hariri, A. R., Bookheimer, S. Y., & Mazziotta, J. C. (2000). Modulating emotional responses: Effects of a neocortical network on the limbic system. *Neuroreport, 11,* 43–48.

Haworth, C. M. A., Wright, M. J., Martin, N. W., Martin, N. G., Boomsma, D. I., Bartels, M., . . . & R. Plomin. (2009). A twin study of the genetics of high cognitive ability selected from 11,000 twin pairs in six studies from four countries. *Behavioral Genetics, 39,* 359–370. doi:10.1007/s10519-009-9262-3

He, D., Fan, C. Y., Niu, G. F., Lian, S. L., & Chen, W. (2016). The effect of parenting styles on adolescents' cyberbullying: The mediating role of covert narcissism. *Chinese Mental Health Journal, 24*(1), 41–44.

Heatherton, T. F. (2011). Neuroscience of self and self-regulation. *Annual Review of Psychology, 62,* 363–390.

Heatherton, T. F., Macrae, C. N., & Kelley, W. M. (2004). What the social brain sciences can tell us about the self. *Psychological Science, 13*(5), 190–193.

Heilig, M. (1960). U.S. Patent No. 3050870. Washington, DC: US Patent and Trademark Office.

Heim, M. (1995). The design of virtual reality. In M. Featherstone & R. Burrows (Eds.), *Cyberspace/cyberbodies/cyberpunk: Cultures of technological embodiment* (pp. 65–77). London, UK: Sage Publications.

Herwig, U., Kaffenberger, T., Schell, C., Jancke, L., & Bruhl, A. B. (2012). Neural activity associated with self-reflection. *BMC Neuroscience, 13.* doi:10.1186/1471-2202-13-52

Heyes, C. (1995). Self-recognition in mirrors: Further reflections create a hall of mirrors. *Animal Behavior, 50,* 1533–1542.

Hick, J. (1976). *Death and eternal life.* New York, NY: Harper & Row.

Hill, M. D., Jouppi, N. P., & Sohi, G. S. (Eds.). (2000). *Readings in computer architecture.* San Diego, CA: Academic Press.

Hoeft, F., Watson, C. L., Kesler, S. R., Bettinger, K. E., and Reiss, A. L. (2008). Gender differences in the mesocorticolimbic system during computer game-play. *Journal of Psychiatric Research, 42,* 253–258.

Hoffman, D. M., Girshick, A. R., Akeley, K., & Banks, M. S. (2008). Vergence-accommodation conflicts hinder visual performance and cause visual fatigue. *Journal of Vision, 8*(3). doi:10.1167/8.3.33

Hoffman, H. G., Doctor, J. N., Patterson, D. R., Carrougher, G. J., & Furness, T. A., III. (2000). Virtual reality as an adjunctive pain control during burn wound care in adolescent patients. *Pain, 85*(1–2), 305–309.

Hofstadter, D. (2007). *I am a strange loop.* New York, NY: Basic Books.

Hong, S. B., Kim, J. W., Choi, E. J., Kim, H. H., Suh, J. E., Kim, C. D., . . . & Yi, S. H. (2013). Reduced orbitofrontal cortical thickness in male adolescents with internet addiction. *Behavioral and Brain Functions, 9*(11), 9081–9089.

Hood, B. (2012). *The self illusion: How the social brain creates identity.* New York, NY: Oxford University Press.

Howell, R. (2006). Self-knowledge and self-reference. *Philosophy and Phenomenological Research, 72,* 44–70.

Howell, E. (2010). Dissociation and dissociative disorders: Commentary and context. In E. Petrucelli (Ed.), *Knowing, not-knowing and sort-of-knowing: psychoanalysis and the experience of uncertainty* (pp. 83–98). London, UK: Karnac Books.***

Huang, E., & Yu-Ting, H. (2013). Interactivity and identification influences on virtual shopping. *International Journal of Electronic Commerce Studies, 4,* 305–312.

Hudson, H. (2001). *A materialist metaphysics of the human person.* Ithaca, NY: Cornell University Press.

Huffman, K., & Dowdell, K. (2015). *Psychology in action.* West Sussex, UK: Wiley-Blackwell.

Hunt, H. T. (1995). *On the nature of consciousness.* New Haven, CT: Yale University Press.

Huntjens, R. J. C., Peters, M. I., Postma, A., Woertman, L., Effting, M., & van der Hart, O. (2005). Transfer of newly acquired stimulus valence between identities in dissociative identity disorder (DID). *Behaviour Research and Therapy, 43,* 243–255.

Ichbiah, D. (2005). *Robots: From science fiction to technological revolution.* New York, NY: Abrams.

Impey, C. (2010). *How it ends: From you to the universe.* New York, NY: Norton.

Indian, M., & Grieve, R. (2014). When Facebook is easier than face-to-face: Social support derived from Facebook in socially anxious individuals. *Personality and Individual Differences, 59*(2), 102–106.

Ipsos MediaCT. (2015). *The 2015 essential facts about the computer and video game industry.* Entertainment Software Association. Retrieved from https://templatearchive.com/esa-essential-facts/

Ishiguro, H. (2007). Scientific issues concerning androids. *International Journal of Robotics Research, 26*(1), 105–117.

Jakobsson, M., & Taylor, T. L. (2003). The Sopranos meets EverQuest: Social networking in massively multiplayer online games. *FineArt Forum 17*(8), 81–90. Retrieved from http://mjson.se/doc/sopranos_meets_eq_faf_v3.pdf

James, W. (1892). *Principles of psychology.* New York, NY: Henry Holt.

Jansari, A. S., Froggatt, D., Edginton, T., & Dawkins, L. (2013). Investigating the impact of nicotine on executive functions using a novel virtual reality assessment. *Addiction, 108,* 977–984.

Jansz, J. (2005). The emotional appeal of violent video games for adolescent males. *Communication Theory, 15*(3), 219–241.

Jansz, J., & Martis, R. G. (2007). The Lara phenomenon: Powerful female characters in video games. *Sex Roles, 56*(3–4), 141–148.

Jeffery, M. (1999). *The human computer.* London, UK: Warner Books.

Jenkins, A. C., & Mitchell, J. P. (2011). Medial prefrontal cortex subserves diverse forms of self-reflection. *Social Neuroscience, 6,* 211–218.

Johannson, R. S., & Westling, G. (1987). Signals in tactile afferents from the fingers eliciting adaptive motor responses during precision grip. *Experimental Brain Research, 66,* 141–154.

Johnson, G. M., & Johnson, J. A. (2008). Internet use and complex cognitive processes. In P. Kommers and P. Isaías (Eds.), *Proceedings of the IADIS International Conference e-Society* (pp. 83–90). N.p.: IADIS.

Johnson, M. K., Nolen-Hoeksema, S., Mitchell, K. J., & Levin, Y. (2009). Medial cortex activity, self-reflection and depression. *Social, Cognitive and Affective Neuroscience, 4,* 313–327.

Johnson, M. K., Raye, C. L., Mitchell, K. J., Touryan, S. R., Greene, E. J., & Nolen-Hoeksema, S. (2006). Dissociating medial frontal and posterior cingulate activity during self-reflection. *Social, Cognitive and Affective Neuroscience, 1,* 56–64.

Joinson, A. N. (2004). Self-esteem, interpersonal risk, and preference for email to face-to-face communication. *Cyberpsychology, Behavior and Social Networking, 7*(4), 472–478.

Jones, C. M., Scholes, L., Johnson, D., Katsikitis, M., & Carras, M. C. (2014). Gaming well: Links between videogames and flourishing mental health. *Frontiers in Psychology, 5.* doi:10.3389 /fpsyg.2014.00260

Jovanovski, D., Zakzanis, K., Campbell, Z., Erb, S., & Nussbaum, D. (2012). Development of a novel, ecologically oriented virtual reality measure of executive function: The Multitasking in the City Test. *Applied Neuropsychology: Adult, 19,* 171–182.

Jovanovski, D., Zakzanis, K., Ruttan, L., Campbell, Z., Erb, S., & Nussbaum, D. (2012). Ecologically valid assessment of executive dysfunction using a novel virtual reality task in patients with acquired brain injury. *Applied Neuropsychology, 19,* 207–220.

Junco, R. (2012). Too much face and not enough books: The relationship between multiple indices of Facebook use and academic performance. *Computers in Human Behavior, 28*(1). doi:10.1016/j.chb.2011.08.026

Kanai, R., Bahrami, B., Roylance, R., & Rees, G. (2011). Online social network size is reflected in human brain structure. *Proceedings of the Royal Society B. Biological Sciences, 279*(1732), 1327–1334. doi:10.1098/rspb.2011.1959

Kane, R. (2005). *A contemporary introduction to free will.* New York, NY: Oxford University Press.

Karoub, J. (2002, December 29). Micro-electro-mechanical systems prosthetic helped save amputee on September 11. *Small Times.* Retrieved June 26, 2005, from www.smalltimes .com/Articles/Article_Display.cfm?ARTICLE_ID=267684&p=109 [no longer accessible]

Kätsyri, J., Hari, R., Ravaja, N., & Nummenmaa, L. (2013). The opponent matters: Elevated fMRI reward responses to winning against a human versus a computer opponent during interactive video game playing. *Cerebral Cortex, 23*(12), 2829–2839.

Kaufman-Osborn, T. (1997). *Creatures of Prometheus.* Lanham, MD: Rowman and Littlefield.

Kawamura, K., Rogers, T., Hambuchen, A., & Erol, D. (2003). Toward a human-robot symbiotic system. *Robotics and Computer Integrated Manufacturing, 19,* 555–565.

Keenan, J. P., Freund, S., Hamilton, R. H., Ganis, G., & Pascual-Leone, A. (2000). Hand response differences in a self-face identification task. *Neuropsychologia, 38,* 1047–1053.

Keenan, J. P., McCutcheon, B., Freund, S., Gallup, G. G., Sanders, G., & Pascual-Leone, A. (1999). Left hand advantage in a self-face recognition task. *Neuropsychologia, 37,* 1421–1425.

Keenan, J. P., & Wheeler, M. (2003). Self-face processing in a callosotomy patient, *European Journal of Neuroscience, 18*(8), 2391–2395.

Kendall, L. (2002). *Hanging out in the virtual pub: Masculinities and relationships online.* Berkeley: University of California Press.

Kennedy, H. (2002, December). Lara Croft: Feminist icon or cyberbimbo? On the limits of textual analysis. *Game Studies, 2*(2). Retrieved from www.gamestudios.org

Kent, S. L. (2001). *The ultimate history of video games.* Roseville, CA: Prima.

Khan, A. F. U. (1995). The ethics of autonomous learning systems. In K. Ford, C. Glymour, and P. Hayes (Eds.), *Android epistemology* (pp. 253–265). Cambridge, MA: MIT Press.

Kilroe, P. (2000). The dream as text, the dream as narrative. *Dreaming, 10*(3), 125–137.

Kim, J., & Lee, J. R. (2011). The Facebook paths to happiness: Effects of the number of Facebook friends and self-presentation on subjective well-being. *Cyberpsychology, Behavior, and Social Networking, 14*(6), 359–364.

Kim, K., & Johnson, M. K. (2010). Extended self: Medial prefrontal activity during transient association of self and objects. *Social, Cognitive and Affective Neuroscience, 7*, 199–207.

Kim, Y., & Sundar, S. S. (2012). Visualizing ideal self vs. actual self through avatars: Impact on preventive health outcomes. *Computers in Human Behavior, 28*(4), 1356–1364.

Kircher, T. T. J., Senior, C., Phillips, M. L., Benson, P. J., Bullmore, E. T., Brammer, M., . . . & David, A. S. (2000). Towards a functional neuroanatomy of self processing: Effects of faces and words. *Cognitive Brain Research, 10*, 133–144.

Kirschner, P. A., & Karpinski, A. C. (2010). Facebook and academic performance. *Computers in Human Behavior, 26*(6), 1237–1245.

Klein, S. B. (2010). The self: As a construct in psychology and neuropsychological evidence for its multiplicity. *WIREs Cognitive Science, 1*, 172–183.

Klein, S. B. (2013). Images and constructs: Can the neural correlates of self be revealed through radiological analysis? *International Journal of Psychological Research, 6*, 117–132.

Klein, S. B., & Gangi, C. E. (2010). The multiplicity of self: Neuropsychological evidence and its implications for the self as a construct in psychological research. *Annals of the New York Academy of Sciences, 1191*, 1–15.

Klein, S. B., & Nichols, S. (2012). Memory and the sense of personal identity. *Mind, 121*, 677–702.

Knobe, J., & Nichols, S. (2008). *Experimental philosophy*. Oxford, UK: Oxford University Press.

Knobe, J., & Nichols, S. (2011). Free will and the bounds of the self. In R. Kane (Ed.), *The Oxford handbook of free will* (pp. 87–101). New York, NY: Oxford University Press.

Koch, C. (2004). *The quest for consciousness: A neurobiological approach*. Englewood, CO: Roberts.

Koepp, M. J., Gunn, R. N., Lawrence, A. D., Cunningham, V. J., Dagher, A., Jones, T., . . . & Grasby, P. M. (1998). Evidence for striatal dopamine release during a video game. *Nature, 393*(6682), 266–268.

Kohut, H. (1977). *The restoration of the self*. Madison, WI: International Universities Press.

Kollock, P., & Smith, M. A. (1999). Communities in cyberspace. In M. A. Smith & P. Kollock (Eds.), *Communities in cyberspace* (pp. 3–25). London, UK: Routledge.

Kotler, S. (2014, July 28). The innovation turbo-charge: How to train the brain to be more creative. *Forbes*. Retrieved from https://www.forbes.com/sites/stevenkotler/2014/07/28/the-innovation-turbo-charge-heightened-creativity-with-flow/#693c2f2d238a

Kozinets, R., Gretzel, U., & Dinhopl, A. (2017). Self in art/self as art: Museum selfies as identity work. *Frontiers in Psychology, 8*, 731.

Kruger, J., Caruana, F., Dalla Volta, R., & Rizzolatti, G. (2010). Seven years of recording from monkey cortex with a chronically implanted multiple microelectrode. *Frontiers in Neuroengineering, 3*, 1–9.

Kühn, S., & Gallinat, J. (2014). Amount of lifetime video gaming is positively associated with entorhinal, hippocampal and occipital volume. *Molecular Psychiatry, 19*(7), 842–847.

Kühn, S., Gleich, T., Lorenz, R. C., Lindenberger, U., & Gallinat, J. (2014). Playing *Super Mario* induces structural brain plasticity: Gray matter changes resulting from training with a commercial video game. *Molecular Psychiatry, 19*(2), 265–271.

Kurzweil, R. (1996/2005). *The singularity is near*. New York, NY: Viking.

Lambert, A. (2013). *Intimacy and friendship on Facebook*. New York, NY: Macmillan.

Lane, R. D., Fink, G. R., Chau, P. M.-L., & Dolan, R. J. (1997). Neural activation during selective attention to subjective emotional responses. *NeuroReport, 8*, 3969–3972.

Langley, P., Simon, H., Bradshaw, G., & Zytkow, J. (1987). *Scientific discovery: Computational explorations of the creative processes.* Cambridge, MA: MIT Press.

Leary, M. R., & Allen, A. B. (2011). Personality and persona: Personality processes in self-presentation. *Journal of Personality, 79*(6), 889–916.

Leary, M. R., & Buttermore, N. E. (2003). Evolution of the human self: Tracing the natural history of self-awareness. *Journal for the Theory of Social Behaviour, 33*, 365–404.

Leary, M. R., & Tangney, J. P. (2012). The self as an organizing construct in the behavioral and social sciences. In M. R. Leary & J. P. Tangney (Eds.), *Handbook of self and identity* (2nd ed., pp. 1–20). New York, NY: Guilford Press.

Lee, S., Quigley, B. M., Nesler, M. S., Corbett, A. B., & Tedeschi, J. T. (1999). Development of a self-presentation tactics scale. *Personality and Individual Differences, 26*, 701–722.

Legrand, D., & Ruby, P. (2009). What is self-specific? Theoretical investigation and critical review of neuroimaging results. *Psychological Review, 116*, 252–282.

Lenat, D. B. (1976). *AM: An artificial intelligence approach to discovery in mathematics as heuristic search* (Unpublished doctoral dissertation). Stanford University, CA.

Leshikar, E. D., & Duarte, A. (2013). Medial prefrontal cortex supports source memory for self-referenced material in young and older adults. *Cognitive, Affective and Behavioral Neuroscience, 14*(1), 236–252. doi: 10.3758/s13415-013-0198-y

Levy, D. (2007). *Love + sex with robots.* New York, NY: Harper.

Levy, S. (1992). *Artificial life: The quest for a new creation.* New York, NY: Pantheon.

Li, C., Shi, S., & Dang, J. (2014). Online communication and subjective well-being in Chinese college students: The mediating role of shyness and social self-efficacy. *Computers in Human Behavior, 34*(5), 89–95.

Li, R., Polat, U., Makous, W., & Bavelier, D. (2009). Enhancing the contrast sensitivity function through action video game training. *Nature Neuroscience, 12*, 549–551.

Li, R., Polat, U., Scalzo, F., Bavelier, D. (2010). Reducing backward masking through action game training. *Journal of Vision, 10*, 1–13.

Libet, B. (2004). *Mind time.* Cambridge, MA: Harvard University Press.

Lieblich, A. E., and Josselson, R. E. (2013). Identity and narrative as root metaphors of personhood. In J. Martin and M. Bickhard (Eds.). *The psychology of personhood* (pp. 203–222). New York, NY: Cambridge University Press.

Lindsay, R. K., Buchanan, B. G., Feigenbaum, E. A., & Lederberg, J. (1993). DENDRAL: A case study of the first expert system for scientific hypothesis formation. *Artificial Intelligence, 61*, 209–261.

Ling, R., Baron, N. S., Lenhart, A., & Campbell, S. W. (2014). "Girls text really weird": Gender, texting and identity among teens. *Journal of Children and Media, 8*(4), 423–439.

Lipson, H., & Pollack, & J. B. (2000). Automatic design and manufacture of robotic lifeforms. *Nature, 406*, 974–978.

Liu, Q. Q., Sun, X. J., Zhou, Z. K., & Niu, G. F. (2015). Self-presentation on social network sites and ego identity: Mediation of online positive feedback. *Chinese Journal of Clinical Psychology, 23*(6), 1094–1097.

Liu, Q. X., Chen, W., & Zhou, Z. K. (2015). Internet use and online altruistic behavior in college students: The role of internet use self-efficacy and gender. *Psychological Development and Education, 6*, 685–693.

Locke, J. (1847/1979). *An essay concerning human understanding.* New York, NY: Oxford University Press.

Lou, H. C., Luber, B., Crupain, M., Keenan, J. P., Nowak, M., Kjaer, T. W., . . . & S. H. Lisanby. (2004). Parietal cortex and representation of the mental self. *Proceedings of the National Academy of Sciences, USA, 101*, 6827–6832.

Lynch, K. M., & Mason, M. T. (1995). Stable pushing: Mechanics, controllability, and planning. *International Journal of Robotics Research, 15*(6), 533–556.

Lynn, S. J., Berg, J., Lilienfeld, S. O., Merckelbach, H., Giesbrecht, T., Accardi, M., & Cleere, C. (2012). 14 dissociative disorders. In M. Hersen & D. C. Beidel (Eds.), *Adult psychopathology and diagnosis* (7th ed., pp. 497–538). New York, NY: Wiley.

Ma, N., Baetens, K., Vanderkerckhove, M., Kestemont, J., Fias, W., & Van Overwalle, F. (2013). Traits are represented in the medial prefrontal cortex: An fMRI adaptation study. *Social, Cognitive, and Affective Neuroscience, 9*(8). doi:0.093/scan/nst098

Mackie, D. (1999). Personal identity and dead people. *Philosophical Studies, 95*(3), 219–242.

Maillot, P., Perrot, A., & Hartley, A. (2012). Effects of interactive physical activity video-game training on physical and cognitive function in older adults. *Psychology and Aging, 27*(3), 589–600.

Malloy, K. M., & Milling, L. S. (2010). The effectiveness of virtual reality distraction for pain reduction: A systematic review. *Clinical Psychology Review, 30*(8), 1011–1018.

Manson, J., & Wrangham, R. W. (1991). Intergroup aggression in chimpanzees and humans. *Current Anthropology, 32*, 369–390.

Mar, R. A., & Oatley, K. (2008). The function of fiction is the abstraction and simulation of social experience. *Perspectives on Psychological Science, 3*(3), 173–192.

Mark, G., Gudith, D., & Klocke, U. (2008). The cost of interrupted work: more speed and stress. *Proceedings of the SIGCHI Conference on Human Factors in Computing Systems 8*(11), 107–110. Retrieved from http://dl.acm.org/citation.cfm?id=135072

Marks, I. M. (1987). *Fears, phobias, and rituals.* New York, NY: Oxford University Press.

Markus, H. R., & Kitayama, S. (1991). Culture and the self: Implications for cognition, emotion, and motivation. *Psychological Review, 98*(2), 224–253.

Martin, J., & Bickhard, M. H. (Eds.). (2013). *The psychology of personhood: Philosophical, historical, social-developmental, and narrative perspectives.* Cambridge, UK: Cambridge University Press.

Martinelli, P., Sperduti, M., & Piolino, P. (2013). Neural substrates of the self-memory system: New insights from a meta-analysis. *Human Brain Mapping, 34*, 1515–1529.

Maslow, A. H. (1970). *Motivation and personality.* New York, NY: Harper & Row.

Mason, M. F., Norton, M. I., Van Horn, J. D., Wegner, D. M., Grafton, S. T., & Macrae, C. N. (2007). Wandering minds: The default network and stimulus-independent thought. *Science, 315*, 393–395.

Matsuba, M. K. (2006). Searching for self and relationships online. *CyberPsychology and Behavior, 9*(9), 275–284.

McCain, J. L., Borg, Z. G., Rothenberg, A. H., Churillo, K. M., Weiler, P., & Campbell, W. K. (2016). Personality and selfies: Narcissism and the Dark Triad. *Computers in Human Behavior, 64*, 126–133. doi:10.1016/j.chb.2016.06.050

McCormick, B. H., & Mayerich, D. M. (2004). Three-dimensional imaging using knife-edge scanning microsocopy. *Microscopy and Microanalysis, 10*(2), 1466–1467.

McCrae, R. R., & Costa, P. T., Jr. (2013). Introduction to the empirical and theoretical status of the five-factor model of personality traits. In T. A. Widiger & P. T. Costa Jr. (Eds.), *Personality disorders and the five-factor model of personality* (3rd ed., pp. 15–27). Washington, DC: American Psychological Association.

McGee, M. J. (2014). Is texting ruining intimacy? Exploring perceptions among sexuality students in higher education. *American Journal of Sexuality Education, 9*(4), 404–427.

McGinn, C. (1987). Could a machine be conscious? In C. Blakemore and S. Greenfield (Eds.), *Mindwaves* (pp. 279–288). Oxford, UK: Blackwell.

McGonigal, J. (2011). *Reality is broken: Why games make us better and how they can change the world.* New York, NY: Penguin Books.

McGuire, P. K., Silbersweig, D. A., & Frith, C. D. (1996). Functional neuroanatomy of verbal self-monitoring. *Brain, 119,* 907–917.

McKenna, K. Y. A., Green, A. S., & Gleeson, M. J. (2002). Relationship formation on the internet: What's the big attraction? *Journal of Social Issues, 58,* 9–32.

McMahan, A. (2003). Immersion, engagement, and presence: A method for analyzing 3-D video games. In M. J. P. Wolf & P. Bernard (Eds.), *The video game theory reader* (pp. 67–86). New York, NY: Routledge.

McPherson, T. (2000). I'll take my stand in Dixie-net: White guys, the South, and cyberspace. In B. E. Kolko, L. Nakamura, & G. B. Rodman (Eds.), *Race and cyberspace* (pp. 117–131). New York, NY: Routledge.

McWilliams, N. (2011). *Psychoanalytic diagnosis: Understanding personality structure in the clinical process.* New York, NY: Guilford Press.

Mehdizadeh, S. (2010). Self-presentation 2.0: Narcissism and self-esteem on Facebook. *Cyberpsychology, Behavior and Social Networking, 13,* 357–364.

Melhuish, C. R. (2001). *Strategies for collective minimalist mobile robots.* Suffolk, UK: St. Edmundsbury Press.

Melucci, A. (1997). Identity and difference in a globalized world. In P. Werbner & T. Modood (Eds.), *Debating cultural hybridity: Multi-cultural identities and the politics of anti-racism* (pp. 58–69). London, UK: Zed Books.

Mengel, F. (2014). Computer games and prosocial behavior. *PLoS One, 9*(4). doi:10.1371/journal.pone.0094099

Merricks, T. (1998). There are no criteria of identity over time. *Noûs, 32,* 106–124.

Miller, B. L., Seeley, W. W., Mychack, P., Rosen, H. J., Mena, I., & Boone, K. (2001). Neuroanatomy of the self: Evidence from patients with frontotemporal dementia. *Neurology, 57,* 817–821.

Minsky, M. (1985). *The society of mind.* New York, NY: Touchstone.

Mischel, W. (1968). *Personality and assessment.* New York, NY: Wiley.

Mishra, B., & Silver, N. (1989). Some discussion of static gripping and its stability. *IEEE Systems, Man, and Cybernetics, 19*(4), 783–796.

Modecki, K. L., Minchin, J., Harbaugh, A. G., Guerra, N. G., & Runions, K. C. (2014). Bullying prevalence across contexts: A meta-analysis measuring cyber and traditional bullying. *Journal of Adolescent Health, 55*(5), 602–611.

Moore, C., & Lemmon, K. (Eds.). (2001). *The self in time: Development perspectives.* Hillsdale, NJ: Erlbaum.

Moran, J. A., Kelley, W. M., & Heatherton, T. F. (2013). What can the organization of the brain's default mode network tell us about self-knowledge? *Frontiers in Human Neuroscience, 7.* doi:10.3389/fnhum.2013.00391

Moravec, H. (1990). *Mind children: The future of robot and human intelligence.* Cambridge, MA: Harvard University Press.

Morf, C., & Mischel, W. (2012). The self as a psycho-social dynamic processing system: Toward a converging science of selfhood. In M. R. Leary & J. P. Tangney (Eds.), *Handbook of self and identity* (2nd ed., pp. 21–49). New York, NY: Guilford Press.

Morf, C. C., & Rhodewalt, F. (2001). Unraveling the paradoxes of narcissism: A dynamic self-regulatory processing model. *Psychological Inquiry, 12,* 177–196.

Morf, C. C., Torchetti, L., & Schürch, E. (2011). Narcissism from the perspective of the dynamic self-regulatory processing model. In W. K. Campbell & J. D. Miller (Eds.), *The handbook of narcissism and narcissistic personality disorder: Theoretical approaches, empirical findings, and treatment* (pp. 56–70). Hoboken, NJ: Wiley.

Mori, M. (2012). The uncanny valley. Translated by K. F. MacDorman & N. Kageki. In. *IEEE Robotics and Automation*, 19(2): 98–100. doi:10.1109/MRA.2012.2192811

Mosig, Y. D. (2006). Conceptions of self in Western and Eastern psychology. *Journal of Theoretical and Philosophical Psychology, 26*, 39–50.

Murray, J. H. (1997). *Hamlet on the holodeck: The future of narrative in cyberspace.* New York, NY: Simon & Schuster.

Muusses, L. D., Finkenauer, C., Kerkhof, P., & Righetti, F. (2013). Partner effects of compulsive internet use: A self-control account. *Communication Research, 42*(3), 365–386.

Myers, D. G. (2001). *Psychology.* New York, NY: Worth.

Nadkarni, A., & Hofmann, S. G. (2012). Why do people use Facebook? *Personality and Individual Differences, 52*(3), 243–249.

Nahmias, E. (2006). Folk fears about freedom and responsibility: Determinism vs. reductionism. *Journal of Cognition and Culture, 6*(1–2), 215–237.

Nakamura, L. (1995). Race in/for cyberspace: Identity tourism and racial passing on the internet. *Works and Days, 25*(26), 181–93. Retrieved from https://pdfs.semanticscholar.org/3531/da9329d2b7158bd697e1aa8ef073f78de6fb.pdf

Nakamura, L. (2002). *Cybertypes: Race, ethnicity, and identity on the internet.* New York, NY: Routledge.

Napier, J. (1980). *Hands.* Princeton, NJ: Princeton University Press.

Nardi, B., Ly, S., & Harris, J. (2007, January). Learning conversations in *World of Warcraft*. Paper presented at Proceedings of Hawaii International Conference on Systems Science, Big Island, HI.

Navarrete, C. D., McDonald, M. M., Mott, M. L., & Asher, B. (2012). Virtual morality: Emotion and action in a simulated three-dimensional "trolley problem." *Emotion, 12*(2), 364–70.

Neuhouser, F. (1990). *Fichte's theory of subjectivity.* New York, NY: Cambridge University Press.

Nesse, R. (1999). Proximate and evolutionary studies of anxiety, stress and depression: Synergy at the interface. *Neuroscience and Biobehavioral Reviews, 23*(7), 895–903.

Nicolelis, M. A. L., Dimitrov, D., Carmena, J. M., Crist, G., Kralik, J. D., & Wise, S. P. (2003). Chronic, multisite, multielectrode recordings in macaque monkeys. *Proceedings of the National Academy of Sciences, 100*(19), 11041–11046.

Nietzsche, F. (1883/1999). *Also sprach Zarathustra I-IV.* G. Colli & M. Montinari (Eds.). Munich, Germany: Deutscher Taschenbuch.

Nitsche, M. (2008). *Video game spaces: Image, play, and structure in 3D game worlds.* Cambridge, MA: MIT Press.

Niu, G. F., Sun, X. J., Zhou, Z. K., Kong, F. C., & Tian, Y. (2016). The impact of social network site (Qzone) on adolescents' depression: The serial mediation of upward social comparison and self-esteem. *Acta Psychologica Sinica, 48*(10), 1282–1291.

Niu, G. F., Sun, X. J., Zhou, Z. K., Tian, Y., Liu, Q .Q., & Lian, S. L. (2016). The effect of adolescents' social networking site use on self-concept clarity: The mediating role of social comparison. *Journal of Psychological Science, 39*(1), 97–102.

Noe, A. (2017, August 4). Technology gets under the skin. *Cosmos and Culture*, NPR. Retrieved from www.npr.org/sections/13.7/2017/08/04/541106998/technology-gets-under-the-skin

Nolfi, S., & Floreano, D. (2000). *Evolutionary robotics: The biology, intelligence, and technology of self-organizing machines.* Cambridge, MA: MIT Press.

Noonan, H. (2003). *Personal identity* (2nd ed.). London: Routledge.

Noonan, M. P., Kolling, N., Walton, M. E., & Rushworth, M. F. S. (2012). Re-evaluating the role of the orbitofrontal cortex in reward and reinforcement. *European Journal of Neuroscience, 35*(7), 997–1010.

Nordhausen, C. T., Maynard, E. M., & Normann, R. A. (1996). Single unit recording capabilities of a 100 microelectrode array. *Brain Research, 726,* 129–140.

Northoff, G., Heinzel, A., de Greck, M., Bermpohl, F., Dobrowolny, H., & Panksepp, J. (2006). Self-referential processing in our brain: A meta-analysis of imaging studies on the self. *NeuroImage, 31*(1), 440–457.

Ochsner, K. N., Beer, J. S., Robertson, E. R., Cooper, J. C., Kihlstrom, J. F., D'Esposito, M., & Gabrieli, J. D. E. (2005). The neural correlates of direct and reflected self-knowledge. *Neuroimage, 28,* 797–814.

O'Doherty, J. E., Ifft, P. J., Zhuang, K. Z., Lebedev, M. A., & Nicolelis, M. A. L. (2010, November). Brain-machine-brain interface using simultaneous recording and intracortical microstimulation feedback. Talk presented at the Annual Meeting of the Society for Neuroscience, San Diego, CA, conference poster no. 899.15.

Olson, E. (1997). *The human animal: Personal identity without psychology.* New York, NY: Oxford University Press.

Olson, E. (2007). *What are we? A study in personal ontology.* New York, NY: Oxford University Press.

Olson, E. (2015). Personal identity. In Edward N. Zalta (Ed.), *Stanford encyclopedia of philosophy* (Winter 2012 ed.). Retrieved from https://plato.stanford.edu/archives/win2012/entries/davidson/

Omohundro, S. M. (2007, October 7). The nature of self-improving artificial intelligence. Paper presented at 2007 Singularity Summit, San Francisco, CA, transcript. *Medium.* Retrieved from https://medium.com/@emergingtechnology/the-nature-of-self-improving-artificial-intelligence-2a4b69bdd160

Ortiz de Gortari, A. B., & Griffiths, M. D. (2016). Prevalence and characteristics of game transfer phenomena: A descriptive survey study. *International Journal of Human-Computer Interaction, 32*(6), 470–480.

Ortiz de Gortari, A. B., & Griffiths, M. D. (2017). Beyond the boundaries of the game: The interplay between in-game phenomena, structural characteristics of video games, and game transfer phenomena. In J. Gackenbach & J. Bown (Eds.), *Boundaries of self and reality online: Implications of digitally constructed realities* (pp. 97–122). London, UK: Academic Press.

Ortiz de Gortari, A. B., Oldfield, B., & Griffiths, M. D. (2016). An empirical examination of factors associated with game transfer phenomenon severity. *Computers in Human Behavior, 64,* 274–284.

Ou, C. X. J., & Davison, R. M. (2011). Interactive or interruptive? Instant Messaging at work. *Decision Support Systems, 52*(1), 61–72.

Pagel, J. F. (2017). Internet dreaming: Is the web conscious? In J. Gackenbach & J. Bown (Eds.), *Boundaries of self and reality online: Implications of digitally constructed realities* (pp. 279–296). London, UK: Academic Press.

Panksepp, J. (2005). Affective consciousness: Core emotional feelings in animals and humans. *Consciousness and Cognition, 14*(1), 30–80.

Parfit, D. (1986). *Reasons and persons.* New York, NY: Oxford University Press.

Paris, J. (2014). Modernity and narcissistic personality disorder. *Personality Disorders: Theory, Research, and Treatment, 5*(2): 220–226.

Park, N., Lee, S., & Chung, J. E. (2016). Uses of cellphone texting: An integration of motivations, usage patterns, and psychological outcomes. *Computers in Human Behavior, 62,* 712–719.

Parsons, T. D. (2017). *Cyberpsychology and the brain: The interaction of neuroscience and affective computing*. New York, NY: Cambridge University Press.

Pennebaker, J. W. (2004). *Writing to heal: A guided journal for recovering from trauma and emotional upheaval*. Oakland, CA: New Harbinger.

Peperkorn, H. M., Diemer, J., & Mühlberger, A. (2015). Temporal dynamics in the relation between presence and fear in virtual reality. *Computers in Human Behavior, 48*, 542–547.

Perry, B. D., Pollard, R. A., Blakley, T. L., Baker, W. L., & Vigilante, D. (1995). Childhood trauma, the neurobiology of adaption and "use-dependent" development of the brain: How "states" become "traits." *Infant Mental Health Journal, 16*, 271–291.

Perry, J. (1979/1993). The problem of the essential indexical. In J. Perry, *The problem of the essential indexical* (pp. 33–53). New York, NY: Oxford University Press.

Perry, J. (1986/1993). Thought without representation. *Supplementary Proceedings of the Aristotelian Society, 205–255*.

Phillips, M. L., Medford, N., Senior, C., Bullmore, E. T., Suckling, J., Brammer, M. J., . . . & David, A. S. (2001). Depersonalization disorder: Thinking without feeling. *Psychiatry Research: Neuroimaging, 108*(3), 145–160.

Picard, L., Mayor-Dubois, C., Maeder, P., Kalenzaga, S., Abram, M., Duval, C., . . . & Piolino, P. (2013). Functional independence within the self-memory system: Insight from two cases of developmental amnesia. *Cortex, 49*, 1463–1481.

Pinker, S. (2003). *The blank slate: The modern denial of human nature*. New York, NY: Penguin Books.

Platek, S. M., & Gallup, G. G. (2002). Self-face recognition is affected by schizotypal personality traits. *Schizophrenia Research, 57*, 81–85.

Platek, S. M., Myers, T. E., Critton, S. R., & Gallup, G. G. (2003). A left-hand advantage for self-description: The impact of schizotypal personality traits. *Schizophrenia Research, 65*, 147–151.

Ponce, J. (1999). Manipulation and grasping. In F. C. Keil and R. A. Wilson (Eds.), *The MIT encyclopedia of cognitive sciences* (pp. 508–511). Cambridge, MA: MIT Press.

Posner, M. I., & Peterson, S. E. (1990). The attention system of the human brain. *Annual Review of Neuroscience, 13*, 25–42.

Posner, M., & Rothbart, M. K. (2000). Developing mechanisms of self-regulation. *Development and Psychopathology, 12*, 427–441.

Postrel, V. (2011). *The future and its enemies: The growing conflict over creativity, enterprise and progress*. New York, NY: Touchstone.

Poundstone, W. (1985). *The recursive universe*. New York, NY: Morrow.

Powers, M. B., & Emmelkamp, P. M. (2008). Virtual reality exposure therapy for anxiety disorders: A meta-analysis. *Journal of Anxiety Disorders, 22*(3), 561–569.

Preston, J. M. (2017). Games, dreams and consciousness: Absorption and perception, cognition, emotion. In J. Gackenbach & J. Bown (Eds.), *Boundaries of self and reality online: Implications of digitally constructed realities* (pp. 205–238). London, UK: Academic Press.

Preston, J. M., & Cull, A. (1998). Virtual environments: Influences on apparent motion aftereffects. Paper presented at the annual meeting of the Canadian Psychological Association, Edmonton, AB.

Przybylski, A. K., Weinstein, N., & Murayama, K. (2017). Internet gaming disorder: Investigating the clinical relevance of a new phenomenon. *American Journal of Psychiatry, 174*(3), 230–236.

Rahula, W. (1974). *What the Buddha taught*. New York, NY: Grove.

Raichle, M. E. (2015). The brain's default mode network. *Annual Review of Neuroscience, 38*, 443–447.

Rand, A. (1961). *The virtue of selfishness*. New York, NY: Signet Classics.

Ray, T. S. (1991). An approach to the synthesis of life. In C. Langton, C. Taylor, J. Farmer, & S. Rasmussen (Eds.), *Artificial life II* (pp. 371–408). Redwood City, CA: Addison-Wesley.

Re, D. E., Wang, S. A., He, J. C., & Rule, N. O. (2016). Selfie indulgence: Self-favoring biases in perceptions of selfies. *Social Psychological and Personality Science, 7*(6), 588–596.

Rebato, C. (2015, March 4). HTC Vive: Virtual reality that's so damn real I can't even handle it. *Gizmodo* [blog]. Retrieved from http://gizmodo.com/htc-vive-virtual-reality-so-damn-real-that-i-cant-even-1689396093

Reed, C. L., & Farah, M. J. (1995). The psychological reality of the body schema: A test with normal participants. *Journal of Experimental Psychology: Human Perception and Performance, 21,* 334–343.

Reid, E. (1999). Hierarchy and power: Social control in cyberspace. In M. A. Smith & P. Kollock (Eds.), *Communities in cyberspace* (pp. 107–133). London, UK: Routledge.

Reid, E. M. (1996). Text-based virtual realities: Identity and the cyborg body. In P. Ludlow (Ed.), *High noon on the electronic frontier: Conceptual issues in cyberspace* (pp. 327–345). Cambridge, MA: MIT Press.

Reid, T. (1785/1969). *Essays on the intellectual powers of man*. B. Brody (Ed.). Cambridge, MA: MIT Press.

Reinders, A. A. (2008). Cross-examining dissociative identity disorder: Neuroimaging and etiology on trial. *Neurocase, 14*(1): 44–53.

Reissman, C. K. (2004). Narrative analysis. In M. S. Lewis-Beck, A. Bryman, & T. Futing Liao (Eds.), *The Sage encyclopedia of social services research methods* (pp. 705–709). Thousand Oaks, CA: Sage Publications.

Renison, B., Ponsford, J., Testa, R. Richardson, B., & Brownfield, K. (2012). The ecological and construct validity of a newly developed measure of executive function: The virtual library task. *Journal of the International Neuropsychological Society, 18,* 440–450.

Renoult, L., Davidson, P. S. R., Palombo, D. J., Moscovitch, M., & Levine, B. (2012). Personal semantics: At the crossroads of semantic and episodic memory. *Trends in Cognitive Sciences, 16,* 550–558.

Reynolds, C. W. (1987). Flocks, herds, and schools: A distributed behavioral model. In *SIGGRAPH '87: Proceedings of the 14th Annual Conference on Computer Graphics and Interactive Techniques* (pp. 25–34). New York, NY: ACM.

Rid, T. (2016) *Rise of the machine: A cybernetic history*. New York, NY: Norton.

Rivero, T. S., Nunez, L. M. A., Pires, E. U., & Francisco, O. (2015). ADHD rehabilitation through video gaming: A systemic review using PRISMA guidelines of the current findings and the associated risk of bias. *Frontiers in Psychiatry, 6.* doi:10.3389/fpsyt.2015.00151

Roberts, S. (2018). Tim Schafer talks Psychonauts 2 and more remasters of Lucasarts adventure games. PCGamer. https://www.pcgamer.com/tim-schafer-talks-psychonauts-2-and-more-remasters-of-lucasarts-adventure-games/.

Robertson, B. (2001). Immersed in art. *Computer Graphics World, 24*(11). Retrieved from www.cgw.com/Publications/CGW/2001/Volume-24-Issue-11-November-2001-/immersed-in-art.aspx

Rogers, C. R. (1961). On *becoming a person: A psychotherapist's view of psychotherapy*. New York, NY: Houghton Mifflin.

Ronchi, A. M. (2009). *Eculture: Cultural content in the digital age*. New York, NY: Springer.

Rorty, R. (1980). *Philosophy and the mirror of nature*. Princeton, NJ: Princeton University Press.

Rosen, L. (2012). *iDisorder: Understanding our obsessions with technology and overcoming its hold on us*. New York, NY: Palgrave Macmillan.

Ross, C. A., Miller, S. D., Bjornson, L., Reagor, P., & Fraser, G. A. (1991). Abuse histories in 102 cases of multiple personality disorder. *Canadian Journal of Psychiatry, 36,* 97–101.

Rothbaum, B. O., & Schwartz, A. C. (2002). Exposure therapy for posttraumatic stress disorder. *American Journal of Psychotherapy, 56*(1), 59–75.

Rothblatt, M. (2014). *Virtually human: The promise—and the peril—of digital immortality.* New York, NY: St. Martin's Press.

Rotter, J. B. (1990). Internal versus external control of reinforcement: A case history of a variable. *American Psychologist, 45,* 489–493.

Rubenstein, M., Cornejo, A., & Nagpal, R. (2014). Programmable self-assembly in a thousand-robot swarm. *Science, 345*(6198), 795–799. doi:10.1126/science.1254295

Ruby, P., & Decety, J. (2001). Effect of subjective perspective taking during simulation of action: A PET investigation of agency. *Nature Neuroscience, 4,* 546–550.

Rudder, C. (2014). *Dataclysm: Who we are (When we think no one's looking).* New York, NY: Crown.

Russell, S., & Norvig, P. (2003). *Artificial intelligence: A modern approach.* Englewood Cliffs, NJ: Prentice Hall.

Ryan, R. M., Rigby, C. S., & Przybylski, A. (2006). The motivational pull of video games: A self-determination theory approach. *Motivation and Emotion, 30,* 344–360. doi:1007/s11031-006-9051-8

Sadler, M. E., Hunger, J. M., & Miller, C. J. (2010). Personality and impression management: Mapping the Multidimensional Personality Questionnaire onto 12 self-presentation tactics. *Personality and Individual Differences, 48*(5), 623–628.

Sainsbury, M. (2011). English speakers should use "I" to refer to themselves. In A. Hatzimoysis (Ed.), *Self-knowledge* (pp. 246–260). Oxford, UK: Oxford University Press.

Sampasa-Kanyinga, H., & Lewis, R. F. (2015). Frequent use of social networking sites is associated with poor psychological functioning among children and adolescents. *Cyberpsychology, Behavior, and Social Networking, 18*(7), 380–385.

Samsonovich, A. V., & Nadel, L. (2005). Fundamental principles and mechanisms of the conscious self. *Cortex, 41,* 669–689.

Sarkis, S. (2014, July 18). Internet gaming disorder in DSM-5. *Psychology Today.* Retrieved from https://www.psychologytoday.com/blog/here-there-and-everywhere/201407/internet-gaming-disorder-in-dsm-5

Schaefer, M., Flor, H., Heinze, H., & Rotte, M. (2007). Morphing the body: Illusory feeling of an elongated arm affects somatosensory homunculus. *Neuroimage, 36,* 700–705.

Schaefer, M., Heinze, H., & Rotte, M. (2009). My third arm: Shifts in topography of the somatosensory homunculus predict feeling of an artificial supernumerary arm. *Human Brain Mapping, 30*(5), 1413–1420.

Scharkow, M., Festl, R., & Quandt, T. (2014). Longitudinal patterns of problematic computer game use among adolescents and adults: A 2 year panel study. *Addiction, 109*(11), 1910–1917.

Schechner, R. (1988, January). Playing. *Play and Culture, 1,* 3–20.

Schilbach, L., Eickhoff, S. B., Rotarska-Jagiela, A., Fink, G. R., & Vogeley, K. (2008). Minds at rest? Social cognition as the default mode of cognizing and its putative relationship to the "default system" of the brain. *Consciousness and Cognition, 17*(2), 457–467.

Schroeder, B. L., & Sims, V. K. (2017). Texting as a multidimensional behavior: Individual differences and measurement of texting behaviors. *Psychology of Popular Media Culture.* doi:10.1037/ppm0000148

Schwartz, H. (1996). *The culture of the copy: Striking likenesses, unreasonable facsimiles.* New York, NY: Zone Books.

Schwerin, A. (2012). *Hume's labyrinth: A search for the self.* Newcastle upon Tyne, UK: Cambridge Scholars.

Searle, J. R. (1980). Minds, brains, and programs. *Behavioral and Brain Sciences, 3,* 417–457.

Sedikides, C., & Skowronski, J. J. (2003). Evolution of the symbolic self: Issues and prospects. In M. R. Leary & J. P. Tangney (Eds.), *Handbook of self and identity* (pp. 594–609). New York, NY: Guilford Press.

Seeley, W. W., Menon, V., Schatzberg, A. F., Keller, J., Glover, G. H., Kenna, H., . . . & Greicius, M. D. (2007). Dissociable intrinsic connectivity networks of salience processing and executive control. *Journal of Neuroscience, 27*, 2349–2356.

Serruya, M. D., Hatsopoulos, N. G., Paninski, L., Fellows, M. R., & Donoghue, J. P. (2002). Instant neural control of a movement signal. *Nature, 416*, 141–142.

Sextus Empiricus. (1949/2000). *Against the professors* (R. Bury, Trans.). Cambridge, MA: Harvard University Press.

Shiban, Y., Schelhorn, I., Pauli, P., & Mühlberger, A. (2015). Effect of combined multiple contexts and multiple stimuli exposure in spider phobia: A randomized clinical trial in virtual reality. *Behaviour Research and Therapy, 71*, 45–53.

Shoemaker, S. (1970). Persons and their pasts. *American Philosophical Quarterly, 7*, 269–285.

Shu, Y., Pi, F., Sharma, A., Rajabi, M., Haque, F., Shu, D., Leggas, M., . . ., & Guo, P. (2014). *Advances in Drug Delivery Review, 66*, 74–89.

Siderits, M., Thompson, E., & Zahavi, D. (2011). *Self, no self: Perspectives from analytical phenomenological and Indian traditions.* Oxford, UK: Oxford University Press.

Simola, J., Kuisma, J., Oörni, A., Uusitalo, L., & Hyönä, J. (2011). The impact of salient advertisements on reading and attention on web pages. *Journal of Experimental Psychology: Applied, 17*(2), 174–190.

Singer, W. (1996). Neuronal synchronization: A solution the binding problem? In R. Llinas & P. S. Churchland (Eds.), *The mind-brain continuum: Sensory processes* (pp. 100–130). Cambridge, MA: MIT Press.

Skulmowski, A., Bunge, A., Kaspar, K., & Pipa, G. (2014). Forced-choice decision-making in modified trolley dilemma situations: A virtual reality and eye tracking study. *Frontiers in Behavioral Neuroscience, 8*. doi:10.3389/fnbeh.2014.00426

Slater, D. (2013). *Love in the time of algorithms: What technology does to meeting and mating.* New York, NY: Current Books.

Slater, M., Perez-Marcos, D., Ehrsson, H. H., & Sanchez-Vives, M. V. (2009). Inducing illusory ownership of a virtual body. *Frontiers in Neuroscience, 3*(2), 214–220. doi:10.3389/neuro.01.029.2009

Slater, M., Spanlang, B., Sanchez-Vives, M. V., & Blanke, O. (2010). First person experience of body transfer in virtual reality. *PloS One, 5*(5). doi:10.1371/journal.pone.0010564

Small, G. W., Moody, T. D., Siddarth, P., & Bookheimer, S. Y. (2009). Your brain on Google: Patterns of cerebral activation during internet searching. *American Journal of Geriatric Psychiatry, 17*, 116–126.

Small, G. W., & Vorgan, G. (2008). *iBrain: Surviving the technological alteration of the modern mind.* New York, NY: HarperCollins.

Smith, P. K., Mahdavi, J., Carvalho, M. Fisher, S., Russell, S., & Tippett, N. (2008). Cyberbullying: Its nature and impact on secondary school pupils. *Journal of Child Psychology and Psychiatry, 49*(4), 376–385.

Snowdon, P. (1990). Persons, animals, and ourselves. In C. Gill (Ed.), *The person and the human mind.* Oxford, UK: Clarendon Press.

Sofka, S. (2015, November 28). Watch this guy walk across the *Fallout 4* wasteland using the Virtuix Omni treadmill. *Nerdist* [blog]. Retrieved from https://archive.nerdist.com/watch-this-guy-walk-across-the-fallout-4-wasteland-using-the-virtuix-omni-treadmill/

Someya, T., Sekitani, T., Iba, S., Kato, Y., Kawaguchi, H., & Sakurai, T. (2004). A large-area, flexible pressure sensor matrix with organic field-effect transistors for artificial skin applications. *Proceedings of the National Academy of Sciences U.S.A., 101*(27), 9966–9970.

Sorokowska, A., Oleszkiewicz, A., Frackowiak, T., Pisanski, K., Chmiel, A., & Sorokowski, P. (2016). Selfies and personality: Who posts self-portrait photographs? *Personality and Individual Differences, 90,* 119–123.

Sparrow, B., Liu, J., & Wegner, D.M. (2011). Google effects on memory: Cognitive consequences of having information at our fingertips. *Science, 333*(6043), 776–778.

Spence, S.A., Brooks, D.J., Hirsch, S.R., Liddle, P.F., Meehan, J., & Grasby, P.M. (1997). A PET study of voluntary movement in schizophrenic patients experiencing passivity phenomena (delusions of alien control). *Brain, 120,* 1997–2011.

Sperry, R.W., Zaidel, E., & Zaidel, D. (1979). Self recognition and social awareness in the disconnected minor hemisphere. *Neuropsychologia, 17,* 153–166.

Spreng, R.N., Mar, R.A., & Kim, A.S. (2009). The common neural basis of autobiographical memory, prospection, navigation, theory of mind, and the default mode: A quantitative meta-analysis. *Journal of Cognitive Neuroscience, 21*(3), 63–74.

Sridharan, D., Levitin, D.J., & Menon, V. (2008). A critical role for the right fronto-insular cortex in switching between central-executive and default-mode networks. *Proceedings of the National Academy of Sciences, 105*(34), 12569–12574.

Staniloiu, A., & Markowitsch, H. (2014). Dissociative amnesia. *Lancet: Psychiatry, 1*(3), 226–241.

Steele, J.D., Lawrie, S.M. (2004). Segregation of cognitive and emotional function in the prefrontal cortex: A stereotactic meta-analysis. *NeuroImage, 21*(3), 868–875.

Steers, M.L.N., Wickham, R.E., & Acitelli, L.K. (2014). Seeing everyone else's highlight reels: How Facebook usage is linked to depressive symptoms. *Journal of Social and Clinical Psychology, 33*(8), 701–731.

Steffgen, G., Silva, M.D., & Recchia, S. (2007). Self-concept clarity style (SCSS): Psychometric properties and aggression correlates of a German version. *Individual Differences Research, 5,* 230–245.

Steffner, D., & Schenkman, B. (2012). Change blindness when viewing web pages. *Work, 41,* 6098–6102.

Steinberg, M. (1994). *Interviewer's guide to the structured clinical interview for DSM-IV. Dissociative disorders.* Rev. ed. Washington, DC: American Psychiatric Press.

Steiner, D. (1996). IMAGINE: An integrated environment for constructing distributed intelligence systems. In G.M.P. O'Hare and N.R. Jennings (Eds.), *Foundations of distributed artificial intelligence* (pp. 345–364). New York, NY: Wiley.

Steinhart, E.C. (2014). *Your digital afterlives: Computational theories of life after death.* New York, NY: Palgrave Macmillan.

Steinkuehler, C., & Williams, D. (2006). Where everybody knows your (screen) name: Online games as "third places." *Journal of Computer-Mediated Communication, 11*(4), 885–909.

Sterling, B. (1992). *The hacker crackdown: Law and disorder on the electronic frontier.* New York, NY: Bantam Books.

Steuer, J. (1992). Defining virtual reality: Dimensions determining telepresence. *Journal of Communication, 42*(4), 73–93.

Stieler-Hunt, C., Jones, C.M., Rolfe, B., & Pozzebon, K. (2014). Examining key decisions involved in developing a serious game for child sexual abuse prevention. *Frontiers in Psychology, 5*(73). doi:10.3389/fpsyg.2014.00073

Stockburger, A. (2007). Playing the third place: Spatial modalities in contemporary game environments. *International Journal of Performance Arts and Digital Media, 3*(2–3), 223–236.

Stone, L. (2009). *Continuous partial attention*. Retrieved from www.lindastone.net/qa/continuous-partial-attention

Strack, F., & Deutsch, R. (2004). Reflective and impulsive determinants of social behavior. *Personality and Social Psychology Review, 8*, 220–247.

Strawson, G. (2009). *Selves: An essay in revisionary metaphysics*. New York, NY: Oxford University Press.

Strobach, T., & Schubert, T. (2015). Experience in action games and the effects on executive control. *Inquisitive Mind, 8*. Retrieved from https://www.in-mind.org/article/experience-in-action-games-and-the-effects-on-executive-control

Sturman, D. J., & Zeltzer, D. (1994). A survey of glove-based inputs. *IEEE Computer Graphics and Applications, 14*(1), 30–39.

Sugiura, M., Kawashima, R., Nakamura, K., Okada, K., Kato, T., Nakamura, A., . . . & Fukuda, H. (2000). Passive and active recognition of one's own face. *NeuroImage, 11*(1), 36–48.

Suler, J. R. (1980). Primary process thinking and creativity. *Psychological Bulletin, 88*(1), 144–165.

Suler, J. R. (2004). The online disinhibition effect. *CyberPsychology and Behavior, 7*, 321–326.

Suler, J. R. (2016). *Psychology of the digital age: Humans become electric*. New York, NY: Cambridge University Press.

Suler, J. R. (2017). The dimensions of cyberpsychology architecture. In J. Gackenbach & J. Bown (Eds.), *Boundaries of self and reality online: Implications of digitally constructed realities* (pp. 1–26). London, UK: Academic Press.

Sung, Y., Lee, J., Kim, E., & Choi, S. M. (2016). Why we post selfies: Understanding motivations for posting pictures of oneself. *Personality and Individual Differences, 97*, 260–265.

Sutherland, I. E. (1968). A head-mounted three dimensional display. In *Proceedings of the 1968 Fall Joint Computer Conference, Part I* (pp. 757–764). Washington, DC: Thomson Book.

Swann, W. B., Jr., & Bosson, J. K. (2010). Self and identity. In S. T. Fiske, D. T. Gilbert, & G. Lindzey (Eds.), *Handbook of social psychology* (pp. 589–628). New York, NY: Wiley.

Swinburne, R. (2013). *Mind, brain, and free will*. Oxford, UK: Oxford University Press.

Symons, C. S., & Johnson, B. T. (1997). The self-reference effect in memory: A meta-analysis. *Psychological Bulletin, 121*, 371–394.

Tamir, D. I., & Mitchell, J. P. (2012). Disclosing information about the self is intrinsically rewarding. *Proceedings of the National Academy of Sciences, 109*(21), 8038–8043.

Taylor, C. (1977). What is human agency? In T. Mischel (Ed.), *The self: Psychological and philosophical issues* (pp. 103–135). Oxford, UK: Blackwell.

Taylor, D. M., Tillery, S. I., & Schwartz, A. B. (2002). Direct cortical control of 3D neuroprosthetic devices. *Science, 296*, 1829–1832.

Taylor, T. L. (2002). Living digitally: Embodiment in virtual world. In R. Schroeder (Ed.), *The social life of avatars: Presence and interaction in shared virtual environments* (pp. 40–62). London, UK: Springer-Verlag.

Teilhard de Chardin, P. (1955). *The phenomenon of man*. New York, NY: Harper & Row.

Teriman, D. (2006, April 12). Phony kids, virtual sex. *CNet*. Retrieved from http://news.com.com/Phony+kids,+virtual+sex/2100-1043_3-6060132.html

Tesser, A. (2002). Constructing a niche for the self: A bio-social, PDP approach to understanding lives. *Self and Identity, 1*, 185–190.

Tesser, A., Millar, M., & Moore, J. (1988). Some affective consequences of social comparison and reflection processes: The pain and pleasure of being close. *Journal of Personality and Social Psychology, 54*(1), 49–61.

Thompson, A. (1998). On the automatic design of robust electronics through artificial evolution. In M. Sipper, D. Mange, & A. Prez-Uribe (Eds.), *Proceedings of the 2nd International*

Conference on Evolvable Systems: From Biology to Hardware (LNCS, 1478) (pp. 13–24). London, UK: Springer-Verlag.

Tononi, G., & Koch, C. (2008). The neural correlates of consciousness. *Annals of the New York Academy of Sciences, 1124*, 239–261.

Torchia, J. (2008). *Exploring personhood: An introduction to the philosophy of human nature.* Plymouth, UK: Rowman and Littlefield.

Torley, V. J. (2015, August 14). Physicist Paul Davies' killer argument against the multiverse. *Uncommon Descent.* Retrieved from https://uncommondescent.com/intelligent-design /physicist-paul-davies-killer-argument-against-the-multiverse/

Tracy, J. L., Robins, R. W., & Tangney, J. P. (Eds.). (2007). *The self-conscious emotions: Theory and research.* New York, NY: Guilford Press.

Turk, D. J., & Heatherton, T. F. (2003). Out of contact, out of mind: The distributed nature of the self. *Annals of the New York Academy of Sciences, 1001*, 65–78.

Turk, D. J., Heatherton, T. F., Kelley, W. M., Funnell, M. G., Gazzaniga, M. S., & Macrae, C. N. (2002). Mike or me? Self recognition in a split-brain patient. *Nature Neuroscience, 5*(9), 841–842.

Turkle, S. (1995). *Life on the screen: Identity in the age of the internet.* Cambridge, MA: MIT Press.

Turkle, S. (1997). Constructions and reconstructions of self in virtual reality: Playing in the MUDs. In S. Kiesler (Ed.), *Culture of the internet* (pp. 143–155). Mahwah, NJ: Lawrence Erlbaum Associates.

Turkle, S. (2011). *Alone together: Why we expect more from technology and less from each other.* New York, NY: Basic Books.

Twenge, J. M., & Campbell, W. K. (2003). "Isn't it fun to get the respect that we're going to deserve?" Narcissism, social rejection, and aggression. *Personality and Social Psychology Bulletin, 29*, 261–272.

Ullman, S., & Richards, W. (1984). *Image understanding.* Norwood, NJ: Ablex.

Valkenburg, P. M., & Peter, J. (2011). Online communication among adolescents: An integrated model of its attraction, opportunities, and risks. *Journal of Adolescent Health, 48*(4), 121–127.

Valkenburg, P. M., Schouten, A. P., & Peter, J. (2005). Adolescents' identity experiments on the internet. *New Media and Society, 7*(3), 383–402.

van Kerkoerle, T., Self, M. W., Dagnino, B., Gariel-Mathis, M., Poort, J., van der Togt, C., & Roelfsema, P. R. (2014). Alpha and gamma oscillations characterize feedback and feedforward processing in monkey visual cortex. *PNAS, 111*(40), 14332–14341.

Varakin, D. A., Levin, D. T., & Fidler, R. (2004). Unseen and unaware: Implications of recent research on failures of visual awareness for human-computer interface design. *Human-Computer Interaction, 19*(4), 389–422.

Velliste, M., Perel, S., Spalding, M. C., Whitford, A. S., & Schwartz, A. B. (2008). Cortical control of a prosthetic arm for self-feeding. *Nature, 453*, 1098–1101.

Virtuix. (2014, December 16). *Virtuix omni.* Retrieved from www.virtuix.com/

Vogeley, K., Bussfeld, P., Newen, A., Hermann, S., Happé, F., Falkai, P., . . . & Zilles, K. (2001). Mind reading: Neural mechanisms of theory of mind and self-perspective. *NeuroImage, 14*, 170–181.

Vogeley, K., & Fink, G. R. (2003). Neural correlates of the first-person perspective. *Trends in Cognitive Neuroscience, 7*, 38–42.

Vogeley, K., & May, M. (2004). Neural correlates of first-person perspective as one constituent of human self-consciousness. *Journal of Cognitive Neuroscience, 16*(5), 817–827.

Vohs, K. D., & Baumeister, R. F. (Eds.). (2011). *Handbook of self-regulation: Research, theory, and applications* (2nd ed.). New York, NY: Guilford Press.

Voiskounsky, A. (2008). Flow experience in cyberspace: Current studies and perspectives. In A. Barak (Ed.), *Psychological aspects of cyberspace: Theory, research, and applications* (pp. 70–101). New York, NY: Cambridge University Press.

Waggoner, Z. (2009). *My avatar, my self.* Jefferson, NC: McFarland.

Walker, J. (2003, August). Performing fictions: Interaction and depiction. *Fine Art Forum, 17*(8). Retrieved from www.fineartforum.org/Backissues/Vol_17/index.html

Walther, J. (1996). Computer-mediated communication: Impersonal, interpersonal, and hyperpersonal interaction. *Communication Research, 23*(3), 3–43.

Wang, S. S., & Stefanone, M. A. (2013). Showing off? Human mobility and the interplay of traits, self-disclosure and Facebook check-ins. *Social Science Computer Review, 31*(4), 437–457.

Warwick, K. I. (2004). *I, cyborg.* Urbana: University of Illinois Press.

Watts, D. J., & Strogatz, S. H. (1998). Collective dynamics of "small-world" networks. *Nature, 393,* 440–442.

Wegner, D. (2002). *The illusion of conscious will.* Cambridge, MA: MIT Press.

Weiss, G. (2000). *Multiagent systems: A modern approach to distributed artificial intelligence.* Cambridge, MA: MIT Press.

Wertheim, M. (1999). *The pearly gates of cyberspace: A history of space from Dante to the internet.* New York, NY: Norton.

Wiley, J. (2012). *Theory and practice in the philosophy of David Hume.* New York, NY: Palgrave Macmillan.

Wilson, L. (2003, August). Interactivity or interpassivity: A question of agency in digital play. *Fine Art Forum, 17*(8). Retrieved from www.fineartforum.org/Backissues/Vol_17/index.html

Wittgenstein, L. (1963). *Philosophical investigations.* Oxford, UK: Blackwell.

Woeste, H. (2009). A history of panoramic image creation. Retrieved from www.graphics.com /article-old/history-panoramic-image-creation

Wolf, M. (Ed.). (2001). *The medium of the video game.* Austin: University of Texas Press.

Ybarra, O., & Winkielman, P. (2012). On-line social interactions and executive functions. *Frontiers in Human Neuroscience, 6.* doi:10.3389/fnhum.2012.00075

Yee, N. (2006). Motivations for play in online games. *CyberPsychology and Behavior, 9*(6), 772–775.

Yee, N., & Bailenson, J. (2007). The Proteus effect: The effect of transformed self-representation on behavior. *Human Communication Research, 33*(3), 271–290.

Yuan, K., Qin, W., Wang, G., Zeng, F., Zhao, L., Yang, X., . . . & Gong, Q. (2011). Microstructure abnormalities in adolescents with internet addiction disorder. *PloS One, 6*(6). doi:10.1371/ journal.pone.0020708

Yuan, K., Qin, W., Yu, D., Bi, Y., Xing, L., Jin, C., & Tian, J. (2015). Core brain networks interactions and cognitive control in internet gaming disorder individuals in late adolescence /early adulthood. *Brain Structure and Function, 221*(3): 1427–1442. doi:10.1007/s00429-014-0982-7

Yudkowsky, Eliezer. (2001, June 15). Creating friendly AI 1.0: The analysis and design of benevolent goal architectures. Singularity Institute, San Francisco, CA. Retrieved from https:// intelligence.org/files/CFAI.pdf

Zadro, L., Williams, K. D., & Richardson, R. (2004). How low can you go? Ostracism by a computer is sufficient to lower self-reported levels of belonging, control, self-esteem, and meaningful existence. *Journal of Experimental Social Psychology, 40*(4), 560–567.

Zanon, M., Novembre, G., Zangrando, N., Chittaro, L., & Silani, G. (2014). Brain activity and prosocial behavior in a simulated life-threatening situation. *Neuroimage, 98,* 134–146.

Zheng, X. L. (2012). A structural equation model for the relationship between optimism, anxiety, online social support and internet altruistic behavior. *Chinese Journal of Special Education, 11,* 84–89.

Zheng, X., & Gu, H. (2012). Personality traits and internet altruistic behavior: The mediating effect of self-esteem. *Chinese Journal of Special Education, 2*, 69–74.

Zhou, Z., Tang, H., Tian, Y., Wei, H., Zhang, F., & Morrison, C. (2013). Cyberbullying and its risk factors among Chinese high school students. *School Psychology International, 34*, 630–647.

Zywica, J., & Danowski, J. (2008). The faces of Facebookers: Investigating social enhancement and social compensation hypotheses; predicting Facebook and offline popularity from sociability and self-esteem, and mapping the meanings of popularity with sematic networks. *Journal of Computer Mediated Communication, 14*(1), 1–34.

INDEX

abomination, 261, 271

Abraham Maslow, 54, 60, 61

absorption, 172–173; games, 173

activation likelihood estimation, 98

active externalism, 45;

Adler, 9

age play, 218

agency, 38–41, 81, 83–84, 97, 223

agent, 8, 13, 177

aggression, 7, 169, 190, 275

Albert Badura, 68

Albert Einstein, 16

Aleph state, 287

alters, 73

altruism, 211, 223

alts, 213–215

Android, 13

anterior cingulate cortex, 86

anterior insula, 76

anthropic mechanism, 17;

anthropomorphism, 129

anticritical view, 35

Antonio Damasio, 90–97

Aristotle, 23, 24; monism, 23; hierarchy of souls, 23;

artificial agents, 83, 237

artificial chromosomes, 134

artificial consciousness, 229, 235, 243

Artificial General Intelligence (AGI), 141, 245–246

Artificial Intelligence (AI): 229–230, 244–245, 252–253, 255, 268; friendly (FAI), 254;

Distributed Artificial Intelligence (DAI), 250–251

artificial life (A-life), 229–230, 233

Artificial self, 2, 11, 12, 13, 51, 53, 258, 260–261, 269, 271

artificial skin, 110–111

asexual reproduction, 7

Asimov's laws of robotics, 61

asomatognosia, 82

asynchronic, 205

asynchronous communication, 153

attention, 41, 50–51, 140, 168, 172, 238, 241

attentional blink, 140

attractiveness rule, 249

augmented reality (AR), 198–200

autobiographical memory, 3, 84, 85

autonomic arousal, 224

autonomous systems, 254

autonomy, 61

autopagnosia, 82

avatars, 11–12, 83, 126, 144, 176–198, 207, 213; projections, 188;

awareness: 88–89, 93, 101, 242: self-, 3, 51, 242, 263; conscious-, 25, 41, 90, 233, 281, 286

basic spaces, three types of, 201

Battlezone, 206

beman, 257–258

beme, 256, 260

Bemetic Intelligence via Neural Architecture at forty-eight teraflops (BINforty-eight), 256–257, 259, 269

bilateral inferior occipital gyrus, 83
binding problem, 89
binocular disparity, 207, 227
biological collectives, 133
biological naturalism, 243
Blue Gene computer, 266
body, 91
boid, 249, 250
bots, 214
Brain and Internet Addiction Disorder, 76
Brain computer interface (BCI), 119–121, 123
Brain machine interface (BMI), 119, 123, 150
Brain Research through Advancing Innovative
    Neurotechnologies (BRAIN) program, 265
brittleness, 244
Bruner, 62
brute physical view, 35
Buddhist psychology, 9
bulletin board systems (BBS), 205

Carl Rogers, 9, 54, 58, 59, 60
Carl Sagan, 16
Cartesian theater, 87
categories for gamers, 178; explorers, 178; achiev-
    ers, 178; socializers, 178; killers, 178–179
Catholic Church, 4
cellular automata (CA), 230–231
cerebellum, 82
change blindness, 168
character, 3
chatbot, 245–248, 262
child play, 218
Chinese room scenario, 239
Cicero, 4, 70
cingulate, 93
cochlea, 109
Cognition Engine, 245
cognition, 50, 51
Cognitive Behavioral Therapy (CBT), 75, 76
cognitive theory of self, 65
collective robot systems, 132
colliculi, 96
Commodore 64, 206
competence, 61
complexity, 229, 230, 237, 281, 282, 283, 284,
    289. See also complexity approach, 240
compromised identities, 74, 75
computation, 33, 53, 236, 287

computational economies, 250
computer emulation, 252
computers, 40, 41
computronium, 286
conceptions of self, 30, 97;
connectome, 265–266
consciousness neurons, 101
consciousness, 5, 40, 41, 45, 87, 233–235, 242–
    243, 259–260, 263, 281, 284, 290
consequentialist approach, 131
constructionist approach, 162
controlled self, 71
cool systems, 53, 54
cooperative symbiotic behavior, 232
core self, 93
corporeal, 229, 233
cortical midline structures, 96
cyber-Dixies, 216
Cyberball, 225
cyberbeings, 258, 261
cyberbullying, 139, 164–165
cyberconsciousness, 258–260
cybernetic organism (cyborg), 11, 103–106, 108;
    animal, 104–105; feedback, 103–104, 123
cyberpsychology, 69, 143–146, 289; identity
    dimension, 143–144; social dimension, 144;
    interactive dimension, 145; reality dimension,
    145–146; physical dimension, 146
cyberspace, 57–58, 70, 145–146, 148, 205

Damasio's theory of self, 237
damnation, 252, 282
Daniel Dennett, 28, 86
David Hume, 26; empiricism, 26
decision-making, 32, 42, 172, 238, 253
Deep brain stimulation (DBS), 107
Default mode network (DMN), 155
degrees of freedom, 112, 115
deontological approach, 131
Depersonalization Disorder, 72
depersonalization, 72, 73
derealization, 73
determinism, 18, 42
digital social self, 70
digital: divide, 259; ghost, 262–263; immortal-
    ity, 262
dimension, 144; text dimension, 144–145; sen-
    sory dimension, 145; temporal dimension,

Dissociative Amnesia, 72
Dissociative disorders, 72, 78
Dissociative Fugue, 72
Dissociative Identity Disorder, 73, 78, 91
divergent evolution, 286
Doer, 54
domain-general reasoning, 253
domain-specific AI, 4
Doom, 170, 206
dorsal anterior cingulate cortex, 76, 77
dorsolateral prefrontal cortex, 77
Douglas Hofstadter, 65
dream states, 146, 242
dualism, 22, 263
dynamism, 273. See also dynamical systems, 274

EchoPixel system, 224
ecological validity, 225
ego, 9, 23, 55, 56, 67, 71, 215
Electrocardiography (ECoG),119, 121–122
electrode array, 106, 119
Electroencephalography (EEG), 119, 122–123
embodiment, 184, 234, 248
emotional robots, 129
emotions, 28, 51, 55, 57–58, 129, 234, 237, 272–273, 278
enhanced abilities, 103
enlightenment, 10
episodic autobiographical memory, 97
episodic memory, 84
ergodic literature, 192
Erik Erikson, 54, 56, 57
escapism, 200
Eterni.me, 256
evolution and freedom, 42, 43
evolution of free will, 43
evolution, 6
evolutionary robotics, 134–135, 237
evolvable hardware, 135–136
executive agent, 49
executive processes, 50
executive system, 76, 77
explanatory gap, 234
explicit systems, 54
exposure therapy, 225–226
extended consciousness, 94
extended self, 47

external locus of control, 69
externalism, 45

fantasy self, 71
Field Programmable Gate Arrays (FPGAs), 135
First Person Point-of-View (POV), 184–185, 194
first-person perspective, 84, 85
first-person shooter (FPS), 140, 170, 196, 201
fission, 36;
five aspects of self, 49
Five-factor model, 63, 64, 65, 66, 161, 165, 172, 187, 190
Fleshism, 261
flocking behavior, 249
flow, 145, 207
Flynn effect, 139
four perspectives of self, 51, 52, 53
free will, 42
frontopolar gyrus, 83
functional organization, 244
functionalist, 66, 243, 244, 289. See Also functionalism, 66, 263

Gaius, 3
Game of Life, 230–231. See also stable shapes, 231; oscillators, 231, R Pentominos, 231, gliders, 231
Game Transfer Phenomena (GTP), 175
gender swapping, 215
General intelligence, 141
Genetic Algorithm (GA) program, 134
genetic engineering, 270, 275, 286
genotype, 135, 232
Gestalt law of proximity, 9
Gestalt psychology, 70
Gettysburg!, 201
global workspace theory, 281
globus pallidus, 82
goal-directedness, 241
God mode, 185
God, 4
Goldilocks effect, 75, 188
Google Cardboard, 209
griefing, 220

haptic sensation, 227
hdentity, 2, 3, 37; dynamic, 2; personal, 2; social, 2;

Headsight, 208
Helsinki Declaration of Ethical Principles for Medical Research Involving Human Subjects, 260, 266
Henri Maillardet, 15
hippocampus, 124
Homo Sapiens, 2
homunculus problem, 88, 89
homunculus, 13, 14
hot systems, 53, 54
HTC Vive, 209
Human Brain Project, 265–266
human, 2
Humanistic psychology, 58
hyperlinks, 167

Id, 55–56, 215
ideal self, 59, 60
identity crisis, 56
idiosyncratic, 180; environmental, 181; power,181; seductive, 181; odd and shocking,
iDisorders, 142
illusion of free will, 43, 44
Implanted Pulse Generator (IPG), 107
implicit systems, 54
inattentional blink, 168
indestructible robot, 236
inferior parietal cortex, 83
infinity, 288
information processing perspective,68
information-processing perspective, 68, 230, 281
inner life, 5
insula, 83, 96
intelligence, 132, 163, 240–241, 244, 270, 273
intentionality, 5, 241
interactivity, 144, 207, 209
internal locus of control, 69
Internalism, 45
Internet Addiction Disorder (IAD), 75, 76, 78
internet addiction, 75–76, 219. See also internet addictive disorder, 76, 219
Internet Gaming disorder (IGD), 76, 77
Internet trolls, 70
interoceptive signals, 96

introspection, 39
ISAC, 130–131

Jaques de Vaucanson, 15
Jean-Jaques Rousseau, 5
Jewish folklore,14
John Locke, 5, 25
John Suler, 69
Julien Offray de La Mettrie, 17

Kilobots, 133
kinesthesis, 110–111
Kismet, 129–130
Knife-Edge Scanning Microscope (KESM), 265

labyrinth types: linear paths, 202; maze path, 203; rhizome, 203
lachine, 11
language, 7, 47, 239
lateral left premotor cortex, 83
lateral temporal cortex, 83
left anterior insula, 81
left hemisphere, 81
left inferior parietal lobule, 83
left posterior cingulate cortex, 83
left prefrontal cortex, 82
LifeNaut program, 256–257
lingual gyrus, 82
local field potential, 119
locus of control, 69
Lord of the Rings, The, 201, 205
love, 218, 260, 277–278
low-bandwidth, 145

Machine racism, 129
Marry Wollstonecraft Shelly, 14
Maslow's: hierarchy, 60–61, 223, 280; pyramid, 279
Massive multiplayer online (MMO) games, 179
Massively Multiple Online Games (MMOGs), 200
Massively Multiple Online Role-Playing Games (MMORPGS, 200
material self, 27
Matrioshka brains (MBrains), 286–287
Media Multitaskers (MMTs), 168
medial prefrontal cortex, 81

mental time travel, 6

mentalizing network, 156

merged group mind, 285

metacognition, 40

metaverse, 205

Microsoft HoloLens, 199

midbie, 212

middle temporal gyrus, 82

mimesis, 182

mind uploading, 22, 33, 229, 263, 287. See also
  whole-brain emulation, 287

mindclone, 229, 256–262

mindfile, 256, 258

mindware, 261

model of self-memory processing, 97

Modernist, 67, 71,

modular prosthetic limb, 114

molecular self, 69

Monism, 23, 263

Moore's law, 252, 284

moral responsibility, 4

morphological freedom, 268

mortality, 236

motivation, 51, 151, 223, 279

Multi-Agent Systems (MAS), 37, 232, 250

Multiple drafts model of consciousness, 88

Multiple occupancy view, 36

Multiple-selves' hypothesis, 78

multiplicity of self, 99, 100

Multitasking in the City Test (MCT), 226

multiverse, 287–288

nanorobotics, 136–137

Narcissistic Personality Disorder, 74, 75, 78,
  161

narration, 61, 62, 63, 66

narrative functioning, 62

nature-versus-nurture, 269

negative digital self, 70

neural map, 93; first-order maps, 93, 94; second-order maps, 93, 94

Neural model of self, 90

neural prosthetic, 119, 227

neural synchronization, 87, 89

neurostimulator, 107

newbie, 212. See Also noob, 212

noncollision rule, 249

nonergodic literature, 192

nonpersons, 4

Nonplayer characters (NPCs), 192–194, 196

nucleus accumbens, 77

object, 90, 91

objective phenomena, 234

Oculus Rift, 209, 221

oldie, 213

Omega Point, 284, 287

online altruistic behavior, 165

online anonymity, 152, 165

online dating, 157–159

online-disinhibition effect, 145, 152–153

orbitofrontal cortex, 76, 77

organism, 90, 91

other aware, 54

out-of-control self, 71

panoramic paintings, 207

paradigmatic functioning, 62

parallel processing, 87, 89

parasite, 232, 282

parietal lobe, 82, 83

Patternism, 10, 65

periaqueductal gray, 96

Persistence question, 35

person, 2, 3

persona-play, 211. See also role-play, 211

personality, 3, 54–55

personhood, 3, 4

Peter Strawson, 5

phenotype, 135, 232

phobia, 224–225

Pierre-Simon Laplace, 17

piezoelectric effect, 111

Plato, 22–23

Point of View (POV), 184–185, 203

Pokemon Go, 199–200

polymodal convergent zones, 96

Pong, 170, 202, 206

Position Exchange Theory (PET), 8, 223

positive digital self, 70

postcentral gyrus, 83

posterior insula, 83

posthuman, 269

Postmodernism, 29, 67, 71

powered exoskeleton, 117

preattentive and attentive processing, 41

prereflective self-consciousness, 41
privacy, 259
proprioception, 110–112
prosthetics, 104, 108, 114–116
Proteus effect, 186
protoself, 92
psyche, 141–142, 191
Psychodynamic psychology, 55–56, 70
psychological continuity view, 35
psychological self, 83
pulvinar, 81
punctuated equilibrium, 232
pure ego, 27, 70
putamen, 81

qualia, 234, 263

Radio-Frequency Identification (RFID), 107
Real self, 59–60, 71
reaper, 232
reciprocal altruism, 6–8, 223
Reciprocal determinism, 68
reentrant, 90
reflexive consciousness, 50
reflexive thinking. 50
regulation, 50–51
relatedness, 61
Rene Descartes, 5, 24–25, 37
replication theory of resurrection, 264
replication, 18; duplication, 18; identical
    twins, 18; cloning, 18; nonidentical
    copy, 18
restored function, 103
retina, 108
right anterior cingulate, 82, 84
right frontal cortex, 81
right inferior parietal cortex, 83
right lateral parietal cortex, 81
right limbic system, 82
right precuneus, 83
right supramarginal gyrus, 83
right temporoparietal junction, 86
RoboCup, 133
roboethics, 259
robot ethics, 131
robot, 11, 15, 83; Karel Capek, 15
robotic psychology, 278
robotics, 125
role identity, 223

Romans, 3
Rubber hand illusion, 116

safe-AI scaffolding strategy, 255
salience network, 76–77, 225
salvation, 282
Sansar, 221–222
SAS cube, 209
schema, 167–168
schizophrenia, 83
Second Life (SL), 183, 200, 206, 210–211, 213–
    216, 218–223
second order desires, 39, 40
self concept clarity, 164
self concept fragmentation hypothesis, 164
self construal, 164
self expression by proxy, 144
self presentation, 159, 163; assertive, 159; defen-
    sive, 159; positive, 163
self-actualization, 60
self-assembly, 133; molecular, 133
self-aware, 54, 81
self-brain system, 80
self-concept, 58
self-consciousness, 41
self-control, 51
self-determination theory, 61
self-efficacy, 68
self-esteem, 27
self-feelings, 27
self-identification, 38, 39
self-reference effect, 84
self-reference, 65, 84
self-referential processing, 95
self-seeking and Self-preservation, 27
self, 5, 9, 10, 49, 50, 80, 289, 290. See also self-
    actualization, 58–61, 223, 280; self-organiza-
    tion, 229; self-organizing emergent proper-
    ties, 285
selfies, 150–152; motivation to take, 151
semantic autobiographical memory, 97
semantic memory, 85
Sensorama simulator, 208
sentient self, 70
sex, 217, 276–277
sexual reproduction, 7
shallow me, 75
shallowing hypothesis, 149
Sigmund Freud, 9, 54, 89

SimCity 2000, 206
SimEarth, 206
simulacrum, 201
singularity, 229, 251–253
six facets of identity, 62
sixteen basic personality traits, 63, 65
Skandhas, 9, 10
social exclusion, 225
social gravity, 219
social memory, 166
social monitoring, 165
Social Networking Sites (SNSs), 154–155, 160,
    162–164
social perspective, 68
social psychology, 8
social self, 27, 54, 223
social stimulation, 130
social-cognitive theory of self, 68, 71
Socrates, 22–23
somatosensation, 110
somatosensory system, 91–92; visceral/intero-
    ceptive division, 91; vestibular, 91–92; musc-
    uloskeletal/proprioceptive system, 91–92;
    fine touch, 91
Space Invaders, 121, 202, 206
specialized system, 80
spiritual Self, 27
split-brain, 36, 37, 81
Star Trek: The Next Generation, 208
state-trait debate, 64
statists, 273
stereoscope, 207–208
strange loops, 66
Structuralism, 69
subjective first-person self, 100
subjective phenomena, 234, 263
Sugarscape, 232
Superego, 55, 56, 215
superintelligence, 252–253, 268, 273, 285
superior colliculus, 93
supplemental motor area, 77
swarm behavior, 249
Sword of Damocles system, 208
symbiosis, 74
symbiotic me, 74

Tamagotchi, 278
techno virgins, 277
technological neuroses, 142

teleoperation, 125
telepresence, 125
telerobotics, 125–126
temporal structure, 90
temporal synchrony, 90
terrarium, 264
texting, 148–150; issues, 148–149; relation-
    ships, 149–150
thalamus, 93
The body transfer illusion, 116
The disillusioned me, 75
The extended mind thesis, 45, 46, 47
The Golem project, 134–135
The KIP model, 179
The Palace, 179–184
Theory of Mind (TOM), 155
theory of self, 26, 27
third path, 252, 282
third person perspective, 85
Third person point-of-view (POV), 184–185,
    194
third spaces, 218
third-person neutrally instantiated systems of
    self, 100
Thomas Hobbes, 5
Thomas Jefferson, 5
Tierra, 231–233
time and indeterminacy, 37, 38
tniversal mechanism, 17
too many thinker's problem, 37
traits, 10, 63, 64, 65, 71, 85
transactive memory, 166
transcendence, 280–281
transcendent me, 69, 70
transgenderism, 215
transhumanism, 268–269. See also transhu-
    manist, 22, 269–271, 285
Transhumanist Declaration, 268
trophy friends, 142
tser immersion, 190
Turing Test, 235, 245, 247
Turing's Various Disabilities Argument, 243

Ultimate Display, The, 206–207
Utah array, 119

valuation, 236
value, 131, 279–280, 283
ventral emotional salience network, 225

ventral tegmental area, 77
ventromedial prefrontal cortex, 77
vergence-accommodation effect, 227
video game addiction, 77, 78
video game spaces: rule-based space, 203; mediated space, 203; play space, 204; social space, 204
video games, 169–175; violence, 169, 171, 194; decision making in, 172
Video role-playing games (v-RPGs), 186, 190–193, 195, 202
virtual behaviors, 183–184
virtual body, 96
virtual reality (VR), 198, 208–210, 221, 224, 253, 289

Virtual Reality Addiction Disorder (VRAD), 77
virtual reality exposure therapy (VRET), 226
virtual terrorism, 220
virtue, 131, 279
vividness, 207
volition, 240–241
Voxel, 98, 122

white matter, 83
whole-brain emulation, 65
Wilhelm Wundt, 39
William James, 26, 27
Willing and doing self, 70
working memory, 95

Founded in 1893,
UNIVERSITY OF CALIFORNIA PRESS
publishes bold, progressive books and journals
on topics in the arts, humanities, social sciences,
and natural sciences—with a focus on social
justice issues—that inspire thought and action
among readers worldwide.

The UC PRESS FOUNDATION
raises funds to uphold the press's vital role
as an independent, nonprofit publisher, and
receives philanthropic support from a wide
range of individuals and institutions—and from
committed readers like you. To learn more, visit
ucpress.edu/supportus.

Made in United States
North Haven, CT
22 January 2022